Y0-BSN-647

WITHDRAWN

Incendiary Weapons

SIPRI

Stockholm International Peace Research Institute

SIPRI is an independent institute for research into problems of peace and conflict, especially those of disarmament and arms regulation. It was established in 1966 to
commemorate Sweden's 150 years of unbroken peace.
The Institute is financed by the Swedish Parliament.
The staff, the Governing Board and the Scientific Council
are international. As a consultative body, the Scientific
Council is not responsible for the views expressed in the
publications of the Institute.

SIPRI

Stockholm International Peace Research Institute

Sveavägen 166, S-113 46 Stockholm, Sweden
Cable: Peaceresearch, Stockholm   Telephone: 08-15 09 40

Incendiary Weapons

A SIPRI MONOGRAPH

Stockholm International Peace Research Institute

The MIT Press
Cambridge, Massachusetts and
London, England

Almqvist & Wiksell
International
Stockholm, Sweden

First published by the Stockholm International Peace Research Institute
in cooperation with
Almqvist & Wiksell International
26 Gamla Brogatan, S-111 20 Stockholm

The MIT Press
28 Carleton Street
Cambridge, Mass. 02142

and

126 Buckingham Palace Road
London SW1 W9

ISBN 0 262 19139 3

*Library of Congress Catalog
Card Number: 75-11515*

Printed in Sweden by
Almqvist & Wiksell, Uppsala 1975

PREFACE

This book describes the uses and effects of incendiary weapons, including napalm and phosphorus weapons.

Before 1939 incendiary weapons were generally regarded as illegal and inhumane, in the same category as weapons, such as mustard gas, which cause chemical burns.

The question of illegality was, however, totally ignored during World War II when a definite policy of incendiary bombing emerged. Some authors have argued that the practice of states during this period made the use of incendiary weapons legal.

A recent survey of the literature on the existing laws of war made by the United Nations Secretariat (United Nations, 1973 c), shows that the legal status of incendiaries is still equivocal. While there is no specific prohibition of incendiary weapons in international law, some states, in their military legal instructions, nevertheless apply certain restrictions in the use of these weapons.

Further, the use of napalm and other incendiary weapons has been deplored in several resolutions of the UN General Assembly. In view of the extensive use of these weapons in recent armed conflicts it is high time to clarify their status in an international legal document (a suggestion already made by the UN Secretary-General in 1969).

This book attempts to provide basic factual information required to evaluate incendiary weapons in the light of humanitarian concerns and military demands.

Chapter 1 describes the rise of incendiary weapons from biblical times up to the modern era, together with attempts to restrain the use of these weapons by legal and disarmament measures.

Chapter 2 examines technical questions such as the principles of heat and combustion and the composition and construction of incendiaries. The advantages and disadvantages of the various weapons for particular tactical purposes are discussed. The chapter concludes with a brief description of various measures for protection against incendiary attack.

In chapter 3 medical problems arising from the effects of excessive heat on the human body are considered. Most doctors agree that a severe burn wound is the most serious trauma to which the human being can be subjected. The effects of burns are consequently described in some detail, as are the very extensive requirements for medical treatment. Effects of particular incendiary weapons are described, as well as the problems arising from mass burns casualties whether from "conventional" or thermo-nuclear attack. It is concluded that the suffering, both short- and long-term, caused by incendiary weapons, is so great that it is difficult to see that it can ever be justified by considerations of "military necessity."

Chapter 4 presents evidence which suggests that incendiary weapons may frequently produce toxic effects. In some cases these toxic effects aggravate the sufferings of disabled men; in other cases they may lead to a long-drawn-out and unnecessarily painful death. Though these effects may be "secondary" they may in certain circumstances be the predominant cause of death and injury.

It appears that incendiary weapons have only a limited place in contemporary military doctrines, since in their role as weapons of mass destruction they have been superseded by nuclear weapons. "Hard" targets are relatively immune to incendiary weapons, while "soft" targets (such as men and light vehicles) are readily destroyed by conventional weapons.

In fact, incendiary weapons have rarely been used in isolation—rather have they been used together with other munitions to enhance their combined effects. But it is doubtful whether this "increase in effectiveness" has ever been quantified, if indeed it exists. The case presented here is that the unnecessary suffering caused by incendiaries far outweighs any putative military advantages to be gained from them.

There are a few cases, and a few only, where incendiaries might arguably be less indiscriminate and more humane than other weapons. But the historical record has shown that incendiaries have been used overwhelmingly in circumstances where very serious legal and humanitarian objections can be put forward.

In the first place, incendiary bombs (including napalm bombs) have been used in huge numbers against cities, towns and villages where indiscriminate effects on the civilian population are inevitable and perhaps even deliberate (for example, where the intention has been to affect morale and/or industrial production, or to force people to leave their homes). In the second place, napalm bombs and flamethrowers have been used largely against personnel, causing unnecessary suffering. Because of difficulties of interpretation in the field of rules regarding the use of specific weapons a total prohibition of incendiary weapons (including pyrophoric incendiaries, such as white phosphorus, zirconium and uranium) is to be preferred. Failing this they should be prohibited for use where they may affect human beings or cause damage to the environment (including the man-made environment) or natural resources.

At the present time the most appropriate forum for arriving at such a prohibition is the Diplomatic Conference on the Geneva Conventions (see chapter 1). A prohibition of incendiary weapons (and of other classes of inhumane and/or indiscriminate weapons) could be incorporated into the texts of Draft Protocols I and II, or as an annex to them. Alternatively a third Additional Protocol might be a possible approach, not so much because it has inherent merits as in order to prevent further delays to the adoption of the first two. A fourth possibility would be for the Conference to adopt one or more Declarations, the procedure adopted at St Petersburg and the Hague when exploding and dum-dum bullets were prohibited. This device has the attraction of technical simplicity but might be more readily rejected by those states which are reluctant to agree to a ban.

This book was written by Dr Malvern Lumsden, a member of the SIPRI research staff.

June 1975 *Frank Barnaby*
Director

ACKNOWLEDGEMENTS

Background material on legal aspects (chapter 1) was provided by Dr Fritz Kalshoven (University of Leiden), Professor B. V. A. Röling (University of Groningen) and Dr Ian Brownlie (University of Oxford). Anu-Mai Köll (University of Stockholm) researched the use of incendiaries in many of the smaller conflicts (chapter 1). Dipl. ing. Gert H. Buck (Buck KG Chemisch-technische Werke, Munich) gave advice on technical matters dealt with in chapter 2. Dr John Constable (Massachusetts General Hospital) provided background material for chapter 3 and further advice was received from Professor Sten-Otto Liljedahl (Linköping, Sweden). Professor Karl-Heinz Lohs (Institute for Chemical Toxicology, Leipzig) assisted in the preparation of chapter 4 and Magnus Groth (Uppsala University) researched the question of white phosphorus burn toxicity (appendix 4A). SIPRI gratefully acknowledges the contributions of these experts but retains full responsibility for the publication.

CONTENTS

9

10

TABLES AND FIGURES

FIGURES

Chapter 4. Toxic effects of incendiary weapons on the human body

TABLES

Chapter 1. The rise of incendiary weapons

I. *Introduction*

Serious attempts have been made throughout history to limit the military use of technology by legal and humanitarian constraints. These attempts have been at best modest, at worst ineffectual; frequently they have also been hindered by a lack of insight into emerging technologies—technologies which often make the political constraints obsolete by the time they are enacted. One of the lessons of a historical survey might be that in order to be effective, political or legal restrictions must be one step ahead of the technology they are trying to hold in check rather than one step behind.

The purpose of this chapter is to outline the historical interplay between the rise of incendiary weapons and attempts to constrain their use.[1] Particular topics such as the current state of incendiary technology and the effects of incendiary weapons are discussed in detail in subsequent chapters.

II. *The origins of incendiary warfare and the laws of war*

Early incendiary warfare

The use of fire in war has a long history. Around 500 BC the earliest known military manual, *The Art of War,* by the Chinese author Sun Tzu Wu, described the use of incendiary arrows. The Bible relates how Samson affixed firebrands to the tails of foxes and released them amongst the cornfields of the Philistines (Judges 15:3–5). Lucretius, in approximately 60 BC wrote:

> Weapons of ancient times were hands and nails and teeth.
> Then axes hewn from trees of the forests.
> Flame and fire as soon as men knew them.

Thucydides describes the use of a great bellows to project flames, made by the Spartans in 42 BC:

---

[1] The UN Secretary-General's report (United Nations, 1973 *a*) describes technical and military aspects of incendiary weapons. Their legal status is discussed in a second report (United Nations, 1973 *c*).

They sawed in two and scooped out a great beam from end to end and fitted it nicely together again like a pie, hung by chains at one end a cauldron. Now the beam was plated with iron and an iron tube joined it to the cauldron. This they brought up from a distance upon carts to the part of the wall principally composed of vines and timber and when it was near, inserted huge bellows into their end of the beam and blew with them. The blast, passing closely confined into the cauldron, which was filled with lighted coals, sulphur and pitch, made a great blaze and set fire to the wall. The defenders could not hold it and left it and fled. In this way the fort was taken.

A device known as a siphon, which was fitted either with a hand pump or some form of mechanical pump, was also used as an early form of flame projector. The siphon was sometimes fitted to a specially constructed ship with an impressive animal head of brass or iron on the prow through the mouth of which could be projected an incendiary liquid that was ignited as it left the apparatus. Two hundred such ships were used in one expedition in the tenth century against the Arabs in Sicily (Partington, 1960). What later became known as Greek fire was usually thrown in earthenware pots and ignited by incendiary arrows, although the large barrels thrown by ballistae (described by de Joinville trans. Evans, 1938) were ignited before launching.

A Chinese technical manual from 1044, the *Wu Ching Tsung Yao,* gives the composition of an incendiary powder for use with incendiary arrows or balls fired from catapults. It also describes a fire-pot and incendiaries attached to birds and animals (Partington, 1960).

Until the tenth century Greek fire was mostly used in naval battles, though it was sometimes also projected from ships at buildings on shore. It went out of use in naval battles in about 1200. Known to the English as "wild fire" it remained in use in land battles and was used by Edward I at Stirling in Scotland in 1304 (Hime, 1915). It was used at the siege of Constantinople in 1453, along with gunpowder and cannon.

During the Siege of Malta in 1565 a variety of incendiary weapons were employed by the defenders. These included: small earthenware pots filled with an incendiary mixture, which could be thrown by hand like grenades; trumps—tubes made of hollowed-out wood or metal and filled with an incendiary—which often had an additional device for firing lead bullets; and firework hoops, constructed of light wood impregnated with a mixture of inflammable substances and gunpowder. All these devices had a considerable effect on the invading Turkish troops whose long robes readily caught fire (Bradford, 1964).

Incendiary arrows were last used by English archers in a siege of 1627. Berthelot (1893) reported that flame projectors were used at Le Havre in 1758 and that he himself had seen the Prussians use them when they attacked Paris in 1870.

But fire was also used for defence as well as attack. In attempting to breach walled cities, large wooden siege towers were sometimes rolled up to the walls as a platform from which to launch an attack over the walls. The defence against such towers often involved the use of burning oil. An Arab author gave the following account of an incident during the siege of Acre (1190–91):

The men from Damascus, in order to deceive the Christians, first threw pots with naptha and other things, not kindled, against one of the towers, which produced no effect. The Christians, full of confidence, climbed triumphantly to the highest stage of the tower, calling out in derision. The men from Damascus, waiting until the contents of the pots had soaked into the tower, at the right moment threw onto it a well-burning pot. At once fire broke out over the whole tower and it was destroyed. The fire was so quick that the Christians had no time to climb down and they and their weapons were all burnt up. The other two towers were similarly destroyed. (Cited in Partington, 1960).

It is reported that some 20 000 barrels of petroleum were used by Shawar to burn down the city of Fustat (Cairo) in 1168 to prevent its recapture by the Franks.

Some of the early incendiary weapons were relatively effective, given the level of technological development of the times, and many were undoubtedly spectacular in operation. Yet it is doubtful whether such weapons enjoyed more than marginal success against seasoned troops, once they overcame their initial apprehension. Fire was most successful as a weapon where it was directed at inflammable targets such as wooden vehicles, ships, siege towers and buildings. But, while incendiary agents were potentially effective against this type of target, limitations inherent in their delivery systems restricted their application. The flame pumps and projectors used in early naval warfare had relatively large capacity but limited range and accuracy. Incendiary arrows had greater range and accuracy but limited incendiary capacity.

In practice, therefore, the major uses of early incendiary weapons were probably either against troops or against large, inflammable targets at close range, such as wooden ships, siege towers or houses. In some historical periods it was common practice to loot and burn conquered towns, killing their inhabitants:

Civilian losses were particularly heavy during the Thirty Years' war . . . By 1639 the devastation had reached its peak. Hundreds of villages were put to the torch. One Swedish general, for example, razed 800 Bohemian villages. It has been estimated that altogether during the war the Swedes razed and destroyed 1 976 castles, 1 629 towns and 18 310 villages. In such warfare civilians perished wholesale. It is accepted that during the looting of Magdeburg alone, 30 000 civilians were slaughtered. The population of Bohemia dropped from 4 000 000 to 800 000. The losses among the civilian population during the war were measured in millions (Urlanis, 1971, p. 273).

The development of incendiary weapons was paralleled, moreover, by the discovery, in the fourteenth century, of gunpowder. This mixture of saltpetre (potassium nitrate), charcoal and sulphur produces such a pressure of gases on combustion that, when harnessed in a tube, it acts as a propellant for bullets or shells. This discovery signalled the birth of the gun, which to this day is the dominating weapon on the battlefield.

In addition to being used as a propellant, gunpowder could be used as an explosive. In large quantities it could do considerable damage to solid structures. In small quantities—as when used in exploding bullets—the mixture of flame and blast could create a very nasty wound.

Then, at the beginning of the twentieth century, military technology took another great leap forward. In 1900 a retired German general, Graf von Zeppelin, flew his first airship. Parallel to this development of lighter-than-air craft was the emergence of heavier-than-air machines, employing the internal-combustion engine and heralded by the Wright brothers in 1903. These parallel developments—the airship, the aeroplane, and the exploitation of large oil reserves to supply the demands of the internal-combustion engine—together coalesced into new dimensions of warfare.

Early development of the laws of war

Two opposing philosophical schools of thought arose in the nineteenth century, concerning the uses to which it was thought the rapidly developing military technology should be put.

On the one hand the military philosophy of the Prussian soldier Carl von Clausewitz emphasized that war was no longer to be considered an irrational act or a natural calamity but was the result of the use of force to achieve political ends:

... to introduce into the philosophy of War itself a principle of moderation would be an absurdity ... if we find civilized nations do not put their prisoners to death, do not devastate towns and countries, this is because their intelligence exercises greater influence on their modes of carrying on War, and has taught them more effectual means of applying force than these rude acts of mere instinct (von Clausewitz, 1832; trans. J. J. Graham, 1908; Penguin edition, 1968, pp. 102–103).

On the other hand there were those who not only advocated a principle of moderation, but managed to persuade governments to agree to national and international rules for the conduct of war. One of the early advocates of moderation was Francis Lieber, a native of Germany, who emigrated to the United States, where, during the carnage of the American Civil War, he helped to draw up the first national military legal code, published by order of the President of the United States as General Order No. 100. Similar legal codes were subsequently adopted by the armed forces of most other military powers.

Also about this time, a young Swiss, Henri Dunant, was moved by his experiences at the Battle of Solferino to propose the establishment of an international organization to assist the wounded and prisoners in time of war (Dunant, 1859). This proposal led to the First Geneva Convention of 1864 and to the establishment of the International Committee of the Red Cross.

In 1868 the major European powers signed the Declaration of St. Petersburg, which had as its object the prevention of "the employment of arms which uselessly aggravate the sufferings of disabled men, or render their death inevitable." From this fundamental principle, the Declaration went on to prohibit a specific class of weapons, namely the employment by the military or naval troops of the contracting parties of any projectile of a weight below 400 grams which was "either explosive or charged with fulminating or inflammable substances.".

In the Declaration of Brussels of 1874, the powers reaffirmed this prohibition and added to it a more general prohibition of "the employment of weapons, projectiles or substances calculated to cause superfluous injuries" (Article 13 e).

The type of wound that the signatories had in mind was that caused by small calibre projectiles filled with gunpowder or some similar composition which could explode or burn on hitting the victim. The wounds caused by such projectiles were large and lacerated and there was little that the surgeons could do to prevent death from loss of blood or disease. The wounds created by such missiles were usually greater than those created by low velocity inert bullets, which were in general regarded as, if not humane, at least as adequate for the task of putting a man out of action.

It is of considerable significance, in view of the fact that certain modern weapons also create large and lacerated wounds or burns, that exploding and incendiary bullets were the very first weapons subjected to a prohibition. The Peace Conference at the Hague in 1899 added expanding and dum-dum bullets to the prohibitions of the St. Petersburg declaration.

Dum-dum, which gave its name to soft-nosed bullets whose jackets do not fully cover the lead core, was the name of a town on the outskirts of Calcutta where an arsenal produced bullets of this kind for use by British colonial forces against local resistance. The Proceedings of the 1899 Hague Conference record that the British delegate, Sir John Ardagh,

adds that there is a difference in war between civilized nations and against savages. If, in the former, a soldier is wounded by a small projectile, he is taken away in the ambulance, but the savage, although run through two or three times, does not cease to advance. For this reason the English delegate demands the liberty of employing projectiles of sufficient efficacy against savage races.

This view was opposed by the Russian delegate who condemned it as "contrary to the humanitarian spirit which rules this end of the nineteenth century" (Scott, 1920, p. 287).

Though in this instance the British delegate was outvoted, the sentiments to which he gave expression continue to have relevance for the development of the law of armed conflicts. The British delegate attempted to make a distinction between conflicts between "civilized nations" (that is, the contracting parties to the international conventions) and conflicts with "savage races" who, since they were not signatories to the conventions, were not

19

protected by international law. A similar distinction is maintained today, where, in an effort to extend the scope of the four Geneva Conventions of 1949, the International Committee of the Red Cross (ICRC) has proposed two additional protocols: one is to cover international armed conflicts (that is conflicts between High Contracting Parties) and the other non-international armed conflicts (that is conflicts, usually in developing countries, between popular movements and a central government).

Neither the First Hague Conference of 1899, nor the Second Hague Conference of 1907 made specific reference to incendiary weapons, which at that time had been eclipsed first by gunpowder and then by high explosives. But the two Hague conferences laid down certain additional principles of the law of armed conflicts.

1. In 1899 the Conference had agreed to prohibit for a period of five years "the launching of projectiles or explosives from balloons, or other new methods of similar nature" (Hague Declaration IV, *1*), thereby taking note of the potential development of aerial warfare. In 1907 the prohibition was renewed, in Declaration XIV, "for a period extending to the close of the Third Peace Conference"—a Conference which has yet to be held!

2. The 1907 Conference added several specific rules to the established principle that weapons should not cause superfluous injury, including a rule that it was forbidden to employ poison or poisoned weapons (Article 23 *e* of the Hague Regulations). They also formulated the general principle that "the right of belligerents to adopt means of injuring the enemy is not unlimited" (Article 22).

3. The preamble to the Declaration of St. Petersburg had established the principle that "the only legitimate object which States should endeavour to accomplish during war is to weaken the *military forces* of the enemy" (italics added). The Hague Regulations added to this principle a specific prohibition against attacking towns or villages which are undefended.

4. The Second Hague Conference adopted a clause proposed by one of the three Russian delegates, which stated that:

Until a more complete code of laws of war has been issued ... the inhabitants and the belligerents remain under the protection and rule of the principles of the law of nations, as they result from the usages established among civilized peoples, from laws of humanity, and from the dictates of public conscience (Hague Convention No. IV, preamble, para. 8).

In effect, that clause established the principle that existing specific laws of war are provisional and require complementing; but that fundamental laws of humanity always apply to both combatants and civilians.

The subsequent history of the use of incendiary weapons emphasizes the need for reaffirming these fundamental principles and the necessity of drawing up a more complete code of the laws of war.

III. *Flame weapons in World War I*

At the outbreak of World War I, the Germans modified for military purposes the civilian Zeppelin fleet they had been building up. These modified Zeppelins were used at first for reconnaissance, and, by December 1914, for bombing. Between January and September 1915 they bombed three British coastal towns, as well as London on two occasions. In 1916 no less than nine Zeppelins made a consorted attack on the town of Shrewsbury, killing 59 people.

In the meantime, the French and British had also developed military air services. Already in 1914, several squadrons were flying along the French front lines on reconnaissance missions. In 1915 they encountered the first resistance in the form of a German fighter aircraft armed with a machine gun. As planes became more powerful, it became possible to equip them with larger calibre guns which were used not only against other aircraft but also against troops on the ground.

By 1917 the Germans had developed the Gotha plane which could carry between 300 and 500 kg of bombs, depending on the amount of fuel carried. London was raided successfully on 13 June. Nearly two tons of bombs were dropped in the area of Liverpool Street Station, one bomb falling on an infant's school in Poplar. One hundred and sixty-two people died and 432 were wounded. Another 57 people were killed and 193 injured in a further attack on the working-class East End of London on 7 July. For these raids both explosive and incendiary bombs were used.[2]

The attacks on the civilian population of London had a number of short-term and long-term consequences. According to Allen (1972), the morale of the working class in London was by 1917 at "a low ebb consequent on the carnage being suffered in France, which struck them more than the rich, as the ordinary soldiers were being used as cannon fodder in greater numbers than the officer class" (Allen, 1972, p. 17). The effect of the bombs, which killed a large number of children in Poplar, London, was to precipitate rioting, strikes and arson, and Lloyd George, the Prime Minister, "no doubt saw the possibility of revolution" (Allen, 1972, p. 17).

Pressed to take political action, he invited the South African General, Jan Smuts, to lead a committee to report on the future of British air power. The conclusions of this committee were to have far-reaching consequences; they recommended abolishing the army and navy air services and establishing an independent air force which would contain an independent bombing force to attack targets in Germany.

These early bombing efforts were no doubt regarded by the military commanders of the time as field experiments rather than as mature means of combat; the casualties claimed were relatively modest compared with the enormity of the slaughter of World War I as a whole: the total number of

---

[2] This account is taken from Allen (1972), pp. 5–17.

people killed by air raids throughout Europe was about 5000 for the whole period of the war (Urlanis, 1971).

On the ground, armies also experimented with flame weapons. The first practical model of an incendiary artillery shell was developed by the French in 1878, and incendiary artillery shells, mortar shells and grenades were used by several of the combatants during World War I (Greene, 1966). Incendiary shells usually contained a solution of white phosphorus in carbon disulphide and bundles of impregnated cloth. When the shell exploded, the bundles would be spread out and ignited (Hanslian, 1937).

White phosphorus not only has an incendiary effect but creates dense white smoke as well. In some attacks white phosphorus was released with chlorine as well as high explosives. For example, along one 28 km long front at Loos on 25 September 1915, the British fired 5500 gas tanks containing some 150 tons of chlorine, 1100 smoke pots, 25000 white phosphorus hand grenades, 10000 high explosive mines from Stokes mortars and 1000 mines from catapults and smaller projectors (Hanslian, 1937).

Between July and November 1918, the period of US participation in World War I, the Americans used 440153 white phosphorus hand grenades in addition to 363776 zinc tetrachloride hand grenades used to produce smoke. They also used 542 Mark I incendiary bombs and 2104 Mark II bombs (Farrows, in Hanslian, 1937).

The Japanese are credited with the first use of compressed gas to project an inflammable liquid (during the Russo-Japanese war of 1905). The Germans also developed flamethrowers during that period, and a portable flamethrower (or *Flammenwerfer*) became standard equipment for the first time in 1912 (Fisher, 1946). It was first used against the French near Melancourt on 26 February 1915. On 30 July 1915 flamethrowers were used to rout the British in their trenches near Ypres (Heon, 1964).

The value of flame at the time was principally psychological—the fiery spurt of burning oil, the roar of the flame, and the billowing clouds of black smoke had a terrifying effect on troops in the trenches. But the portable equipment was cumbersome, resupply was difficult, the field of fire was small, and the range rarely exceeded 30 yards. Furthermore, the operator of the portable apparatus was easily distinguished and highly vulnerable to small arms fire ... The flame projector, with all its faults, became a responsibility of the chemical warfare services (Kleber & Birdsell, 1966, p. 15).

The flame projector was never used by American troops in World War I (Sorenson, 1948; Kleber and Birdsell, 1966) because US military experts at the time were not impressed by its performance.

There is little doubt that flame was overshadowed on the battlefield by chemical weapons such as mustard gas, which claimed up to 5 per cent of the total hospital admissions in 1918 compared with burns and scalds which, even including all causes, hostile and non-hostile, came to only approximately 0.5 per cent. Probably a greater proportion of victims of flamethrower attack died before they reached hospital than did the victims of chemical attack.

Although incendiary weapons played a relatively minor role in World War I, they did merit specific consideration in a number of the post-war disarmament efforts; however, the problem of gas warfare was to dominate these discussions.

IV. *The inter-war period, 1920–1938*

Legal developments

The disarmament efforts between the wars may be grouped into three phases. The first phase was concerned with the series of peace treaties which legally terminated hostilities. The peace treaties of Saint-Germain (Article 135), Neuilly (Article 82), Trianon (Article 119) and Sèvres (Article 176) repeated the formulation of Article 171 of Treaty of Versailles prohibiting chemical weapons, but added to this the prohibition of *flamethrowers*.

The 1923 Draft Rules on Aerial Warfare

The second phase was aimed at broaching the subject of what to do about two of the most threatening developments to emerge during the war, aerial warfare and chemical warfare. Although there were laws for war waged on land and sea, there was no law for air warfare. The initial attempt to draw up rules of air warfare was made in 1923 by a commission of lawyers at the Hague (*American Journal of International Law*, **17**, Supplement, 1923). The commission laid down detailed proposals regarding the problem of aerial bombardment which, while not specifically referring to incendiary bombs, clearly covered their use. The commission also touched upon another problem, namely, the use of small incendiary projectiles which were prohibited for use on land by the St. Petersburg Declaration. During World War I the use of such projectiles to bring down aircraft became common practice; therefore, the commission proposed a formulation that "the use of tracer projectiles, whether incendiary or explosive, by or against an aircraft is not forbidden".

Since the Draft Rules have never been adopted, there is still no law of air warfare, an omission which is no less glaring more than 50 years later.

The 1925 Geneva Protocol

Shortly afterwards, in 1925, the Geneva Protocol prohibiting chemical and bacteriological weapons was signed. During World War I, chemical agents were the cause of greater numbers of casualties than were incendiary weapons and thus gained wider attention in post-war discussions. The Protocol refers to the use in war of asphyxiating, poisonous or other gases and of all other analogous liquids, materials or devices. There is no positive indication that such a formulation was intended to include incendiary weapons. On the other hand, the military practice of many states has traditionally been to include incendiary warfare under the purview of the chemical warfare services; moreover incendiary weapons may produce asphyxiating gases (see chapter 4). It is quite feasible, therefore, that the expression "analogous" was intended to cover weapons like incendiaries which might be used more extensively in future conflicts.[3]

However, since there was never any positive indication that the intention of the Geneva Protocol was to prohibit incendiaries, it is not surprising that the adoption of the Protocol did not have any prohibitory effect on the use of incendiary weapons *per se*.

The 1931–1933 League of Nations Disarmament Conference

The disarmament conference of the League of Nations took place in Geneva from 1931–33 after many years of preparatory effort. This conference undertook the more ambitious task of bringing about substantial disarmament as a basis for a more peaceful world. It was addressed to all classes of armaments.

In March 1933, the delegation of the United Kingdom submitted to the General Commission a draft disarmament convention which contained provisions concerning chemical, incendiary and bacteriological warfare. The relevant provisions of this draft convention were as follows:

Article 49

The prohibition of the use of incendiary weapons shall apply to:
  1. *The use of projectiles specifically intended to cause fires.*
  The prohibition shall not apply to:

(a) Projectiles specially constructed to give light or to be luminous and generally to pyrotechnics not intended to cause fires, or to projectiles of all kinds capable of producing incendiary effects accidentally;

(b) Incendiary projectiles designed specifically for defence against aircraft, *provided that they are used exclusively for that purpose.*

  2. *The use of appliances designed to attack persons by fire,* such as flame-projectors (League of Nations, Series of Publications: 1933. IX, 2; Conf. D. 157 (1); italics added).

Despite a number of reservations, the British draft was unanimously accepted as a basis for a future convention.[4]

---

[3] The Protocol, like all such documents, was presumably a compromise between more or less restrictive points of view; the content of an open term like "analogous" may have been accorded more specific content by some of the signatories to the Protocol than by others.
[4] The provisional text of the draft convention, prepared in the light of the modifications adopted in the first reading and of the amendments presented by the delegations and published on 22 September 1933 (Conference Document 163 (1)), contained a proposal by the Little Entente to delete paragraph three of Article 47, on the right to retaliate (Conference document C. G. 123).

But the conference never reconvened. Its collapse brought to nothing the League's efforts to go beyond the Geneva Protocol of 1925.

With all its shortcomings, the text of the convention, if it had been adopted, would have constituted a considerable advance, when compared to the 1925 Geneva Protocol. In particular it would have:

(*a*) prohibited not only chemical and biological but also incendiary weapons;

(*b*) prohibited preparations for chemical, incendiary and bacteriological warfare in time of peace as well as in time of war, including the training of armed forces in the use of banned weapons;

(*c*) instituted some international supervision and governmental control of substances used for protective experiments;

(*d*) enabled states to submit complaints about possible breaches of the prohibition;

(*e*) introduced some procedure for establishing the fact of the use of the prohibited weapons.

To suggest that incendiary weapons were a major concern in these negotiations would be misleading. Incendiary weapons, though viewed with some horror, were regarded by many military experts as somewhat ineffective and only marginally useful. But, to those military authorities who were prepared to use weapons against unprotected civilian populations, incendiary weapons offered certain attractions, due to the propensity of fire to cause panic and to spread. The Special Committee of the Disarmament Conference, in terms which in retrospect appear far-sighted, had drawn attention to these uses of incendiary weapons. But the Draft Disarmament Convention was overtaken by political events; Hitler's rapid rise to power and the forces behind it brought their deliberations to nought.

Military developments

British air power in Western Asia, 1916–1940

During and after World War I, the colonial powers, Britain and France, competed to establish their hegemony over large areas of the Middle East from the Mediterranean to the Northwest Frontier of India. Their efforts met with resistance from the local peoples.

In the face of a deteriorating situation, Winston Churchill was transferred from the Air Ministry to the Colonial Office in the early spring of 1921. The British rulers were faced with a rebellion in Mesopotamia (Iraq) which was costing £30 million a year to put down (Payne, 1966). Churchill summoned a meeting of high officials, including T. E. Lawrence[5] and Air Marshall Sir Hugh Trenchard. Apparently on Lawrence's recommendation (he was then in the Royal Air Force), the RAF was given the task of conducting punitive campaigns on the Northwest Frontier, the Middle East and Somaliland (Divine, 1966; Allen, 1972). Operations of this kind had been carried out as early as 1916 in Sudan (Slessor, 1956) and continued until World War II.

These events contributed to the development of the concept of air warfare in two ways. First, this appears to have been the earliest attempt to use air power in an attempt to "pacify" resistance to colonial rule—a use of air power which later became a prominent one. Second, the "effectiveness" of British bombs and machine guns against almost defenceless villages, apparently convinced Trenchard of the omnipotence of bombers—a conviction which was to become the doctrine of the Royal Air Force during World War II.

Ethiopia, 1935–1936

In a telegram on 30 December 1935 the Emperor of Ethiopia informed the Secretary-General of the League of Nations that the Italian troops invading his country had made use of asphyxiating and poison gases. (For an account of these episodes, see SIPRI, 1971*a*, 1971*b*.)

In a memorandum by the Ethiopian National Red Cross Society, addressed to the International Committee of the Red Cross on 2 March 1936, attention was drawn to consignments of *inter alia* incendiary weapons, including 3 227 incendiary bombs on 4 January 1936 and 185 flamethrowers on 19 January.

Detailed allegations and refutations were made on the question of the use of gas, particularly mustard gas which causes chemical burns. A large number of burn cases reported by various observers were attributed to mustard gas, air-dropped in large containers by the Italians. However, in a statement of 10 June 1936, a Belgian lieutenant, Armand Frère, formerly military adviser to the army of Ras Desta (the son-in-law of the Emperor), claimed that he had never seen victims of gas attacks:

What the Ethiopians took for gas bombs were *merely incendiary bombs,* which, after exploding, left greenish yellow traces giving off a smell of slow combustion powder; this had nothing to do with gas and was quite harmless to the touch (SIPRI, 1971, Vol. IV, p. 185; after League of Nations, Appendix I, 1: Document C. 280. M. 170, 1936. VII; italics added).[6]

A major problem with flamethrowers in World War I had been that they were heavy and cumbersome to carry, and the duration and range of the

---

[5] T. E. Lawrence ("Lawrence of Arabia") had played an active role in the Middle East during World War I. He is the author of the book, *The Seven Pillars of Wisdom,* and has become something of a legend.
[6] A similar "explanation" has been given with regard to allegations of the use of poison gas in Yemen; see p. 64.

flames was short, due to the small amount of fuel that could be carried and the limited power of equipment small enough to be portable. By mounting flamethrowers on tanks, a much more powerful device could be used, and a fuel capacity of several hundred litres could be carried (*Revue Militaire d'Information*, No. 225, 1954; Sorenson, 1948).

According to Kleber & Birdsell (1966), the Italians were the first to employ a flamethrower mounted on a tank, in Ethiopia in 1935. The following year they demonstrated flamethrowers mounted on other combat cars and armoured vehicles.

The Italians also capitalized on their almost uncontested control of the air over Ethiopia. Bombardment from aircraft was used as a means of terrorizing Ethiopians, both troops and civilians. Incendiary bombs were used in tactical support; in addition, according to many reports, undefended Ethiopian towns were bombed. Except for Addis Ababa most of the centres of Ethiopia were subjected to substantial bombing, often with incendiaries.

Replying to allegations of incendiary bombing, the Italian Embassy in London issued a statement saying that "the use by the Italian air forces of incendiary bombs against concentrated Ethiopian troops was a reprisal against the use by Ethiopians of dum-dum bullets"[7] (*New York Times*, 8 December 1935).

The city of Harar, which at that time had a normal population of 40 000, was left in flames after a two-and-a-half-hour attack with incendiary bombs in March 1936 (*New York Times*, 30 March 1936).

The Italian activities in Ethiopia were widely deplored and they aroused sufficiently strong opposition to lead to the adoption of sanctions against Italy by the League of Nations.

Of particular interest here is the fact that in October 1935 the committee established by the League to coordinate sanctions against Italy adopted a proposal which, in placing an embargo on shipments of certain categories of arms to Italy and Italian possessions, included flamethrowers on the list of prohibitions. In the same category were placed mustard gas, lewisite, ethyldichlorarsine and all other products destined for chemical or incendiary warfare (League of Nations, 1935, *Official Journal*, Special Supplement No. 145. Co-ordination Committee. Second Meeting [Private]).[8]

Since the League sanctions were applied half-heartedly and never included military measures, they failed to stop aggression and the use of chemical and incendiary weapons. On 6 July 1936 the League Assembly

---

[7] This reasoning is interesting since it would seem to be based on the supposition that both dum-dum bullets and incendiary bombs were regarded as illegal means of warfare.

[8] Against paragraphs 1 and 2, the following remark was made: "It should be observed that the utilization of these articles has been and still is, prohibited under the Convention of June 17th, 1925. These articles are only mentioned above because their manufacture being free (the more so, as in many instances they serve various purposes), the Committee desires to emphasize that the export of such products could in no circumstances be tolerated." (League of Nations, *Official Journal*, Special Supplement No. 145. Co-ordinating Committee. Fourth Meeting)

abrogated the restrictive measures (League of Nations, 1936, *Official Journal,* Special Supplement No. 150).

The Spanish Civil War, 1936–1939

The Spanish Civil War provided a further opportunity to test incendiary weapons in combat and to develop tactics as a prelude to World War II. Both sides received outside help: the Nationalists from Germany and Italy, the Republicans from the Soviet Union. New Soviet bombers, the SB-2s, with a 500 kg bomb load were mainly used for tactical bombing of targets such as Nationalist airfields, though towns were bombed as well.

On the Nationalist side, Germany introduced flame tanks (Kleber & Birdsell, 1966) and the German Condor Legion flew in Junkers 52/3Ms and the new Heinkel He 111B-2s. These, too, were used for bombing targets such as airfields and for other tactical uses. During these operations, thermite bombs were used. Nationalist planes also bombed towns with incendiaries, frequently in combination with machine-gun strafing as in the case of the attack on the Aragonian town of Gijon on 15 October 1937.

There are indications that some of the attacks on towns were designed as experiments to guide the planning of the German Luftwaffe which was in the process of a massive expansion. This view is supported by a statement of Goering who, as chief of the Luftwaffe, was in charge of supplying aid to France (*Nuremberg Trials, IX,* pp. 280–81).

Thomas (1961) reports that the German officers were interested in seeing the reaction of a civilian population to a carefully planned attempt to set fire to a city. The bombing of Madrid concentrated on hospitals and other buildings whose destruction would be most likely to cause panic.

Perhaps the most thorough experiment of this kind was the destruction of the Basque town of Guernica on 26 April 1937.

At half past four in the afternoon, a single peal of church bells announced an air raid. There had been some raids in the area before, but Guernica had not been bombed. At twenty minutes to five Heinkel 111s began to appear, first bombing the town and then machine-gunning its streets. The Heinkels were followed by the old spectres of the Spanish war, Junkers 52s. People began to run from the town. These also were machine gunned. Incendiary bombs, weighing up to 1 000 1b [454 kg], and also high explosives, were dropped by waves of aircraft arriving every twenty minutes until a quarter-to-eight. The centre of the town was then destroyed and burning. 1 654 people were killed and 889 wounded (Thomas, 1961, p. 419).

The Sino-Japanese War, 1937–1945

During the first stage of the war, when the League of Nations was still functioning, it condemned the cruelty of the Japanese campaigns, in particular the bombings of the most densely populated Chinese towns: Canton, Nanking, Yenchow and others. The question of regulating or inhibiting aerial warfare was also raised. Incendiary weapons were not discussed separately, though allegations of incendiary bombing were made in passing.

The Japanese, militarily the stronger party with a superior air force, were accused of using incendiaries against population centres as well as flamethrowers in combat (*The Sino-Japanese conflict and the League of Nations,* Press Bureau of the Chinese Delegation, Geneva, 1937).

Towards the end of World War II as allied forces sought to dislodge the Japanese from the Asian mainland, Chinese cities were again bombed, this time by US aircraft. Hankow was bombed exclusively with incendiary bombs on 18 December 1944 (see below, p. 36).

Incendiary weapons on the eve of World War II

By the late 1930s several states had demonstrated their readiness to use both portable and mechanized flamethrowers and incendiary bombs. The British, the French and the Russians, for their part, having made limited use of these weapons during World War I, maintained similar weapons in their arsenals.

As for the United States, it appears that prior to World War II there was little military interest in incendiary munitions:

Incendiary artillery, mortar shells, and grenades were used tactically [in World War I] but these and the bombs were not particularly effective. Because of this, there was a considerable lack of interest in the further development of incendiary munitions in the US ... Most military experts were of the opinion that high-explosive munitions offered far more potential because they could destroy targets by blast and start fires as a secondary effect (Greene, 1966, p. 895).

However, this assessment was not shared by the US Army Chemical Warfare Service, which several years before World War II initiated a project to develop an effective incendiary bomb.

Further, between the two world wars the major powers had developed doctrines for the use of air power which were to have a major impact on the course of World War II. According to Jackson (1970), the Soviet Union learned from the Spanish Civil War the need to develop an aircraft designed for support of ground troops, a lesson which was to provide the Soviet Union with the world's most formidable short-range attack force, as well as dictating the tactical thinking of the Red Air Force's strategists for years to come. Because of this thinking, the Soviet Union did not develop heavy long distance bombers at that time.

The German Air Force, on the other hand, developed its *Blitzkrieg* tactic of heavy forward bombing of strategic targets in advance of ground troops, a method used with great success in the early part of World War II.

The British Royal Air Force adopted a doctrine of *independent* air power—that is, independent of ground operations—which, although derived as an "economy" measure in wars of pacification, came to dominate British air warfare against Germany. But it was not until 1942 that they produced the heavy bombers required to pursue this policy. The United States, on the other hand, was the only power to have a heavy bomber (the B-17) operational at the beginning of the war.

V. *The rise of incendiary weapons in World War II*

Within a short time of the outbreak of World War II, flamethrowers were used in ground combat and incendiary bombs were dropped from the air. The early use in Europe stimulated research and development elsewhere which were to be significant later:

By mid-1940 intelligence reports revealed that the Germans had employed flamethrowers in Poland, in their attack on the Belgian fort of Eben Emael, and in their drive across the Low Countries and France. As these reports, often undocumented, were scattered and usually highly coloured, doubt remained as to the extent of Axis preparation for the employment of flamethrowers. But that such weapons might be useful could no longer be denied by American planners (Kleber & Birdsell, 1966, p. 535).

The outbreak of war in Europe called attention as never before to the possibilities of aerial incendiaries. German planes began to shower London with magnesium electron bombs and 100-kilo oil bombs, and the English replied with their 4-pound magnesium munition. The United States Army could no longer afford to neglect the development and production of incendiary bombs (*Ibid.*, p. 617).

At this time, too, Soviet planes dropped 41 000 incendiary bombs and 55 000 high explosive bombs on 690 targets in Finland, killing 956 people (Pajari, 1971). The Finns, in turn, replied with improvised "Molotov cocktails" against Soviet ground forces in the bitter Winter War.[9]

The use of incendiary weapons during World War II demonstrated to all parties their awesome possibilities. The weapons were developed from the unreliable devices of World War I to major weapons of tactical and strategic warfare.

During World War II the military uses of incendiary weapons became more differentiated. Metal or oil incendiary bombs were used for "strategic bombing" of built-up areas, that is as what subsequently became known as "weapons of mass destruction". Lighter-case oil incendiary bombs (napalm bombs, or "fire-bombs") were used for tactical missions against troops or light army equipment on the ground. Flamethrowers were mainly used for special purposes such as attacks on troops in pill-boxes or caves, though occasionally they were used in major assaults. These various uses are described in more detail below.

Area bombing

During World War II the concept of deploying concentrated air power as an independent means of carrying the war to the heartland of an industrial country became a major strategy. Incendiary bombs played an important part in this strategy. Strategic area bombing generated at the time, and continues to generate, considerable controversy, arising from doubts both

---

[9] In February 1944, during the Continuation War, the Soviet Air Force dropped a further 15 300 bombs on Helsinki, about half of them incendiaries, killing 145 people (Mäkelä, 1967).

as to its military effectiveness as a means of winning wars, and as to its moral and legal position.

It is beyond the scope of this study to examine in detail the questions posed by strategic area bombing as a means of war. Nevertheless, because of the important part played by incendiary bombs in this strategy it is necessary to examine some of the rationale and consequences of strategic area bombing.

In the early part of World War II cities were bombed indiscriminately—the Germans bombed Polish cities and later Rotterdam,[10] French and Belgian harbour towns,[11] and then across the Channel in England while the British bombed Wilhelmshaven, Cuxhaven, Berlin and other German targets.[12]

As the war proceeded and capability expanded, bombing attacks were directed at important port cities and centres for the production of aircraft engines or other military equipment and munitions.[13] The attacks were also indiscriminate in their effects, since navigational and bombing methods were highly inaccurate. They had little military effect since bomb loads were small and air defences good.[14] Each of the major powers in turn discovered that it could not afford the losses associated with daylight raids with unescorted bombers over enemy heartlands.

[10] This attack was an example of "coercive warfare". Dutch resistance to the German offensive was stronger than expected and the Germans issued an ultimatum to the defenders of Rotterdam to surrender or be bombed. As the time limit ran out the defenders did surrender, but the bombers were already on their way. Forty-three of them received the order not to bomb and turned back but the remaining 57 He-111 bombers had already dropped 98 tons of high explosive bombs (Middlebrook, 1973). Though incendiaries were not used, a 2.9 km² area of the city caught fire making 75 000 people homeless (Rumpf, 1952).

[11] Ostend, Dunkirk, Calais, Boulogne and Le Havre (Rumpf, 1952).

[12] The British tried to bomb Wilhelmshaven on 4 September 1939 only two days after they entered the war (Hampe, 1963). The German planes first attacked British airfields. Hitler directed that "the Air Force is, in the first place, to prevent the French and British Air Forces from attacking the German Army and the German *Lebensraum* (air space) ..." (Shirer, 1962, p. 590). The German Air Force bombed London in December 1940 and May 1941, after Churchill had ordered attacks on Berlin in August 1940 (Webster & Frankland, 1962).

[13] On 14 November 1940 the city of Coventry, a centre for the production of aircraft engines and other important engineering products, was bombed with 500 tons of high explosives and more than a thousand incendiary bombs. Four hundred people were killed and a twelfth of the city destroyed, but production in the aircraft engine factory was only broken off for a week. This attack was followed by others in Liverpool, Birmingham, Sheffield, Manchester, Leeds, Glasgow and elsewhere (Rumpf, 1952).

The British bombers retaliated with a raid on 16 December 1940, when 134 aircraft dropped incendiary bombs on Mannheim. Berlin, Hamm, Essen, Düsseldorf, Hanover, Bremen, Cologne and Hamburg were also bombed in this early period.

[14] Of the one-and-a-half-million men in the Luftwaffe at the outbreak of war, nearly two-thirds were anti-aircraft personnel (Verrier, 1968).

"For its part, the British Government, in expectation of terror bombing of London, had ordered Fighter Command to be concentrated in the south of England; the radar stations gave early warning only to the south, east and north-east ... In the event, therefore, the radar and fighter shield for London proved, with the great success of Bomber Command in sinking the barge concentrations, an effective defence against invasion" (Verrier, 1968, p. 76).

In these circumstances attention turned in some quarters towards the feasibility of large-scale night raids. These, too, proved costly of men and aircraft, but more to the point here is that, with the equipment then available, it was not possible to locate "precision" targets at night. Hence the rationale of area bombing was developed.

Lord Cherwell, scientific adviser to the British government, produced a cabinet paper which formed the basis of the bombing policy in early 1942, and which has been summarized by another government scientist as follows:

It described, in quantitative terms, the effect on Germany of a British bombing offensive in the next eighteen months (approximately March 1942–September 1943). The paper laid down a strategic policy. The bombing must be directed essentially against German working-class houses. Middle-class houses have too much space around them, and so are bound to waste bombs; factories and "military objectives" had long since been forgotten, except in official bulletins, since they were much too difficult to find and hit (Snow, 1962, p. 47).

This policy was energetically pursued by the newly appointed Commander-in-Chief of Bomber Command, Sir Arthur Harris, until the end of the war, apparently in spite of subsequent directives putting more emphasis on industrial and transportation targets. The first major night raids were on Lübeck (28–29 March 1942) and Rostock (23–26 April 1942); though these old medieval towns were largely destroyed, the Heinkel and Arado aircraft factories were not, according to Rumpf (1952).

The German aircraft and other war production continued to increase to the point where the bombing offensive was being seriously compromised. The Casablanca Conference in early 1943 led to agreement on a Combined Bomber Offensive by British and US forces, the mission of which was

to accomplish the progressive destruction and dislocation of the German military, industrial and economic system, and the undermining of the morale of the German people to a point where their capacity for armed resistance is fatally weakened. This is construed as meaning so weakened as to permit initiation of final combined operations on the Continent (*The Combined Bomber Offensive from the United Kingdom* (Pointblank) *as approved by the Combined Chiefs of Staff, 14 May 1943.* In Webster & Frankland, 1961).

After this preamble, the directive went on to specify six target areas: small submarine construction yards and bases; the German aircraft industry; industries manufacturing ball-bearings, synthetic rubber and tyres; oil installations and military transport vehicles. There was no further discussion of "morale" but the respective roles of the British and US forces were spelt out:

... when precision targets are bombed by the (US) Eighth Air Force in daylight, the efforts should be complemented and completed by RAF bombing attacks against the surrounding industrial area at night. Fortunately the industrial areas to be attacked are in most cases identical with the industrial areas which the British Bomber Command has selected for mass destruction anyway (*Ibid.*).

Indiscriminate effects of incendiary bombing: I. Dresden, Germany, 1945.

"A total of 190 335 tons of incendiaries and 292 000 tons of high explosives were dropped by the Royal Air Force on German cities. The USAF added a further 80 000 tons ..." (p. 33).

"At the time of the attack on Dresden it was overfilled with an unknown number of refugees from the Eastern front. For this reason it was particularly difficult to estimate the number of casualties. Estimates ranged from under 100 000 dead to 300 000." (p. 34)

(Photo: ADN)

Indiscriminate effects of incendiary bombing: II. Shizuoka, Japan, 1945.

"US air forces dropped 160 800 tons of bombs on the Japanese home islands, most of them incendiaries ... A total of more than 40 per cent of the housing in some 65 cities was destroyed and an estimated five to six hundred thousand civilians died." (p. 36)

(Photo: Mainichi Newspapers)

Indiscriminate effects of incendiary bombing: III. Tokyo, Japan, 1945.

"The death rate of Tokyo was higher than that of Hiroshima or Nagasaki ..."
(p. 37)

(Photo: Mainichi Newspapers)

Indiscriminate effects of incendiary bombing: IV. South Viet-Nam, 1966.

"It is likely that the total tonnage of air-dropped napalm, phosphorus and other incendiary munitions actually expended in Indo-China exceeded 400 000 tons ..." (p. 52) "Greater quantities of incendiary munitions have been used in South Viet-Nam than in any other country in any other war ... it is clear that many civilian casualties have resulted from this massive use of incendiaries." (p. 59)

Photo shows napalm (black smoke) and phosphorus bombs (white smoke) exploding in a village 70 km from Bien Hoa. Four A-1E aircraft were used in the attack, two loaded with six 500-lb general purpose bombs and six 260-lb fragmentation bombs, and two loaded with six 500-lb napalm cannisters and eight 100-lb white phosphorus bombs. While one aircraft engaged in a bombing run, a second strafed the target with cannon fire. Each napalm aircraft made two tree-top level passes, dumping a mixture of napalm and phosphorus on each pass. A post-strike assessment showed 29 buildings destroyed and five damaged. (*Aviation Week & Space Technology,* 21, 28 February 1966)

(Photo: James H. Pickering/*Aviation Week*).

Thus the rationale of strategic bombing had two components. First, there was still the hope of affecting the enemy's means of production, even if specific industrial targets could not be located or only at great cost. Modern industries depend on the continued supply of materials and parts from subcontractors, and on a large working force living in the neighbourhood. Area attacks were expected to occasion some direct damage to important industries, to destroy feeder companies and lines of communication, and to cause casualties to the working force.

Second, from the earliest days there was a psychological component.[15] It was hoped that area attacks on cities would lower the morale of the population, which might diminish war production and even lead to capitulation. The emphasis given to the "success" of such attacks in the propaganda on the home front suggests that they were also used to boost domestic morale (Verrier, 1968) and that of the political leaders.

Experiments with incendiary weapons proved that they were not very successful against industrial targets, unless these were particularly inflammable, but that they could be effective against small inner-city residential and commercial properties, since these buildings readily took fire and rapidly spread. With the shift towards the area bombing of working-class residental areas, incendiary bombs became a major weapon. A total of 1 136 000 tons of bombs were dropped on German targets by the Western allies; of these, 190 335 tons were incendiaries and 292 000 tons were high explosive (HE) and fragmentation bombs dropped by the Royal Air Force on German cities. The USAF added a further 80 000 tons to the latter total (USSBS, 1945; Blackett, 1948; Harris, 1947; Rumpf, 1961).

At first incendiary bombs were dropped at the beginning of a raid to mark the target for the following planes. Later, as photographic reconnaissance showed large areas which could be burned out, the proportion of incendiaries dropped on German cities was increased from about 25 or 30 per cent to about 70 per cent (Fisher, 1946).

High explosive and fragmentation bombs added to the effects of the incendiaries in a variety of ways:

The high explosives were dispatched in Germany to perform the multiple duties of breaking water mains, blocking streets, keeping the fire guards under cover, inflicting civilian casualties, lowering morale, puncturing occasional reinforced concrete buildings and harassing fire-fighters with delayed action explosives after the attack. It was thought that the greatly increased havoc and confusion caused by the fires in Japan would counteract the lack of high explosive bombs (Bond, 1946, p. 174).

The bombing of an already burning area with HE serves to impede the efforts of local fire fighters, but heavy demolition bombs are also effective means for extinguishing fires. Fragmentation bombs have been found to be reasonably satisfactory in restraining firemen without impeding the progress of the fires. These of course must be detonated while the fire fighting is in progress, that is some time after the

[15] The British carried out a psychological warfare leaflet raid over Germany the day after they entered the war and these raids continued (Verrier, 1968).

incendiary bombs have been dropped. Delayed action bombs dropped at random throughout the area also add to the uncertainty and confusion of the defence (Fisher, 1946, p. 9).[16]

The US Strategic Bombing Survey (USSBS) estimated that in 49 of the larger German cities, 2 164 800 dwelling units out of 5 554 500 (39 per cent) were destroyed or seriously damaged, in addition to large areas of commercial and public buildings (USSBS, 1945). Frequently fire accounted for 75–80 per cent of the damage, particularly in those areas where fire-storms occurred.

The USSBS reported fire-storms in Hamburg, Kassel, Darmstadt and Dresden (USSBS, 1945) but Bond (1946) notes that, as this survey was incomplete, there may have been others; for instance, the fire chief of Stuttgart reported fire-storm conditions there. The greatest loss of life occurred in Hamburg and in Dresden.

Hamburg was bombed many times, but the most devastating raids were carried out on 24/25 and 27/28 July and 3/4 August 1943 by the British Commonwealth air forces. In each of these three raids an average of 700 aircraft dropped 1 300 tons of high explosive bombs, 500 tons of 30-1b oil incendiary bombs, and 600 tons of 4-1b magnesium-thermite bombs (Bond, 1946). German reports also speak of phosphorus bombs bursting in the air and scattering particles of burning phosphorus (Miller, 1972). An estimated 55–60 per cent of the city was destroyed, 75–80 per cent of it by fire, including 32.5 km^2 completely burned out. Fire fighting was limited because the high explosive bombs burst water mains in 847 places (Bond, 1946); in some areas fire hoses went dry within 8 minutes (Miller, 1972). It was estimated that 60 000–100 000 people were killed and 750 000 of a population of 1 760 000 made homeless (USSBS, 1945).

Dresden was attacked during the night of 13/14 February 1945 by the British air forces and the following day by the USAAF. The rationale for this attack remains obscure: unlike Hamburg, Dresden was a cultural rather than an industrial centre, and the railway junctions received little damage. At the time of the attack it was overfilled with an unknown number of refugees from the Eastern front. For this reason it was particularly difficult to estimate the number of casualties. Estimates ranged from under 100 000 dead to 300 000 (*New York Times,* 2 January 1946). Irving (1963) settles for a figure of 135 000.

The capital city of Berlin proved harder to burn, with the result that twice as many incendiary bombs per given area were dropped (Bond, 1946).

[16] The British apparently learned to use delayed action bombs from the Germans: "The use of approximately 10 per cent delay action bombs is recommended in view of the difficulties experienced by the railway authorities from the small number of similar bombs dropped in England, especially if set to explode at frequent intervals and so prevent or seriously interfere with fire fighting, repair and general traffic organisation" (Directive, 9 July 1941, from Air Vice-Marshal N. H. Bottomley (Deputy Chief of the Air Staff) to Air Marshal Sir Richard Peirse, in Webster & Frankland, 1961, Vol. IV, p. 140).

Though no fire-storm is reported, about 60–70 per cent of the city was destroyed, about three-quarters of the damage being caused by fire (USSBS, 1945).

The human cost of these attacks is incalculable. Apart from the direct casualties the scale of destruction was sufficient to have numerous indirect effects on the society. At the end of the war the occupation authorities in Berlin reported an infant mortality rate of 359.4 per thousand (*UN Statistical Yearbook,* 1948), a rate about three times greater than in the poorest developing countries (the normal infant mortality rate in Berlin before the war was less than 60 per thousand). Infant mortality rates of this order of magnitude indicate a complete breakdown of normal health, sanitation and food distribution facilities.

While there is no doubt as to the extent of the destruction of the German cities, there is considerable doubt as to the effect on the course of the war.

The British Bombing Survey Unit concluded that

... area attacks against German cities could not have been responsible for more than a very small part of the fall which actually had occurred in German production by the spring of 1945, and ... in terms of bombing effort, they were also a very costly way of achieving the results which they did achieve (BBSU, *The Strategic Air War,* p. 97; cited in Frankland & Webster, 1961, p. 49).[17]

The attempt to "dehouse" the German population proved less successful than expected since German cities proved to have an "elasticity" of 25 per cent—that is, the population of a given city remained the same until more than 25 per cent of the houses were destroyed, since the remaining houses absorbed the homeless part of the population. The equivalent figure in Japan was 10 per cent (Iklé, 1958).[18]

There was little evidence to suggest that lowered morale due to bombing had a significant effect on the German capacity to make war; indeed, ironically perhaps in view of the emphasis on the morale effects of area bombing, the evidence points to greater morale effects of precision bombing on particular armaments factories:

[17] The US Strategic Bombing Survey estimated that the percentage loss in total German production attributable to strategic bombing was 2.5 in 1942; 9.0 in 1943; 17.0 in 1944 and 6.5 in 1945 (January to April). The British Bombing Survey Unit estimated that war production (as opposed to total production) was never reduced by more than 3.8 per cent (Frankland & Webster, 1961, vol. IV, p. 49). The US Strategic Bombing Survey reported with regard to the Hiroshima atomic attack:
"The bulk of the city's output came from large plants located on the outskirts of the city; one half of the industrial production came from only five firms. Of these larger companies, only one suffered more than superficial damage. Of their working force, 94 percent were uninjured. Since electric power was available, and materials and working force were not destroyed, plants ordinarily responsible for three-fourths of Hiroshima's industrial production could have resumed normal operation within 30 days of the attack had the war continued" (USSBS, "The Effect of Atomic Bombs on Hiroshima and Nagasaki", in Bond, 1946).
[18] F. C. Iklé's study on *The Social Impact of Bomb Destruction* (1958) was based on classified work for the US Air Force and US Army. The author is presently Director of the US Arms Control and Disarmament Agency.

Daylight raids with conventional bombs against defense plants create a localized danger which leads to absenteeism in the factories rather than flight from the city. Such absenteeism occurred during World War II . . . (Iklé, 1958, p. 30).

Incendiary bombs were used in Asia with much the same rationale as in Europe—as weapons of mass destruction. The US incendiary raids on Japan were preceded by bombing raids in Burma, Thailand, Indo-China, South China and throughout the Pacific. The assault on Iwo Jima, for example, was preceded by a 10-week bombardment in which incendiary clusters formed a significant part of the bomb load (Kleber & Birdsell, 1966). An attack on Hankow, China, on 18 December 1944, was noteworthy in that it consisted *only* of incendiary bombs (Fisher, 1946). Also of note is the fact that an occupied town was chosen for the experiment. Forty to fifty per cent of the target area was destroyed though "some bombs were dropped in areas inhabited by Chinese civilians" (Craven & Cate, 1953, Vol. V. p. 166).

US air forces dropped a total of 656 000 tons of bombs in the Pacific area, of which 160 800 tons were dropped on the Japanese home islands (Craven & Cate, 1950). Most of the bombs dropped on Japan were incendiaries. The most devastating raid was that on Tokyo on 9/10 March 1945.[19] The official US Air Force historians described it as follows:

The area attacked was a rectangle measuring approximately four by three miles. It was densely populated, with an average of 103 000 inhabitants to the square mile (one ward, the Asakusa, averaged 135 000) and a "built-upness", or ratio of roof space to total area, of 40 to 50 per cent, as compared to a normal American residential average of about 10 per cent. The zone bordered the most important industrial section of Tokyo and included a few individually designated strategic targets. Its main importance lay in its home industries and feeder plants; being closely spaced and predominantly of wood-bamboo-plaster construction, these buildings easily kindled and the flames spread with the rapidity of a brush fire in a drought, damaging the fire-resistive factories . . .
Police records show that 267 171 buildings were destroyed—about one-fourth of the total in Tokyo—and that 1 008 005 persons were rendered homeless. The official roll of casualties listed 83 793 dead and 40 918 wounded. It was twentyfive days before all the dead were removed from the ruins . . .
It was good propaganda to picture LeMay[20] as a modern Nero . . . and there are passages in Tacitus' famous account of the disaster of 64 A.D. that might have been applied to that of 10 March. But the physical destruction and loss of life at Tokyo

---

[19] There was a small incendiary raid on Nagasaki the previous summer (Craven & Cate, 1953). Smaller raids with high explosive bombs continued throughout the autumn in 1944. The first night raid on Tokyo was on 29–30 November (Guillain, 1947). At the end of January 1945, 15 B-29s dropped high explosive bombs in the heart of Tokyo. The raids continued in February. The significance of the 9 March raid was that many more aircraft were involved, and the strong wind caused the fire to spread rapidly and with great intensity.
[20] General Curtis E. LeMay, Commanding General XXI Bomber Command, 1945; Chief of Staff, US Army Strategic Air Forces in the Pacific, August 1945 (Hiroshima, Nagasaki); Commander in Chief, Strategic Air Command, 1948–57; Chief of Staff, US Air Force, 1961–64. Asked about how to solve the problem of the Viet-Nam war he replied: "My solution? Tell the Vietnamese they've got to draw in their horns and stop aggression or we're going to bomb them back into the Stone Age" (cited in Greene, 1967).

exceeded that of Rome (where ten out of fourteen wards of a much smaller city were consumed) or that of any of the great conflagrations of the Western world—London, 1666 (436 acres, 13 200 buildings); Moscow, 1812 (38 000 buildings); Chicago, 1871 (2 124 acres, 17 450 buildings); San Francisco, 1906 (4 square miles, 21 188 buildings). Only Japan itself, with the earthquake and fire of 1923 at Tokyo and Yokohama, had suffered so terrible a disaster. No other air attack of the war, either in Japan or Europe, was so destructive of life and property (Craven & Cate, 1953, Vol. V, pp. 616–17).

According to official US figures, the death toll in Tokyo was higher than that in Hiroshima or Nagasaki.[21] Indeed fire was the major cause of death from the two atomic bombs (see chapter 3), which are also in this respect incendiary weapons.[22]

The Tokyo raid was followed by large-scale incendiary attacks on Nagoya, Kobe, Osaka, Yokohama and Kawasaki, the most important industrial cities. By 14 August, 58 other Japanese cities had been fire-bombed (Craven & Crate, 1953). A total of more than 40 per cent of the housing in some 65 cities was destroyed and an estimated five to six hundred thousand civilians died (Mainichi Newspapers, 1971).

In spite of the huge death tolls resulting from area bombing in both Germany and Japan, it seems impossible to draw conclusions about the impact on either civilian morale or on political leadership. Although attacks on cities caused some industrial damage, Albert Speer, the German minister responsible for war production, concluded after the war that bombing aimed at specific economic targets was more effective than attacks on towns and cities (in Webster & Frankland, 1961, Vol. IV.)

The flamethrower in World War II

On 10 May 1940 the Germans employed flamethrowers in their attack on the Belgian fort of Eben Emael. The flame tank Pzkw II, which had been developed during the Spanish Civil War, was used again in breaking through the Maginot Line on 19 June 1940 and in 1941 in the invasion eastward into Russia. A new flame tank, the Pzkw III, was introduced in 1943.

[21] Guillain (1947) reports that "after the war I learned that, according to official Japanese documents seized by the American command [secret documents which belonged to the Japanese government during the war and which were not drawn to the attention of the Americans] the definitive total was 197 000 dead or missing . . . [compared with] about 130 000 in Hiroshima—half dying immediately, the other half later, as a result of their injuries" (trans. J. Schiffman, in Livingston, Moore & Oldfather, 1973).
[22] It is estimated that the effect of the Hiroshima bomb could have been achieved by placing approximately 975 tons of incendiary bombs and 325 tons of high explosive bombs in the target area. To ensure this tonnage in the target area, it is estimated that a total of 1 600 tons would have to have been dropped. To these bomb loads, about 500 tons of fragmentation bombs would be required to inflict a comparable number of casualties (US Strategic Bombing Survey, in Bond, 1946).

The British established a Department of Petroleum Warfare,[23] which also had the function of exploring possible uses of petroleum as a weapon. A great variety of ingenious devices were produced ranging from a rifle which fired milk bottles filled with phosphorus to enormous systems of stationary flame devices, at 7000 sites mainly in southern England, and at 2000 sites in Scotland (Banks, 1946). The Germans were said to have used similar devices in their defensive warfare against the Russians later in the war. Stationary flame devices were deployed by the Germans along the French coast (Hajek, 1957).

Portable flamethrowers were developed by the Germans, Russians, French and Americans.

The British developed a portable flamethrower called the "Lifebuoy":

'Lifebuoys' were used in most of the main theatres of war. Perhaps their most spectacular employment was by the Chindits in the Burmese jungle, where Orde Wingate's quick appreciation of their possibilities in tip and run raids on the Japanese camps led to intensive efforts to get them out to him in time for their use in his adventurous airborne descents. But they were too complicated for real reliability and for such close combat work absolute dependability in all conditions, from the frosts of Germany, to the steamy heat of the Tropics, was essential. They suffered from some unpopularity and steps were actively in hand at the end of the war to supply a lighter and more reliable model (Banks, 1946, pp. 63–65).

Following the example of Germany and Italy, Britain, the United States and the Soviet Union all developed mechanized flamethrowers during World War II. British and Canadian engineers developed a lighter mechanized flamethrower, called the Ronson, 1300 of which the Canadians procured and used in many actions in the Low Countries (Banks, 1946). This was the forerunner of the Wasp (Mark I) flame gun of which 1000 were ordered and went into production in March 1943. A flamethrower version of the Churchill tank, known as the Crocodile, was developed and in April 1943 a decision to produce 250 was made. The order was increased by stages to 750 and in April 1945 a further order for 250 for India was placed, bringing the total to 1000, of which 800 had been delivered by the end of hostilities (Banks, 1946).

In 1943 under the Allied Aid Agreement, a unit of British Crocodiles was shipped by the Petroleum Warfare Department to the Soviet Union for training purposes. Experience gained with these machines contributed to the design of new equipment for the OT-34 flamethrower tank which was first used against the Germans in 1944 (Milsom, 1970).

The first successful use of a portable flamethrower by US forces occurred on 15 January 1943 at Guadalcanal in the Pacific, where the Japanese

[23] The Petroleum Warfare Department was established on 9 July 1940 with a staff of 10 persons "in three small rooms with no technical knowledge and no more stock in trade than the consuming zeal of Mr. Geoffrey Lloyd [Secretary for Petroleum in the British Government] and the vision of Lord Hankey" (Banks, 1946, p. 29).

positions were well protected against artillery and mortar fire (Kleber & Birdsell, 1966).

The subsequent history of the use of flamethrowers is complicated by technical questions of inadequate product development and supply. As improvements were introduced, the use of the flamethrower spread through the Pacific region.

The flamethrower proved its effectiveness anew in May 1944 on Wakde Island ... To do the job the company used dynamite, bazookas, white phosphorus grenades, and flamethrowers, but only the flamethrowers proved successful against both caves and tunnels. On at least eight separate occasions flamethrower assaults either killed the Japanese defenders outright or drove them from their hiding places into the open, where they became easy targets for riflemen (*Ibid.*, p. 551).

Flamethrowers were also used in street fighting in Manila (Kleber & Birdsell, 1966).

In the European theatre of operations, US forces made little use of the flamethrower, although they were equipped with the weapon. It was not used at all in the invasion of North Africa and only once in Sicily, where it was used to burn wheat fields hiding enemy soldiers (*Ibid.*).

There were occasional uses in French towns in street fighting. Flamethrowers were used in Brittany in August and September 1944, with results which seemed to differ from those in the Pacific. On one occasion:

A short burst of fire directed at each pillbox in turn resulted in the hasty surrender of the occupants. The psychological effect of the flamethrowers was the determining factor in the success of the operation. Not one enemy soldier had been burned (*Ibid.*, p. 598).

The mechanized flamethrower played an even smaller role in the European theatre than did the portable flamethrower, though some British and Canadian forces used them extensively (Wilson, 1956), sometimes in collaboration with US forces.

US authors offer two possible explanations for the apparent discrepancy between the Pacific and the European theatres: the terrain and the enemy. Jungle terrain permitted the flamethrower to get closer to the target than was possible in the more open terrain of Europe. On the other hand, the Japanese soldier was said to be less likely to surrender than his German counterpart, who might give up a position when confronted by a flamethrower.

Tactical use of napalm bombs during World War II

The tactical use of napalm bombs evolved during the later stages of World War II. Unlike the other incendiary weapons, which were first developed in Europe and Japan, napalm was a US invention (Fieser, 1943), and the technique of napalm bombing was a US tactic, largely dependent upon the establishment and maintenance of control of the airspace over the battlefield.

Napalm bombs at that time were filled in the field, using expendable, auxiliary fuel tanks wired up to an incendiary grenade or part of a magnesium incendiary bomb. Following the D-day invasion intensive fire bomb missions were inaugurated by US air forces in Europe. As napalm was not used by ground forces at the anticipated rate, a further 50 000 gallons (190 000 litres) were transferred to the air forces (Kleber & Birdsell, 1966).

Napalm bombs and M-76, 500-1b oil bombs were dropped on supply dumps, troop concentrations, convoys and vehicles. They were used extensively against German forces as they tried to escape encirclement at Falaise; against German motor transportation and armoured concentrations in wooded territory during the Ardennes counter-offensive; and on marshalling yards at St. Quentin in France (Kleber & Birdsell, 1966).

In the Pacific theatre the napalm bomb was also widely used. In some battles this use reached enormous proportions. During the Luzon campaign, for example, a total of 4 million litres of napalm was dropped on the Japanese by US air units (Kleber & Birdsell, 1966).

Altogether during World War II, the US Army Air Force dropped about 14 000 tons of napalm bombs, over two-thirds of them in the Pacific area (Kleber & Birdsell, 1966).

US military experts concluded that napalm bombs were most effective against human targets and in addition had a terrorizing effect, though prisoners of war stated that widely dispersed napalm bomb hits had little or no effect on morale (*Ibid*).

The napalm bomb developed from birth to maturity in the short space of some three years. It was used mainly in the "far off" Pacific theatre and perhaps therefore failed to achieve the attention it deserved in the post-war legal and humanitarian discussions. Subsequently such attention was diverted by the so-called "Cold War", enabling greatly increased use of the weapon in the Korean War and subsequently elsewhere in Asia.

VI. *The post-World War II period, 1946–1974*

The immediate post-war legal discussions

Incendiary weapons, which had been widely regarded as illegal prior to World War II (Noel-Baker, 1958), were used by all major combatant parties during the war.

As had been the case in previous conflicts, the post-war period generated much political and legal activity. This activity was concerned in the first place with retribution for crimes committed by the defeated powers—the Nuremberg and Tokyo war crimes tribunals. Subsequently through the auspices of the United Nations, the Convention on the Prevention and Punishment of the Crime of Genocide was adopted in 1948. Under the auspices of the International Committee of the Red Cross, the four Geneva Conventions of 12 August 1949 were adopted.

The issues raised by the systematic bombing of civilian populations and the use of means of combat which caused needless injury during the war were not raised—at least not sufficiently to find expression in the Geneva Conventions. Nevertheless, some consideration was given to the problems raised by "weapons of mass destruction" in disarmament discussions.

A United Nations General Assembly resolution of December 1946 asked for the elimination of all weapons adaptable, either then or in the future, to mass destruction. Weapons of mass destruction were defined in the US revised draft resolution of 8 September 1947 as including:

atomic explosive weapons, radioactive material weapons, lethal chemical and biological weapons, and any weapons developed in the future which have characteristics comparable in destructive effect to those of the atomic bomb or other weapons mentioned above (UN document S/C. 3/SC. 3/7/Rev. 1).

During the discussion, the Soviet representative criticized this definition as too restrictive. During World War II, he said, Germany had used weapons other than atomic bombs, with mass destructive effect on populations and cities far from the field of battle. He instanced the flying bomb and rocket as weapons of mass destruction, though they contained neither radioactive nor lethal chemical or biological components. It was his view that an attempt to establish two lists, one consisting of atomic weapons and other weapons of mass destruction, and another consisting of conventional weapons, would be a wrong approach. This view was opposed by the British delegate who claimed that the 14 000 V-weapons dropped on England had killed 56 000 persons, or four persons per weapon.[24]

The US revised draft was accepted by the working committee. Subsequently, the definition was accepted by the Commission on Conventional Armaments on 12 August 1948 (UN document S/C 3/SR. 13).[25]

Little further progress was made by the Commission in its study of armaments. Its work was overshadowed by political and military developments both in Europe and in Asia.

The Greek Civil War, 1944–1949

The Greek Civil War broke out in the aftermath of World War II. In 1947, in accordance with the Truman Doctrine, the USA decided to send large-scale military aid in the form of equipment and advisors to support the Greek National Army (GNA).

The Civil War was largely fought as a guerilla war. The rebel Greek

[24] Other figures suggest that the V-rockets killed about 13 500 in London and 3 700 in Antwerp at a rate of about one death per rocket (*Underrättelser från flygvapnet,* Stockholm, October 1948).

[25] The USSR and the Ukrainian SSR abstained.

Democratic Army (GDA) at times held large parts of the countryside. It used largely outdated equipment but there is one account of a spectacular raid on a train in northern Greece, where the GDA used flamethrowers (O'Ballance, 1966, p. 163).

Although materially far better off, the GNA also had outdated arms and equipment. In 1947 vigorous intervention by the United States resulted in a reorganization of the GNA with training programmes and a flow of advanced weapons including napalm.

Though US combat troops were not involved, the Joint US Military Advisory and Planning Group, which had a decisive influence over the command of the GNA, gained experience in the use of napalm and other means of warfare in counter-guerilla operations.

The war in Indo-China, 1946–1954

Early in 1950 the French Air Force in Indo-China carried out experiments with napalm bombs, which they called "special antipersonnel bombs" (Chassin, 1954). The Commander of the French Air Force, General Chassin described them as "a terrible weapon".

By the beginning of 1951, the development of the "special antipersonnel bomb", made from wing-tanks filled with napalm for use by fighter-planes, was completed. The story of the new weapon, used on a large scale in the battle of Vinh-Yen in January 1951, has been told from both sides (Chassin, 1954; Fall, 1961).

A Viet-Minh officer's diary gives the following account:

Hell comes in the form of large, egg-shaped containers, dropping from the first plane, followed by other eggs from the second and third plane. Immense sheets of flames, extending over hundreds of meters, it seems, strike terror in the ranks of my soldiers. This is napalm, the fire which falls from the skies.

Another plane swoops down behind us and I feel its fiery breath touching my whole body. The men are now fleeing in all directions and I cannot hold them back. There is no way of holding out under this torrent of fire which flows in all directions and burns everything in its passage. On all sides flames surround us now. In addition, French artillery and mortars now have our range and transform into a fiery tomb what had been, ten minutes ago, a quiet part of the forest.

... [The platoon commander's] eyes were wide with terror. "What is this? The atomic bomb?"

"No, it is napalm."

(cited by Fall, 1961, pp. 34–35).

The effects of napalm on Viet-Minh troop concentrations seem to have had a decisive influence on the French victory in the battle of Vinh-Yen. The special antipersonnel bomb became a very important weapon in French warfare. However, the Viet-Minh rapidly changed their tactics, no longer showing up in large concentrations which were an easy target for aircraft. But the superior mobility and camouflage techniques of the Viet-Minh did not diminish the French aerial bombardments. Instead they were extended over

42

large areas where the enemy was believed to be hiding, beneath the forest cover. Incendiary weapons could have a double effect—destroying the cover, as well as the enemy.

Napalm bombs were at first used for close air support of ground forces. Later they were employed in offensive air operations with the apparent intention of making a psychological impact on the population. Because of the highly inflammable building materials of South-East Asian villages, the effect of napalm bombing was both devastating and indiscriminate. The effectiveness of napalm for burning woods and crops was discovered and used, although not on a large scale. However, this was the main strategy recommended by General Chassin for future guerilla wars. According to him, the French forces had not realized the necessity of this strategy soon enough (Chassin, 1954, p. 238*ff.*).

Malaya, 1948–1960

In 1951, the British conducted tests at Song-Song Island Bombing Range, where various types of bombs were dropped into the jungle on the island to measure the damage caused. However, the military experts concluded that napalm was ineffective for igniting tropical rain forest (Peterson, Reinhardt & Conger, 1963, pp. 49–51) and plant-killing chemicals were adopted instead.

In the Malayan War the bombing of troops on the ground was not very common since the guerillas of the Malayan Races Liberation Army (MRLA) were contained throughout the whole war in tiny guerilla units. The total amount of air-dropped munitions was 33 000 tons over a ten-year period (Air Commodore A. D. J. Garrisson, in Peterson, Reinhardt & Conger, 1963). Thus the British decision not to include napalm as part of their normal armoury was in marked contrast to the French strategy in Indo-China pursued at the same time.

The Korean War, 1950–1953

Napalm bombs were used extensively by UN forces in Korea.[26] The US Far East Air Force (FEAF) used a total of 32 557 tons of napalm (Futrell, 1961), which made up some 6.8 per cent of the total tonnage of FEAF ordnance delivered. Napalm bombs were also dropped by US Navy and Marine

---

[26] According to one source, the maximum US monthly production rate during the Korean War was 2 000 napalm bombs and 20 500 high explosive bombs (Aviation Studies [International] Ltd, *Armament Data Sheets,* Section 16, p. 4, 1972). However, already in June 1950 the US Far East Air Materiel Command was authorized to procure napalm tanks in Japan, the first of many locally procured supplies that had previously been procured only in the USA. By the end of June 1951 the newly established Procurement and Industrial Planning Directorate had completed 1 536 procurement actions, totalling $25 855 860. There is some irony in the fact that one of the first stimuli to rebuilding the Japanese economy should come from the production of napalm bombs to be used to destroy towns and industries (many of them built by the Japanese) in newly-liberated Korea.

aircraft. In addition, incendiary cluster bombs and large oil bombs were used for attacks on larger targets, and ground flame weapons were used extensively in ground operations.

Because of the highly mobile nature of the fighting in the first year of the war, napalm was mostly used aginst concentrations of troops, columns of trucks and armoured vehicles, and suspected enemy gun positions.

The effectiveness of napalm may well have been misjudged by US troops in the field:

Enemy prisoners of war, however, indicated that they did not fear napalm very much unless it was dropped directly on them. Otherwise, the Reds said that they could run away from the napalm blast. This, in fact, was probably why United Nations airmen and ground troops liked napalm: they saw it make enemy soldiers run and concluded that it must be highly effective (Futrell, 1961, p. 90).

There was a widely held view that napalm weapons were necessary to combat "hordes" of soldiers. There is little doubt that United Nations air action contributed to the tremendous toll of Korean and Chinese troops (and civilians). Yet napalm was only one of a considerable armoury of weapons dropped from the air.

The Chinese "hordes" did not materialize because of a whole complex of factors, including limited Chinese interest in intervention, restricted logistic facilities, severe weather conditions and heavy casualties. Napalm bombs were no doubt a contributing factor but can hardly have been decisive.

During the Korean War, napalm bombs were also successful against Soviet-built T-34 tanks.

In the early days at Taegu the Mustangs used light-case 500-pound bombs filled with thermite and napalm with great success against both tanks and troops. The Russian-built tanks had a good bit of rubber in their treads and even a near miss with flaming napalm would usually ignite and destroy the armoured tank. (Futrell, 1961, p. 90).

Because of the particular configuration of the Soviet-built T-34 tanks, napalm incendiary mixture had been the most effective destroyer of Red armour (*Ibid.,* p. 330).

Modern tanks are not nearly so susceptible to napalm attack.

There is considerable evidence to support allegations that even tactical uses of napalm are frequently indiscriminate in their effects. This indiscriminate type of warfare seems to have been extensive in Korea. For example, on 31 January 1951, crews of B-26 bombers[27] reported a "scarcity of targets at Hamhung". According to one of the crew members "It's hard to find good targets, for we've burned out almost everything" (Fifth Air Force operational summary, 31 January 1951, in *New York Times,* 1 February 1951). The same communiqué reported "large fires in villages in the western sector following attacks with rockets, napalm and machine guns".

[27] A typical bomb load for a B-26 light bomber was: 28 100-1b demolition bombs, four napalm tanks, and nearly 6 000 rounds of .50 ammunition for its 16 machine guns (*Air Clues* (UK), April 1954).

A front line correspondent of the *New York Times,* who was with an armoured column when it took a village about this time, wrote:

A napalm raid hit the village three or four days ago when Chinese were holding up the advance, and nowhere in the village have they buried the dead because there is nobody left to do so. This correspondent came across one old woman, the only one who seemed to be left alive, dazedly hanging up some clothes in a blackened courtyard filled with the bodies of four members of her family.

The inhabitants throughout the village and in the fields were caught and killed and kept the exact postures they had held when the napalm struck—a man about to get on his bicycle, fifty boys and girls playing in an orphanage, a housewife strangely unmarked . . . There must be almost two hundred dead in the tiny hamlet (G. Barrett, *New York Times,* 9 February 1951).

The Korean correspondent of the BBC described the results of this kind of warfare:

In front of us a curious figure was standing a little crouched, legs straddled, arms held out from his sides. He had no eyes, and the whole of his body, nearly all of which was visible through the tatters of burned rags, was covered with a hard black crust speckled by yellow pus . . . He had to stand because he was no longer covered with a skin, but with a crust-like crackling which broke easily . . . *I thought of the hundreds of villages reduced to ash which I personally had seen and realized the sort of casualty list which must be mounting up along the Korean front* (Cutforth, 1952; italics added).

Napalm and other incendiary bombs were also used for large-scale area attacks in Korea. According to one recent writer:

Following a careful study of the five major target systems selected for attack it was quickly realised that since industries and communications complexes within these areas were grouped so closely together, little advantage would be derived from a programme of precision bombing . . . Area bombing with widespread use of incendiary bombs was thought to be a far more effective solution . . . (Jackson, 1973, pp. 56–57).

Testifying before a US Senate Committee, Major General Emmet O'Donnell Jr., who had been commander of the US Far East Air Force Bomber Command, described his intentions as follows:

General O'Donnell: It was my intention and hope, not having any instructions, that we would be able to get out there and . . . go to work on burning five major cities in North Korea to the ground, and to destroy completely every one of about 18 major strategic targets . . . We were not at that time permitted to do it . . .

The main cities were Pyongyang, first, the capital, Seishin, Rashin, Wonsan, and Chinnampo . . .

Senator Stennis . . . Now, as a matter of fact, Northern Korea has been virtually destroyed, hasn't it? Those cities have been virtually destroyed.

General O'Donnell: Oh, yes, we did it all later anyhow . . . I would say that the entire, almost the entire Korean Peninsula is just a terrible mess. Everything is destroyed. There is nothing standing worth the name . . . Just before the Chinese came in we grounded. There were no more targets in Korea.

Chairman Russell: . . . I think you have demonstrated soldierly qualities that endeared you to the American people (US Senate Committee on Armed Services and Committee on Foreign Regulations, 1951, pp. 3063–3114).

In November 1950 an attack by 79 B-29 Superfortresses and some 300 fighter-bombers was launched on Sinuiju, a Korean city just across the border from Antung, the Chinese town from where General MacArthur had reported anti-aircraft fire on four occasions. According to the account in the *New York Times* (9 November 1950), the attack began in the morning "when fighter planes swept the area with machine guns, rockets, and jellied gasoline bombs." These were followed by "ten of the Superforts [which] dropped 1 000-pound high explosive bombs on railroad and railway bridges across the Yalu River and on the bridge approaches". Later, "the remaining planes used incendiaries exclusively on a two-and-a-half mile built-up area along the southeast bank of the Yalu." A total of 630 tons of bombs and 85 000 incendiaries were dropped on the city, which, it was claimed, was 90 per cent destroyed, although General Stratemeyer, the Commander of the Far East Air Forces maintained that the bombing was only aimed at targets of a military nature. By 10 November, the *New York Times* (11 November 1950) reported "in the fourth incendiary raid since Sunday, B-29 Superforts . . . plastered the town of Uiju on the Yalu's south bank ten miles upstream from the burned-out city of Sinuiju, site of the principle bridge to Manchuria."

On 24 November, the day a Chinese delegation arrived at the UN for negotiations, General MacArthur launched his "home-by-Christmas" offensive. (Later it transpired that this offensive had been postponed since 15 November, the day the Chinese had been originally scheduled to arrive at the UN [*New Yorker,* 10 March 1951].) The offensive precipitated heavy fighting. Within a month the UN forces were in full retreat, during which they carried out a "scorched earth policy". Pyongyang, which had been in UN hands since October, was evacuated on 4 December, and set afire.

On 6 December the US Republican party leader Harold E. Stassen, after a meeting with General MacArthur, criticized the directives under which UN forces were operating. He proposed an unconditional ceasefire ultimatum. If this was not agreed to, the Supreme Commander should be allowed to retaliate "by striking in any manner any objects of military significance either in Korea or in China." Air bombardment and blockade should be "supplemented by orders to General Douglas MacArthur to withdraw land forces from Korea in as orderly a manner as possible in favour of long-range attacks." It seems this is what General MacArthur himself had in mind. The withdrawal continued and major bombing attacks were launched:

Sixty-three B-29's on 3 January and 60 B-29's on 5 January [1951] strewed incendiary bombs over the North Korean capital city. Snow-covered roofs checked the spread of the conflagration, and only 35 per cent of the city's built up area was destroyed, but the Red radio at Pyongyang bitterly reported that "the entire city burned like a furnace for two whole days" (Futrell, 1961, p. 258).

In January 1951 a bill was put to Congress to reorganize the US Air Force, one aim of which was "to have an authority in Washington that could stop an atom-bomb strike even after the planes had left a distant base" (Associated

Press, *New York Herald Tribune* [International Edition], 12 January 1951). Major General O'Donnell, Commander of Bomber Command, was relieved of his post, and "strategic bombing" in Korea was ended, along with the "planned withdrawal."

It appears that from this point on, though bombing did not cease in Korea, it was referred to as "interdiction", that is, cutting of communications or "close air support of ground troops", rather than as strategic bombing. (Even the later attacks on such obviously strategic targets as hydroelectric dams were described as interdiction.)

Large-scale area attacks were repeated at intervals throughout the war. In April 1952 the industrial city of Chongjin was attacked simultaneously by naval and aerial bombardment during which napalm was dropped. The capital city, Pyongyang, was attacked on several occasions in July and August 1952.

The strikes on the capital city . . . continued the rest of the day (11 July 1952). A total of 1 400 tons of bombs and 23 000 gallons of napalm were delivered upon Pyongyang's targets during an 11-hour period by 1 254 aircraft (Cagle & Manson, 1957, p. 453).

According to plan, the Fifth Air Force light-bomber wings commenced their night attacks against Communist communication centres on 20 July. Employing M-20 incendiary clusters and M-76 fire-bombs, [the planes] arrived at heights of about 4 000 feet, at five-minute intervals to bomb targets marked for them by the incendiary bombs carried by pathfinder lead crew. Once the fire got going, each bomber added to the conflagration . . . From their beginning the light bomber fire raids were marked with success (Futrell, 1961, p. 483).

These incendiary raids were comparable in scale to those on German and Japanese cities during World War II—area raids with no pretension to be aimed at precise military targets. It seems unlikely in these circumstances that the population was reassured by the psychological warfare leaflets emphasizing the military nature of the targeting.

UN forces in Korea also used flamethrowers, as well as a number of other ground flame devices, including flame land-mines, flame fougasses, napalm bunker bombs and Husch flares.

It was during the Korean War that the use of ground flame weapons against close formation infantry attacks developed (US Army, 1960).

Another technique developed was that of napalm "Golden Rain", created by spraying a napalm mixture into the air above enemy troop positions (Miller, 1958). But Karig, Cagle and Manson (1952) described the flamethrower as "the weapon the North Koreans hate most".

The ICRC's Draft Rules, 1955–1958

Following the conclusion of the wars in Korea and Indo-China, the International Committee of the Red Cross (ICRC) undertook to codify areas of the international law of armed conflicts which had not been adequately covered in the four conventions of 1949. A first version of the *Draft Rules for the*

Protection of the Civilian Population from the Dangers of Indiscriminate Warfare was published in 1955. The articles on prohibited weapons did not mention incendiaries (ICRC, 1955, Part I, General Principle No. IV; Part II, Articles 10–11). The ICRC later explained that such a reference had been omitted because "the terrible damage to the civilian population [caused] by incendiary bombs was mainly due to their indiscriminate use", a matter which was dealt with in another part of the Draft Rules (ICRC, 1958 a, p. 106).

In the second version, published in 1958 under the title *Draft Rules for the Limitation of the Dangers Incurred by the Civilian Population in Time of War,* the ICRC adopted a different course and proposed a prohibition against the use of

weapons whose harmful effects—resulting in particular from the dissemination of incendiary, chemical, bacteriological, radioactive or other agents—could spread to an unforeseen degree or escape, either in space or in time, from the control of those who employ them, thus endangering the civilian population (ICRC, 1958 a, Article 14).

The ICRC explained in the commentary that while the protection of the civilian population had been the main motive for Article 14, the prohibition proposed was meant to be total and would therefore apply just as much to the use of the said agents against military forces.

In the event, these efforts of the ICRC led to nothing. The only time the Draft Rules were the object of serious discussion was at the XIXth International Conference of the Red Cross in New Delhi in 1957. The discussion of Article 14 concentrated entirely on the question of nuclear weapons. Incendiary weapons were not so much as mentioned in the debate (ICRC, 1958 b).

Nevertheless, the proposed text of the 1958 Draft Rules retains considerable relevance today. If adopted it would have added, to the generally accepted rule that weapons should not cause superfluous injury, a second general principle: that weapons should not be indiscriminate in their effects, either in time or space. In the absence of such rules, incendiary bombs continued to be used.

Algeria, 1954–1961

During the Algerian war of liberation French forces used napalm bombs and 20 mm high-explosive-incendiary ammunition in attacks from the air on guerilla units. Napalm bombs dropped from aircraft were a means of attacking forces in mountain areas. The 20 mm guns were mounted on helicopters, replacing .50 calibre inert ammunition; the 3–5 metre lethal area of a 20 mm shell was considered an advantage for this kind of attack (General Ezanno, in Peterson, Reinhardt & Conger, 1963).

In some larger operations considerable amounts of napalm were used. On one occasion, a napalm attack was launched against a gathering of soldiers in the Kabylian region. According to a French general, "at the end of the operation we found something like three hundred soldiers completely burned" (General Giroult, in Peterson *et al.*, 1963). It is interesting that this general was asked whether he was able to distinguish the guerilla armed forces from the civilian population, to which he replied that he could since they were in organized military units (*katibas*) and in uniform. He also emphasized a second important aspect of this kind of pacification operation: administering to the needs of the civilian population, in particular with medical aid. The French forces, he said, had 600 military doctors and 250 nurses in the most remote villages.

Napalm was also used to destroy large numbers of villages. In many cases the villages were first emptied and the people moved forcibly to regroupment centres before their homes were destroyed. In other cases military commanders were "obliged to clear the villages by air" (Commandant d'Aviation Pierre Clostermann, in Favrod, 1962).

Cuba, 1956–1959, 1961

Napalm bombs are reported to have been among the weapons used by the Batista régime (from 1956–59) in its unsuccessful attempts to suppress the revolution led by Fidel Castro. In one large-scale offensive carried out by Batista's forces "the air force failed to distinguish between Batistianso and rebels, and some of the former were killed by napalm bombing" (Thomas, 1971, p. 998).

According to some Cuban sources napalm bombs were also used during the Playa Giron (Bay of Pigs) invasion in April 1961 (Herrera, 1972; Cuban Embassy, Stockholm, personal communication, 29 November 1974).

The war in Indo-China, 1961–1975

The most extensive use of incendiary weapons has been in the war in Indo-China from 1961 until the present day. This was particularly so during the period of active engagement of US ground, sea and air forces from 1961–1973. During this period all categories of munitions, including incendiary munitions, were used in quantities two or three times the total used by US forces in World War II (US Senate Committee on Foreign Relations, 1971).

Table 1.1 shows the tonnages of munitions dropped from the air by US and allied forces in Indo-China from 1963–72. No complete figures have been published on the quantities of incendiary munitions used, though some figures for napalm appeared in earlier years. SIPRI estimates based on these earlier figures are included in the table.

Another indication of the quantities of munitions expended in the Indo-China War is the year-by-year US purchases of various munitions. These figures roughly follow actual use over a period of years but may not reflect actual use in a given year. This is because there is normally a larger stock of

Table 1.1. Estimated use of napalm bombs in Indo-China, 1963–1973 (March)[a]

Year	Total air munitions (tons)	Fighter-bomber (FB) munitions (tons)	Napalm bombs (tons)	Napalm bombs as percent of FB tonnage
1963	. .	. .	2 181	. .
1964	. .	. .	1 177	. .
1965	321 009	289 000	17 659	6.1
1966	439 856	336 848	54 620	16.2
1967	842 680	581 971	(62 218)	(11.6)
1968	1 273 931	688 069	(70 871)	(10.3)
1969	1 217 887	666 086	(66 000)	(9.9)
1970	804 542	396 264	(39 250)	(9.9)
1971	626 279	300 939	(29 816)	(9.9)
1972	949 949	399 888	(37 989)	(9.5)
1973	174 410	63 447	(5 710)	(9.0)
Total	**6 650 543**	**3 722 512**	**(388 091)**	**(10.4)**

[a] Previous estimates were published in the *SIPRI Yearbook 1973*. These revised estimates are based on new figures for the total air munitions and fighter-bomber munitions published by the US Department of Defense in June 1973. The estimates of napalm use are computed from the partial data given in the sources below, taking into account the tonnages of munitions dropped by fighter-bombers, and the decline in napalm use for close air support as US troops were withdrawn.

Sources: International Herald Tribune, 11 December 1967; *San Francisco Chronicle,* 19 March 1968; Office of the Assistant Secretary of Defense, Public Affairs, letter to Professor J. B. Neilands, University of California, 18 August 1971; US Department of Defense, Press release, June 1973.

any given standardized munition (known in the USA as War Readiness Material, WRM). Usage in a particular year may exceed current procurement so that part of the WRM is used up and a larger procurement is made the following year to cover both the increased use and to replenish the WRM. Also, obsolete munitions may be used up from stocks without new procurement, whereas new munitions may be acquired at first in small numbers for testing in combat, and then in much larger numbers than are immediately used in order to build up a stock. With these factors in mind it will be seen that the US procurement of napalm bombs over the ten-year period 1964–73 amounts to approximately 400 000 tons (table 1.2). This figure, therefore, gives support to the SIPRI estimate of total use in Indo-China during this period.

Some napalm bombs are filled during production. Others are shipped empty and filled in the theatre of operations. In 1965 the US Air Force procured 8 784 000 lbs (3 921 tons) of a napalm-thickening agent called "Alecto" (napalm-B) and 350 000 gallons (1 484 000 litres) of "Instantgel". In 1966 the USAF procured 6 200 607 lbs (2 768 tons) of "Incendagel", 1 266 667 lbs (565 tons) of M-4 napalm thickener and 8 378 000 lbs (3 740 tons) of napalm-B thickener. Thickening agents are usually mixed in the proportion of about one part thickener to nine parts fuel, though some napalm-B compositions may have more thickener (see chapter 2). In 1967

Table 1.2. US procurement of napalm bombs, fiscal years 1964–1973.

Bomb type (nominal weight)	1964	1965	1966	1967	1968	1969	1970	1971	1972	1973	Total
					Numbers of napalm bombs procured						
250-lb[a]	..	45 730	..	..	..	..	..	..	..	..	45 730
500-lb[b]	..	51 170	164 000	..	..	17 130	91 362	..	54 800	59 400	437 862
750-lb[c]	27 229	42 421	211 900	104 549	72 800	167 258	21 138	56 400	..	..	703 695
750-lb (empty)[d]	..	..	..	..	..	12 000	12 000	12 000	15 204	..	51 204
560-lb[e]	..	25 000	53 250	63 830	3 456	31 200	35 600	17 400	..	..	229 736
Total (number)	27 229	164 321	429 150	168 379	76 256	227 588	160 100	85 800	70 004	59 400	1 468 227
					Tonnage of napalm bombs procured[f]						
Total (tons)	9 117	36 979	123 513	50 963	25 239	71 431	40 246	27 252	17 323	13 259	415 322

[a] BLU-10.
[b] BLU-11, BLU-23, BLU-32.
[c] BLU-1, BLU-27.
[d] BLU-27.
[e] MK-77 (US Navy).
[f] Tonnage calculated on basis of nominal weights, not actual weights.

Source: US Department of Defense, 1973.

Table 1.3. US procurement of incendiary cluster bombs, fiscal years 1968–1973

Bomb type	1968	1969	1970	1971	1972	1973
CBU-52/53/54	692	. .	3 050	4 900	18 960	22 950
M-36 750-1b[a]	. .	8 150	12 346	18 002	. .	. .

[a] In the years prior to 1969 existing stocks were used up but new supplies were not procured.
Source: US Department of Defense 1973.

the US Congress appropriated $5 541 000 for the purchase of 26 461 615 lbs (11 810 tons) of napalm-B, but this quantity was not procured.

Though napalm bombs have been the predominant incendiary munition during the Indo-China War, the US and allied forces also made limited use of magnesium-thermite incendiary cluster bombs. A representative of the US Defense Department testified before a Congressional Committee in 1970 that stockpiles of World War II incendiary cluster bombs had been depleted by 1968 and that production was restarted in 1969 (US Senate Committee on Armed Services, 1971).

In addition the USA procured, and apparently tested in Indo-China, a number of new types of incendiary cluster bombs (the CBU-52, CBU-53 and CBU-54). Some of these new types of bombs produce pyrophoric fragments on impact with the target.[28] Table 1.3 shows the number of incendiary cluster bombs procured during the period.

White phosphorus bombs of World War II type were procured periodically throughout the Indo-China War (table 1.4). In addition small numbers of white phosphorus cluster bombs (CBU-13/As and CBU-22/As) were also procured for use as "massive aerial munitions" (Beller, 1969, p. 158). White phosphorus aircraft rockets, mainly 2.75 inch (70 mm) were procured extensively. Not only did the procurement of 2.75 inch rockets increase with the escalation of the war in Indo-China but the proportion of white phosphorus warheads (as compared with fragmentation and flechette warheads) also increased from 8.3 per cent in 1966 to 88.5 per cent in 1970.

Beller (1969) reports in his history of the US Army Materiel Command that white phosphorus rocket warheads were obtained by emptying and reconditioning stocks of conventional high explosive/fragmentation warheads and refilling them with white phosphorus. Both 6 1b (2.7 kg) and 10 1b (4.5 kg) shells were used for this purpose, but by 1968 the larger size had come to predominate.

Taken together, therefore, it is likely that the total tonnage of air-dropped napalm, phosphorus and other incendiary munitions actually expended in Indo-China exceeded 400 000 tons by 15 August 1973, when the US Senate voted a bombing halt by US aircraft.

[28] *Aerospace Daily* (26 December 1972) reported that the US Air Force was buying 732 941 lbs (333 155 kg) of zirconium sponge particles, "the incendiary elements of CBU-54 cluster bombs ... a reflection of the stepped up operations in Southeast Asia."

Table 1.4. US procurement of white phosphorus (WP) bombs and aircraft rockets, fiscal years 1965–1973

Type	1965	1966	1967	1968	1969	1970	1971	1972	1973
AN-M47A4 100-1b WP bomb	85 000	13 660	. .	. .	10 300	6 700	. .	1 430	2 460
CBU-13/22 WP cluster bomb	. .	5 321	6 841					. .	. .
2.75 in. WP rocket[a]	80 000	287 968	374 500	778 729	847 500	288 900	394 608	113 884	. .

[a] Procurement for US Air Force only; does not include purchases for US Navy aircraft.

Source: US Department of Defense, 1973.

It is more difficult to estimate the quantities of ground flame weapons used in the war in Indo-China, but some indications are given by the procurement information which is available.

The US Army purchased 800 million lbs (357 000 tons) of incendiary thickening oil in 1967 and a further 425 million lbs (190 000 tons) in 1969, which when dissolved in petrol could produce as much as ten times that amount of incendiary agent. Again it may be assumed that these purchases bear some relation to their use by the military in the following year, and that during the period in question this type of munition was destined in the main for employment in Indo-China.

Thickened incendiary oils may be used in improvised incendiary mines and grenades, and in portable and mechanized flamethrowers. In order to simplify the construction of improvised mines, the USA introduced in 1968 the M-4 Destroyer files, small igniting devices which could be readily fitted to, for example, oil drums filled with napalm. About that time the XM-54 "pop-up" plasticized white phosphorus antipersonnel mine was also introduced, intended to "supplement or replace flame field expedients" (US Army, 1969, p. 49), but this mine does not appear to have been procured in significant numbers.

In 1969 very large quantities of manufactured incendiary grenades were purchased, including 394 million AN-M 14 thermite incendiary grenades and 379 million M-34 white phosphorus grenades. In 1970 a further 320 000 themite grenades and 1 343 white phosphorus grenades were purchased.

The XM-191 portable flame weapon was introduced in 1969. Instead of firing a stream of burning napalm like conventional flamethrowers, it fires up to four small rockets containing a thickened pyrophoric fuel which ignites on impact with the target. In 1969, 44 420 of these 4-round rocket clips were acquired (32 480 for the US Army and 11 760 for the US Marine Corps) and in 1970, 103 644 were procured (43 644 for the Army and 60 000 for the Marine Corps).

These new munitions gradually came to replace ground flame weapons derived largely from World War II and Korean War technology. Because of the different nature of these weapons it is difficult to aggregate the quantities of ground flame weapons procured during the period.

No figures have been published on the tonnages of various kinds of ground munitions actually expended in Indo-China. Figures made available to the US Senate Committee on Foreign Relations (1971) showed that the total tonnage for all surface-launched munitions between 1965–70 (5 888 433 tons) somewhat exceeded the tonnage of air-dropped munitions (5 556 100 tons).[29] Incendiary munitions made up less than 10 per cent of those dropped by aircraft, but it is not known what proportion of ground munitions they accounted for.

A few instances have been reported of the use of flame weapons by the forces of the National Liberation Front (NLF) in South Viet-Nam. A guide to the Soviet- and Chinese-supplied weapons used by these forces shows that they are in general blast and fragmenting types of munition (McClean, 1971). Cushmac (1968) reports that a few examples of Soviet- or Chinese-made portable flamethrowers were captured in South Viet-Nam. US casualties from booby traps constructed out of unexploded US white phosphorus and other munitions have also been reported (Curreri, Asch & Pruitt, 1970).

Since the type of warfare has been somewhat different in the various countries of Indo-China it is convenient to review them separately.

South Viet-Nam

Napalm bombs and other incendiary munitions were used in South Viet-Nam mainly for close air support, air strikes and the destruction of both food supplies and forest cover.

Where Republic of Viet-Nam (RVN) or US troops were under attack, or met with armed opposition while engaged in "search and destroy" operations, it was common practice to call in ground attack aircraft. Napalm bombs were often the preferred weapon for use in close combat, since they could be dropped from low level with less danger to the aircraft or to the government or US forces than with fragmentation or high explosive bombs, which have a less clearly prescribed effective radius. Close air support, which made up not more than 10 per cent of fighter-bomber activity, is said by US military spokesmen to have been the major use of napalm bombs, a statement which is consistent with the estimates of napalm use given in table 1.1. Some of the civilian (and military) casualties which have been reported have been the result of accidental drops of napalm bombs by aircraft engaged in close support operations.[30]

---

[29] By mid-1973, US and allied forces had expended some 15 million tons of munitions in Indo-China, of which the US Air Force alone had dropped more than 6.5 million tons (US Department of Defense, press release, June 1973).

[30] Butterfield (1972) reports that accidental napalm bombing of "friendly" forces or civilians "is not a rare occurrence, but such mistakes are seldom reported in the official United States or South Vietnamese daily military communiques." He records an example from the previous

Table 1.5. Summary of air attacks and napalm bombs dropped by US Pacific Fleet Aircraft, April–July 1965[a]

Targets	Air attacks on targets		Napalm bombs on targets	
	No.	Per cent	No.	Per cent
Barracks/administration building	486	5.3	3	0.2
Factory	4	0.1	4	0.4
Vehicle park	18	0.2	4	0.4
Trucks	278	3.0	4	0.4
Communications station	63	0.7	6	0.5
Road choke point	502	5.5	8	0.7
Warehouse	101	1.1	12	1.0
Radar site	245	2.7	14	1.2
Road reconnaissance	130	1.4	14	1.2
Industrial area	29	0.3	16	1.3
Village	320	3.5	17	1.5
Army supply dump/ammunition depot	287	3.1	55	4.7
Army supply building	624	6.8	72	6.2
Troop positions	2 383	26.0	300	25.8
Billeting/military area	3 676	40.2	634	54.5
Total	**9 146**	**100.0**	**1 163**	**100.0**

[a] Does not cover attacks by US Air Force or RVN Air Force, which may have been directed at a different distribution of targets.

Source: Kusterer (1966).

Napalm and phosphorus bombs have also been used for air strikes against targets in areas where ground troops did not have access, or prior to ground operations. Little information has been published about the proportion of different types of target attacked, but in one study Kusterer (1966) showed that the majority of napalm bombs dropped by US Navy aircraft in a four month period were on rear-area targets, including villages.

Incendiary cluster bombs of the type dropped on cities during World War II and the Korean War were used in Viet-Nam on certain kinds of tactical target, such as trucks. They were also used on several occasions in attempts to burn forested areas (see below, p. 57*ff*). White phosphorus munitions were used for marking targets and providing smoke screens. They were also used for attacks on personnel (reported for the first time by UPI, *New York Herald Tribune,* european edition, 22 March 1965) and as incendiary weapons against inflammable targets (such as bamboo huts), often together with napalm, since white phosphorus, which ignites spontaneously, helps to ensure the ignition of the napalm (Beller, 1969).

In the early 1960s reports began to filter through to the West in the press

day, not officially reported, where nine paratroopers were killed and 21 wounded. In selected data released by the US delegation at the Lucerne Conference of Government Experts (ICRC, 1974), 53 cases of US soldiers burned by napalm were recorded; this was a limited sample, mainly resulting from two accidents, not a record of all such cases. The US Army Institute of Surgical Research (1972) recorded 32 patients with napalm burns received from Viet-Nam from 1965–71; an unknown number of "more severly injured patients with significant complications ... expired" before admission to the burns centre in Texas.

and other mass media about the use of incendiaries and in particular napalm by US troops in Viet-Nam (*New York Times,* 19 January, 7 July, 25 July 1962; 8 April 1963). The increasing number of these reports contributed to a wave of public concern. This public interest, in turn, led to a number of investigations (for example, Rusk, 1967) and it is possible that these were instrumental in the formulation of more restrictive "rules of engagement" which may have been subsequently adopted concerning the use of napalm. In 1967 a team of US doctors reported that they found only a few cases of war-related burns in the RVN hospitals they visited, and doctors on the spot described a reduction in the number of civilian war-related burn casualties from 1966 to 1967. Other reasons for the decline in observed civilian napalm casualties may have been that by 1967 civilians had learnt to take better precautions and many civilians had fled from the countryside where napalm attacks were carried out.[31]

It has sometimes been argued by official spokesmen that the number of civilian napalm casualties was not as high as has sometimes been thought. This may be so, though a consideration of the method of attack also suggests other explanations for the small numbers of civilian casualties observed in RVN government hospitals.

First, napalm attacks were usually carried out in areas not under government control, and hence victims of attacks might not have been seen by outside observers. Second, the chance of surviving such an attack must have been small, since people running from the flames would be hit by fragments or shot by aircraft cannons; the best chance of survival would be to flee the area before the attack, as indeed several million people did. Third, the chance of being wounded *only* by napalm—rather than by fire from burning buildings or clothes, or by blast, fragments or bullets—was small. Fourth, the chance of surviving a rough journey of many hours or perhaps days to an RVN government hospital with a severe burn was also small, even if a person wounded in an NLF area should wish to try to reach an RVN hospital.[32] Fifth, the rural Viet-Namese civilian is particularly liable to

[31] Speaking before a US Senate Committee, Dr John Constable reported seeing 38 cases of war-caused burns in a survey of some 1 100 civilian war casualties in 35 of the 44 provincial hospitals he visited. Dr Herbert L. Needleman reported seeing napalm burns, identified as such by the physician in attendance, in every one of six hospitals he visited in the northern part of South Viet-Nam. Dr Theodore Tapper reported that at the hospital of Can Tho in the Mekong Delta over a hundred cases of napalm burns had been recorded during 1966 (US Senate Committee on the Judiciary, 1968).

Statistics from the RVN and the US Agency for International Development on new refugees registered with the government showed 772 000 in 1965 and 906 000 in 1966, but a decline to 463 000 in 1967 and 494 000 in 1968 (US Senate Committee on the Judiciary, 1974).

The Senate Subcommittee on Refugees estimated a cumulative total one year after the Paris Agreements of 10 470 000 displaced persons in South Viet-Nam, including those not registered with the government and repatriates from Cambodia.

[32] Dr Frank Ervin described a typical delay of 8 to 36 hours before war-wounded South Viet-Namese could reach hospital (US Senate Committee on the Judiciary, 1968). A delay of this length greatly increases the mortality of severe burns or other wounds.

succumb to the effects of a severe burn (or other severe trauma).[33] Finally, there are reports that very severely burned persons might not be admitted to RVN hospitals (which could do little to save them), nor might persons with burns which were not critically serious.[34]

In view of the reports of attacks on villages, therefore, it is legitimate to advance these explanations against those which seek to minimize the number of civilian casualties. However, due to the exigencies of war, and no doubt to a certain official reticence on the matter, there is insufficient data to test these hypotheses. The modest number of civilian napalm casualties reported officially in RVN hospitals does not *prove* that more have died in the field; but neither does it *disprove* that larger numbers of civilian casualties have occurred.

Whether or not there was a decline in the number of civilian napalm casualties after 1967, civilian casualties were widely reported in the world press during 1972. Some of these casualties resulted from RVN aircraft dropping napalm on their own side and on civilians (*New York Times,* 9 June 1972), while others resulted from napalm strikes on villages where NLF guerillas had been reported (*Le Monde,* 10 December 1972).

Incendiary weapons were also used as part of a strategy of "area denial".[35] A great effort was made to destroy villages, crops, and the cover provided by large areas of forest, by defoliation, burning and finally by scraping away vegetation with bulldozers.

Several experimental attempts to burn forests in Viet-Nam were made by US forces under the direction of the Advanced Research Projects Agency of the Department of Defense.

The venture began in 1965 in response to complaints from field commanders that other methods of defoliation were too slow and too inefficient to expose the forest floor to aerial view. The Defense Department theorized that forest fires would quickly wipe

---

[33] Young children and old people, who make up the majority of the village population, have a higher mortality from burns (see chapter 3). In addition, the rural population is weakened by poor nutrition and disease (Dudley, Knight, McNeur & Rosengarten, 1968). Several doctors reported that they had not seen burns of more than 20 or 30 per cent of the body surface area in South Viet-Namese hospitals, though more serious burns must be assumed to have occurred (US Senate Committee on the Judiciary, 1968).

[34] Dr Tapper reported two cases of patients with phosphorus burns covering 50 or 60 per cent of the body who reached hospital but were sent home to die. He also reported that the Da Nang surgical hospital would not admit patients with less than 15 per cent third degree burns because of overcrowding (*Ibid*).

[35] An earlier reference to the concept of "area denial" is to be found in a document entitled "Program of Action to Prevent Communist Domination of South Vietnam" prepared by the Vietnam Task Force, a group of high US officials, set up by President Kennedy on 20 April 1961. The programme, which was circulated by General Edward Landsdale of the Central Intelligence Agency (CIA), recommends, *inter alia,* "the application of technological area denial techniques (e.g. CW, BW, light plastic, air droppable mines, fluorescent materials, etc.)". The document was reproduced in a study for the US Senate Committee on Foreign Relations (1972).

out all vegetation, from the under canopy to the ground and called in its Advanced Research Projects Agency to figure out a way. The agency, in turn, contracted with Forest Service, which sent over men from its fire research laboratories in Montana and California (Reinhold, 1972).

Two classified studies of fires in tropical areas were made for the US Department of Defense by Bachelder & Hirt (1966) and the US Department of Agriculture, Forest Service (1966). In the meantime, a number of attempts were made to initiate fire-storms in forest areas, using magnesium incendiary bombs dropped by B-52 strategic bombers, following defoliation of the trees by chemicals (*St. Louis Post Dispatch*, 28 January 1967; McConnell, 1970; Reinhold, 1972; Shapley, 1972; *Newsweek*, 7 August 1972). In "Operation Sherwood Forest" in 1965 and 1966 attempts were made to burn a forested area near Saigon. In January–April 1967, areas in War Zones C and D, to the north-east of Saigon, were bombed with incendiaries during "Operation Pink Rose" (McConnell, 1970). In one day's attack, B-52s dropped incendiaries on an area of four square miles (*St. Louis Post Dispatch*, 28 January 1967). Though these attacks were said to be in areas which were not permanently inhabited, *Keesing's Contemporary Archives* (1967, p. 22573) reports that 6 000 people were made homeless following the attacks on the "Iron Triangle" (the Boi Loi woods), which was cleared with huge bulldozers, following defoliation and burning in early 1967.

US Defense Department spokesmen quoted by Reinhold (1972) asserted that these experiments were unsuccessful, as the tropical forest did not burn. According to *Keesing's* (op. cit.) the guerillas were officially acknowledged as having returned to the Iron Triangle within a month.

There appears no doubt that a large number of civilians lost their homes and means of livelihood in these experiments, and a great deal of forest was burned. Reinhold refers to an area the size of the city of Philadelphia. Thomas O. Perry, of the Harvard University Forest, writing in *Science* (10 May 1968), gives a figure of "some 100 000 acres" (about 40 000 hectares). These events were not disclosed to the general public until 1972. Within a week of these disclosures the US Senate voted to curtail any military expenditure for the creation of such fires as a weapon of war (*International Herald Tribune*, 19 July 1972).

In 1968 a third and much larger episode took place, in the U Minh forest (the "Forest of Darkness") in the extreme south of the Mekong Delta, which had been described as the "Vietcong's strongest fortress in South Vietnam ... communist-held since the Vietminh grasped it from the French" (*Sunday Times*, 14 April 1968).

There are conflicting reports of the origins of this fire, which may have been started accidentally or by natural causes. Whatever the origins, however, it was utilized for military ends:

It was three weeks before the allies realized the importance of what was happening— and made the burning of the U Minh a matter of military policy. While the Vietcong frantically tried to dig firebreaks and remove their supplies to safer grounds, US jets roared down over the Delta to feed the fire with napalm and white phosphorus rockets (*Time,* 26 April 1968).

Time (26 April 1968) and *Keesing's* (1968, p. 23140-41) indicate that in addition to air and naval bombardment, land-based artillery was also used to keep the fires going. B-52 heavy bombers were directed towards areas at the edge of the forest (*St. Louis Post Dispatch,* 13 April 1968).

All the accounts agree that the forest continued burning for about six weeks:

It destroyed 20 years' worth of Communist building and hoarding, setting off secondary explosions of ammunition or fuel at a rate of three an hour, denuding the enemy's protective cover completely. It will take at least a year for the forest to turn green once more, and five years before anyone, including the Viet Cong, can hope to use it as a hiding place again (*Time, op. cit.*).

Clearly, this was a much more significant action than the "unsuccessful experiments" of spring 1966 and spring 1967.

In other operations, growing crops were destroyed in the fields by bombing, burning and spraying with chemicals or by combinations of these methods (some napalm compositions contain sodium, enabling them to burn on the water of a paddy-field). Incendiary weapons were recommended for the destruction of harvested rice (US Army, 1969), but full information on the extent of these operations is not available.

The use of ground weapons in Viet-Nam has received less attention in the news media than aerial bombing. Mechanized flamethrowers on land vehicles and river boats were used for much the same purposes as napalm bombs, mainly supporting ground forces engaged in search and destroy operations. A US Army study team evaluated the use of mechanized flamethrowers operating in pairs and reported that they were "extremely useful when employed against dug-in ... positions, particularly when the positions were in dense thickets or scrub growth" (Dryer, 1965; from unclassified author's abstract in *Technical Abstracts Bulletin,* no. 367371). The team recommended that the flame vehicle, the M-132, be introduced into the US Military Assistance Program for South Viet-Nam, with four flamethrowers and two service units to be issued to each armoured cavalry squadron. A small number of these flamethrowers has been supplied even after the ceasefire. Flamethrowers mounted on boats were used in patrolling the rivers of the Mekong Delta; they could fire a stream of burning napalm at targets on the bank up to 200 metres away, and had a much greater fuel capacity than flamethrowers on land vehicles.

In sum, greater quantities of incendiary munitions have been used in South Viet-Nam than in any other country in any other war. Whatever the military effects, it is clear that many civilian casualties have resulted from this massive use of incendiaries.

North Viet-Nam

The US air war against North Viet-Nam appears initially to have had three goals. First it was hoped to prevent, or at least reduce, the supply of men and equipment to the NLF forces in South Viet-Nam. The Joint Chiefs of Staff recommended 94 targets that they believed to be militarily significant, such as airfields, ports, rail and highway systems, bridges, barracks and assembly points. Not all of these targets were initially authorized for attack by the White House.

Second, the gradual escalation approach was adopted by the US civilian leadership, contrary to military counselling, in the hope that the bombing would influence North Viet-Namese leaders, while avoiding the appearance of a direct confrontation with the Soviet Union or China. That is, the bombing was intended as a tool in a strategy of "coercive warfare".

Third, in the context of the rapidly deteriorating political and military situation in South Viet-Nam and the real prospect of a total collapse of South Viet-Namese (government) resistance (Sullivan *et al.,* 1968, p. 68), President Johnson was advised, early in 1965, that "morale in South Vietnam could be revived only if we bombed military targets in North Vietnam. This would assure Saigon of our determination to stay the course ..." (Goodwin, 1966, p. 31). That is, the bombing was not so much intended to break down the morale of leaders in Hanoi as to boost the morale of the leaders in Saigon.

Some six months later *Newsweek* reported

Since February ... US aircraft have flown nearly 20 000 missions against Communist North Vietnam, blasting away with bombs and napalm at military targets from the 17th parallel to the very border with Communist China (*Newsweek,* 11 October 1965).

Much of the bombing of North Viet-Nam was directed either at structures and installations of various kinds, for which high explosive munitions were most appropriate, or at anti-aircraft defences, for which fragmentation bombs were used increasingly. However, in certain areas where military personnel and supplies were gathered before moving to the battle front, napalm bombs were also used (US Commander in Chief, Pacific, 1968). The late Minister of Health of the Democratic Republic of Viet-Nam reported in *Le Monde* (25 November 1967) that

In districts close to the fighting 5–10% of our wounded have napalm burns ... Napalm is dropped in jet containers and is used in the bombing of our towns. Casualties also result from the use of phosphorus and magnesium packed into shells which are fired from naval guns, and guns whose range extends over the 17th parallel (Pham Ngoc Thach, interview with Dr. Escoffier-Lambiette, in *Le Monde,* 25 November 1967).

Gestewitz (1968) reports that the number of napalm casualties among military personnel in North Viet-Nam, particularly in the southern parts of the country, rose from 2 per cent in 1965 to 12 per cent in 1966, but declined to 9 per cent in 1967. At the same time the total number of attacks and the total tonnage of bombs increased greatly, so that the total number of napalm casualties was higher in 1967 than in 1966. Similar findings were reported for the civilian population. The proportion of civilian casualties from incendiary bombs rose from 0.3 per cent in 1965 to 13 per cent in 1967. Of those who died immediately (civilian and military), 8 per cent died from burns.

A British surgeon who visited North Viet-Nam in March 1967 reported that while anti-personnel pellet bombs "appeared to have been used over North Viet-Nam for about a year, the even more barbarous method of napalm bombing has only been widely used in the South" (Birnstigl, 1968, p. 8). Some Western doctors did report seeing relics of napalm bombing, but mainly in the areas near the 17th parallel (Harvey, 1968). Other sources give an impression of a somewhat greater use of napalm. *Vietnam Courier* (8 April 1968) reported that napalm "has also been extensively employed against North Vietnam", while a Soviet reporter who visited North Viet-Nam in 1968 recalled "whole districts burned up by napalm—brown, lifeless land" (*Soviet Weekly*, 15 July 1972). A possible explanation of the apparent discrepancies in these reports may be that napalm was used more in the border crossing areas than elsewhere in North Viet-Nam.

Though many towns in North Viet-Nam have been very largely destroyed by US bombing, there is no evidence that incendiary bombs were used for systematic area attacks.[36] Nevertheless, some magnesium-thermite incendiary cluster bombs of the type used on European cities during World War II were apparently used in some attacks on North Viet-Nam. For example, M-126 bombs, used in the M-36 cluster, were dropped in an attack in Quang Binh province on 21 September 1971 (*Vietnam Medical Aid News Bulletin (London)*, No. 20, Summer 1972). There are reports that napalm bombs were used in the bombing of major cities in the 1972 air offensive. The Agence France Presse correspondent in Hanoi, Joel Henri, reported in June 1972 that the textile industry town Nam Dinh had been bombed for the third time in a month, using napalm and fragmentation bombs in addition to high explosive bombs, and causing many civilian casualties (*Dagens Nyheter*, 13 June 1972).

The USA estimated that 52 000 civilians had died from US air strikes by the time of the bombing halt in 1968 (*Congressional Record*, 11 May 1972, p. E5063). It is not known what the reliability of this estimate is, or how many died in subsequent attacks.

---

[36] Professor Telford Taylor, chief legal counsel for the prosecution at the Nuremberg trials, reported after a visit to Hanoi during the Christmas 1972 bombing raids that the total destruction was not so great as World War II bombing raids on German cities because incendiary bombs were not used on Hanoi, though the raids caused extensive destruction of many non-military facilities (*International Herald Tribune*, 3 January 1973).

Laos

Incendiary bombs were widely used by government and US air forces in Laos until 1973. A report prepared by the staff of the US Senate Subcommittee reported that bombing in Laos was increased in four stages, beginning about May 1964.

The fourth phase, beginning early in 1969, saw the heaviest bombing, following the bombing halt over North Viet-Nam. According to refugee reports, during this phase the aircraft came daily, dropping napalm, phosphorus and anti-personnel bombs (US Senate Committee on the Judiciary, 1970). The bombing of Laos reached a peak in 1970–71 and was terminated in February 1973.

While it is known, for instance, that in addition to napalm and phosphorus, magnesium-thermite incendiary cluster bombs were used in an attempt to stop trucks transporting supplies to South Viet-Nam (US Senate Committee on Armed Services, 1971), there is little general information available about the quantities of incendiary bombs used in Laos, about their military effects and about their effects on the civilian population.

A report prepared for the US Senate Committee on Foreign Relations (1971) describes the complex "Rules of Engagement and Operational Authorities" by which the US Embassy in Vientiane controlled the attacks by US aircraft. In some specially designated areas all munitions could be used without special authorization with the sole exception of napalm. In other areas, napalm could be used against certain kinds of targets. Though these rules were at that time stricter than they had been some years previously, they did not prevent some attacks on unauthorized targets. Nor did they apply to the Royal Lao Air Force, which attacked targets, including the town of Saravane, out of bounds to US aircraft. After the ceasefire it was reported that

... contrary to US claims made during the war that few people lived in Pathet Lao areas—an allegation that US officials used in order to justify the bombing of these areas—the US Mission in Vientiane now estimates a population of 750 000 to 1 000 000 people under Pathet Lao control, or some one-third of the Laotian population (US Senate Committee on the Judiciary, 1974, p. 102).[37]

A study mission sent by the Senate Subcommittee on Refugees reported that physical rehabilitation of war victims was urgently needed, because there was a higher proportion of civilian casualties than in South Viet-Nam and even more limited medical resources.

Khmer Republic (Cambodia)

Following the extension of the Indo-China War to Cambodia, similar means of warfare were employed, including the use of napalm bombs and

---

[37] Pathet Lao officials quoted by this report claimed that about 1.5 million (that is, half the population) were under their control.

flamethrowers. Between April 1970 and March 1973 the US Air Force dropped an estimated 78 154 tons of munitions on Cambodian targets (US Department of Defense, press release, June 1973), and presumably these raids included a similar proportion of napalm to that used in Viet-Nam and Laos. In addition, the Khmer (Cambodian) Air Force has used napalm, dropped from its propellor-driven fighter-bomber planes (*International Herald Tribune*, 11 January 1974). The fighting has been very severe and has taken a heavy toll of the civilian population (US Senate Committee on the Judiciary, 1974).

Thailand, 1968–1973

Anti-government guerillas in the north, north-east and south of Thailand have been met with air attacks, during which napalm, defoliants and other munitions were used by government forces, aided by US military personnel (*Le Monde*, 20 April 1968; *Le Monde Diplomatique*, July 1973).

Arab-Israeli Wars, 1947–1974

Incendiary weapons of various kinds have been used in all the wars between Israel and the Arab states.

In 1947 neither side had more than a few World War II fighter aircraft. Egyptian Spitfires carried out some ground attacks on Jewish settlements and even on Tel Aviv, but on 1 June Israeli planes dropped incendiary and high explosive bombs on Amman. Later some other towns were attacked. On the ground improvised incendiary grenades and a single flamethrower were used by the Israelis against the Syrians (O'Ballance, 1956). Fieser (1964), the inventor of napalm, provided information on an incendiary anti-tank grenade to the Israelis.

According to some foreign military observers, the Israeli use of napalm in 1956 contributed to victory by constituting a shock for which the Egyptian soldiers were not prepared (Baer, 1957).

In the war of June 1967, Israel used napalm extensively against Egyptian troops fighting in the Sinai desert, as well as on some civilian targets. On one occasion four Israeli jet aircraft dropped napalm bombs on the August Victoria Hospital in Jerusalem. Since patients and staff were sheltering in the basement, no-one was hurt, but a wing of the building was destroyed (*The Economist*, 1 July 1967; *Life Magazine*, 3 July 1967).

On 15 February 1968 Israeli planes attacked more than 15 villages and refugee camps along the River Jordan with napalm, killing 56 people, including 46 civilians, injuring 82, including 55 civilians, and sending some 70 000 people fleeing towards Amman (*Le Jour* (Beirut), 16 February 1968; *L'Orient* (Beirut), 18, 22 February 1968). On 4 August the same year Israeli planes carried out a napalm raid on Slat (Jordan), killing 28 people, 22 of them civilians, and injuring 82 (*Arab Report & Record*, 1–15 August 1968, p. 220).

During the "War of Attrition" in 1969–70, Israeli aircraft dropped napalm bombs and delayed-action fragmentation bombs in the heavily populated Nile Delta area. A number of these raids were observed by UN observation posts and reported to the Security Council (UN Doc. S/7930/Add. 465; 19 December 1969). On 12 February 1970 Israeli Phantom jets bombed the Egyptian iron works at Abu Zabal. President Nasser alleged on 1 May that napalm bombs had been used in this raid (*The Times* (London), 2 May 1970), though Israeli Defence Minister Dayan, in response to questions in the Israeli parliament, denied that this was so. At the same time, Dayan confirmed that napalm bombs had been dropped elsewhere in the Nile Delta (*Dagens Nyheter,* 6 March 1970).

Napalm raids against villages and refugee camps suspected of harbouring Palestinian guerillas have been reported periodically since that time (*Neues Deutschland,* 28 February, 1972; *Dagens Nyheter,* 28 October, 1972).

In the war of October 1973 napalm was reported to have been used by both sides. As in previous full-scale engagements, Israel made extensive use of ground-attack aircraft, using napalm as well as other weapons. Egypt made little use of its air force, but some napalm casualties from Egyptian or Syrian attack have been reported (*Dagens Nyheter,* 29 October 1973). An extensive system of static flame projectors was reported to have been deployed on the Israeli side along the Suez front; but this was rendered inoperative at the start of hostilities by Egyptian sappers who blocked the nozzles with cement (*Sunday Times,* 16 December 1973).

Palestinian spokesmen have reported the use of napalm in Israeli air raids on villages and refugee camps in southern Lebanon suspected of harbouring guerillas (*The Times* (London), 22 May 1974).

Yemen 1962–1969

Following a *coup d'état* against the Imam of Yemen, there was a prolonged civil war between Royalist forces and the armed forces of the new military government. The Royalist forces were backed by Saudi Arabia and received material aid from several western countries. The United Arab Republic intervened on the government side, sending an expeditionary force equipped with aircraft and napalm. Material aid also came from the Soviet Union. Egyptian involvement seems however to have ceased following the UAR defeat in the Six Day War in 1967.

Use of napalm in Egyptian air raids against Royalist territory is mentioned by several reporters (for example, O'Ballance, 1971, p. 126; Schmidt 1968, p. 169). At times it appeared that all the villages in the contested areas had had to be abandoned because of the bombardments; the inhabitants had to live in caves in the hills.

In 1963 there was a UN investigation of allegations, made by the Royalist side, that the Egyptians were using poison gas in their bombs. There was no conclusive evidence in this case, but the suggestion was made that the burns in question had been caused by napalm, which was not forbidden, and that the damage done was consequently not so alarming from a legal point of view.

In the British House of Commons, Prime Minister Edward Heath said that the British ambassador in Cairo had told the Egyptian government of 'the extreme seriousness' with which the British government would view the use of gas, should it be confirmed, and noted that Egyptian authorities had suggested that the reported incidents were probably caused by napalm, not gas (Schmidt, 1968, p. 259).

Iraq, 1961–1970, 1974

Kurds, living in northern and eastern parts of Iraq, have been fighting an intermittent war for autonomy against the government of Iraq during the whole of the 1960s. They accused the government of attacking Kurdish villages with napalm in the course of this war. An instance of this was published in *Le Monde* of 27 June 1969 from a communiqué issued by the headquarters of the Kurd autonomists: "Faced with the successive defeats of Iraqi ground troops, the air force ... attacked fifty-seven Kurd localities, bombing them with napalm and acids."

Following the renewal of fighting in 1974 the Kurds issued further press reports alleging the use of napalm. For example, a spokesman for the Kurdish Democratic Party reported that several towns were bombed between 24–28 April 1974, and that napalm was dropped during an attack on the town of Qaladiza, with 35 000 inhabitants; as many as a hundred children were said to have been killed (*Dagens Nyheter,* 29 April 1974). Periodic reports of the use of napalm have appeared since that time. According to a report from *Reuters,* a senior doctor at a refugee camp for Kurdish refugees on the Iranian side of the border claimed that napalm had been used against civilians, though he had only seen a few victims in the border area (*Dagens Nyheter,* 4 September 1974).

Cyprus, 1964, 1974

On 7, 8 and 9 August 1964 the Turkish Air Force intervened in Cyprus where fighting was going on between the Cyprus National Guard and Turkish Cypriot forces.

Napalm bombs as well as rockets and machine guns were used in these air attacks, which also caused civilian casualties (Republic of Cyprus Public Information Office, 1969).[38]

The military occupation by Turkish forces of part of Cyprus in the summer of 1974 was accompanied by air attacks during which the use of napalm was again reported *(International Herald Tribune,* 22 July 1974). In

---

[38] A photograph of the remains of a napalm bomb dropped by Turkish planes on a village in the Paphos area appeared in a brochure published by the Union of Journalists of Athens Daily Newspapers (*Satan Storms Cyprus,* Athens, 1966). It was a 750-1b type E-74 napalm bomb manufactured by the American Stove Co., and still marked "Property of US Air Force".

the course of one attack three Austrian soldiers of the United Nations force were killed by a napalm bomb, an incident which was "profoundly deplored" by the Security Council in a resolution of 15 August 1974.

India-Pakistan, 1971

On 10 December 1971 Pakistan protested strongly to the International Committee of the Red Cross in Geneva that the Indian Air Force had dropped napalm bombs, causing terrible suffering among civilians. The Pakistani government alleged that this was a contravention of the Geneva Convention and hoped that the ICRC would make representations to those responsible (*The Times* (London) 11 December 1971).

Angola, 1961–1974

The first reports of the use of napalm in Angola were made in 1961, when refugees from the Luanda area crossed into the Congo (now Zaire). According to their reports, collected by missionaries and other observers, not only were people attacked by Portuguese planes but vegetable gardens were burned with napalm, creating a food shortage (Dr David Grenfell, in Davidson, 1972). A Swedish journalist, among others, reported that many villages were bombed and also that the dry savannah grass was set afire with napalm bombs, causing miles of fires in Northern Angola. Some 215 000 Angolan refugees were reported in the Congo by September 1962 (Statement by Baptist Missionary Society, London, 15 September 1962; cited in Davidson, 1972).

There was little sign of military activity after this period until guerilla operations were initiated in 1966. In 1968 the Portuguese launched a major counterattack and in 1971 reports appeared of the combined use of incendiary bombs and chemical defoliants aimed at destroying crops such as cassava and sweet potato in the field and burning surrounding forest (*Le Monde*, 9 July 1971; *The Times* London, 22 July 1971). A leader of the popular Movement for the Liberation of Angola (MPLA) spoke of a systematic attempt to destroy the crops in the areas controlled by the MPLA in order to force the population out of those areas into "strategic hamlets" under Portuguese military control (*Africasia*, 25 April 1971). According to *Frankfurter Rundschau* (4 June 1971), the deputy military commander of Angola, Commandente Machado da Silva, confirmed the use of napalm, though he denied that it was used against human life; large stocks of napalm bombs were to be seen at air bases in Luso and Gago Coutino by the side of bombers ready for take-off.

The use of napalm in Angola by Portuguese forces was reported to the Security Council by Pascal Luvalo, a representative of the MPLA, on 1 February 1972 (UN Press Release, SC/3302, 1 February 1972).

Guinea-Bissau, 1962–1974

Guerilla warfare began in Guinea-Bissau in a small way in 1962. Napalm was used by Portuguese forces in an effort to maintain their colonial rule. An eyewitness account by a western journalist is given by Davidson (1969) who even recorded the markings on a fragment of a napalm cannister he found after an attack: FCM-1-55 NAPALM 300 kg—350 1 M/61. According to Davidson, the Portuguese used a large amount of napalm and there were many victims to be seen in the clinics and hospitals in the areas held by the PAIGC.[39]

The late leader of the PAIGC reported ''The Portuguese have used napalm for years. They bomb our villages and burn our crops, and attack our schools, and hospitals ...'' (Interview with Amilcar Cabral, *The Guardian* (UK), 26 October 1971).

In an interview in the newspaper *Corriere della Sera* (16 July 1973), an Italian missionary gave dates and other information of napalm bomb attacks on villages (see also *Le Monde,* 18 July 1973).

The use of napalm by Portuguese forces in Guinea-Bissau has been reported to the Fourth Committee (non-autonomous territories) of the United Nations General Assembly.

Mozambique, 1964–1974

Guerilla fighting started in 1964 under the leadership of FRELIMO.[40] The movement developed slowly and in 1970 Portuguese forces undertook a major counteroffensive, Operation Gordian Knot. As in the other Portuguese colonies in Africa, napalm bombs were one of the weapons used by airborne Portuguese forces. The *Standard* (Tanzania) on 3 November 1972 published a picture of a napalm victim with the text ''Napalm is a deadly poison used by Portuguese terrorists against the Mozambican people. This victim's picture ... speaks more loudly than a thousand people behind microphones ...''

Chad, 1970

In 1970 French forces assisted the government of Chad in military operations to put down an armed rebellion. Several allegations of the use of napalm and flamethrowers were made as a result of these events. On the night of 29–30 August 1970, the Armée National Tchadienne was reported to have attacked the town of Fada with flamethrowers (*Tchad* (collective authorship), 1971). In October 1970 a violent napalm bombardment in the Zouar region was reported (*Ibid.*). The use of napalm was denied by the French government (*Ibid.*).

---

[39] The African Party for the Independence of Guinea and Cap Verde.
[40] Front for the Liberation of Mozambique.

Southern Africa

The South African minister of defence has on several occasions announced that South Africa is manufacturing napalm bombs from raw materials available in the Republic (*Daily Telegraph*, 13 March 1968; *Sunday Times*, 25 October 1970).

In Rhodesia, where there has been more organized guerilla activity, it has been suggested that napalm may also be made available to government forces.

Napalm and CS-gas are said to be produced by African Explosives and Chemical Industries at Umboginini in Natal. According to some reports this is the source of at least some of the napalm used by Portuguese forces in Angola and Mozambique (*Örebrokuriren*, (Sweden) 29 January 1973), though a representative of the PAIGC has said that no South African napalm has been used in Guinea-Bissau as far as he knew (G. Fernandes, 14 April 1973, personal communication).

Peru, 1965

Napalm was reported to have been used by government and US Special Forces troops engaged in the suppression of guerilla activity in the mountains (*Le Monde*, 24, 25 August, 1965).

Bolivia 1967

Air attacks with napalm bombs against the mountain hiding places of guerillas were reported in Bolivia (*New York Times*, 31 March 1967).

Guatemala, 1967

The Vice President of Guatemala, Clemente Marroquin Rojas, is reported as having stated in an interview with Inter Press Service that a squadron of US aircraft piloted by US personnel had for some time flown from bases in Panama, delivered loads of napalm on targets suspected of being guerilla hideouts and flown back to their bases in Panama without landing on Guatemalan soil (*NACLA Newsletter*, 15 September 1967).

Venezuela, 1969

It was officially announced for the first time that the Venezuelan Air Force had bombarded guerilla positions in the east of the country in February 1969, though the munitions were not specified. Previously a number of opposition political leaders had alleged that napalm bombs had been used (*Le Monde*, 9–10 February 1969).

Non-governmental use of incendiary weapons

Only governments have the resources to use incendiary—or any other— weapons on a large scale. However, because of the simplicity of construction, improvised incendiary weapons have been used by a wide variety of non-governmental groups and individuals. A few random examples illustrate their widespread usage.

West German police extinguished an incendiary device burning in a British Army car parked outside a military headquarters (*The Times* (London), 6 October 1973). A bus driver in Jerusalem put out the flames of a fire bomb placed beside his bus, presumably by an Arab guerilla or sympathizer (*The Times* (London) 11 December 1972). In Paris Molotov cocktails were hurled at police trying to break up a clash between left-and right-wing political groups; ten policemen were admitted to hospital with serious burns (*International Herald Tribune,* 22 June 1973).

In Spain a number of bookstores have been attacked with firebombs by a group calling itself the "National Socialist Action Group", described as right-wing extremists retaliating against the left-wing Basque separatist movement (*International Herald Tribune,* 11 August 1973). In South London, England, a wave of petrol bomb attacks was reported against small businesses run by immigrants of Asian origin (*Sunday Times,* 18 March 1973). Incendiary devices have also been used in Northern Ireland; in one incident the British Army defused five incendiary devices concealed in books in a public library (*International Herald Tribune,* 24 February 1973).

VII. *Recent legal developments at the UN and the ICRC*

The UN report on incendiary weapons

At the 1968 International Conference on Human Rights held in Teheran, the Secretary-General of the United Nations was asked to study steps to secure the better application of existing humanitarian international conventions and rules in all armed conflicts.

In October 1972 the Secretary-General's report on *Napalm and Other Incendiary Weapons and All Aspects of Their Possible Use* was published (United Nations, 1973 a). Its main conclusion was that the destruction caused by incendiaries is often indiscriminate and more damaging to the civilian population than to the military. The report drew attention to the social and economic consequences of incendiary warfare, particularly the marked disparity between the abilities of the developed and the underdeveloped countries both to inflict and to repair the economic damage that may result from incendiary attack. Furthermore it pointed out that the production of incendiary weapons of even greater destructiveness continues, with the possibility of subsequent proliferation of these weapons to an increasing number of states.

The report suggested that the use of incendiary weapons may be part of a more general problem—the increasing mobilization of science and technology for war purposes:

New weapons of increased destructiveness are emerging from the research and development programmes at an increasing rate, alongside which the long upheld principle of the immunity of the non-combatant appears to be receding from the military consciousness. These trends have very grave implications for the world community. It is therefore essential that the principle of restraint in the conduct of military operations, and in the selection and use of weapons, be researched with vigour. Clear lines must be drawn between what is permissible in time of war and what is not permissible (*Ibid.*, para. 190).

The report emphasized "the necessity of working out measures for the prohibition of the use, production, development and stockpiling of napalm and other incendiary weapons" (*Ibid.*, para. 193).

Following the publication of the report, the General Assembly, in a resolution of 29 November 1972, deplored the use of napalm and other incendiary weapons in armed conflicts and requested the Secretary-General to make the report widely available (see appendix 1C). The Secretary-General was further requested to report on the comments of governments to the 28th session of the General Assembly (United Nations, 1973 *b*).

The resolution was passed by 99 votes in favour and none against, with 15 nations abstaining (Australia, Belgium, Canada, France, Greece, Israel, Italy, Japan, Luxembourg, the Netherlands, New Zealand, Portugal, South Africa, the United Kingdom and the United States).

The vote of 99 nations in favour of a resolution deploring the use of incendiary weapons in armed conflicts indicated a widespread aversion to such weapons. It remained to write such an aversion into international law.

As a further step in this direction, the General Assembly in Resolution 3032 (XXVII) of 18 December 1972 urged all governments and the International Committee of the Red Cross to continue their efforts to ensure that new rules applicable in armed conflicts would be adopted.

The International Committee of the Red Cross (ICRC)

At the present time efforts are being made to reaffirm and develop the international humanitarian law of armed conflicts by modernizing the four Geneva Conventions of 1949. The International Committee of the Red Cross (ICRC) has produced two Draft Additional Protocols which have been refined through the work of two conferences of Government Experts, held in Geneva in 1971 and 1972 (ICRC, 1973 *a*). These Draft Protocols were the subject of Diplomatic Conferences in Geneva in the spring of 1974 and 1975. Among the subjects covered in these negotiations was the question of the restriction or prohibition of use of certain specific weapons, including incendiary weapons.

The XXI International Conference of the Red Cross, held at Istanbul in 1969, urged the ICRC to draw up concrete rules to supplement the international humanitarian law of armed conflicts already in force and to hold consultations with government experts on these proposals.

In pursuance of this mandate, in 1971 the ICRC convened a Conference of Government Experts to "reaffirm and develop the international humanitarian law of armed conflicts" (ICRC, 1971).

The ICRC subsequently agreed to take up a proposal by 19 states to convene a special group of experts to examine in more detail the question of particular conventional weapons which may cause unnecessary suffering or have indiscriminate effects. The work of these experts resulted in the publication of a report by the ICRC in 1973 (ICRC, 1973c). The report sought to describe the use and effects of a range of "antipersonnel" weapons such as high-velocity small arms, fragmentation weapons, delayed action weapons, and certain potential developments such as laser weapons.

Following the publication of this report further action was urged by the XXII International Conference of the Red Cross, meeting in Teheran in November 1973, to take the form of a full-scale Conference of Government Experts on the question of weapons which may be inhumane or indiscriminate in their effects.

The Conference of Government Experts on the Use of Certain Conventional Weapons was held at Lucerne, Switzerland, from 24 September to 18 October 1974 (ICRC, 1975). Incendiary weapons were the first item on the agenda.

Unlike the previous reports on incendiary weapons, this conference had the benefit of the presence of experts of some of the states which have been the major users of incendiary weapons. These states reasoned that, while incendiary weapons could be used indiscriminately and had been so used on some occasions in the past, when used discriminately against battlefield targets there was no evidence of significant civilian casualties. There was general agreement that burn injuries were among the most severe to which the human being could be subjected; but it was argued that certain incendiary weapons were, unfortunately, a military necessity in certain battlefield situations. The debate was marred by a continuing lack of precise information on the severity of wounds caused by incendiary weapons compared with those caused by other weapons, and on the actual numbers of civilian casualties resulting from the use of incendiary weapons.

The report of the Conference of Government Experts was presented to the United Nations General Assembly, which passed two further resolutions on the subject of napalm and incendiary weapons (appendix 1C). In one resolution governments were urged to compile without delay such supplementary data as may be required by them to focus upon specific proposals for prohibitions and restrictions of use of incendiary weapons. In the second resolution, the use of napalm and other incendiary weapons was condemned in circumstances where it may affect human beings or cause damage to the environment and/or natural resources; all states were urged to refrain from production, stockpiling, proliferation and use of such weapons pending conclusion of agreements on their prohibition.

71

VIII. *Summary*

This survey of the use of incendiary weapons cannot claim to be complete and may, because of the sparse nature of some of the reporting, contain inaccuracies. A number of other possible instances of the use of incendiary weapons, particularly napalm bombs in "pacification" operations, have been received in private communications, but have not been publicly documented; these attacks have usually been in areas to which outside observers do not have access. It is also possible that not all the allegations made by various parties cited here can be substantiated.

Nevertheless, in spite of these uncertainties, the general trends emerging from this survey are likely to be close to the historical record. Until World War I, incendiary weapons had a long history of battlefield use, both against persons and against inflammable targets, such as transport carts, ships, siege towers, and wooden buildings. These uses were for a time eclipsed by the rise of explosives and long range projectiles. During World War I mechanical flamethrowers were used in short-range ground operations, and incendiary bombs were dropped from aircraft on towns. Between the wars the technique of replacing ground troops with air power was developed for "pacification" operations in western Asia and parts of north-east Africa, operations of the type in which napalm bombs were later to be used; both ground and air flame weapons were used in the Italian invasion of Ethiopia. The technique of bombing cities was developed further in the Spanish Civil War and in the Sino-Japanese War. By the beginning of World War II, the major military powers were equipped with the basic technology and tactics of modern incendiary warfare; during the war, incendiary weapons were used both as weapons of mass destruction and as battlefield support weapons. It was also during World War II that the napalm bomb was developed.

Following World War II, the napalm bomb was used increasingly in air attacks in close support of ground troops, and in air strikes independent of ground operations in rear areas. Very large quantities of napalm were used by US and allied forces in Korea and Indo-China and by French forces in Indo-China and Algeria. Napalm bombs became a standard weapon for combating movements of armed resistance to colonial or central government. In these pacification operations napalm was used in air attacks in an effort both to substitute for as well as to support ground troops. Improvised incendiary devices, such as "Molotov cocktails", have been used not only by large armies but also by small groups of guerilla fighters and individuals.

Several attempts have been made to restrict or prohibit the use of incendiary weapons by international agreement; indeed the disarmament conference of the League of Nations seemed close to success in 1933. But just as the awesome use of gas during World War I overshadowed incendiary weapons in the post-war legal discussions, so did the atom bomb over-shadow them in the legal negotiations after World War II. Chemical and nuclear weapons continue to receive priority in disarmament negotiations.

In the meantime, incendiary weapons—and a great variety of new types of "conventional" weapons—are being used to kill and maim combatants and civilians. As a result there is a renewed effort to bring incendiary weapons, along with other conventional weapons which may be inhumane or indiscriminate, to the forefront of international negotiations in an attempt to restrict or prevent their further use on humanitarian grounds.

Appendix 1A

Incendiary weapons of World War I and World War II

In this appendix brief descriptions of incendiary weapons associated with World War I and World War II are given in tabular form. The incendiary agents referred to, as well as more modern incendiary weapons such as those used in Korea and Indo-China, are described in chapter 2.

Details regarding actual historical uses of each weapon are not always available, and the period between entry into service and obsolescence of weapons varies considerably. For these reasons some weapons are listed which were developed in the years prior to a war, even though they were used up or superseded by new designs early in the war, while other weapons listed were developed under the pressures of a particular war but did not always reach the war theatre in time for operational service. This kind of information is indicated where possible.

Information regarding incendiary weapons is widely scattered and different sources are not always consistent. One reason for this may be that very often a particular weapon is modified continuously during a war lasting several years. For example, a bomb casing may be strengthened, so that later models are heavier, or other incendiary agents may be used, due to shortages of raw materials or new discoveries. This kind of variation may have led to occasional errors in the technical details presented.

The tables can claim to be reasonably complete with regard to flamethrowers and incendiary bombs. A number of representative artillery rounds and grenades are included in the World War I table, but after that period no attempt has been made to include these munitions, due to the great variety of types.

Table 1A.1. Incendiary weapons of World War I

Type	Notes
France	
455 g hand or rifle grenade	Contained 300 g white phosphorus
605 g hand or rifle grenade	Contained 470 g white phosphorus
75 mm artillery shell	Contained 920 g white phosphorus and molasses
75 mm artillery shell	Contained 800 g white phosphorus dissolved in carbon disulphide; projectile weighed 5.3 kg
75 mm artillery shell	Impregnated incendiary bundles in white phosphorus and carbon disulphide solution; each bundle weighed 45 g and burned for 70–80 seconds
75 mm artillery shell	Contained 700 g white phosphorus, carbon disulphide and tar oil; projectile weighed 5.2 kg
120 mm artillery shell	Contained 2.2 kg of incendiary agent consisting of 58 impregnated incendiary bundles in white phosphorus and carbon disulphide solution; projectile weighed 17.7 kg
155 mm artillery shell	Contained 3 kg of incendiary bundles in white phosphorus and carbon disulphide solution; projectile weighed 43 kg
155 mm artillery shell	White phosphorus only
3.25 kg incendiary bomb	White phosphorus and molasses
5.5 kg incendiary bomb	Filled with nitrobenzene and nitrogen tetroxide
Germany	
13 cm artillery shell	Contained thermite and sodium
15 cm artillery shell	Contained white phosphorus
17 cm artillery shell	Contained thermite and sodium
Portable flamethrower	
United Kingdom	
450 g hand and rifle grenade	Contained 315–335 g white phosphorus
4 in incendiary mine	Filled with thermite or white phosphorus
8 in incendiary mine	Filled with raw petroleum or amyl acetate and balloon dope
Portable flamethrower	
6½ oz Mk IV incendiary bomb	"Baby Incendiary Bomb;" consisted of a tin-plate body containing Daisite (17.5 per cent aluminium; 57.5 per cent hammer scale; 25 per cent sulphur) and a starter mixture (60 per cent barium nitrate; 20 per cent sulphur; 20 per cent aluminium); inner tube fitted with special 12-bore shot gun cartridge and cap; lead weight and striker in base.
4.5 in howitzer shell	Incendiary composition containing aluminium
8 in howitzer shell	powder, potassium nitrate, sulphur and antimony sulphide
18-pounder artillery shell	Contained thermite or white phosphorus
United States	
75 mm antiaircraft shell	Contained red lead and magnesium; for use against airships
Russia	
76 mm artillery shell	Contained 930 g thermite composition; projectile weight, 4.7 kg

Sources: Hanslian (1937); Prentiss (1937); Greene (1947).

Table 1A.2. Incendiary weapons of World War II

Type	Notes
Germany	
FlaW-41 portable flamethrower	Weighed 18.5 kg; fuel capacity, 7 litres; range, 30 metres
FlaW-46 portable flamethrower	Weighed 3.1 kg; fuel capacity, 1–1.5 litres; range 30–40 metres
Pzkw II mechanized flamethrower	Fuel capacity, 850 litres; range 40 metres
Pzkw III mechanized flamethrower	Fuel capacity, 1 000 litres; range, 80 metres; introduced 1943
Sd-122 mechanized flamethrower	Fuel capacity, 320 litres; range, 60–80 metres
AbwFnw-42 stationary flamethrower	System using combustion gases from a pyrotechnic charge to force incendiary fuel through a nozzle; capacity, 25 litres, range 45–60 metres; in use towards end of war; similar to Soviet FOG-2
1 kg incendiary bomb	Magnesium case containing thermite
2.2 kg incendiary bomb with fragmentation attachment	Magnesium case with thermite filler (1 kg incendiary bomb) with TNT explosive pellet in screw-on antipersonnel section
25 kg incendiary bomb	Thermite bomb, introduced prior to World War II
50 kg C-50 *Sprengbrand* bomb	Combined explosive and incendiary bomb, with thermite "firepots" as incendiary agent
50 kg incendiary bomb	Incendiary solution consisting of 86 per cent benzene thickened with 10 per cent rubber and ignited by 4 per cent white phosphorus
110 kg C-250 Flam incendiary bomb	Thickened oil with TNT burster; some later versions thickened with polystyrene
220 kg C-500 Flam incendiary bomb	As above
ABB-500 incendiary cluster bomb	500 kg bomb containing 1 kg magnesium/thermite bombs
32 cm incendiary rocket	Range, 2 000 metres
Italy	
CV-33 Mechanized flamethrower	Incendiary fuel capacity, 450 litres; range 30–40 metres
Fiat-Ansaldo M-33 mechanized flamethrower	Range, 50–60 metres
Fiat-Ansaldo M-35 mechanized flamethrower	Range, 50–60 metres
1 kg incendiary bomb	Magnesium case, thermite filler
2 kg incendiary bomb	Thermite and oil filler
2 kg incendiary bomb	Magnesium, mercuric oxide and nitrobenzene filler
20 kg incendiary bomb	Thermite
62 kg incendiary bomb	Thermite filler
100 kg incendiary bomb	Combined incendiary and fragmentation bomb
Japan	
1 kg incendiary bomb	Red phosphorus filling
60 kg incendiary bomb	Paraffin, paraffin wax and thermite filling
60 kg incendiary bomb	Combined incendiary and high explosive bomb containing picric acid and crepe rubbet pellets impregnated with white phosphorus dissolved in carbon disulphide

Table 1A.2. Incendiary weapons of World War II

Type	Notes
70 kg incendiary bomb	Contained many small Elektron containers filled with thermite
70 kg incendiary bomb	Magnesium bomb filled with oil and asphalt; some versions had case made of lithium

United Kingdom

Type	Notes
Lifebuoy portable flamethrower	Weight, 28 kg; fuel capacity, 19 litres; range, 36 metres
Akpak portable flamethrower	Weight, 21.8 kg; fuel capacity, 18 litres; range, 36 metres
Ronson mechanized flamethrower	Incendiary fuel capacity, 250 litres; range, 45 metres
MK I Wasp mechanized flamethrower	Incendiary fuel capacity, 1 400 litres; range, 90 metres
MK VIII Crocodile mechanized flamethrower	Incendiary fuel capacity, 1 900 litres; range, 130 metres; modified Churchill tank
Fougasse	Oil drum (eg. 170 litre) filled with thickened or unthickened oil and explosive charge, added just before use through pipe welded onto drum; variations included "Demi-gasses" (tar barrels connected to a detonating device), "Hedge-hoppers" (fougasses which could be thrown 5–6 m into the air before exploding) and "Cliff-hoppers" (fougasses perched on the edge of cliffs)
Static Flame Trap	Large tank of petrol which could flood a low-lying stretch of road through perforated pipes; ignited by guard with incendiary grenade
Sea Flame Barrage	System for pumping large quantities of oil onto the sea and igniting it with phosphorus pellets and other means; plan for 50 miles approved, but only 10 miles built
INC-4 lb (1.7 kg) incendiary bomb	250 g of incendiary mixture consisting of 36.3 per cent petrol; 10 per cent caoutchouc; 2–3 per oxide; 20.2 per cent aluminium; 5.1 per cent binder
INC-30 lb (14 kg) incendiary bomb	3.5 litres of incendiary oil consisting of 87–88 per cent petrol; 10 per cent caoutchouc; 2–3 per cent white phosphorus
INC-30 lb (14 kg) incendiary bomb	3.5 litres of incendiary oil consisting of 78 per cent benzene; 5 per cent synthetic rubber; 17 per cent phosphorus
I-30 lb Mk-1 incendiary bomb	3.5 litres of petrol and thermite
Lc-250 lb (110 kg) incendiary bomb	55 litres of petrol, paraffin, oil and textile waste
Lc-250 lb incendiary bomb	55 litres of petrol (94 per cent) thickened with rubber (6 per cent)
INC-4000 lb (1 800 kg) incendiary bomb	Approximately 800 litres of benzene and synthetic rubber
SBC 250 lb incendiary cluster bomb	Could be loaded with 90 INC-4 lb incendiary bombs or 8 INC-30 lb incendiary bombs

United States

Type	Notes
M-1 portable flamethrower	Early model (produced 1942, first used in combat 15 January 1943) firing unthickened fuel to a distance of 15 metres

Table 1A.2. Incendiary weapons of World War II

Type	Notes
M1A1 portable flamethrower	Remodeled M-1, designed to fire thickened fuel (napalm) to a distance of 40–45 metres; fuel capacity, 17 litres; weight, 30 kg
M2-2 portable flamethrower	Weight, 32 kg; fuel capacity, 17 litres; range, 40–45 metres
Satan mechanized flamethrower	M-3 tank modified (in Hawaii by US Marine Corps) to take British Ronson flame gun; used compressed carbon dioxide as propellant, giving range of 60–80 metres; fuel capacity, over 700 litres; only a few were made
POA-CWS "75" H-1 mechanized flamethrower	M-4 tank modified (in Hawai (H-1) by Chemical Warfare Service (CWS) Pacific Ocean Area (POA)) to take Ronson flame gun, disguised in 75 mm gun barrel; fuel capacity, 1 200 litres; range, 60–80 metres; 8 produced for Iwo Jima, 54 for Ryukyus attacks, where they discharged some 850 000 litres of napalm in 600 operations
E7-7 mechanized flamethrower	Flamethrower originally designed for modified M5A1 light tank; fuel capacity, 465 litres; range with thickened fuel, 105–130 metres. M5A1 was taken out of service before E7-7 became operational but flame gun was modified for use in M-4 tank (see below)
M5-4 mechanized flamethrower	Modified M-4 tank, using flamethrower from E7-7
Mk-I incendiary dart	Consisted of elongated 12-bore shot gun shell filled with incendiary agent made up of magnesium and/or magnesium powder, oil and asphalt and an oxidizer (sodium or barium chlorate); scatter-type bomb, 61 in cluster, intended for readily inflammable targets such as dry grain fields; developed before outbreak of war
Mk-II incendiary dart	Consisted of zinc case 5 cm in diameter 38 cm long with cast steel nose to aid penetration of buildings; contained thermite and oil, weighed 2.7 kg, intended for use against built-up areas; developed prior to outbreak of war
Mk-II M1 incendiary bomb	18 kg bomb containing thermite and solid oil, pre-war development
Mk-III incendiary bomb	45 kg bomb containing thermite and solid oil, pre-war development
50-1b bomb with "Wet incendiary filling"	Standard bomb case filled with balls of cotton waste in carbon disulphide and turpentine, or carbon disulphide, benzene and crude paraffin (kerosene); pre-war development
50-1b bomb with "Dry incendiary filling"	Standard bomb case filled with celluloid spheres, 5 cm in diameter, containing solid oil and wrapped in cotton waste saturated in molten aluminium nitrate; each sphere was then coated in a mixture of trinitrotoluene and naphthalene and sprinkled with black powder; pre-war development
M-47 incendiary bomb	Bomb of 100 lb (45 kg) nominal weight, filled with various agents. Early incendiary filling of petrol and rubber; later filled with napalm, IM or PT1, or white phosphorus or plasticized white phosphorus; four modifications, A1–A4, the latter in service until 1970s; first US incendiary bomb developed after outbreak of war
M-50 incendiary bomb	4 lb (1.7 kg) bomb with 285 g thermate in magnesium case
M-50X incendiary bomb	Same as above with tetryl or tetrylotol explosive charge
M-52 incendiary bomb	2 lb (0.9 kg) bomb containing thermite in magnesium body

Table 1A.2. Incendiary weapons of World War II

Type	Notes
M-52X incendiary bomb	Same as above with tetryl explosive charge
M-54 incendiary bomb	4 lb (1.7 kg) magnesium bomb containing thermate
M-54X incendiary bomb	Same as above with tetryl explosive charge
M-69 incendiary bomb	6 lb (2.8 kg) bomb filled with napalm or IM, with white phosphorus igniter; produced as an alternative to magnesium bombs for use against light wooden buildings
M-69X incendiary bomb	Same as above with explosive charge
M-74 incendiary bomb	10 lb (4.5 kg) bomb filled with about 1.3 kg of "goop", napalm, PT1 gel or IM, with 170 g white phosphorus igniter
M-74X incendiary bomb	Same as above with explosive charge
M-76 incendiary bomb	500 lb (224 kg) bomb containing thickened oil (PT1)
M-126 incendiary bomb	Modified M-50 with fin assembly; still in use early 1970s
M-3 incendiary cluster bomb	
M-6 incendiary cluster bomb	100 lb (45 kg) bomb containing 28 M-50 and 6 M-50X bomblets
M-7 incendiary cluster bomb	500 lb (224 kg) bomb containing 102 M-50 and 26 M-50X bomblets
M-8 incendiary cluster bomb	100 lb (45 kg) bomb containing 28 M-54 and 6 M-54X bomblets
M-9 incendiary cluster bomb	500 lb (224 kg) bomb containing 102 M-54 and 26 M-54X bomblets
M-12 incendiary cluster bomb	100 lb (45 kg) bomb containing 14 M-69 bomblets
M-19 incendiary cluster bomb	500 lb (224 kg) bomb containing 38 M-69 bomblets
M-31 incendiary cluster bomb	500 lb (224 kg) bomb containing 38 M-74 bomblets
M-32 incendiary cluster bomb	500 lb (224 kg) bomb containing 108 M-50 bomblets
M-35 incendiary cluster bomb	750 lb (340 kg) bomb containing 182 M-126 bomblets; still in use early 1970s
M-36 incendiary cluster bomb	750 lb (340 kg) bomb containing 182 M-126 bomblets
75 gallon (315 l) napalm bomb	Bomb improvised in field from droppable fuel tank
100 gallon (420 l) napalm bomb	Bomb improvised in field from droppable fuel tank
108 gallon (455 l) napalm bomb	Bomb improvised in field from droppable fuel tank
110 gallon (465 l) napalm bomb	Bomb improvised in field from droppable fuel tank
165 gallon (695 l) napalm bomb	Bomb improvised in field from droppable fuel tank
M-116	First specifically designed and standardized napalm bomb, 3.5 m long and 47 cm in diameter, weighing approximately 24 kg empty and 300 kg filled with 100 gallons (424 litres) of napalm-thickened aviation fuel; fuses in nose and tail, with longitudinal TNT burster and white phosphorus igniter
Soviet Union	
ROKS-1 portable flamethrower	Early model, introduced in 1940, ignited by glowing bark
ROKS-2 portable flamethrower	Later model with compressed air system, ignited by mechanical pyrotechnic spark device; weight, 23 kg, fuel capacity 10 litres, range 35 metres
ROKS-3 portable flamethrower	Similar to above
LPO portable flamethrower	No separate gas chamber—generates gas by combustion of pyrotechnic fuel cartridge at base of fuel tank; pressurizing cartridge ignited by electrical system powered by four dry batteries; the gas generated ruptures diaphragm, forcing thickened fuel (OP-2 napalm) through non-return valve into hose of flame gun; the fuel is

79

Table 1A.2. Incendiary weapons of World War II

Type	Notes
	ignited by ignition cartridge; has three disposable fuel tanks, which are refilled and fitted with new pressurizing and ignition cartridges and diaphragms after use; each fuel tank contains 3.9 litres and can be fired only once; total weight, 22.7 kg; range 70 m. Latest known model, LPO-50, believed still in service with some Soviet-supplied forces in mid-1960s.
OT-26 mechanized flamethrower	Pre-war model built into T-26A tank in 1933; incendiary fuel capacity of only 60 litres
OT-130 mechanized flamethrower	Pre-war model built into T-26B-2 tank in 1937, with 400 litres of unthickened fuel and range of 40 m; used in Manchuria in 1939, Finland, 1939–40, and against the Germans in 1942
OT-133 mechanized flamethrower	Later version of above, based on T-26C tank, introduced during Soviet-Finnish war
BT-5-OT mechanized flame-thrower	Flamethrower version of BT-3 tank, using flame gun from OT-133; appears to have been experimental version only, 1937–40
(OT-28 mechanized flamethrower)	Some German sources have reported a flamethrowing version of the T-28 medium tank in the early part of the war, but these reports have not been confirmed
OT-34 mechanized flamethrower	Flamethrower version of the T-34 tank; early models fitted with ATO-41 flame gun, with 100 litres fuel capacity, later models with ATO-42 flame gun, with 200 litres fuel capacity. The OT-34 could fire 6 shots of two seconds duration to a distance of some 120 m; first used against the Germans in 1944
KV-8 mechanized flamethrower	ATO-42 flame gun fitted to a KV-IC heavy tank, with fuel capacity of 570 litres and range of 120 metres
SPS stationary flamethrower	Early model of Soviet fougasse, using combustion gases from rapidly burning powder to force incendiary fuel through nozzle; named after the inventors, Stolycin, Povarnin & Stranded, who invented a system of this kind in 1916, using a piston; this arrangement was developed further in the first Five-year Plans following the Revolution
FOG-2 stationary flamethrower	This model, introduced in 1942, dispensed with the piston, operation being similar to the LPO flamethrower. It contained 20–30 litres fuel and weighed 60–100 kg
ZAB 100 CK incendiary bomb	Thermite
ZAB 300–500 TS incendiary bomb	Contained large numbers of balls of compressed thermite

Sources: Banks (1946), Bond (1946), Greene (1947), Kleber & Birdsell (1966), Konupka (1960), US War Department (1943).

Appendix 1B

Large-Scale fires

Fires in urban areas

During and after World War II extensive studies were carried out on the factors which had influenced the spread of fires in urban areas. The following types of large-scale fire were distinguished:

1. Isolated multiple fires. In many cities, such as Munich and Berlin (Bond, 1946), fires initiated by incendiary bombs did not in general spread to other areas due to the presence of physical features such as stone or brick walls, broad avenues or canals which acted as firebreaks.

2. Coalescing multiple fires. Where the individual fires were undisturbed by surface winds, a pillar of smoke, hot air, vapours and gases could rise almost vertically several thousand metres above the ground. As the fires gained in intensity, the gases within this pillar might ignite. The vapours would condense on contact with colder layers of air, forming clouds, and where the air was humid the fumes from the fire would spread out horizontally, in some cases precipitating oily droplets of condensed hydrocarbon vapours back into the fire or surrounding areas.

3. Fire-storms. In certain conditions the convection column of rising hot air and smoke could draw in cold fresh air at ground level with gale forces of up to 25 metres per second. Even at a distance of three kilometres from the fire in Hamburg, the wind velocity increased from three to 14 metres per second. The inrushing wind had the same effect on the fire as a bellows, increasing the intensity and temperature of the fire. Bond (1946) reports that the fire-storm areas of Hamburg could not be approached for two days because of the temperature.

4. Conflagrations. With a strong wind the fire could coalesce into an advancing front, preceded by a turbulent mass of preheated vapours. The column of smoke would slant forwards, depositing firebrands which ignite combustible materials in its path, in advance of the main body of fire. The great city fires of the past have been of this kind, as are large forest fires. The main example during World War II was the Tokyo fire of 9–10 March 1945, when incendiary bombs dropped over an area of 20 square kilometres caused a conflagration which completely destroyed 40 square kilometres of the city (Sanborn in Bond, 1946).

Fires in rural areas

The few known scientific studies of the military uses of large-scale fires in rural areas have been withheld from the public, and therefore little is known about specific wartime instances of such fires.[1] However, it may be assumed that they resemble peacetime fires of the same type.

1. Fires of crops. The tactic of setting fire to an enemy's cornfields seems to be as old as recorded history (see p. 15). The British *Manual of Air Tactics* of 1937 advocated the tactic as a means of punishment, "having been used for that purpose in outlying areas against primitive peoples" (Webster & Frankland, 1961, vol. I, p. 104, footnote). The same tactic was recommended by the British Ministry of Economic Warfare in June 1940 for use against Germany, but tests on British crops showed poor results and the British concluded that the tactic had not accomplished much in Germany either (Webster & Frankland, *op. cit.*, p. 295). It appears that in temperate zones growing crops usually have too high a moisture content to be readily ignited. In exceptionally dry conditions, or in other areas such as the Mediterranean, ripe seed crops may be destroyed by fire.

2. Fires in savannah or bush country. Some tropical areas are characterized by large expanses of dry grassland interspersed by bushes. Fires in this type of terrain are a periodically occurring natural phenomenon, and relatively easy to generate artificially for military purposes as well.

3. Forest fires. Forest fires are of three main types: surface, crown and ground. Ground fires, in which the top layer of humus in the soil catches fire, have the most serious long-term effects on the soil as the texture is broken down making the soil liable to erosion; surface fires are the most common type and also do the most short-term damage; crown fires may kill adult trees and leave an area of dead trunks.

Tropical rain forests have a structure different from those in temperate zones. They are characterized by several layers of vegetation but dead vegetation decays so rapidly that there is little or no litter on the forest floor to feed a surface fire. The high water content of the plant material and the high humidity of the air makes ignition of rain forests difficult, if not impossible.

Newspaper reports of the "Sherwood Forest" and "Pink Rose" operations in Viet-Nam claimed that the intention was to try to create fire-storms, by simultaneously igniting many points with magnesium-thermite incendiary bombs, but this was denied by the Defense Department spokesman, J. W. Friedheim, who claimed that the aim had been to clear the foliage (*New York Times*, 24 July 1972).

---

[1] A study entitled "Forest fire as a military weapon" was carried out by the US Forest Service in 1966 and 1967, funded by the US Department of Defense Advanced Research Projects Agency (ARPA). The agency refused the request of a US Congressman to declassify this report, on the ground of "the probable negative diplomatic impact if the report were to be released for open publication", while at the same time asserting that the experiments on forest fires had proved negative (S. J. Lukasik, Director of ARPA. Letter to Hon. Les Aspin, US House of Representatives, 17 September 1973). A number of hypothetical studies of forest fires resulting from nuclear attacks have been published, for example Ayres (1965).

Appendix 1C

*Resolutions of the United Nations General Assembly
on napalm and other incendiary weapons and related topics*

Resolution no. and date of adoption	Subject and contents of resolution	Voting results
2674 (XXV) 9 December 1970	Considers that air bombardments of civil populations and the use of asphyxiating, poisonous or other gases and of all analogous liquids, materials and devices, as well as bacteriological (biological) weapons, constitute a flagrant violation of the Hague Convention of 1907, the Geneva Protocol of 1925 and the Geneva Conventions of 1949.	*In favour* 77 *Against* 2: Brazil,[a] Portugal *Abstentions* 36: Argentina, Australia, Austria, Belgium, Cambodia, Canada, Central African Republic, Colombia, Costa Rica, Denmark, Dominican Republic, El Salvador, Finland, France, Guatemala, Guyana, Haiti, Honduras, Iceland, Ireland, Israel, Italy, Lesotho, Luxembourg, Malawi, Netherlands, New Zealand, Norway, Paraguay, Spain, Sweden, Thailand, UK, USA, Uruguay, Venezuela *Absent:* Albania, Bolivia, Botswana, Ceylon, Equatorial Giunea, Fiji, Laos, Maldives, Malta, Mexico, South Africa, Trinidad and Tobago
2677 (XXV) 9 December 1970	Calls upon all parties to any armed conflict to observe the rules laid down in the Hague Conventions of 1899 and 1907, the Geneva Protocol of 1925, the Geneva Conventions of 1949 and other humanitarian rules applicable in armed conflicts, and invites those states which have not yet done so to adhere to those conventions; expresses the hope that the conference of government experts to be convened in 1971 by the International Committee of the Red Cross will consider further what development is required in existing humanitarian laws applicable to armed conflicts and that it will make specific recommendations in this respect.	*In favour* 111 *Against* 0 *Abstentions* 4
2852 (XXVI) 20 December 1971	Invites the International Committee of the Red Cross to continue the work that was begun with the assistance of government experts in 1971 and to devote special attention, among the questions to be taken up, to the need to ensure better application of existing rules relating to armed conflicts, particularly the Hague Conventions of 1899 and 1907, the Geneva Protocol of 1925 and the four Geneva Conventions of 1949; and to the need for a reaffirmation and development of relevant rules, as well as other measures to improve the protection of the civilian population during armed conflicts, including legal restraints and restrictions on certain methods of warfare and weapons that have proved particularly perilous to civilians, as well as arrangements for humanitarian relief.	*In favour* 110 *Against* 1 *Abstentions* 5

Resolution no. and date of adoption	Subject and contents of resolution	Voting results
2918 (XXVII) 14 November 1972	Requests the Secretary-General to prepare, as soon as possible, with the help of governmental qualified consultant experts, a report on napalm and other incendiary weapons and all aspects of their possible use.	*In favour* 98 *Against* 6: Brazil, Portugal, South Africa, Spain, United Kingdom, United States *Abstentions* 8: Belgium, France, Guatemala, Honduras, Italy, Luxembourg, Uruguay, Venezuela *Absent:* Bolivia, Colombia, Costa Rica, Democratic Republic of Yemen, Dominican Republic, El Salvador, Equatorial Guinea,[b] Gambia, Guyana,[b] Haiti, Lesotho,[b] Malawi, Maldives, Mali, Malta, Nicaragua, Niger,[b] Paraguay, Sri Lanka, Togo[b]
2932 A (XXVII) 29 November 1972	Condemns the continuation by Portuguese military forces of the indiscriminate bombing of civilians, the wholesale destruction of villages and property and the ruthless use of napalm and chemical substances in Angola, Guinea (Bissau) and Cape Verde and Mozambique.	*In favour* 99 *Against* 0 *Abstentions* 15: Australia, Belgium, Canada, France, Greece, Israel, Italy, Japan, Luxembourg, Netherlands, New Zealand, Portugal, South Africa, United Kingdom, United States *Absent:* Albania, Botswana, Dahomey, Equatorial Guinea, Gabon, Gambia, Guinea, Haiti, Honduras, Malawi, Morocco, Nepal, Nicaragua, Saudi Arabia, Sierra Leone, Somalia, Trinidad and Tobago,[b] Yemen
3076 (XXVIII) 6 December 1973	Deplores the use of napalm and other incendiary weapons in all conflicts; welcomes the report of the Secretary-General on napalm and other incendiary weapons and all aspects of their possible use; takes note of the views expressed in the report regarding the production, development and stockpiling of these weapons; requests the Secretary-General to circulate the report to the governments of member states for their comments and to report on these comments to the 28th General Assembly.	*In favour* 103 *Against* 0 *Abstentions* 18: Belgium, Bulgaria, Byelorussian SSR, Central African Republic, Czechoslovakia, France, German Democratic Republic, Greece, Hungary, Israel, Italy, Mongolia, Poland, Saudi Arabia, Ukrainian SSR, USSR, United Kingdom, United States *Absent or not participating in the vote:* Bahamas, Chile, Ecuador, Equatorial Guinea, Gambia, Guyana, Iceland, Kenya,[b] Lebanon, Malawi, Maldives, Mauritius, Nigeria, Swaziland

Invites the Diplomatic Conference on the Reaffirmation and Development of International Humanitarian Law Applicable in Armed Conflicts to consider the question of the use of napalm and other incendiary weapons, as well as other specific conventional weapons which may be deemed to cause unnecessary suffering or to have indiscriminate effects, and to seek agreement on rules prohibiting or restricting the use of such weapons.

85

Resolution no. and date of adoption	Subject and contents of resolution	Voting results
3255 A (XXIX) 9 December 1974	Notes with appreciation the expressed readiness of the International Committee of the Red Cross to convoke another Conference of Government experts and urges all Governments to compile without delay such supplementary data as may be required by them to focus upon specific proposals for prohibitions or restrictions	*In favour* 108 *Against* 0 *Abstentions* 13: **Bulgaria**, Byelorussian SSR, Czechoslovakia, France, German Democratic Republic, Hungary, Israel, Mongolia, Poland, Ukrainian SSR, USSR, United Kingdom, United States *Absent or not participating in the vote:* Bahamas, Bhutan, Chad, Equatorial Guinea, Gabon, Grenada, Guinea, [b] Guinea-Bissau, Jamaica, Lesotho, Maldives, Mali, Mauritius, [b] Saudi Arabia, South Africa, Swaziland, Togo.
3255 B (XXIX) 9 December 1974	Deeply disturbed at the continuing use of napalm and other incendiary weapons, condemns the use of napalm and other incendiary weapons in circumstances where it may affect human beings or may cause damage to the environment and/or natural resources; urges all States to refrain from production, stockpiling, proliferation and use of such weapons, pending conclusion of agreements on the prohibition of these weapons; invites all Governments, the International Committee of the Red Cross, the specialized agencies and the other international organizations concerned to transmit to the Secretary-General all information about the use of napalm and other incendiary weapons in armed conflicts; and requests the Secretary-General to prepare a report on this subject.	*In favour* 98 *Against* 0 *Abstentions* 27: Australia, Austria, Belgium, Bulgaria, Byelorussian SSR, Canada, Czechoslovakia, Denmark, France, German Democratic Republic, Germany (Federal Republic of), Greece[b] Hungary, Ireland, Israel, Italy, Japan, Luxembourg, Mongolia, Netherlands, Norway, Poland, Turkey, Ukrainian SSR, USSR, UK, USA. *Absent or not participating in the vote:* Bahrain, Chad, Gabon, Grenada, Guinea,[b] Guinea-Bissau, Jamaica, Lesotho, Maldives, Mali, Saudi Arabia, South Africa, Swaziland.

[a] Later indicated it had intended to abstain. Japan, which had voted in favour, indicated the same.
[b] Later indicated it had intended to vote in favour.

Chapter 2. Incendiary weapons today

I. *Introduction*

The development of incendiary technology has proceeded along two parallel lines. One of these is to maximize the heat and time of combustion of various incendiary agents in order to increase their potential for destructiveness and the other is to diversify and streamline the means of projecting them. In some cases diversification has taken the form of designing incendiary warheads which are compatible with other members of a "family" of munitions fired by the same weapon (for example, incendiary artillery shells). In other cases, weapons specifically designed for incendiary agents have been developed (for example, flamethrowers).

This chapter describes a series of modern incendiary weapon systems together with some current research and development trends. The principles of fire technology are summarized and some methods of protection against incendiary attack are described.

II. *Some elements of combustion technology*

Incendiary agents are substances which *oxidize* (that is, burn) with a powerful *exothermic* (heat-producing) reaction. Inflammable substances only burn in the presence of oxygen (usually provided from the surrounding air) or *oxidizing agents*. These latter react to oxidize other materials, and can be added to explosives and some incendiary agents in order to improve combustion. Examples of common oxidizing agents include chromates, nitrates, chlorates, permanganates and peroxides.

The *rate of combustion* is an important variable in the military context. Where combustion is slow, the gases produced dissipate unless confined, but when the combustion is rapid the great quantity of gas produced in a small space will generally cause an explosion. This is the basis of explosive and propellant technology. Incendiary agents differ from explosives in that combustion is sustained for a relatively long period of time (minutes instead of micro-seconds) during which the gradients of heat dissipation can be overcome, thus increasing the likelihood of igniting secondary fires in inflammable substances such as wood, plastics or asphalt. For this reason incendiary agents of the napalm type contain components designed to slow down the rate of burning.

Heat is transferred to the target by *radiation, convection* or *conduction*.

Damage from radiant heat is unlikely at more than a few metres from the source, since it is very rapidly dissipated unless the energy source emits radiant heat at a very high intensity, as in the case of nuclear or thermonuclear explosions, and/or for a long period.

Convection is the form of heat transfer which predominates in fires caused by most incendiary weapons. Incendiary bombs, for instance, are usually designed to penetrate the roofs of houses and ignite on the lower floors. The flames and hot gases produced rise through the upper floors and roof, setting fire to inflammable materials in their path.

Heat is conducted readily by many metals whereas many non-metallic substances, such as asbestos or plastics, are heat insulating. If a substance is both a poor conductor and inflammable, it may ignite at the point of contact with the heat source. Since conduction is a more effective means of transferring heat downwards than convection, some incendiary agents are designed to form metal slags as products of combustion. The red-hot embers of these slags can then cause damage to equipment they come into direct contact with by conduction downwards.

In addition to igniting inflammable materials, the heat generated by incendiary weapons may be sufficient to decompose many plastics, fuse glass, detemper light steels and melt some metals. Equipment or structures composed of a variety of materials may be deformed by the uneven forces of expansion, in some cases leading to fissures or structural collapse. The expansion of liquids or gases may rupture containers. (Physiological effects of heat are described in the next chapter.)

III. *Incendiary agents*

Metal incendiaries

Magnesium

Metal incendiary agents have the advantage of very high burning temperatures and ease of manufacturing and handling. The most common pure metal incendiary agent is magnesium. A German magnesium bomb was perfected in the spring of 1918 but not brought into use until 1939 (Fisher, 1946). Magnesium incendiary cluster bombs were used extensively during World War II and have continued in use as recently as the Viet-Nam War.

When raised to ignition temperature (623°C), magnesium burns with a very hot, bright flame to form a white smoke of magnesium oxide, releasing 6 000 kilocalories of heat per kilogram weight of magnesium.

Temperatures up to 1 980°C may be reached, which is sufficient to melt mild steels. This is advantageous in attacks against vehicles, rolling stock, railyards, factories and so on. Magnesium tends to scatter burning pieces and drops of molten metal which are effective in igniting combustible material. This scattering effect may be increased by the addition of an explosive charge.

Fire-fighting measures are complicated by the fact that, in contact with burning magnesium, water may produce an explosive mixture of hydrogen and other gases. Chemical fire extinguishers which contain carbon tetrachloride (pyrene) or carbon dioxide may generate a mixture of the toxic gases phosgene, chlorine, hydrochloric acid and carbon monoxide (US Departments of the Army, Navy and the Air Force, 1968, p. 80; Mendelson, 1971). Particles of magnesium burning in the skin may react with the moisture of the body with localized formation of hydrogen gas, resulting in further tissue necrosis (US Departments of the Army, Navy and the Air Force, *op. cit.*)

Aluminium

Aluminium is an important constituent of many incendiary agents. It can be used in its pure metal state; as an alloy with magnesium; as a constituent of thermite; in the form of the napthenate, palmitate, or laurate in napalm; in organometallic compounds such as triethyl aluminium, and in powder form it can be mixed with some napalm compositions. Burning aluminium produces more heat per kilogram (7 000 kcal/kg) than magnesium and as much as some carbon fuels but it is more difficult to ignite. It may be mixed with the oxidizing agent iron oxide to produce thermite although then it produces less heat.

Pyrotechnic incendiary agents

Pyrotechnic or combustible-oxidizing incendiary agents are compositions which incorporate an oxidizing agent to ensure efficient initial combustion independently of the air supply. In general they burn rapidly and generate high temperatures. The major application of these agents is as fire-starters. Once the fire has been initiated, however, a supply of air is necessary for continued combustion.

A pyrotechnic mixture used extensively in small arms incendiary projectiles is two parts by weight of magnesium and 17 parts by weight of barium peroxide. The magnesium powder is mixed with alcohol and compressed. Other mixtures include red lead and magnesium, and red lead and aluminium. A mixture of potassium nitrate, sulphur and antimony powder has sometimes been used as a primer to ignite incendiary compositions.

A composition known as "Scheelite" (after its inventor, Dr Scheele) was used to some extent during World War I. It consisted of one part hexamethylene-tetramine and two parts sodium peroxide. When ignited with sulphuric acid it reacted very rapidly in the open, generating considerable heat and flames. When confined it exploded. (Prentiss, 1937).

Thermite

The most common pyrotechnic incendiary agent is thermite, which is essentially a mixture of powdered ferric oxide and powdered or granular aluminium. When raised to the combustion temperature an intense reaction occurs whereby the oxygen in the ferric oxide is transferred to the aluminium, producing molten iron aluminium oxide and releasing 758 kilocalories per gram molecule.

This exothermic reaction may produce a temperature of about 2 400°C under favourable conditions. The white hot molten iron and slag may itself prolong and extend the heating and incendiary action.

Thermite was used for industrial purposes, such as welding railway lines, before World War I. It was used quite extensively as a military incendiary agent during World War I by most of the major combatants. Commercial thermite is simply a loose mixture but for military purposes a binder was necessary to prevent separation of the constituents. Sodium or potassium silicate or sulphur were usually used for this purpose. Where a concentrated incendiary effect was required, the silicate binder was more effective, since the molten products were able to penetrate metal and prolong the incendiary action. Where a scattering action was required, sulphur was used, as in the French "Daisite", since this composition burns with explosive violence and spatters small drops over a large area. Celluloid was also used as a binder, chiefly by Germany. Other substances including resins, paraffin and pitch, have also been tried as binders.

Other pyrotechnic mixtures been used as igniters for thermite. Where a scattering effect was desired a rapid igniter was used, such as the British "Ophorite", consisting of nine parts magnesium powder to 13 parts potassium perchlorate. This was used extensively by British and US forces during World War I in incendiary shells and also in certain types of gas shell (Prentiss, 1937).[1]

A number of modifications of thermite were tried during and after World War I. Copper, nickel, manganese and lead oxides were tried in place of iron oxide but had no greater effect. The Germans used a mixture of manganese oxide and magnesium in certain early incendiary bombs. Later in the war the British introduced "flaming thermite" composed of three parts powdered aluminium, six parts barium nitrate and eight parts ferrous oxide. This was compressed to half the original volume and used in the small "Baby Incendiary Bombs" (see appendix 1 A).

Thermate is the general name given to a number of mixtures of thermite and pyrotechnic additives, several of which were developed before and during World War II. A pyrotechnic agent containing barium nitrate was used in the M-8 illuminant flare. This was then combined with thermite and

[1] Ophorite was also the cause of several very serious accidents in manufacturing and loading plants during World War I (Prentiss, 1937).

90

called "Therm-8" and later "Thermate", TH-1. Later variations included TH-2, TH-3 and TH-4.

Thermite does not have the same ability as magnesium or oil incendiary agents to start secondary fires because its heat of combustion is comparatively low and because it burns so quickly (Greene, 1966). However, the high temperature produced by burning thermite is sufficient to melt iron or steel with which it comes in contact (Fisher, 1946), and it is very effective as an igniter for magnesium bombs. It is still used in handgrenades and bombs.

Oil-based incendiary agents

Commercial aviation or motor vehicle fuels are preferred for use in incendiary weapons because first, as hydrocarbons, they release large amounts of thermal energy on combustion and second, they are readily available.

High temperatures of from 800–1 200°C are produced by the burning hydrocarbon vapours. However, the temperature of the liquid fuel under the burning vapours may only reach its boiling point of 130°C. This is an important consideration for military use because heat in a fire caused by incendiaries is primarily transferred by convection, that is upwards and away from the target.

Even before World War II petroleum fuels had been used in flamethrowers, bombs, shells and mines. Sometimes lighter petroleum fractions were thickened with heavier oils or tar. These weapons were spectacular, but while they could be effective against personnel, they had only limited effect on equipment. Indeed, they were said by some writers to be equally dangerous to friend and foe alike because of their low viscosity:

When used in bombs the petroleum fuels were atomized excessively by the explosive force of the burster, resulting in a relatively ineffective instantaneous flash or fireball. Likewise, when used in flamethrowers the range was short due to excessive burning of the fuel before it reached the target and also due to the inability of the liquid rod to withstand the impact with air when projected at high velocities (Hollingsworth, 1951, p. 26).

Napalm

Napalm is now used as a general term for a class of thickened oil incendiary agents. During World War I a group at the American University in Washington DC had begun research on the problem of increasing the viscosity of petroleum incendiary agents. They experimented with some 40 compounds as potential thickeners, including sodium stearate; however, this research lapsed after 1919 (Greene, 1947). In the period between the two world wars there seems to have been little research interest in oil-based incendiaries in the USA. However, investigations continued in the UK, so that at the beginning of World War II the British appear to have been the only military power with an effective oil-based incendiary composition, in the form of petroleum thickened with rubber. Incendiary bombs filled with this mixture were effective fire-starters, and early in the war the Americans imported the British technology. They filled 10 000 M-47 bomb containers (originally intended for mustard gas or other vesicants) with a solution of 8 per cent crepe rubber in gasoline, which was found to give efficient gasoline gels (Hollingsworth, 1951). The US Chemical Warfare Service shipped these bombs to the Far East in 1941, but they were lost in transportation due to hostile action (Fieser, 1964). Following the success of the Japanese offensive, supplies of rubber to the Western powers became severely restricted, so that substitutes had to be devised (Fieser, 1952).

Although Germany, Italy, Japan and the Soviet Union produced some oil bombs and flamethrowers, the subsequent development of oil-based incendiary agents was largely undertaken by the USA and the UK, who cooperated closely on this question during World War II.[2] US research concentrated on the development of incendiary bombs while the British worked on flamethrowers; yet the petroleum thickener developed by the USA for use in bombs proved to be a major factor in the advance of flamethrowers. The work of the US Chemical Warfare Service was supplemented by that of a number of teams in other government institutions, industry and universities (Brophy, Miles & Cochrane, 1959). In the UK the work was carried out by sections of the Petroleum Warfare Department, in cooperation with experts from the oil industry and others (Banks, 1946).

The basic alternatives to rubber as petroleum thickeners were soap gels, elastomer thickeners (certain polymers), napalm thickeners, solid thickeners, and emulsions (Beerbower & Philippoff, 1968).

The soap gel was utilized in some 200 000 "fougasses" which were deployed in defensive positions in the United Kingdom. These consisted of drums filled with petrol and fuel oil, gelled with a calcium soap formed by the action of cresylic acid in coal tar on lime.

During World War II, essentially all suitable polymers were required for high priority production of other materials which precluded their use as incendiaries. The solid thickeners were not suitable, and the emulsions had a high degree of flashing (instantaneous flame rather than slow burning). In practice therefore, napalm thickeners were the only ones available to the Western powers during World War II.

The research which lead to the discovery of napalm was directed by the Harvard University professor, Louis F. Fieser, who successfully developed a petroleum gel fulfilling requirements established by the Chemical Warfare Service. Although napalm derives its name from aluminium napthenate and

[2] Towards the end of World War II, the Germans tried some thickeners, the most successful of which was said to be aluminium alcoholate. However, this was not as effective as the American napalm, and the range was little greater than American unthickened fuels. Neither did the Japanese develop thickeners, though a few flamethrowing vehicles were captured by US forces towards the end of the war (Brophy, Miles & Cochrane, 1959).

aluminium palmitate, two constituents of a gel which was initially regarded as satisfactorily filling the requirements, the final "production model" substituted lauric acid for palmitic acid, since the former was readily available from coconut oil, to which the United States had ready access.

A precipitation method appeared the most successful means of production, using two parts coconut oil acid, one part napthenic acid and one part oleic acid. The precipitate was a brownish-white, dry, non-sticky powder.

When an amount of napalm powder sufficient to produce a 12 % solution is poured into gasoline and given one stir, solvation occurs rapidly and the swollen solvated particles soon fill the container with material of apple sauce consistency, which is pourable. After aging for a few hours without attention, the gel reaches its final form, in which it is tough, strong, and sticky (Fieser, 1964, p. 32).

Fieser *et al.*, (1946)[3] described the relative contributions of the two components of the napalm gel as follows:

One is aluminium laurate or a saturated fatty acid soap containing at least 40–50 per cent of this substance or of a functionally related acid soap; this component is a relatively high-melting-point solid that, by itself, produces only thin and unstable gels. The second component is an aluminium soap or soap selected from the group including cyclo-paraffinic and unsaturated acids—that is, an aluminium napthenate oleate, oleate-linoleate, etc. By itself, the aluminium soap comprising the second component is either a resinous gum or a low-melting-point solid, and most soaps of this type yield hydrocarbon gels only by heat treatment or by special processing; the resulting gels are not very full-bodied. The combination of an aluminium soap of the laurate type with one or more soaps of the napthenate-oleate type gives a thickening agent of distinctive and superior properties not found in either component and when prepared by the precipitation process, the soap is a solid of sufficiently high softening point to withstand elevated drying and storing temperature.

Fieser applied for a US patent on 1 November 1943 (published as US Patent No. 2 606 107, 5 August 1952) for a wide range of variations of this basic principle of incendiary gels. These variations included the substitution of coconut oil with purely synthetic equivalents; the addition of lamp black to increase the burning time; compositions more able to stand the force of dispersal by an explosive charge, and so on.

Depending on the proportion of thickener added—usually between 6 and 12 per cent—more or less viscous napalm compositions could be produced for applications ranging from flamethrowers to handgrenades and airdropped bombs.

As an incendiary agent, napalm proved to have many advantages over unthickened fuels. Most significant was the increase in burning time from a few seconds (or even microseconds if the fuel was sufficiently atomized) to several minutes, depending on the composition and other factors. This greatly increased the probability of igniting other inflammable materials in the target area. The thickened oil spread much more effectively than metal

---

[3] This article is of historical importance in describing the chemical research leading to the development of napalm by the original researchers.

incendiaries, and in more effective quantities than was the case with unthickened fuels. The visco-elasticity of napalm greatly extended the range of the jet of flaming fuel projected by flamethrowers. Less of the fuel burned before reaching the target, which made these weapons safer to use as well as more effective.

With the increasing use of napalm during World War II a number of technical refinements were introduced. Some early types of US napalm standardized for use in the field were M1, M2 and M4. A number of alternatives to napalm gels were developed by other research groups. The most often used was based on an acrylic resin, polyisobutyl methacrylate (IM). Another synthetic acrylic resin which was used in some compositions was polymethyl methacrylate (Perspex).

IM-gels are more difficult to handle than napalm. Further, as with gels from raw rubber, a liquid component separates out when subjected to high pressure (for example, when forced through the nozzle of a flamethrower), or even from vibration during transportation, limiting their suitability for military use. Many of the IM-filled M-69 incendiary bombs manufactured in the United States and shipped to the UK during World War II were found to be unsatisfactory on arrival (Fieser, 1964).

Napalm was widely used in World War II in M-69 bombs and in flamethrowers. By the end of the war, production of the napalm thickener had reached 35 million kilograms per year; approximately 30 million M-69 bombs (Fieser, 1964, p. 52) and 3.5 million M-47 bombs (Brophy, Miles & Cochrane, 1969) had been produced.

Napalm itself is not self-igniting and this raises the problem for the weapon designer of igniting the napalm from a bomb or flamethrower. Several systems were attempted in flamethrowers. Napalm bombs were sometimes ignited with traditional systems using gunpowder and magnesium. A member of Fieser's research team, E. B. Hershberg, designed an alternative, based on a rod of high explosive (TNT or tetryl) surrounded by white phosphorus. The explosive burst the bomb, at the same time shattering the phosphorus and scattering the napalm. The phosphorus ignited spontaneously and this in turn ignited the napalm. This became the standard arrangement on large napalm tanks dropped by air. Because of this system of ignition, it is common for napalm dispensed by bombs to contain phosphorus, which not only tends to reignite napalm which has been extinguished, but may complicate the physiological effects of napalm on the human body (see chapters 3 and 4).

The success of napalm as an incendiary agent during World War II led to its adoption by many armed forces after the war, for use both in flamethrowers and in bombs. Though these types of napalm may have local brand names (a Swedish napalm thickener is called Alunat; a Soviet one, OP-2), they are essentially the same as Fieser's original aluminium soap composition.

Since World War II a number of other incendiary gels have been produced, using other fatty acids, which are said to gel more easily in petroleum and at lower temperatures, and have physical properties which increase the range of flamethrowers (Naerland, 1967). The incendiary effect is also increased by the inclusion of various additives in the composition. Some of these, such as asphalt, wood dust, lamp black or various resins, increase the burning time. One such composition referred to as US Standard Mixture contains asphalt, together with white phosphorus as an igniter and aluminium perchlorate and calcium perchlorate as oxidizing agents, enabling the flame to reach a temperature of 1 980°C. Another composition, called Supernapalm, contains a self-igniting light metal compound which removes the need for a separate ignition system, and is said to ignite equally well on snow or water (Naerland, 1967).

Other additives include small amounts of peroxides, which induce explosions, and powdered thermite, aluminium or magnesium which increase the downward conduction of heat through the mass of gel to the target underneath, before they themselves ignite, increasing the heat of the flame.

Napalm-B

Napalm-B is a more radical departure from World War II napalm technology since it uses a complex polymer, polystyrene, as a thickener in place of the aluminium salts of napthenic and lauric acids used originally. Chemically speaking, therefore, the term "napalm" is even more inappropriate. Technologically it may be regarded as a "second generation" product.

Napalm-B is a true viscous liquid, not a gel. It consists essentially of 50 per cent polystyrene thickener, 25 per cent benzene and 25 per cent gasoline. It was developed at the Eglin Air Force Base, in cooperation with the Dow Chemical Company's polystyrene section.

Benzene is a highly inflammable liquid which is an excellent solvent for waxes, resins, rubber and other organic materials, but its fumes are toxic. Polystyrene is a synthetic resin made from ethylene. (Brady, 1963).

Polystyrene is the basis of a great many household and industrial plastic products and US production amounted to some 30 million kilograms per month in 1965. When the use of polystyrene in napalm-B became known (*Chemical & Engineering News,* 14 March 1966) it was predicted that as much as 12 million kilograms per month might be used in the production of napalm-B. With this heavy demand the Dow Chemical Co. increased the price of polystyrene.[4]

[4] The Chairman of the Dow Chemical Co. reported in November 1967 that the company's profits were being affected by various forms of protest against its napalm production including boycotts of Dow consumer products, a campaign to convince Dow shareholders to sell their stock, and increased executive time for answering inquiries about napalm. Dow announced that it would continue to make napalm which accounted for 0.5 percent of its $1.4 billion annual sales (*Chemical and Engineering News,* 27 November 1967). However, the company lost the contract in 1969 to the American Electric Company in Los Angeles (*New York Times,* 16 November 1969).

Tests carried out by the US Air Force in 1965 showed that napalm-B (then known as Alecto) had a number of advantages over ordinary napalm and an experimental composition made by the Western Corporation, Westcogel. Napalm-B achieved a somewhat higher maximum temperature (about 850°C compared with 760°C), but burned for between two and three times as long. As a result it caused much greater damage to the target. For example, napalm-B charred pine wood to a depth of approximately 3 mm where conventional napalms deposited a residue which prevented much damage to the underlying wood. Because of the longer burning time, napalm-B was more effective in igniting fuels and lubricating oils in mechanical equipment, melting alloy components, detempering steels, fusing glass and burning rubber. Tests on dummy soldiers showed only slight burning of clothes with conventional napalms but severe burning with napalm-B.

A further difference that was observed was in the area covered by a napalm-B bomb. While the width of the area covered, about 30 metres, was comparable to conventional napalms, the length extended to some 200 metres, compared with 70–100 metres.

Napalm-B also proved to be more stable in storage, so that bombs could be filled in the factory rather than in the field. (Conventional napalm bombs required more preparation in the field than any other air force munition.) It also proved feasible to fill the bomb in the factory with solid pieces of polystyrene which dissolved when the solvent was added in the field, thereby avoiding the need for special mixing equipment (Anderson, 1969).

These findings led the US Air Force to turn to napalm-B as its main incendiary agent (US Tactical Air Command, 1966). Patents on similar compositions were taken out in other countries within a short time (Buck, 1967).

A great many other polymers, such as polyisobutylene, polybutadiene, substituted polybutadiene, polyisoprene, and copolymers of hydrocarbon dienes, may be used as alternative thickeners, while toluene, methyl-ethyl-ketone, and so on may be used as solvents. Characteristic of these thickeners is that they do not separate out in storage or on impact, as often occurred with the original napalm compositions. The jelly-like mass of the incendiary mixture is more adhesive, even sticking to vertical surfaces without dropping down. It is almost impossible to remove, and burns for up to ten times as long as traditional napalm (Buck, 1967).

A great variety of substances can be added to napalm-B-type composi-tions to create particular effects, a common one being dense clouds of black smoke. This effect can be enhanced by the addition of benzene or napth-alene or similar hydrocarbons. The dense smoke is said to increase the psychological effect of the napalm attack and hinders efforts to fight the flames.[5] Conversely, the addition of carbon disulphide greatly reduces the smoke, which can be a military advantage in certain circumstances.

[5] This black smoke may also be a significant casualty-producing agent; see chapters 3 and 4.

Table 2.1. Possible napalm constituents

Hydrocarbon fuels	Motor spirit. Aviation fuel. Paraffin/kerosene. Benzene. Toluene. Xylene. Light petroleum. White spirit. Unrefined crude oil. Refinery residues.
Thickeners	Rubber. Rubber processing residues. Metallic soaps of palmitic, oleic, napthenic and lauric acids. Polymers such as polystyrene and polyisobutylene. Emulsions. Silica gel.
Additives	White phosphorus. Red phosphorus. Magnesium (powder). Aluminium (powder). Other slag formers such as calcium silicate, calcium silicide, ferro-silicon, lithium silicide, diatomaceous earth, and fine brick dust. Viscous or solid hydrocarbons such as napthalene or members of the paraffin group. Asphalt. Wood dust. Phenolo-formaldehyde resins. Benzene sulphohydrazide. Carbon disulphide.

Other substances may be added which produce water-resistant and floatable foams of napalm. Examples of such substances include phenolformaldehyde resins, which may be used in amounts up to 10 per cent by weight and which are capable of forming adhesive crusts, particularly with red hot cinders; and benzene sulphohydrazide, which converts the synthetic resins to foams. In this case the proportion of polymer thickener is reduced to only 1 to 2 per cent by weight (Buck, 1967).

These second generation napalm compositions are also more effective in absorbing slag-forming additives and metals. The addition of powdered inorganic substances such as red phosphorus, finely divided silicon compounds (such as calcium silicide, ferrosilicon or lithium silicide, diatomaceous earth or brick dust) or pulverized light metals (such as aluminium or magnesium) increases the temperature of the mass and results in the production of red hot cinders which prolong the effects and are difficult to extinguish.

A summary of napalm fuels, thickeners and additives appears in table 2.1.

Oil-and-metal incendiaries

The somewhat different properties of oil incendiaries and metal incendiaries have led to various attempts to combine the two. The oil incendiary is used to give a spreading effect; and powdered metal incendiary agents are added to increase the downward conduction of heat from the mass, increase the burning temperature and prolong the effect by producing hot slags of solid oxides.

In an effort to develop an oil-based incendiary agent which could withstand the effects of a high explosive charge, the US Chemical Warfare Service investigated a mixture known as "goop" in 1943. Goop was produced as part of the industrial manufacture of magnesium. The magnesium was so finely divided that it was pyrophoric (self-igniting) and was therefore immediately wetted down in a petroleum fraction of high boiling point to permit processing in the next manufacturing operation. The mixture of magnesium powder and petroleum had a pasty consistency. After experimenting with this mixture in M-47 bombs it was decided to use goop as the filling for 500-lb (223 kg) bombs subsequently designated M-76 (Fieser, 1964).

Pyrogels

Goop was the forerunner of a class of oil-and-metal incendiary agents which became known as *pyrogels*.

Like napalm the pyrogels consist essentially of thickened gasoline. In this case the thickener is usually isobutyl metacrylate and may include natural rubber. A metal incendiary is added to increase the temperature of combustion which may reach as high as 1 600°C, though the pyrogels tend to burn up quicker than napalm. The same type of disseminated incendiary effect is obtained as with napalm-type oil incendiary bombs but asphalt is added as a binder to overcome the shearing strains resulting from high altitude bombings (Hollingsworth, 1951).

Pyrogels used by US forces include:

1. *PTI*, which is a complex mixture based on a paste of magnesium and an oxidizer, bound with petroleum distillate and asphalt. Isobutyl methacrylate is used as a thickener.

2. *PT2*, which contains 5 per cent isobutyl metacrylate as a thickener, together with barium nitrate and a small quantity of asphalt.

3. *PTV*, which is described as an improved oil and metal incendiary mixture composed of 5 per cent polybutadiene, 6 per cent sodium nitrate, and 28 per cent magnesium and a trace of p-aminophenol in 60 per cent gasoline (US Departments of the Army and the Air Force, 1963).

Pyrophoric incendiary agents

All the incendiary agents described so far require an ignition device. Pyrophoric agents are a class capable of igniting spontaneously in air. They are often used as igniters of other incendiary agents and to some extent as antipersonnel weapons or as weapons for use against targets containing highly inflammable substances.

There are three main types of pyrophoric agent: white phosphorus and other inorganic non-metals; finely divided metals; and certain organometallic compounds.

White phosphorus (WP)

The most important pyrophoric incendiary agent is white phosphorus. Chevalier in France noted the incendiary possibilities of white phosphorus in 1789, but it was only used sporadically in warfare until World War I.

During that war it was used extensively in small arms incendiary bullets and in hand and rifle grenades by all the principle belligerents; the French and the Germans used larger calibre phosphorus shells and the British and Americans trench-mortar bombs. Because of the great amount of white smoke produced by white phosphorus, it is used extensively not only as an incendiary but also as a screening and marking agent, and as a combined smoke and antipersonnel agent. It is used in hand grenades, aircraft rockets, bombs, artillery shells and mines.

White phosphorus ignites spontaneously in air, forming a dense white smoke of phosphorus pentoxide, which is subsequently converted by the moisture in the air to acids of phosphorus. These acids are thus present in the smoke as small droplets.

The oxides produced by burning phosphorus provide some protection against fire and for this reason, together with the relatively low temperature of combustion, white phosphorus is not an effective incendiary agent for use against wooden structures and other materials which are difficult to ignite. It has proved to be an effective igniter of oil-based incendiary agents and it is also an offensive agent for use against personnel and readily combustible materials, such as dry grain fields.

The effects of white phosphorus as an antipersonnel agent were demonstrated during World War I.

When scattered from overhead bursts of grenades and trench-mortar bombs, the phosphorus rained down in flaming particles, which stuck to clothing and could not be brushed off or quenched. The larger particles quickly burned through clothing and produced painful burns that were slow and difficult to heal. These properties soon became known to troops and phosphorus was justly dreaded and always caused a demoralizing effect beyond the actual casualties produced (Prentiss, 1937, pp. 251–52).

White phosphorus is insoluble in water but soluble in carbon disulphide. White phosphorus has therefore sometimes been dissolved in carbon disulphide for use in incendiary bombs and shells.

White phosphorus is never found free in nature. An important source for its manufacture is apatite, large deposits of which are found in the USSR, the USA and Morocco. In one manufacturing process the tri-calcium phosphate contained in apatite is heated in the presence of carbon and silica in an electric or fuel-fired blast furnace. Elementary phosphorus is liberated as a vapour and collected under water. If desired the phosphorus vapour and the carbon monoxide produced in the reaction can be directly oxidized in the presence of moisture to form phosphoric acid for making superphosphate fertilizers, which are of increasing importance in world agriculture. Phosphates are also used in detergents and for other purposes. As a result, world production of elementary phosphorus and phosphoric acid is high. In the United States alone some half a million tons a year are produced, of which, in 1965, some 4 per cent (23 600 tons) was for pyrotechnics and munitions (*Chemical & Engineering News*, 14 March 1966).

Elementary white phosphorus contains polymerized P_4 molecules $[(P_4)_x]$. Unpolymerized P_4 exists only in vapourized form and consists of four atoms arranged in a tetrahedron. The weak bonding angle of 60° helps to explain the reactivity of the molecule. If white phosphorus is exposed to sunlight or heated up to 250°C in its own vapour it polymerizes to form larger molecules, with increasing specific gravity, giving yellow, red, violet and black forms of phosphorus. As the molecules grow larger, the toxicity and reactivity decrease, and the red form, for example, does not ignite spontaneously in dry air at room temperature. The solubility also decreases, the difference being sufficiently great to enable a separation of red from white phosphorus by dissolving the white phosphorus in carbon disulphide. As it does not ignite spontaneously and is not toxic, red phosphorus is used in safety matches. Red phosphorus is reconverted to white phosphorus by heating, in the absence of oxygen, to a high temperature. Highly toxic fumes are emitted in the process (Weast, 1968).

For many military purposes so-called "plastic white phosphorus" (PWP) is used. The properties are essentially the same as white phosphorus. Granules of white phosphorus are bound together in a rubbery solution which prevents them breaking up to the same extent when dispersed by an exploding munition. PWP is prepared from a slurry of white phosphorus granules in cold water with a viscous solution of synthetic rubber.

Zirconium

While almost any metal in the finely divided state exhibits pyrophoric properties, a few metals when abraded emit a shower of sparks of sufficient temperature to ignite hydrocarbon vapours. Cerium is the best known metal of this kind for commercial purposes, such as gas lighter flints. For military purposes zirconium is the most used. It has found applications in high explosive and armour-piercing incendiary ammunition, the lining of shaped-charge rounds, and in incendiary cluster bombs.

Though the element was discovered in 1789 it was not prepared in the pure state until 1914. It may be prepared commercially by the reaction of zirconium chloride with magnesium (the Kroll process) and other methods. The principle ore is zircon, deposits of which are found in the United States, Australia and Brazil. A number of special properties, such as exceptional resistance to corrosion and a low absorption cross section, have led to the use of zirconium or alloys containing zirconium, in many specialized applications in the chemical, nuclear and manufacturing industries.

For use in munitions zirconium may be alloyed with other metals such as titanium and lead in approximately equal proportions. Fine particles of the metals may be mixed and bound in a synthetic rubber composition. To give added durability to this incendiary core it may be surrounded by a similarly bound composition of iron and nickel carbonate powder. (Balke & Graff, 1957).

A search for more readily available, less expensive and equally effective alternatives to zirconium was carried out at the University of Denver in the early 1950s (Frankford Arsenal, 1954), but zirconium is still in use. The most promising alternative was titanium, which is used in the construction of high-performance aircraft.

Depleted uranium

In the natural state uranium is a mixture of isotopes from which two, U_{235} and U_{238}, are extracted for use in nuclear reactors and weapons. What remains after the extraction is known as *depleted uranium* which now exists in large quantities and for which few uses have so far been found. One property of uranium is its high density—it is heavier than lead—and this has led to the investigation of its military applications.

Pellets, slugs or flechettes made of uranium have very good powers of penetration. However, uranium is softer than steel so that in the process of penetrating an armoured steel plate it is partially pulverized. Since in this form uranium is pyrophoric (self-igniting), such projectiles have an incendiary as well as a penetrating effect. According to one account of flechettes made of depleted uranium:

... darts penetrate conventional steel plate better than tungsten tipped weapons. The darts also burn as they go through steel plate and spew flames inside the tank (Aviation Studies, 1972).

In the process of burning, toxic compounds are formed (see chapter 4) which may produce delayed effects on personnel exposed to the smoke.

Triethylaluminium (TEA)

A number of organometallic compounds are spontaneously inflammable in air. Others, like organosodium and organopotassium compounds, are not only spontaneously inflammable in air but react violently with water and carbon dioxide (Roberts & Caserio, 1965).

One member of this class of compounds, known to be used as an incendiary agent, is *triethylaluminium* (Al $(C_2H_5)_3$). Similar agents, such as trimethylaluminium or trimethylmagnesium, might also have possible military applications as incendiaries. Diethyl zinc has been employed as an igniter (Fieser, 1964).

Triethylaluminium is a colourless liquid which burns with a bright flame reaching temperatures of up to 2 300°C, which are comparable to those attained by the metal incendiaries. However, it burns very rapidly and the effects on material are limited.

For weapons use it is thickened with polyisobutylene, a very long chain polymer, certain fractions of which are very tacky and are used as adhesives for pressure-sealing tapes (Roberts & Caserio, 1965). Polyisobutylene-thickened TEA is comparable to napalm in that it has two components: a thickener and an inflammable agent. The term "thickened pyrophoric agent" (TPA) is sometimes used for agents of this kind.

Production of TPA is much more complex than that of napalm, limiting it to those nations with an advanced petrochemical industry. Because of the reactivity with air, production is usually carried out in an inert atmosphere of nitrogen or helium. Polymerization of isobutylene is also a complex process, requiring catalysts such as aluminium, titanium or molybdenum. Triethylaluminium is itself used as such a catalyst in the Ziegler polymerization process.[6]

TEA is currently being used in small incendiary rockets which can be fired from the shoulder by a lightweight launcher, designed to replace conventional flamethrowers. It is the incendiary agent in several prototype large calibre incendiary projectiles for use by armoured vehicles.

Experiments have shown that if TEA is thickened with only 1 per cent polyisobutylene (instead of the usual 6 per cent) it is possible to produce a chemical fireball which radiates sufficient thermal energy to destroy or damage military targets. It is reported that such a weapon could cause third degree burns on occupants of bunkers within a few seconds, whether or not the agent hit individuals. Previously only nuclear weapons were able to produce damaging levels of thermal radiation. (US Army Munitions Command, 1972.)

The concept of the "controlled chemical fireball" is said to have significantly advanced the potential effectiveness of incendiary weapons. Theoretical studies have indicated that a great many applications may be possible, since, by changing the blend of the chemical constitutents so as to achieve predetermined rates of combustion, the incendiary agent may be adapted to various operational requirements.

In order to permit safe handling and storage, TEA may be made non-pyrophoric by the addition of soluable diluents (for example, n-hexane). "The diluent is expected to flash off when the flame weapon is employed rendering the basic TEA payload pyrophoric again. An effective delayed, combined flameblast effect should result from the flaming TEA and the deflagrating n-hexane vapor cloud" (US Army Munitions Command, 1973, p. I-D-23).

Inorganic substances which ignite in water

Sodium is a very reactive substance which is never found free in nature. It is not generally used as an incendiary agent as such but, because of its tendency not only to float on water but also to ignite spontaneously in contact with it, it may be added to napalm for use against river targets

---

[6] K. Ziegler and G. Natta received the Nobel prize for their work on polymerization in 1963.

or enemy positions in rice paddy fields or in snow. Sodium is obtained commercially by electrolysis of dry fused sodium chloride.

Potassium also has the property of igniting spontaneously in water. The pure metal is more difficult to obtain than is sodium. Barium, calcium and lithium also ignite in the presence of water, though not as vigorously as sodium. Lithium is the lightest of all metals and has the highest specific heat of any solid. It can burn with a temperature of up to 1 350°C. Lithium was used for the case of a World War II Japanese 70 kg phosphorus incendiary bomb (Konupka, 1960).

New incendiary agents

A great many other substances have been investigated in a search for new incendiary agents. Most interest at the present time seems to be focussed on agents which ignite spontaneously, thereby avoiding the need for a fuse. Agents of this kind are particularly suitable for use in small rockets, artillery projectiles and aircraft bomblets which can be distributed over a large area.

In addition to pyrophoric organometallic compounds of the TEA type, a number of boron compounds are pyrophoric, including aluminium borohydride, pentaborane and the boron alkyls, such as triethylboron. An alternative means of ensuring spontaneous ignition is to utilize a hypergolic oxidizing agent, that is, an agent which generates so much heat while oxidizing a fuel that the fuel ignites. Agents which are hypergolic with petrol are the interhalogens, chlorine trifluoride, bromine trifluoride, and bromine pentafluoride.

Many of these substances have been investigated in the context of rocket propulsion technology, since, chemically, the combustion of rocket fuels is related to the combustion of incendiary agents (Hotzmann, 1969). Though by-products of rocket research may be theoretically of interest as potential incendiary agents, it remains to be seen whether they are feasible economically.

IV. *Incendiary weapons*

Essentially, incendiary weapons are simply containers for an incendiary agent, together with a means of dispersal (for example, an explosive charge or a compressed air spray) and an igniter. However since incendiary weapons are in practice adapted to a wide range of military uses it is convenient to discuss them under different categories.

Improvised incendiary weapons

As petroleum fuels are readily available in most countries it is relatively easy to make a variety of improvised incendiary weapons. Their use is restricted, however, by their limited range. A simple incendiary grenade, the "Molotov cocktail", is made by filling a bottle with petrol and fitting it with a simple fuse. The fuse is lit by hand and when the bottle breaks on the target the fuel is released, burning with considerable force. Such a weapon has little effect in the open, but in a confined space—for instance, in the cockpit of a tank—it can severely burn the crew and possibly cause material damage by igniting combustible substances or even the fuel tank. The flame and smoke may obscure the vision of the crew temporarily, during which time the tank may stop or drive off course, and make a better target for attack with other weapons.

White phosphorus dissolved in carbon disulphide may be used as a spontaneously igniting incendiary agent; this avoids the problem of ignition, but grenades of this kind are difficult to fill and handle safely. Another method of ignition, used in some of the later Soviet grenades of this type during World War II, was to mix powdered potassium permanganate into petrol or diesel oil and then to insert a glass tube containing sulphuric acid into the bottle before use. When the grenade was thrown, the tube and bottle broke, and the sulphuric acid reacted with the permanganate generating sufficient heat to ignite the petrol (Konupka, 1960).

Incendiary mines may be constructed in the field by filling oil drums with a napalm mixture and placing them in a suitable position in the path of advancing troops. They may be useful as warning or illuminating devices in the event of an unexpected attack on an isolated position, particularly at night. Usually such devices are fitted with a high explosive detonator and an igniter of white phosphorus or thermite filings attached to a remote triggering system. A chain of such mines may be connected in series, forming a temporary barrier of fire when they are detonated.

US forces in Korea devised means of increasing the effects of these mines against personnel by tightly winding barbed wire around the outside of the oil drums, and suspending them in trees or bushes some two metres above the ground. When the drum burst the barbed wire would break into fragments (US Department of the Army, 1960).

Incendiary weapons are also suited to certain kinds of sabotage activity. Pocket incendiaries may, for example, be surreptitiously placed in an inflammable target, such as wooden barracks, clothing stores or fuel tanks. Usually such a weapon is designed to ignite after some delay and burn slowly, igniting the surrounding material after the saboteur has got away.

An example of such a weapon is described by Fieser (1964), the inventor of napalm. Following a request during World War II for a light fire-starting device his team developed the "Harvard Candle", consisting of a cylinder of celluloid filled with napalm. It was ignited by a red phosphorus composition in a metal pull cap which served as a scratching disc.[7]

Unexploded white phosphorus bombs or shells (as well as high explosive

---

[7] The same author also describes the use of napalm to sabotage motor vehicles simply by blocking the fuel system. A small quantity of thickener is slipped into the fuel tank, where it gels, sooner or later blocking the fuel pipes or carburettor jets.

munitions) may be picked up by an astute enemy, defused, rewired and used as booby traps. Sixteen of the white phosphorus casualties described by Curreri, Asch & Pruitt (1970) were due to such booby traps (see chapters 3 and 4).[8]

Incendiary grenades and mines

Though improvised incendiary weapons may be used in some circumstances it is more common for conventional armies to rely on standardized, factory-made munitions. Factory-made incendiary grenades usually contain white phosphorus or thermite. Though the ability of white phosphorus to start fires is limited, a US military manual points out that "pieces of WP will burn for about 60 seconds, igniting any flammable substance contacted. Since WP burns the flesh, it is effective against personnel. The effective casualty radius is 15 meters (49.2 feet)." (US Departments of the Army and the Navy, 1971, p. 2–31).

Thermite grenades are more effective in starting fires and can burn through steel plate, such as hatches over fortified positions. They are effective against buildings or equipment, and the burning particles and molten drops may cause casualties. An example of a modern grenade of this kind is the US AN-M14, which contains 700 grams of thermite and can burn for 30–45 seconds at a temperature of up to about 2 200°C. (*Ibid.*, p. 2–29). The unit cost (1972) was about $3.90.

Other modern incendiary grenades include the West German DM-19, weighing 320 grams with a red phosphorus and aluminium incendiary charge weighing 365 grams, reaching 1 200°C; the French 47-mm FLDE hand and rifle grenade; and the Dutch incendiary hand grenade No 12 with a filling of 380 grams incendiary mixture. The Spanish POI, II and III grenades may be filled to order with an incendiary composition. The Federal German army uses several hand-held incendiary grenade launchers, the DM-24, DM-24A1 and the HaFla (see p. 107). They have a range of about 70 metres.

Incendiary grenades may be thrown by hand or launched by hand-fired or automatic launchers. Some infantry grenade launchers are separate weapons, such as the US M-79 40 mm grenade launcher, but it is more common to fit an attachment to an assault rifle. Almost all modern assault rifles are designed to accept a grenade launcher. Grenades may also be launched by rapid-firing automatic launchers mounted on platforms such as helicopters; examples are the US M-75 and XM-129 40 mm grenade launchers.

Factory-made incendiary mines are less common, though the British did manufacture thermite, petroleum and white phosphorus mines during World

---

[8] Enthoven & Smith (1971) report that in 1966 booby traps made from some 27 000 tons of unexploded munitions killed some 1 000 US troops in Viet-Nam; the unobserved air and artillery strikes which provided the unexploded munitions were estimated to have killed less than 100 enemy soldiers.

War I. Most incendiary mines since that time have been of the improvised type, though construction may be simplified by the use of standardized explosive and igniting devices.

An experimental factory-made incendiary mine has been produced more recently in the United States, the primary purpose of which is to replace the improvised devices previously used. It has the advantage of being shipped ready for use, and the filling does not deteriorate with time, as does the fuel of improvised mines. The XM-54 mine contains plasticized white phosphorus and has a projection device, causing it to "pop up" some three metres when activated. It may be triggered by foot pressure or by a trip wire. The mine explodes in the air, discharging white phosphorus and metal fragments over a radius of 25 metres. It weighs nearly 15 kg (US Department of the Army, 1969). A design for a directional flame mine has also been proposed.

Flamethrowers

A flamethrower is a device for projecting a stream of burning incendiary liquid. The liquid is forced by the pressure of compressed gas through a nozzle where it is ignited. The most common systems use air or nitrogen under a pressure of about 135–200 atmospheres and a nozzle of some 8–13 mm or larger, depending on the size of the flamethrower. An operating pressure of 13–30 atmospheres is obtained by means of a reduction valve. Most flamethrowers utilize a separate cylinder of compressed gas, but some types use a pump, or generate gas *in situ* by burning cordite. The rate of fuel discharge may vary from 2–20 litres per second.

A variety of ignition systems has been used in flamethrowers. Some use a jet of hydrogen or petroleum ignited by an electric spark. Others use pyrotechnic and mechanical ignition systems.

Early flamethrowers used unthickened fuel. The development of thickened fuel of the napalm type during World War II doubled the range of flamethrowers. Napalm is very suitable for flamethrower applications because when it is forced at pressure through a nozzle the jelly momentarily becomes as liquid as lubricating oil. Conversely, the napalm gel regains its viscosity when the shearing forces are removed. If it did not, the stream of burning fuel would be shattered by its impact with the air.

Even with thickened fuels the range of portable flamethrowers is still very short and their usefulness is restricted by the need to get close to the target. As a result, since World War II only a few flamethrowers have been developed, most of them based on World War II technology. The Swiss multishot SIFRAG S 55 is an example of this kind. It was introduced about 1957, weighs about 20 kg, and has a fuel capacity of 18 litres. It incorporates a new ignition system, with 10 pyrotechnic cartridges in a magazine from which they can be automatically fired. It has an improved range of up to 80 metres with thickened fuel.

Conventional flamethrowers are cumbersome and the person carrying one makes a conspicuous target for small arms fire. Therefore a number of attempts have been made to produce smaller systems, using one-shot, disposable fuel containers. This method was introduced by Germany at the end of World War II in the FlaW-46. More recently the West German Mauser and IWK (Industriewerke Karlsruhe) companies have each produced small one-shot flamethrowers with a fuel capacity of about 1.8 litres and a range of 40 metres. The French Mle LFP-58 weighs 7.5 kg (6 kg in a light alloy version) and has a capacity of 3 litres of fuel. It can fire one or two shots to a range of about 45 metres. The US M-8 one-shot flamethrower weighs 12 kg and can fire about 8 litres of fuel in one burst of 4–5 seconds. It has a range of 55–65 metres (US Department of the Army, 1960).

A different approach is taken in the West German *Handflammpatrone*, HaFla, developed by Firma Buck. This consists of a small hand-held tube launcher firing an incendiary grenade. The grenade is derived from the *Blend-Brand-Handgranate* (BBH), that is, an incendiary grenade containing a mixture of red phosphorus and a metallic powder such as aluminium, which when ignited produces a ball of fire and smoke which obscures vision and causes incendiary effects.

This system has the disadvantage compared with traditional flamethrowers that it depends on accurate initial shooting to be effective; unlike the jet from a conventional flamethrower the flame cannot be directed after launching.

Another approach to the construction of portable flamethrowers is the US M-202 A1. This weapon also illustrates a trend towards "compatible" weapons systems, where a single delivery system can launch a variety of warheads. The launcher of the M-202 A1, which can also be used for launching anti-tank rocket-assisted projectiles, fires up to four small rockets containing 0.6 litres of TPA (polyisobutylene-thickened triethylaluminium). Fully loaded it weighs a little over 12 kg and the unit cost (1974) is about $855. The range exceeds that of traditional flamethrowers by several hundred metres. The agent ignites on impact rather than at the muzzle of the launcher, as in earlier types, and can give bursts over a radius of 10–20 metres, burning for eight to nine seconds. The small quantity of incendiary agent and the great rapidity with which TPA burns limits the effectiveness of this system. Few armies today put much reliance on portable flamethrowers, though they may be retained for possible use in special circumstances.

Mechanized flamethrowers, too, are characterized by the limited range and duration of fire, and their range of applications is therefore restricted. It appears that only a few new models of mechanized flamethrowers have been developed since World War II.

Currently the USA has two mechanized flamethrowing vehicles. The lighter one, the M-132, is a conversion of the M-113 armoured personnel carrier. The flame gun has a range of up to 210 metres and a maximum duration of 32 seconds.

The M67A1/A2 flamethrower tank is derived from the M-48 medium tank. The main armament is replaced by a dummy 90-mm gun barrel housing a M7A1-6 flame gun, the barrel of which is actually somewhat shorter but with a larger diameter than that of the 90-mm gun. The flame gun barrel has holes in the side for additional ventilation, and holes and drop shields at the bottom for drainage. The fuel capacity is about 1 500 litres and the range up to some 250 metres, with a maximum duration for a single shot of 61 seconds. US Marine Corps battalions have nine of these flamethrowing tanks to 70 regular tanks. There is some possibility that the XM-551 General Sheridan armoured airborne assault vehicle, which has a 152-mm gun, will be produced in a flamethrower version. However, it seems more likely that the use of "encapsulated flame rounds", which are under development, will be preferred, since these would be compatible with the 152-mm weapon system, already designed to fire either the Shillelagh missile or conventional rounds.

The US Navy has mounted flame guns on patrol boats for use against targets along the banks of rivers. The flame guns are the same as those in the M-67 flamethrower tank, two entire flame tank cupolas being built into the foredeck of the boat. The hold of the boat can accomodate up to 27 100-gallon napalm fuel tanks (compared with only four in the M-67 tank itself), giving a fuel capacity of some 11 500 litres. The range of fire of this Mk 1 "Zippo" flamethrowing boat is about 200 metres (*National Defense,* November–December, 1974).

Small calibre incendiary projectiles

Small calibre incendiary projectiles, that is those weighing under 400 grams, were forbidden for use against personnel by the St Petersburg Declaration of 1868. Nevertheless, small calibre projectiles containing incendiary substances have been very widely used for a variety of tactical purposes. A small calibre, inert projectile has only limited effects on a target such as a vehicle or an aircraft when used on its own, but combined with an incendiary and/or explosive agent it may be very effective. Projectiles of this combined type may therefore give the lightly-armed infantryman the ability to attack mechanized targets. Machine guns firing combined action projectiles are standard equipment on most combat aircraft, and are fitted as auxiliary weapons on armoured vehicles. They may also be mounted as primary weapons on light cross-country vehicles, patrol boats or aircraft.

In general, small incendiary projectiles are not large enough to include a sophisticated time or proximity fuse. In some early types the incendiary agent, usually white phosphorus, was ignited as it was propelled from the cartridge. The centrifugal force of a heavy lead stopper forced the white phosphorus through slits in the case, where it ignited in the air, leaving a trail of smoke. It had an incendiary effect on inflammable targets in its path up to about 1 500 metres. Bullets of this kind were used by German and Austrian forces during World War I.

Most modern types of projectile contain an incendiary composition such as red phosphorus, aluminium or magnesium powder, an oxidizing agent and an agent which is ignited by the compression of impact. The pressure of gases ruptures the shell, releasing smoke and flames. The smoke serves to mark the point of impact and the flames ignite combustible substances. Shells of this kind may be very small indeed, such as the Soviet PZ 7.62 mm. They may be effective in destroying easily penetrable and ignitable targets such as a hot motor or aircraft engine. This kind of ammunition was complemented during World War II by penetrating-incendiary and high-explosive-incendiary shells, for use against lightly armoured vehicles. For example, the Soviet B32 bullet had a steel case and a hard steel core. The core was able to penetrate up to 10 mm of armour at 200 metres, and the incendiary agent could set fire to fuel and ammunition inside the target vehicle. A tracer version, the BZT 7.62-mm, emitted a trail of coloured smoke, but had less ability to penetrate armour (7 mm at 200 metres) (Konupka, 1960).

Tracer bullets can be as small as the US 5.56-mm calibre, but incendiary bullets are more usual in the larger 12.7-mm–40-mm calibres. Shells in these calibres are found in a great range of types, combining incendiary (I), high explosive (HE), armour-piercing (AP), and tracer (T) effects, together with various permutations of these such as HEI, APT and API bullets.

In order to increase the effects on the target and the range, there is a trend towards increasing the calibre of the weapons: 20-mm weapons are being replaced by 25-mm and 30-mm; 30-mm weapons by 35-mm or 40-mm, and so on. A further development is to increase the rate of fire in order to increase the probability of hitting the target; modern, multibarrelled cannons may fire several thousand shells per minute.

Another area of active research is the development of small calibre projectiles which are pyrophoric on impact with the target. Among recent projects are the efforts to develop caseless 25- and 30-mm pyrophoric ammunition for the new US F-15 fighter-bomber and AX close support aircraft. Depleted uranium projectiles have been considered for use in the US Bushmaster gun and the CIWS (Close In Weapons System). Projectiles of this kind combine the advantages of high density (greater range and penetration) with a pyrophoric effect.

In spite of the increasing mechanization of armies, a US Army Infantry School design study for the Bushmaster gun estimated that 54 per cent of the potential targets were personnel, and only 29 per cent light armoured vehicles, 13 per cent aircraft (including helicopters), and 4 per cent other vehicles. (US Senate Committee on Armed Services, 1974, part 6, p. 2803).

A modern 20-mm incendiary shell has an effective radius of about 5 metres, and fragments may travel even further from the point of impact. This limited "area" effect gives the exploding munition a greater hit probability than inert ammunition, unless inert bullets can be fired more accurately or in greater numbers. For use against personnel, the blast and fragmentation effects predominate, due to the small quantities of incendiary agent it is possible to put in these small shells; but the incendiary agent may greatly complicate the wounds of those already incapacitated by blast and fragmentation. Some manufacturers advertise that the incendiary composition used in projectiles of this kind produce toxic gases (NWM De Kruithoorn, undated).

Large calibre incendiary projectiles

Attempts to develop effective large calibre incendiary projectiles during World War I did not prove very successful, and since that time projectiles of this kind, with the exception of white phosphorus projectiles, have seen only limited service. White phosphorus projectiles are widely used and are produced in a great range of calibres. They are mainly used for smoke screening and marking, but have a limited incendiary effect which may be used to cause casualties. Phosphorus projectiles listed by US military manuals as "munitions for the defeat of personnel" include the 60-mm and 81-mm mortar projectiles and the 105-mm WP-T M-416 artillery projectile. A 151-mm projectile, the XM-410 has been under development. (US Army Munitions Command, 1972)

A US manual reports that the screening effect of white phosphorus smoke is limited because it burns with such intense heat that the smoke tends to rise rapidly (US Departments of the Army and the Navy, 1971).

Nevertheless, a manual on jungle operations notes that artillery, mortars and rockets are effective methods of employing incendiaries (US Department of the Army, 1969), and new designs for a 60-mm incendiary mortar projectile and a 105-mm artillery projectile have been examined. Advanced development work on the latter was scheduled for the autumn of 1974. A 152-mm prototype, filled with a pyrophoric incendiary agent of the TPA type, proved to be very accurate at a range five times that of conventional mechanized flamethrowers (see p. 107). "Encapsulated flame rounds" of this kind turn any vehicle with a large calibre gun into a flamethrower. (US Army Munitions Command, 1973)

The West German army has an unusual smoke and flame device, the 182-mm *Nebelwerfer* which fires a projectile containing 5.6 kg of smoke and incendiary composition to a range of 220 metres. Temperatures of 1 100–1 200°C can be maintained for about three minutes. The launcher is fired electrically.

Incendiary rockets

A number of incendiary rockets have been developed for use by both ground and air forces. The most common are small, aircraft-launched

110

rockets containing white phosphorus. An example is the US 2.75-inch M-156 10-lb (4.5 kg) aircraft rocket, which may be filled with phosphorus or other chemical filling. It has a limited incendiary and antipersonnel effect, but is claimed to be mainly used for marking targets for attack. In view of the numbers of white phosphorus rockets procured for the Viet-Nam War (see chapter 1) it is curious to note that *Aviation Week & Space Technology* (14 March 1966) reported that for target marking, "the traditional use of . . . smoke rockets sometimes has proved to be of marginal value over the jungles of Vietnam."

The 2.75-inch rocket may also be fitted with a variety of other warheads, including the Mk 5 Mod O HEAT (high explosive anti-tank) warhead. This warhead employs the shaped charge principle, producing a jet of high temperature, high velocity particles which can force their way through armour plate. A US military manual states that "the jet will materially increase the temperature behind the armor and, in the case of a small enclosure such as the inside of a tank, its searing heat normally will kill the occupants" (US Bureau of Naval Personnel, 1970, p. 223).

The USA also developed an 8-inch (20 cm) rocket, the F-42, containing nearly 25 litres of napalm. In addition the new US flamethrower system, the M-202, projects small rockets.

More recently an Israeli 420-mm incendiary rocket containing crude oil has been reported.

Mechanical projection

A catapult designed to project a 200-litre napalm-filled drum was developed in the United States in the early 1960s. It weighed 500 kg and could be airlifted by transport aircraft or helicopter, or could be mounted on a variety of vehicles. It was powered by a 37-mm blank cartridge with a slow-burning powder which drove a piston (*Military Review,* January 1964, p. 94).

Incendiary bombs

Incendiary bombs, ranging in size from a few hundred grams to perhaps 500 kg, have proved to be the most significant of the incendiary weapons. This is due not so much to the capabilities of the bombs themselves but to the range and carrying capacity of modern aircraft. Ground flame weapons have limited incendiary capacity and are restricted in use to points of immediate contact between opposing forces, or, in the case of artillery, to within a few kilometres of the front lines. Aircraft, on the other hand, may carry out attacks far beyond the front lines, on targets which are difficult or impossible to protect from incendiary attack, such as towns, villages, industrial areas, barrack areas, forests and grain fields. Aircraft may also be used to drop incendiaries on troops and other military targets in areas which are inaccessible to ground troops, such as mountain or jungle areas; air attacks may also be carried out as a preliminary to, or in conjunction with, a ground offensive.

The 1933 Disarmament Conference made a distinction between incendiary weapons "specifically intended to cause fires" and those "designed to attack by fire" (see chapter 1). A similar distinction is made in US military terminology between "incendiary bombs" (intended to initiate conflagrations in inflammable target areas) and "fire bombs" (designed to attack personnel, and targets which do not necessarily contain inflammable material, but are nevertheless damaged by heat and flame). Generally speaking, bombs of the first kind are used for attacks in rear areas, whereas bombs of the second kind are used for attacks on battlefield targets. However, this distinction is by no means entirely clear, since incendiary cluster bombs of the type used for attacks on cities during World War II have more recently been used against some tactical targets (columns of trucks), whereas napalm bombs have proved to be most effective against barrack areas.

Incendiary bombs specifically intended to cause fires are of two general types, the intensive type and the scatter type. The intensive type usually consists of a magnesium case filled with thermite which generates a high temperature in a limited area. They may have tail fins or streamers to give them a more stable flight path and a lead weight or steel nose cap to aid penetration of the roofs of houses. They usually weigh one or two kilograms.

One of the earliest bombs of this kind was the British "Baby Incendiary Bomb" (6½ oz Mk IV Incendiary Bomb) which was considered the most effective incendiary bomb of World War I (Greene, 1947). The US military designed a similar but somewhat larger bomb prior to World War II, the Mk II Incendiary Dart. Italy and Germany developed 1-kg and 2-kg incendiary bombs which were tried in Ethiopia and Spain. By 1936 military observers regarded bombs of this type as the principle threat to cities (Greene, 1947). This judgement was confirmed by the events of World War II.

The effectiveness of the intensive-type magnesium bombs in raids on British cities influenced the design of the M-50 bomb produced by the USA. This bomb was succeeded by the M-126 bomb, 182 of which are fitted into the M-36 incendiary cluster bomb. This bomb was used until recently, modified for high-speed delivery by jet aircraft.

Because of other demands of the production of magnesium the USA also developed during World War II a small oil incendiary bomb, the M-69, which was intended as an alternative to the magnesium bomb. It was more of a scatter-type bomb, but was used in great numbers against Japanese cities, which consisted largely of light, wooden buildings, rather than the masonry buildings characteristic of European cities.

A number of scatter-type bombs have been developed, but they have found few applications. During World War II several of the combatants designed small scatterable incendiary "leaflets", consisting of celluloid envelopes containing white phosphorus, intended to set fire to grain fields or forests. Either they proved to be relatively ineffective, or there was some hesitation about using them for fear of reprisals in kind. Whatever the explanation, they saw little use. Other scatter-type bombs contained such incendiary agents as rubber-thickened benzene with white phosphorus as an igniter, or crepe rubber balls in a solution of white phosphorous in carbon disulphide.

Reports during World War II showed that, in general, densely populated working class areas or slum areas ignited more readily than areas of more sparsely distributed large commercial properties or residential suburbs. Conflagrations were more readily started by dropping a large number of small bombs to produce numerous small fires which could then coalesce, rather than by dropping fewer large incendiary bombs. Small incendiary bombs could be distributed over an area by means of a hopper or dispenser installed in or under an aircraft, or by arranging them in clusters. A cluster bomb contains many smaller bombs which it releases at a certain height over the target. In this way it is theoretically possible to match the distribution of bombs to the density of ignition points. The principle of the cluster bomb is also used for distributing chemical and fragmentation munitions over a wide area.

The cluster bomb principle has been developed extensively in the United States in recent years. The US CBU (Cluster Bomb Unit) and CDU series (see table 2.2) now include more than 80 types of incendiary, fragmentation, chemical and smoke bombs. There are five principle types of bomblet dispenser, the SUU-7, SUU-13, SUU-14, SUU-30 and the Tactical Fighter Dispenser (TFD), each of which can be filled with a variety of bomblet types. The SUU-30 operates rather like a pea-pod and is similar in size and shape to a 750-lb (340 kg) bomb. The SUU-7 and SUU-14 consist of horizontal tubes slung under a plane from which the bombs are ejected. The SUU-13 and the TFD consist of vertical tubes from which the bombs are dropped. In addition, the SUU-24 is designed to scatter 4 248 incendiary or fragmentation bomblets from B-47 or B-52 heavy bombers.

Since World War II it has been common practice to combine blast and fragmentation effects with incendiary effects, either in the same munition, or by mixing sub-munitions in a cluster bomb (see appendix 1A). Several modern bomblets combine incendiary and fragmentation effects for example by mixing zirconium with composition-B explosive, as in the BLU-61. Zirconium bomblets, such as the BLU-68, may be mixed with fragmentation bomblets, such as the BLU-63, in a single dispenser, such as the SUU-24.

A further class of incendiary bombs is that which is specifically designed to attack directly by fire independently of the availability of inflammable materials in the target area. To do this they utilize a large quantity of incendiary fuel, usually napalm or phosphorus, in the bomb itself.

113

Table 2.2. Modern US incendiary cluster bombs

Type	Notes
CBU-12	SUU-7 dispenser loaded with 213 BLU-17 white phosphorus bomblets
CBU-22	SUU-14 dispenser with 72 BLU-17 white phosphorus bomblets
CBU-41	750-lb bomb containing 18 napalm-B-filled BLU-53 bomblets
CBU-52	750-lb bomb containing 254 BLU-61 bomblets, producing zirconium fragments
CBU-53	750-lb bomb containing 670 BLU-70 zirconium bomblets
CBU-54	750-lb bomb containing 670 BLU-68 zirconium bomblets
CDU-15	Cannister cluster bomb containing 177 BLU-68 bomblets; used in SUU-24 Hayes dispenser[a]
CDU-17	Cannister cluster bomb containing 177 BLU-70 bomblets; used in SUU-24 Hayes dispenser[a]

[a] The SUU-24 bomb and grenade dispenser (Hayes dispenser) is a 24-cell free fall release dispenser designed for attachment to clip-on bomb racks of B-47 and B-52 bombers. It dispenses BLU-3, BLU-26, BLU-36, BLU-41, BLU-61 and BLU-63 fragmentation bomblets; BLU-68, BLU-69 and BLU-70 incendiary bomblets; and M-40 23-lb (10 kg) fragmentation bombs.

Sources: DMS (1974), Prokosch (1973), Robinson (1973), US Air Force (1970), US Department of the Army (1966, 1970, 1971).

Napalm bombs

During World War II an increasing number of aircraft were fitted with auxiliary fuel tanks which were given a streamlined, "cigar-shaped" form and slung under the fusilage or from the wings. Small fighter or fighter-bomber aircraft, which were increasingly used in ground attack operations, had a limited range when using only internal fuel tanks, and additional outside tanks were a means of increasing the range. These tanks were normally made of light aluminium alloy and could be detached and dropped in flight after use. "Drop tanks" continue to be a standard item of equipment.

Since napalm consisted originally of aviation fuel thickened in the field by the addition of napalm powder, it became a simple matter to convert drop tanks to large incendiary bombs by the addition of the thickening powder and an ignition system. Subsequently a version was standardized as the M-116 bomb. The M-116 bomb was 3.5 metres long and 47 cm in diameter and weighed 23.6 kg empty or approximately 300 kg when filled with 100 gallons (424 litres) of napalm-thickened aviation fuel. On impact, fuses ignited a TNT burster surrounded by a quantity of white phosphorus which ignited the napalm. A fireball which burned with intense heat for 6–10 seconds gave way to a fire of reduced intensity, lasting 6–10 minutes over an elliptical area about 30 metres broad and 90 metres long (US Department of the Army, 1960).

Following World War II, napalm bombs became standard items of equipment in many air forces. Modern napalm bombs (table 2.3) are essentially the same as the M-116 but are modified to make them suitable for use

Table 2.3. Examples of types of napalm bombs

Type	Nominal size	Notes
France		
. .	500 litre	
. .	750 litre	
. .	950 litre	
. .	1 550 litre	
Italy		
. .	110 kg	
. .	160 kg	
Sweden		
m/58	500 kg	Napalm with "Alunat" thickner
UK		
. .	454 litre	Heavy case
. .	500 litre	
USA		
BLU-1	750-lb (340 kg)	Filled with 280 to 359 kg of napalm. Weight of assembly bomb varies from 317 to 397 kg, depending on filler
BLU-10	250-lb (113 kg)	Small version of BLU-1. Filled with 96 kg of napalm
BLU-11	500-lb (227 kg)	Modified version of M116A1 firebomb. Filled with 200 kg napalm. Assembled weight, 228 kg.
BLU-23	500-lb (227 kg)	Small version of BLU-1. Filled with 195 kg of napalm. Assembled weight, 222 kg.
BLU-27	750-lb (340 kg)	Welded version of BLU-1. Filled with 360 kg of napalm B. Assembled weight, 400 kg.
BLU-32	500-lb (227 kg)	Welded version of BLU-23. Filled with 240 kg of napalm B. Assembled weight, 268 kg.
BLU-35	250-lb (113 kg)	Modular.
BLU-51	. .	
BLU-53	20-lb (9.1 kg)	Napalm B-filled. Used in CBU-41 cluster bomb
BLU-65	820-lb (370 kg)	
BLU-74	250-lb (113 kg)	Napalm-B filled. Modular bomb for use in SUU-48 dispenser
BLU-75	. .	
Mk-77 Mod 0	750-lb (340 kg)	
Mk-77 Mod 1	500-lb (250 kg)	
Mk-79 Mod 1	1 000-lb (454 kg)	Fin stabilized
Mk-116	750-lb (340 kg)	Also Mk-116 A1
Mk-122	900-lb (410 kg)	Fireye; improved Mk-79

Sources: Aviation Studies Atlantic, *passim;* DMS, *passim;* Prokosch (1973), Robinson (1973), US Department of the Army (1966, 1970, 1971).

with high performance aircraft. A single fighter-bomber aircraft can normally carry two napalm bombs, though some aircraft carry more.

There is some doubt as to the effectiveness of napalm bombs. They are widely believed to have a substantial impact on the morale of troops confronted by them, as well as causing casualties. They are also believed to be effective against tanks. But Kusterer (1966) reports that a study carried out by the Battelle Memorial Institute (1965) showed that inexperienced troops were the source of most of the stories that napalm was the "most feared" weapon in Korea and Viet-Nam. This would seem to be corroborated by the accounts of Futrell (1961) and Fall (1961) (see chapter 1).

Tests in the United States during the Korean war showed that a single aircraft had difficulty hitting a tank with a napalm bomb, and that against new tanks, with hatches closed and with stowage items (such as ammunition, food or bedding) removed, napalm had little effect. Goats and sheep which were passengers in the radio-controlled tanks were not affected either by heat or oxygen depletion. In order to be effective in combat it was usual practice for a flight of four aircraft to drop all their napalm bombs in the vicinity of a single tank and to combine "the fire-starting ability of napalm with the high-velocity rockets and armour-piercing incendiary .50-caliber machine gun bullets of the entire flight of aircraft" (Dolan, 1952, p. 18). Similarly in attacks on other targets:

[The] most effective technique calls for employment of napalm in connection with high explosive attacks in the form of fragmentation bombs, mortar fire, and artillery fire. The target is first attacked with fragmentation bombs, and mortar and artillery fire combined. This attack is immediately followed by a saturation of fire bombs; then immediately after the fire bomb attack, the high explosive attack is repeated (Dolan, 1952, p. 16).

Thus, though napalm alone may be effective against unprepared troops in the open, it is not a very effective weapon against protected targets unless combined with massive fire from conventional blast and fragmentation munitions. A measure of the size of the increment in military effectiveness has yet to appear in the public literature.

In an effort to increase the effectiveness of napalm bombs, napalm-B was introduced. Napalm-B not only increases the length of the area covered to nearly 200 metres, but it burns for as long as 15 minutes, thereby transferring much more heat to the target. Experiments showed greatly increased damage to military equipment, dummy soldiers, and other targets (US Tactical Air Command, 1966) but indications of the significance of these findings in actual combat have not been published. Any increase in the effectiveness against military equipment would, of course, be matched by an increase in the severity of burns inflicted on human beings.

It is said that the main use of napalm bombs is in close air support of ground forces. However, in the study by Kusterer (1966), cited in chapter 1, only 25.8 per cent of the napalm bomb attacks in a four-month period were against targets classified as "troop positions". The majority of the other targets attacked were of a kind which are typically found at some distance from the front.

A new development is the use of clustered napalm bombs. The SUU-48 dispenser, for example, can release up to five BLU-74 napalm-B bombs either singly, in rapid succession, or all together as a salvo.

Phosphorus bombs

Perhaps the most widely used white phosphorus bomb is the US AN-M-47A4, which is a modified version of the standard 100 lb M-47 bomb. Originally designed during World War II as a carrier for a variety of chemical and incendiary agents, it has continued to be manufactured until quite recently. This bomb contains about 20 kg of plastic white phosphorus and a high explosive burster which spreads particles of burning phosphorus over a radius of some 15 metres (700 m²). It has been used in combination with napalm bombs as well as other munitions.

A smaller white phosphorus bomb, the M-67, was used in some US cluster bombs, and the BLU-17 is used in several modern cluster bombs (CBU-12, CBU-22).

V. *Defensive measures in the event of an incendiary attack*

General principles of fire protection

The general principles of fire protection are (*a*) to prevent ignition (that is, the initiation of the oxidation reaction), and (*b*) to extinguish the fire (that is, the process of oxidation), by excluding oxygen or fuel, or by reducing the temperature to below that required for continued combustion.

Prevention of ignition

Many inflammable materials can be replaced by non-inflammable materials impregnated or coated with flame-retarding substances. Because fire damage is so costly this is an area of growing research and technology (Lyons, 1970). Examples include:

1. *Fire-retarding paint* which contains a high proportion of inorganic phosphate pigments, causing it to foam on exposure to flame. The foam may be hundreds of times thicker than the original film of paint and insulates the underlying material from the heat and flame (*Chemical & Engineering News*, 6 May 1968). Paints of this kind have been applied to bombs to reduce the chance of detonation in the event of a fire.[9]

2. *Impregnating cotton materials* with a variety of substances to make

[9] Following a fire aboard the US aircraft *Forrestal*, when a bomb exploded after 90 seconds, killing the first group of firefighters, the US Navy developed a protective paint which extended the average "cook-off" time of bombs subjected to fire from two minutes to at least five minutes. The outside of the bomb was painted with an intumescent paint (a paint that foams when heated, forming an insulating layer over the surface to which it is applied), and the bomb case was lined with asphalt to which was added a high-melting point wax. (*Ordnance*, January–February 1970).

them fire-resistant. One very effective substance is diammonium phosphate, which is easy to use since it dissolves in water, but has the disadvantage that materials must be re-impregnated after every wash. Permanent flame-proofing of cotton can be achieved, for example, with tetrahydroxymethylene phosphonium chloride (THPC) which reacts with the cellulose when, after impregnation, the cotton cloth is heated to 140°C. However, like other substances which react with the fibre, it has the disadvantage that it reduces the wearability of the cloth. Another approach is to use impregnating substances which dissolve in chlorated organic liquids, such as the perchlorethylene used in "dry cleaning". A substance of this kind which has given good results is tri-2,3-dibromopropyl phosphate (T23P or TBPP) (Miles & Delesanto, 1968; Adler, 1971). This substance has the advantage that even washing the cotton in hot water does not effect the degree of flame-proofing.

In general, flame-retarding substances are rich in phosphorus and halogens. It seems that when cotton fibres impregnated with these substances are exposed to flame, the phosphorus compounds help to prevent ignition by altering the mode of decomposition (pyrolysis) of the cellulose fibre so that less combustible products are formed. Halogen compounds act in the gas phase by inhibiting the flames (Baum, 1973 b).

3. *Fire-resistant artificial fibres.* Many artificial fibres used for clothing materials have a tendency to ignite and flare up rapidly. Nightwear made of materials of this kind has been responsible for many accidents resulting in children being burned from buttocks to neck. A further hazard of some artificial fibres like nylon, is that they melt at about 250°C, so that if they do not catch fire they may cause deep burns from the highly adhesive molten residue. Acetate and rayon fibres are spun from solution, a technique which lends itself readily to the introduction of fire-retarding chemicals, such as T23P (Schappel, 1968). A variety of flame-retardant acetate, rayon and nylon fibres have been produced (Baum, 1973 a; Stepnick, 1973). Some of them have been specifically developed for military applications.[10]

4. *Fire-resistant aircraft fuels.* Fire is a major hazard in aircraft crashes, whether in the civilian or the military sphere. The hazard is more acute in the military context because of the possibility of attack from high-explosive-incendiary shells specifically designed to ignite fuel supplies.[11] As

[10] The US Navy Medical Research Department spent ten years developing a flame resistant nylon substitute for overalls for aircrews. The new material, Nomex, which was adopted as standard in 1967, was produced by a major US company (*Du Pont Magazine,* November–December 1965).

[11] The US Air Force issued design standards (TAC 32–67) in 1967 to stimulate industrial research into this problem. One result was a gel produced by Western Co., which, though normally liquid, thickened instantaneously when subjected to the shearing strains of a bullet. For potential large-scale use in South-East Asia or other theatres of operation, the company estimated that the additional cost of the gel would be 0.7 cents per gallon, based on a consumption of 15 million gallons per month (*Aviation Week,* 10 July 1967).

118

a result there has been a considerable amount of research into possibilities for reducing this hazard. When aircraft fuel tanks are ruptured on crashing or by an anti-aircraft shell, the fuel flows out and vapourizes, forming an explosive mixture with air which is readily ignited by the hot engines. Most approaches to reducing this hazard have therefore concentrated on ways of retaining the fuel in the fuel tank, even if it is holed. Considerable success has been achieved with additives which gel or emulsify the fuel[12] and the injection of a foam which soaks up the fuel like a sponge.[13]

Thus, technical possibilities exist for greatly reducing the fire hazard presented by common materials, both in the military and civilian contexts. However, the addition of fire-retarding chemicals demands a more complex manufacturing process, and therefore a more expensive product.[14] This may well mean that the better protection afforded by these new developments may be confined in the first instance to the armed forces of the richer countries and their allies rather than civilians, particularly those of poorer countries who, in recent conflicts at least, have often been the victims of incendiary attacks.

Fire extinguishing

Several measures can be taken, although the effectiveness of each measure may well depend on the nature of the fire.

1. Douse the fire in cold water. Wetting and emulsifying additives may increase the dousing effect. This method should *not* be employed in the case of a fire caused by electrical short-circuiting, by burning oil or by metal incendiary agents.

2. Prevent fuel from feeding the fire.

3. Blanket the fire physically to exclude oxygen. A small, localized fire may be extinguished by covering it with a wet blanket or asbestos blanket, sand or earth.

4. Lower the oxygen concentration within the fire. A fire in a confined space may be extinguished by closing off all air intakes. Larger fires in buildings may be attacked by diluting the entering air with inert gases such as carbon dioxide or nitrogen.[15]

5. Interrupt the combustion mechanism chemically by means of "flame-quenching" dry chemicals, such as potassium or sodium bicarbonate, and

[12] In one study of several gelling additives, N-coco-γ-hydroxybutyramide (CHBA) was found to give the best results, reducing the amount of flame generated by 85.2 per cent compared with ungelled fuel (Posey & Schleicher, 1966).

[13] Polyurethane foam fillers for fuel tanks used in combat aircraft were also evaluated for commercial aircraft (*Aviation Week,* 13 November 1967).

[14] In the USA, flame-retardant nightwear garments cost about $1 to $1.50 more than inflammable ones in 1973 (Baum, 1973 b).

[15] The exhaust gas of a jet engine has been proposed as a fire extinguisher. The normal oxygen content is 16–17 per cent and this can be reduced to 12 per cent by an after-burner. These gases are very hot—about 1 800°C—and must therefore be cooled to about 100°C by injecting water. This further reduces the oxygen content to 4–5 per cent. Experiments at the British Fire

halogenated hydrocarbon gases and liquids. Chemicals such as carbon tetrachloride have proved more effective than carbon dioxide for extinguishing. However, many of the early chemicals of this class were not only toxic before use, but could produce even more toxic by-products, such as phosgene and chlorine (Haessler, 1973; US Army, 1960). A more recent substitute is bromotrifluoromethane which has greater thermal stability, low toxicity and requires only about one cylinder to do the job of six heavier cylinders of carbon dioxide (Haessler, 1973). Trimethoxyboroxine (TMB) may be used for suppression of metal fires (Botteri & Manheim, 1969).[16]

Fire protection on the battlefield

The protection of troops in the field can be greatly enhanced by using fire-retarding materials for uniforms, coating ammunition with intumescent paints, or gelling fuel in aircraft fuel tanks. Locations with limited space such as naval vessels can be equipped with automatic fire extinguishing systems, fire doors and other means of limiting outbreaks of fire. Armoured vehicles can be constructed to prevent napalm or gases being drawn in through the ventilation system.

Sand and earth are in general the best means of extinguishing burning incendiary agents on the battlefield. Water is not recommended: napalm floats on it, so that using water merely spreads the fuel; other incendiary compositions may contain sodium which ignites in reaction with water. Metal incendiary agents may produce an explosive mixture of hydrogen and air if quenched with water, and may produce a poisonous mixture of gases such as chlorine and phosgene if an attempt is made to extinguish them with carbon tetrachloride (US Army, 1960). White phosphorus may be extinguished with water, or with a 5 per cent solution of copper sulphate. The latter has the advantage that it forms a layer of copper phosphide around the phosphorus particles, preventing re-ignition which might otherwise occur when the phosphorus dries out (*Voennyj Vestnik*, 5 May 1968).

Protection of the civilian population from incendiary attack

Because fire spreads so readily it is particularly difficult to protect a civilian population from incendiary attack. This is illustrated by the experience of the World War II bombing of German cities. Even though these cities were

Research Station with a Viper jet engine producing 45 000 cu. ft/min successfully controlled or extinguished wood and oil fires, and resulted in an atmosphere clear enough for firemen using breathing apparatus to readily locate the fire (Silversides, 1964). The US Naval Research Institute has developed a method for extinguishing fires in submarines by injecting nitrogen (*New Scientist*, 13 September 1973).

[16] The United Kingdom Atomic Energy Authority patented a new dry powder fire extinguisher which produces a foam in the presence of fire. The major constituent is perlite, a natural complex aluminium silicate of volcanic origin. It is viscous and more heat-stable than normal fusible powders and therefore particularly suitable for use against finely divided metals such as zirconium, and it sticks well to hot metal surfaces (*Atom*, February 1970). It should therefore be very effective against modern pyrophoric metal incendiary agents.

built with a high proportion of stone and cement, with relatively wide streets which might act as fire-breaks (compared with large areas of the Japanese cities which consisted of light wooden houses, closely spaced), and even though Germany had modern, well developed fire services (see Rumpf, 1952; Hampe, 1963), it was estimated that incendiaries were 4.8 times as effective as high explosive bombs, judged by the areas destroyed. The reason is that human habitations themselves contain the fuel which, once it is ignited, can destroy them.

Generally speaking, modern fire services can prevent a fire in a single building from spreading to other buildings. The aim of an incendiary attack on an inhabited area is to create many fires simultaneously, far beyond the fire defence capacity. In such circumstances it is not possible to isolate each fire, particularly when explosive bombs contribute to blocking access with rubble, rupturing water pipes, and killing and injuring civil defence personnel. Fire spreads from one building to another until it engulfs whole areas. It may continue to burn for days and smoulder for weeks.

Where mass fires are created in this way normal air raid shelters offer inadequate protection. The greatest risk for the inhabitants of the shelter is that toxic gases, mainly carbon monoxide (see chapter 4), are drawn in through the ventilators. Carbon monoxide can be filtered out by a charcoal filter, as in a gas mask, but where the incoming air exceeds 140°C, the charcoal filter may start to oxidize, producing rather than absorbing carbon monoxide (Nykvist, 1974). If the air temperature rises above 60°C, the inhabitants will die from heat stroke within a few hours or less. The fire also consumes huge quantities of oxygen, which may thus be drawn from the shelter through ventilators, leading to asphyxiation of the occupants. All these causes lead to a typical picture of the ''shelter dead'' (see chapters 3 and 4).

Thus, even with the most advanced techniques of town planning, shelter construction and fire-fighting, only limited protection can be given to the civilian population against incendiary attack. It is clear that in ''under-developed'' countries advanced techniques are not available. Town planning may be almost non-existent, with large numbers of people crowded into simple or makeshift dwellings of inflammable material. Water supplies are often totally inadequate even for normal household use and are certainly insufficient to cope with large-scale outbreaks of fire. Where people have inadequate housing, they certainly do not have access to advanced air raid shelters; similarly, fire services will normally be underdeveloped and lack both personnel and modern equipment.

Chapter 3. Thermal effects of incendiary weapons on the human body

I. *Introduction*

A vital consideration in arguments about military necessity *versus* humanitarian priorities is the medical aspect of the use of incendiary weapons. Such questions as the nature of the casualty effects, the problems of medical treatment, the prospects for the surviving casualties, and the likelihood and the time of death are all relevant to any assessment of the amount of suffering caused to victims of incendiary attack. From the viewpoint of the international laws of war, this amount of suffering has somehow to be weighed against the "military necessity" of the use of incendiary weapons, for it is presumably only in this way that it may be determined whether all or a part of this suffering is "unnecessary".

The traumatic effect of most weapons is to penetrate the skin and damage internal organs. Although the action of flame weapons is essentially to damage only the skin, fire may cause death in a number of ways so that the exact cause may be difficult to determine in a given case. In general, death by fire may be due to the following causes: (*a*) heatstroke, caused by the transfer of heat to the body sufficient to increase the body temperature above a critical level (approximately 43°C), (*b*) pulmonary damage due to inhalation of smoke and toxic fumes, (*c*) carbon monoxide poisoning, (*d*) deprivation of oxygen, and (*e*) severity of the burn wound in terms of depth and the extent of the body surface area affected.

The likelihood of death from burn wounds is also affected by such factors as the age, the general health and the nutritional status of the victim, and the potential risk of infection.

Heatstroke may be an important cause of immediate death from fire, but it is not a significant cause of later death. The same applies to carbon monoxide poisoning and the deprivation of oxygen, since these reactions are also reversible (although some long-term injury may result: see chapter 4). Major factors related to the death rate from burns, after initial survival, are the degree of pulmonary injury and the extent of the body surface area involved. The age of the patient and his general health and nutritional status are additional factors which may influence the prognosis. One analysis of the complications causing or contributing to death due to burns is shown in table 3.1.

Where toxic and respiratory complications are not present, the mortality from burns in individuals of given age and general health depends pri-

Table 3.1. Complications from burning which caused or contributed to death

	Number of cases		Number of cases
Non-bacterial complications		**Bacterial complications**	
Early shock and/or cardiac failure		Septicaemia	60
Early hyperkalaemia	1	Bronchopneumonia	56
Other shock	18	Pyelonephritis	16
Subtotal	19	Meningitis	2
		Peritonitis	2
		Entero-colitis	3
Respiratory complications		Gas gangrene	1
Carbon monoxide	2	Extra-renal abscess	1
Inhalation of smoke	3		
Glottic burns	4	**Total bacterial complications**	141
Obstructive tracheobronchitis	2		
Blast injury to lungs	1		
Congestive atelectasis	9		
Pulmonary oedema	2		
Inhalation of vomit	2		
Subtotal	25		
Acute cardiac complications			
Toxic myocarditis	1		
Cardiac arrest	4		
Subtotal	5		
Renal failure	24		
Hypokalaemia	4		
Pulmonary embolism	5		
Hepatic jaundice	2		
Acute dilatation of the stomach	3		
Paralytic ileus	1		
Agranulocytosis and thrombocytopenia	1		
Haemorrhage from acute duodenal ulcer	1		
Anoxic cerebral softening	1		
Subtotal	42	**Total non-bacterial complications**	91
		Total all cases	232

Source: Sevitt (1966).

marily upon the depth and extent of the burn, because of the physiological importance of the skin as a vital organ of the body. This is true whether death results from inadequately treated shock in the early stages of burn care, subsequent infections or other less frequent causes of death such as burn-induced gastric ulceration. Except for electrical burns, characterized by the deep destruction of muscles and other tissue but with limited skin damage, the causative agent is less important in determining the outlook for a burn patient.

For these reasons, the major thermal effects of incendiary weapons on the human body to be described in this chapter relate to burns of the skin, although reference is also made to the so-called "pulmonary burns", which have now been shown to be due more to the inhalation of smoke and fumes than to actual thermal burns of the lungs. The toxic effects of incendiary weapons are described in chapter 4, where further reference is made to lung irritant effects.

It is sometimes useful to distinguish between *primary* burns, due to the direct effects of an incendiary agent on the body, and *secondary* burns, due to the combustion of clothes, equipment, houses, and so on. Primary burns caused by military incendiary agents are likely to be especially severe since they are the result of extensive technological efforts to increase both the heat of combustion and the burning time. Secondary burns resulting from incendiaries are in principle little different from burns experienced in civilian life, about which there is a voluminous medical literature. In this chapter, the general medical literature on burns is surveyed in order to convey some indication of the complexity and severity of the burn wound and the resulting demands on treatment facilities. More specific effects of the use of incendiary weapons are also described. The chapter concludes with a discussion of some additional factors which complicate medical treatment—and therefore the prognosis for the patient—in wartime conditions.

II. *Pathological effects of burns*

The skin as a vital organ

The significance of the physiological role of the skin is not commonly appreciated. The skin is not only an essential part of the body, but it also has considerable psychological significance to the individual. In both cases this is because the skin forms the interface between the individual and the outside physical and social world.

A living organism may be described as an "open system" maintaining itself in a dynamic equilibrium with its environment. This equilibrium, known as homeostasis,[1] is maintained by balancing many processes, including the ingestion of foodstuffs and the excretion of waste products, the inhalation of oxygen and the exhalation of carbon dioxide, and the imbibing of water in order to compensate for the loss of moisture by evaporation or excretion.

The skin plays a vital role in maintaining homeostasis, particularly in controlling the temperature of the body and in limiting evaporation of moisture from it. When food is metabolized in the body it produces heat enabling the body to maintain the normal temperature of about 37°C. The skin acts as an insulating layer, actively controlling the loss of heat to the surrounding air, and thereby diminishing the food intake needed simply to provide the body's "central heating".

---

[1] *Homeostasis:* The maintenance of a state of equilibrium within the body with respect to temperature, heart rate, blood pressure, water content, blood sugar level, and so on.

124

Preventing water from evaporating from the body is important for three main reasons. First, evaporation has a cooling effect. Without control by the skin the heat loss due to evaporation places excessive demands on the body's capacity to generate heat by metabolism. Second, water is essential for the transport of substances in the body. If water is lost by evaporation, the body fluids become more concentrated, and in an effort to restore the balance, water passes out of the cells into the fluids surrounding them, and may be lost from the body by further evaporation. The cells can only tolerate a minor water loss before they die. Third, the effect of the loss of water, whether due to the loss of circulating blood from damaged blood vessels or by evaporation from open wounds, is to decrease the flow of fluids through major organs such as the brain, heart and kidneys, threatening these major body systems with injury or death.

Further, the skin is a major means of contact with the environment, containing nerve endings which provide the brain with a continual feedback of information about pain, temperature, touch and pressure through proprioceptive sensors. If the skin is removed, these sensors are removed with it, depriving the brain of much of the information necessary for adaptive behaviour.

Although much of the skin is usually clothed for social and practical reasons, it has great psychological importance for the individual since, being the outside of the body, the skin is most accessible to observation and touch by other persons. Damage and deformity to the skin, particularly in such important areas as the head and hands, have far-reaching psychological consequences.

The skin is made up of several layers. The outer layer, the *epidermis*, is composed of non-living, hard-wearing cells and in some parts of the body, such as the soles of the feet, may be quite thick. As these outer cells are worn away, they are constantly replaced by cells from the underlying layer, called the *dermis*. This layer is composed of living cells and contains all the functional components of the skin—small blood capillaries, nerve endings, sweat glands and hair follicles. Dilation of these blood capillaries enables the body to increase the flow of blood at the surface of the body, where heat is more readily dissipated. Contraction of these vessels helps to conserve the heat of the body. Changes in the state of these blood vessels are responsible for changes in the colour of the skin when a person is too hot or too cold. Perspiration from the sweat glands is another means of dissipating heat from the body, while the hair is a means of conserving heat, albeit one which is largely vestigial in man.

Underneath the skin is a layer of adipose tissue, made up largely of cells containing large globules of fat, which also protects and insulates the body. The thickness of this layer varies considerably from one individual to another and in different parts of the body.

Stoll & Green (1959) showed that the receptors in the skin which are effective in mediating the pain sensation have a threshold of approximately 43.2°C.

In a major series of experiments Moritz and his colleagues (Henriques & Moritz, 1947; Moritz & Henriques, 1947; Moritz, 1947) showed that the lower temperature limit for a cutaneous burn due to hot water is approximately 44°C.

At 44°C it took about three hours to raise the temperature of the underlying skin at the dermis-fat interface to 44°C, damaging the full thickness of the skin. At a temperature of 55°C, it took only 0.4 minutes to create the same effect. At 100°C it took only some 0.1 seconds to destroy the epidermis, but in that short time there was no significant temperature increase at the dermis-fat interface. That is, the physiological changes in the skin due to burns depended upon both the temperature and the time of contact with the burning agent: the hotter the agent, the shorter the contact time required to destroy the tissue.

It will be obvious from the description of the functions of the skin that the severity of a cutaneous burn wound depends not only upon the depth of the burn but also upon the extent of the body surface area affected, which determines the loss of fluids and heat and therefore the impact on the major physiological systems of the body.

The depth of burns (degree)

Burns which only injure the epidermis, such as mild sunburn, are known as *first degree* burns (see figure 3.1). They result in temporary erythema (redness), due to dilation of the capillaries, and oedema (swelling). They usually heal within a few days after sloughing off the epidermis, and leave no scar.

Burns which extend into the living layer of the skin, the dermis, are much more serious. It is common to distinguish between *second degree,* or partial thickness, burns, and *third degree*, or full thickness, burns. Second degree burns denote those in which necrosis[2] extends into the dermis, but with the survival of a sufficient foundation of such skin appendages as sweat glands and hair follicles to ensure that the skin regenerates without having to heal from the edges of the wounds. There is a wide variation in the severity of these burns. Some, such as severe sunburn with blistering, will heal within a week or two and leave no scars; others will heal within a month with reasonable care; and still others will not heal spontaneously unless specific treatment is given to prevent the destruction of surviving epithelial[3] cells of the skin by secondary infection and to encourage these cells to grow. Third degree, or full thickness, burns are those in which all the dermis is destroyed.

[2] *Necrosis:* The death of one or more cells or a portion of a tissue or organ.
[3] *Epithelium:* A thin layer of tissue without blood vessels which covers all the free surfaces of the body, including eyes, glands, respiratory passages, and so on.

Figure 3.1 Schematic outline of cross-section of the skin showing degrees of burn[a]

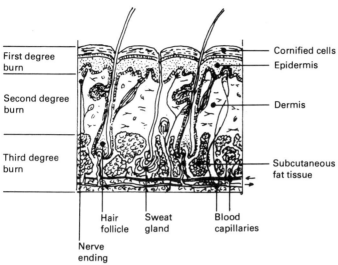

First degree burn

Second degree burn

Third degree burn

Cornified cells

Epidermis

Dermis

Subcutaneous fat tissue

Hair follicle   Sweat gland   Blood capillaries

Nerve ending

[a] First degree, or superficial burns, involve only the epidermis and heal rapidly. Second degree burns damage the upper part of the dermis but islets of living dermal tissue remain and proliferate to cover the area in about 14 days. Third degree, deep, or full thickness, burns extend through the dermis and may extend to underlying tissues. Some authors refer to burns which extend into underlying tissues as fourth and fifth degree burns. In general, third degree burns greater than 1–2 cm² in area require skin transplantation in order to heal.

In addition there may be destruction of the underlying fat, muscle, bone and other tissues. The terms *fourth* and *fifth degree* burns are sometimes used to describe such injuries, although in general this nomenclature is no longer favoured in the international literature, as specific deeper injuries of this sort are better recorded as such.

The depth of the burn is easily misjudged and depends upon the cause, the temperature, the length of exposure, and the thickness of the skin (the soles of the feet, the palms of the hands, and the back being thicker than elsewhere). Intense heat over a short period may produce a burn which *looks* very much like one produced by less heat over a longer period, although the latter may destroy more of the underlying dermal elements. Both first and superficial second degree burns blanche on pressure with an instrument such as a sterile microscope slide; the colour returns when the pressure is released. Third degree burns do not blanche or flush on pressure or release. The persistence of sensation, which is easily tested with a sterile needle, is often helpful in differentiating second and third degree burns, although this test is not completely reliable. Destruction of the full skin thickness kills the nerve endings, resulting in loss of feeling (Phillips & Constable, undated). Even experts may have difficulty in estimating burn depth, and subsequent sepsis[4] may invalidate initially correct judgements by converting a second degree burn to a full thickness injury. This is particularly likely to happen in malnourished anaemic patients, who also commonly have no access to adequate medical facilities. Deep second degree burns often heal with severe scarring.

Deep burns heal only after the dead tissue is removed either by unassisted or natural separation, which usually involves bacterial infection, or by repeated dressings (debridement) or surgical excision. The 'clean' burn wound may then heal by epithelial ingrowth from the edges, if it is less than 1–2 cm² in area, by the effective surgical closure of small wounds, or by the application of skin grafts from other parts of the body.

The cropping of skin grafts leaves painful donor sites, comparable to second degree burns, which usually heal in about two weeks with no more than minimal scarring. Under less than optimal conditions, however, sepsis may intervene and these donor sites, in turn, become areas of full thickness or third degree skin loss. This may account for the reluctance of surgeons to apply skin grafts to burns which otherwise appear to necessitate them when patients are in poor condition and medical facilities are minimal. At present, permanent skin grafts can only be taken from the recipient himself, identical twins excepted.

Second degree burns are characteristically extremely painful until they are essentially healed. Third degree burns, because of the destruction of the nerve endings in the dermis, are characteristically not strikingly painful during the first few days after the injury. With progressive healing and removal of the insensitive overlayer of dead tissue, the wounds become more and more sensitive until covered with grafts or by the ingrowth of epithelium. Daily changes of dressings are excruciatingly painful, equivalent to tearing off the outer, insensitive layer of the skin from the inner, sensitive layer.

The extent of burns

The second factor determining the severity of burns is the extent of the body surface area involved, which is significant for several reasons. The greater the area of skin destroyed, the greater the loss of moisture and heat by evaporation, which are major factors in the pathophysiology of the burn injury. Second, the greater the area involved, the greater the problem of coping with infection. Third, the greater the area of skin destroyed, the less skin is available for grafting—a procedure which is all the more necessary. As a result of these and other factors there is a direct relationship between the extent of a burn of a given depth and the chance of sur-

---

[4] *Sepsis:* The localized or superficial presence of various pus-forming and other pathogenic organisms or their toxins which kill the tissues. The presence of microorganisms or their toxins in the circulating blood may give rise to systemic disease, a condition known as *septicaemia.*

Figure 3.2 The "rule of nines" as a method for estimating the approximate extent of burns in an adult

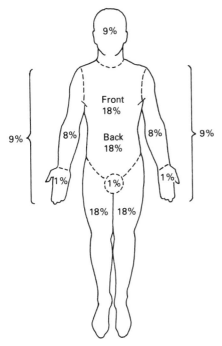

Source: After Berkow (1924).

vival. A convenient means of estimating the extent of body area burned was introduced by Berkow in 1924, and is often presented as the "rule of nines" (figure 3.2). The face or an arm make up approximately 9 per cent of the total body surface area, whereas a leg, the front (chest and abdomen together) or the back each make up about 18 per cent, a multiple of 9. The proportions are only approximate and are somewhat different for a child under five years of age (see table 3.2). The palm of the hand and fingers make up about 1 per cent of the body surface area, so that the extent of the burn may be measured approximately by the number of "hands" required to cover it.

The severity and mortality of burns

As a rough guide, third degree burns of less than 5 per cent of the body surface area may be regarded as light, while those of more than 10 per cent, or first and second degree burns of more than 30 per cent, are regarded as severe. In addition, any third degree burns affecting the face, hands,[5] feet and genitalia are classified as severe, as well as circumferential

[5] Burns of the hands account for approximately one-third and burns of the face for approximately one-quarter of all burns (Tubiana, Baux & Kenesi, 1967; Converse, 1967; Kovaric, Aaby, Hamit & Hardway, 1969). See table 3.10.

Table 3.2. Methods of calculating approximate extent of burns over body surface

Per cent

Area of body surface	Surface area formulae		Rule of nines
	Adult or child over 5 yrs of age	Child under 5 yrs of age	
Head	6	15	9
Anterior trunk	18	18	9×2=18
Posterior trunk	20	20	9×2=18
Both upper arms	7.5 ⎫		
Both forearms	6.0 ⎬ 18	18	9 each=18
Both hands	4.5 ⎭		
Both thighs, incl buttocks	19	13	9 each=18
Both legs	13.0 ⎫ 19	10 ⎫ 16	9 each=18
Both feet	6.0 ⎭	6 ⎭	

Source: Phillips and Constable (undated).

deep burns of the limbs which affect the circulation to the extremities. Arturson (1966) adds to the category of severe burns those which are complicated in the following ways: (*a*) soft tissue wounds and skeletal damage; (*b*) complications of the respiratory passage; (*c*) electrical burns; (*d*) simultaneous radiation injury, and (*e*) burn wounds due to white phosphorus, mustard gas or other chemicals.

First degree burns have no significant mortality. Superficial second degree burns, however extensive, are rarely fatal if some medical care, such as that sufficient to maintain an adequate fluid intake in a hot climate, is available. The percentage of deep second degree and third degree burns in a given individual can be combined for practical purposes in estimating probable mortality, although the mortality from the third degree burn will generally be greater. With *adequate* treatment, deep second and third degree burns of less than 15 per cent are unlikely to cause death, whereas burns of over 50 per cent often do (cf. Bull & Squire, 1949). With ideal treatment young adults with burns of up to 85 per cent of the body, including 70 per cent full thickness burn, have survived (Birke, Liljedahl & Nylén, 1970).

In general, there is a statistical relationship between the extent of the burn and the mortality, which is shown in figure 3.3. The sigmoid relationship has been noted by a number of authors, such as Clarkson & Lawrie (1946). It implies that even for relatively mild burns (e.g. 5–15 per cent in adults aged 15–44 years) a few individuals less able to withstand the physiological stresses resulting from burning will die. A similar relationship has been noted in the case of some other biological phenomena, such as the relationship between mortality and the dose of toxic drugs (cf. Gaddum, 1933). Acceptance of the idea of a sigmoid relationship be-

Figure 3.3. Characteristic relationship between mortality and severity of burn[a]

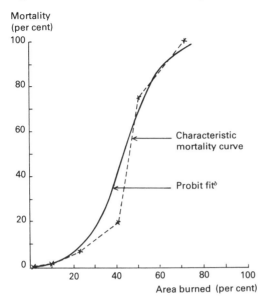

[a] The figure illustrates the typical relationship between the percentage of patients dying (the mortality) and the average area of the body surface burned, which is a measure of the severity of the burn. The data are averages drawn from various groups of patients between 15 and 44 years old (total sample=311 patients).
[b] The real data approximate to an ideal curve indicated by the probit fit. It is assumed that the larger the number of data, and consequently the larger the number of points it is possible to plot, the more the actual data would approach the ideal sigmoid distribution.
Source: Bull & Squire (1949).

tween mortality and burn severity is of great clinical importance, since it suggests that in theory some probability of survival remains even for the most seriously burned patient.

This . . . is preferable to the old idea that a burn of a certain proportion of the body surface was necessarily fatal. If each burned patient is regarded as having a chance of recovery, every effort will be made to help by means of treatment (Bull & Squire, 1949, p. 171).

A mathematical method of analysis, known as probit analysis, was set out by Bliss (1938), among others, and developed by Finney (1947). The method was first applied to burn data by Bull & Squire (1949) and is now common practice.[6] It enables estimates to be made of the severity of a burn likely to produce any level of mortality. For instance, in Bull & Squire's original data (figure 3.4) a 51 per cent burn in the 0–14 age group was likely to

[6] Bull & Squire (1949) described the rationale for this method and constructed an actuarial table from their data for the probability of death (the mortality risk) for an individual of given age and area of burn. Bull & Fisher (1954) published revised estimates for calculating the mortality risk which have since been used as a standard of comparison with other studies.

Table 3.3. LA$_{50}$ for some large treatment series

Age (years)	Baxter & Shires (1968) saline	Bull & Fisher (1954)	Bull (1971) before AgNo$_3$, 1944–64	Bull (1971) after AgNO$_3$, 1965–70	Pruitt et al. (1964) before sulpha-mylon, 1950–60	Birke & Liljedahl (1968) dextran group A, 1954–59	Birke & Liljedahl (1968) plasma group B, 1960–66
under 15	36	49	48	64	49	45	75
15–44	27	46	47	56	56	43	64
45–64	23	27	29	40	29	36	54
over 65	7	10	10	17		23	30

Source: Birke & Liljedahl (1971).

produce death in 50 per cent of the patients treated. The great advantage of this method is that it enables an assessment of the effectiveness of treatment to be made by comparing the *actual mortality* with the *predicted mortality* from the probit analysis. Further, Bull & Squire suggested that

just as the toxicity of a drug is best expressed in terms of the dose needed to kill 50 per cent of a batch of experimental animals (usually known as the Lethal Dose of 50 per cent or L.D. 50), so we may assess the treatment of a series of burned patients in terms of the area of burn producing death in 50 per cent of cases (i.e. Lethal Area for 50 per cent, or L.A. 50) (Bull & Squire, 1949, pp. 166–167).

That is, the greater the LA$_{50}$, the more successful the means of treatment. Table 3.3 shows the results of a series of studies by different authors, some of which indicate progress in the treatment of burns as new methods were introduced.

The influence of age on mortality

The age of the patient is a major factor in the mortality of burns, with the elderly surviving burns less effectively (see figure 3.5). A *very* rough rule for adult patients is that if the age of the patient and the percentage of the body surface area burned added together exceed 100 then survival is unlikely. For example, a 50-year-old patient with a 40 per cent burn may hope to survive; an 80-year-old patient with a 25 per cent burn is unlikely to do so.

In the mortality data provided by Bull & Squire (1949), all children within the age group 0–14 were classified together, and these data indicated a relatively good capacity to survive burn injuries (see figure 3.4). Other authors, by contrast, believe that very young children have less ability to survive burns than do young adults. Data provided by Pruitt, Tumbusch, Mason & Pearson (1964) confirm such a view, and these authors suggest a possible explanation.

The present data on the younger age groups (0–4 and 0–14) . . . would suggest that these younger groups are able to withstand burn injury of up to 30 per cent of the body surface virtually as well as the older groups. Beyond that level, how-

Figure 3.4. Typical mortality curves (deaths in per cent) for burned patients according to age and extent of burn[a]

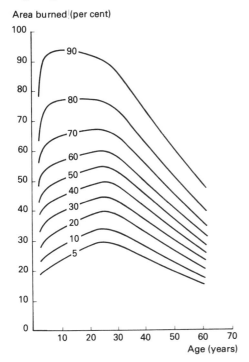

Area burned (per cent)

Age (years)

[a] Data from 1100 patients treated at the US Army Surgical Research Unit, 1950–1960.

Source: Pruitt, Tumbusch, Mason & Pearson (1964).

ever, this group appears significantly less able to withstand comparable percentage area burns. The large area to weight ratio in children may explain this greater effect in terms of mortality of the larger burns in the younger group (Pruitt *et al.*, 1964, pp. 399–400).

The higher susceptibility to burns of very young children is also reported by Winterscheid & Merendino (1960) and Rittenbury, Madox, Schmidt, Ham & Haynes (1966).

Similarly it is well known that older patients tolerate a burn wound very poorly (Moyer, 1954). In one large series, no patient over 65 years with a burn of 25 per cent of the body surface area survived, and as many as 18 per cent of the older patients died with burns of only 4 per cent or less (Rittenbury *et al.*, 1966).

This means that the young adult of military age and standard of fitness is more able to withstand the physiological stresses of the severe burn than the young child or the elderly person. Because of the difference in the age distribution, it is clear that a sample of the general civilian population subjected to burns risks a greater proportion of deaths than a military sample of the same size.

The time taken to die

An important consideration in evaluating the suffering resulting from different weapons is the time taken to die. If a victim is going to die he will in general suffer less if he dies immediately than if he dies slowly. The implication of the legal expression that weapons should not "render death inevitable" is that weapons, where they do not kill immediately, should offer the wounded person a high probability of recovery.

So many factors are involved in different wounds that it is difficult to make meaningful comparisons. However, there are indications that, where adequate medical facilities are available, simple penetrating and blast wounds in general approach the above humanitarian criterion. For example, a study of 45 094 US Army casualties in Viet-Nam between 1965 and 1967 showed that 5 387 (11.9 per cent) were killed in action, 623 (1.4 per cent) died of wounds, and 39 707 (88.1 per cent) survived. Of those who died of wounds in hospital, 62.3 per cent died within the first 24 hours, and it was concluded that a high proportion of these early deaths represented casualties which, in previous wars without highly effective helicopter evacuation, would have been classified as "killed in action". Of the wounded in action 43.3 per cent were returned to duty within the theatre of operations within 30 days and 54.2 per cent were evacuated for further treatment (Whelan, Burkhalter & Gomez, 1968). These figures indicate that, while conventional weapons are by no means "perfect", nevertheless, death tends to be relatively rapid *or* the chances of recovery relatively good.

There are indications that burn wounds, by contrast, conform less to such a humanitarian criterion. While there is little doubt that war burns have a high early mortality, in many cases death may not ensue for days or even weeks. Ironically, the better the treatment available, the more drawn-out the period of dying may be. That there is evidence to support such a conclusion may be seen from the following surveys.

Fifty-one girls of the Hijiyama High School in Hiroshima, Japan, were outdoors in the school grounds, less than one kilometre from the explo-

Table 3.4. Day of death of 51 girls, at the Hijiyama High School, Hiroshima, Japan, who received severe burns from the atomic bomb explosion

Day after the explosion	Daily death rate of the 51 girls
1	10
2	7
3	15
4	9
5	4
6	5
7	1

Source: Oughterson & Warren (1956).

Table 3.5. Average day of death from burns in a five-year survey (1963–1967) of hospitals in Melbourne, Australia[a]

Hospital	Number of patients	Number of deaths	Average post-burn day of dying
1	195	16	17
2	123	10	11.4
3	119	19	18.8
4	144	20	20.9

[a] The original data includes a further 111 patients at four other hospitals. Only five of these patients died.

Source: MacLeod (1970).

sion of the atomic bomb. They were all severely burned, and mortality within one week was 100 per cent. However, only 10 of the girls died on the first day; the largest number died on the third day (table 3.4). At the Kameyama Hospital, also in Hiroshima, peak mortality from burns occurred on the fourth day, although another peak in deaths occurred in the third and fourth weeks, when complications, including those associated with radiation injury, set in (Oughterson & Warren, 1956).

In a recent five-year survey of eight hospitals in Melbourne, Australia, it was found that on average death from burns occurred 10 to 20 days after the injury, depending on the quality of the hospital treatment (see table 3.5). The author concluded:

Table 3.6. Day of death for severely burned patients in Stockholm, Sweden[a]

Case	Age years	Extent of body surface area burned per cent		Post-burn day of dying
		Total	Third degree	
1	22	100	98	11
2	38	95	90	7
3	34	95	75	20
4	60	85	80	32
5	57	80	75	9
6	47	75	70	13
7	44	75	70	10
8	75	70	70	9
9	64	65	60	6
10	58	65	60	14
11	74	60	50	19
12	74	45	45	15
13	79	45	40	38

[a] The original data includes an additional 50 patients, none of whom died. All patients were treated with the modern warm dry air method.

Source: Birke & Liljedahl (1971).

. . . 20 years ago 75 % of deaths occurred from shock in the first three days, [whereas] only the most severely burnt now die at this stage . . . although over recent years the interval before death has been prolonged, there has been little reduction in overall mortality (MacLeod, 1970, p. 776).

Birke & Liljedahl (1971) reported the time of death for a series of civilian burn patients in Sweden (table 3.6). In no case did death occur in less than six days, and even for patients with a very high probability of dying, death was in some cases drawn out to three weeks or one month. The (US) Brooke Army Medical Center (1972) reported that, for patients treated between 1965 and 1971, the average time taken to die was 14.9 days after the burn.

These indications are not conclusive, but they are suggestive of a significant difference between the time of death caused by conventional penetrating and blast weapons and that caused by incendiary weapons. It has not been possible to trace data in the public literature which would enable a clear statement to be made on this aspect of the problem, and further studies are warranted.

Pathophysiology of the surface burn wound

In this section the pathological effects of the burn wound at the physiological level are described briefly. It is important to understand that a surface burn is not simply a matter of damage to an unimportant area of the body: not only is the skin itself an organ of vital importance, as has been explained, but extensive burn wounds cause such extreme disturbances that the whole physiological balance of the body may be upset and major internal organs such as the kidneys, the heart and the digestive system threatened.

Two specialists on burns open a major article with the words:

Patients with extensive deep burns suffer the greatest trauma to which the body can be exposed and have profound metabolic disturbances that persist far into the course [of treatment] (Birke & Liljedahl, 1971, p. 5).

These general metabolic effects are the primary initial causes of death, and present the immediate challenge for treatment.

Physiological changes in the shock phase

The initial phase following a burn wound is usually known as the 'shock phase'.[7] Shock here refers to *hypovolemic*, or *oligaemic* shock, a physiological syndrome resulting from a reduction in the volume of blood. It should be distinguished from the profound mental and nervous effects

[7] The many uses of the term shock make it unsuitable for scientific use. However, the term is still widely used clinically and so it is used here. Simeone (1963) reviews the history of the term and attempts to combine semantic clarity with physiological complexity.

136

consequent upon severe injury or emotional disturbance, resulting from the release of hormones such as adrenaline and histamine into the blood stream which in turn affect the nervous system; such shock is sometimes known as *neurogenic* shock. Both kinds of shock may be present in the burn casualty.

Hypovolemic shock is due to the loss of body fluids by direct flow or by evaporation from the burned surface. In a severe burn, loss of water by evaporation alone may amount to four to five litres per day (Roe, Kinney & Blair, 1964). The reduction in the volume of circulating blood has profound effects on the heart and on the peripheral blood flow. Moncrief (1966) showed that in the immediate post-burn period, the cardiac output of experimentally scalded dogs was reduced to 43 per cent of the pre-burn level, and then further declined to 20 per cent of the pre-burn level, unless the volume of lost fluids was replaced. In order to increase the blood flow to the heart the peripheral blood vessels are constricted, greatly reducing the blood supply to other organs and muscles. Beyond critical levels, the reduced blood flow is insufficient to maintain the supply of oxygen to the heart muscle, and the heart fails. Cardiac arrest is followed within a few minutes by death.

Changes in the electrolyte composition of the body fluids

The site of the burn wound, where the tissue is destroyed, is surrounded by an area of partial injury. In the dead tissue, circulation of blood ceases but in the surrounding area there is increased permeability of the capillaries, leading to an increased flow of water, electrolytes, proteins and other constituents from the blood into the wound, from where they may be lost. The flow of liquids is indicated by seepage from the wound, swelling of the tissue (oedema) or the formation of blisters.

It is thus not only the volume but also the composition of fluids lost that is important since the salts, proteins and other substances which they contain are essential for the normal functioning of the body. Replacement fluids (see below) must contain not only large quantities of water but also balanced amounts of electrolytes, the exact amount and concentration being carefully judged in each individual case. Normally water in the body flows into the cells from the extracellular fluid by osmosis—the flow through a semi-permeable membrane from a weaker to a stronger solution. When water is lost from the body fluids, the concentration of the solution outside the cells becomes greater than that inside, and water flows out, leading to the death of the cells. Any fluid leaked from the wound will contain some sodium ions, and the kidneys remove some sodium too, unless the concentration rises beyond the level with which the kidneys can cope (hypernatriaemia).[8] Thus the burned person may suffer losses of sodium

[8] Hypernatriaemia may also indicate increased secretion of aldosterone, a substance secreted by the adrenal glands which causes retention of sodium ions and the loss of potassium. Aldosterone is normally broken down by the liver or excreted in the urine.

ions from the tissues, even though there may be a higher concentration in the (reduced volume of) body fluids.

The balance of potassium ions is affected somewhat differently. Potassium is normally found in a higher concentration in the intracellular fluid rather than in the extracellular fluid. When the cells are destroyed by heat (or by disease), additional potassium ions are released into the body fluids. Thus there may be an initial rise in the concentration of potassium ions (hyperkalaemia) following a burn. If the kidneys continue to function normally they will remove some of this additional potassium so that, as the tissues are reconstituted, there may later arise a condition of hypokalaemia, due to a shortage of potassium ions. In the first day or two of treatment it is usually unnecessary to replace lost potassium ions (Phillips & Constable, undated), but careful monitoring of electrolyte concentrations in the body fluids remains necessary for some time to avoid shortages later. (Table 3.1 records one death from hyperkalaemia, and four from hypokalaemia.)

Changes in blood protein levels

The major components of the blood are plasma—a fluid which contains dissolved salts, proteins (such as albumins, globulins and fibrinogen) and other compounds—red blood corpuscles, containing the red iron-rich protein haemoglobin, and white corpuscles, whose principal function is to protect the body against the invasion of microorganisms.

Extensive deep burns may result in the loss of as much as 20 per cent of the red corpuscles (Liljedahl, 1967). The red blood cells are broken down, a process known as haemolysis, releasing the haemoglobin into the plasma (a condition known as haemoglobinaemia), from which it may be extracted and be excreted in the urine (a condition known as haemoglobinuria). Removal of red corpuscles from the circulating blood may also result from local thrombosis—the formation of a clot of blood which occludes a blood vessel—in and around the area of burned tissue. Damage to the capillaries in non-burned areas as a result of thrombosis has been demonstrated experimentally by Arturson (1961) and by Birke and his colleagues (1960).

In addition to the loss of blood proteins by direct flow from the wound and by haemolysis, there are other large fluctuations in the levels of blood proteins, which appear to be related to changes at the site of the wound and to the greatly increased metabolic needs of the burned person. Since it is difficult to supply sufficient additional energy from external sources, the body turns to metabolizing its own proteins. The result is a severe initial decrease in the blood protein levels, which in severe burns may be reduced to one-half of normal levels (Liljedahl, 1967). Subsequently, muscle tissue is metabolized, and the patient's weight declines rapidly although the blood protein levels return to normal.

Changes in the kidney function

The kidneys have two major functions. They play a major role in maintaining the water balance of the body. Secondly, they extract a range of waste products from the blood and pass them into the urine which is then excreted. The kidneys consist of large numbers of tubules. In the first part of each tubule, known as the glomerulus, water and waste products are filtered out of the circulating blood. In the last part of the tubule some water is reabsorbed into the blood while the waste products and the remaining water are passed into the bladder as urine. These processes are regulated by hormones, such as those produced by the adrenal glands adjacent to the kidneys.

The decrease in the volume of the circulating blood, due to loss from the burn wound, haemolysis and thrombosis, induces constriction of the blood vessels which further decreases the flow of blood through the kidneys. In the initial postburn phase, the flow of fluids through the kidneys may decrease by 30–50 per cent. The amount of fluid filtered by the glomeruli is reduced by 40–50 per cent, while the resorption of water in the tubules increases as the body attempts to maintain the fluid balance. The higher concentration of waste products may block the filtering action of the tubules, hindering the excretion of waste products into the urine.

The frequency of confirmed kidney damage resulting from larger burn wounds varies between 9 and 12 per cent in various studies (Liljedahl, 1967). Electrical and extensive pulmonary burns are particularly liable to produce physiological disturbances sufficient to result in renal damage (Birke, Liljedahl & Linderholm, 1958; Birke & Liljedahl, 1966). Kidney damage in patients with extensive burns greatly complicates the prognosis, even where an artificial kidney is available. Mortality in these cases is high (Cameron, 1969).

Damage to the digestive system

During the initial phase of the burn injury the muscle wall of the intestines may be paralysed, suspending peristalsis, the normal waves of alternate contraction and relaxation which cause the contents of the alimentary tract to be propelled forward. This may be followed by acute retention of food in the stomach. Changes in the gastro-intestinal tract may cause ulcers, indicated by vomiting of blood and the passage of dark, tarry-coloured stools, due to the presence of blood chemically altered by the intestinal juices (melaena). Gastric and duodenal ulcers arise, in some cases in the surface, and in others, as deep, acute ulcers known as Curling's ulcers. These ulcers may result in dangerous haemorrhages and perforations. The pathogenesis of such ulcers is not fully ascertained although the most widely accepted hypotheses include the effects of histamine, steroids, shock, gastric acid, microemboli and endotoxins as possible causative agents (Friesen, 1950; Moncrief, Switzer & Teplitz, 1964; O'Neill, Pruitt & Moncrief, 1968).

Even in later phases of the burn injury, particularly where chronic infections of the wound develop, difficulties in digestion may create problems in maintaining an adequate nutritional state.

Changes in the hormone balance

The physiological stress due to thermal injury stimulates the production of a number of hormones, particularly those produced by the adrenal glands (Birke *et al.,* 1958; Feller, 1962).

Adrenaline, also known as epinephrine, is released by the medulla of the adrenal glands and stimulates the heart, inhibits the movements of muscle wall of the intestines, relaxes the bronchioles of the lungs and constricts or dilates the blood vessels. Noradrenaline secretion is also increased; this hormone possesses the excitatory function of adrenaline but not the inhibitory functions. The production of corticosteroid hormones by the adrenal glands also increases.

In some cases, however, the stress of thermal injury results in haemorrhage and necrosis of the adrenal glands, which in turn leads to a lack of adrenal hormones sufficient to cause death (Foley, Pruitt, Myers & Moncrief, 1967).

In the first hours after the wound occurs there is a large increase in the concentration of histamine in the blood. Histamine is a hormone which is liberated as a result of injury. It causes itching or pain, dilation of the blood vessels, reddening of the skin, lowered blood pressure, increased gastric secretion and may result in shock-like manifestations. The liberation of large quantities of histamine into the blood may be a possible contributing factor to gastric ulcers and to the general capillary damage evidenced in extensive burns (Liljedahl, 1967). Heparin has been used experimentally in the treatment of burns because of its strong anti-histamine effect. Heparin appears to decrease the size of the burn, shorten the healing time, and significantly relieve the pain (Saliba, 1970; Saliba & Griner, 1970), although its use cannot be prolonged since it interferes with the blood-clotting mechanism.

The problem of heat loss

One of the major functions of the skin is to prevent the evaporation of the body fluids and the loss of heat from the body. Apart from the threat of hypovolemic shock due to loss of fluids, the evaporation of each litre of water requires 580 kilocalories of heat (the latent heat of vaporization of water). Figure 3.5 shows that the rate of evaporation of water for varying areas of burn wound may amount to many litres per day, compared with the rate from the unburned body surface. In an attempt to maintain the normal temperature of the body, the severely burned person uses up large amounts

Figure 3.5. Rate of evaporation of water in three patients with 85, 30 and 25 per cent burn wounds compared with normal values, during first four weeks after injury

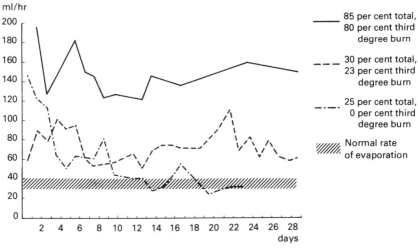

Source: Liljedahl (1971).

of energy. Some calculations of typical energy requirements are given in table 3.7. It will be seen that the severely burned person may use up to twice as much energy as normal just to compensate for the loss of heat by evaporation of water.

The increase in the basal metabolic rate as a result of burn wounds was reported by Cope, Nathanson, Rourke & Wilson (1943). Birke *et al.* (1958) showed that the basal metabolic rate may increase by as much as 100 per cent several weeks after the injury. This increased rate of metabolism

Table 3.7. Average daily rate of evaporation of water from burn wounds of varying extent and corresponding heat loss due to this evaporation, compared with the rate of water evaporation from a normal adult male

Area of third degree burn *per cent*	Loss of water by evaporation *litres/day*	Heat lost due to evaporation[a] *kilocalories/day*
20–40	1–2	580–1 160
40–60	3–4	1 740–2 320
60–90	5–7	2 900–4 060
Normal 70 kg male	approx. 0.85	approx. 490
Normal 70 kg male	basal heat production moderate activity	approx. 1 700 kilocals./day approx. 2 700 kilocals./day

[a] The latent heat of vaporization of water is 580 kilocalories per litre.

Source: Liljedahl (1971).

presents a major problem in treatment, since the severely burned person, who frequently develops complications in the digestive tract, has great difficulty assimilating sufficient quantities of nutrients to provide so much energy.

Where only simple medical facilities are available, it is a common experience that the severely burned person in fact uses up energy faster than he is able to replace it from food and as a result loses weight rapidly. Gestewitz (1968), for example, reports that for burn patients in North Viet-Nam, weight losses may be as much as 1 kg per day, and finally average a loss of 15 per cent of the normal body weight. This remarkable weight loss gave rise to the expression "napalm intoxification" and is very difficult to cope with except in the most advanced treatment centres.[9] Roe *et al.* (1964) showed that slowing down the rate of evaporation decreased the heat loss and lowered the rate of metabolism; this finding led to the method reported by Liljedahl (1967) whereby warm, dry air is pumped into the room in which the patient is treated. This increases the rate of evaporation temporarily, but the wound rapidly dries, and after two days the rate of evaporation, and hence the increased rate of basal metabolism, declines considerably.

Pathophysiology of "pulmonary burns"

In addition to the surface burns described above, fire may cause death or injury by various forms of damage to the lungs and respiratory passages. These injuries are often referred to as "pulmonary burns". Such "burns" have now been recognized as one of the principal causes of death by fire (cf. Phillips & Cope, 1962; Shook, MacMillan & Altemeier, 1968).

It was at first assumed that the victim of pulmonary burns actually suffered burns of the respiratory tract and the lungs, due to the inhalation of flames and hot air. It is now realized that the term is something of a misnomer; thermal injury of the lower respiratory tract is rare, since the flames do not pass beyond the nose and throat, and the heat of the air is rapidly dissipated before reaching the lungs. Only where steam is inhaled does thermal damage to the lungs possibly occur, since steam has a thermal capacity 4 000 times greater than that of dry air (Moritz, Henriques & McLean, 1945).

However, there is no doubt that pulmonary complications are a significant cause of death. In many cases, pulmonary complications arise as a direct sequel to burns of the face, nose, mouth and throat, or the inhala-

---

[9] Horn (1969) gives a vivid account of such a problem in the People's Republic of China: "At a time when he most needed nourishment, the patient's appetite started to flag . . . When this news leaked out the chefs of Shanghai's famous restaurants put their heads together . . . and sent a stream of delicacies to the hospital . . ." (p. 108). Ironically, the answer is not tempting dishes but the intravenous administration of an emulsion of soybean oil and egg yolk (see below, page 169).

Table 3.8. Major cause of death in 38 patients who died as a result of inhalation injury[a]

Autopsy finding	Number of patients who died
Pneumonia	15
Laryngotracheobronchitis	8
Burn wound sepsis	6
Respiratory tract burn	3
Pulmonary oedema	2
Atelectasis	1
Myocardial infarction	1
Cardiac tamponade	1
Gastrointestinal haemorrhage	1
Total	**38**

[a] The data are gathered from the hospital records of the 2 297 patients treated for thermal injuries at the US Army Institute for Surgical Research between 1956 and 1968. Sixty-six patients were identified with inhalation injury, and of these 38 died.

Source: DiVicenti, Pruitt & Reckler (1971).

tion of large amounts of smoke or fumes, particularly in a closed space. While the majority of such injuries occur in confined spaces, one study of 66 patients showed that eight patients sustained smoke inhalation injury from accidents that occurred in open areas (DiVicenti, Pruitt & Reckler, 1971). Mortality in these cases is very high. Of the 66 patients mentioned above, 38 died, a mortality of 57.6 per cent. This may be compared with an overall mortality of 9.6 per cent for thermal injuries treated at the same institution in the last year of the study. The major causes of death in these patients are shown in table 3.8.

However, pulmonary complications frequently accompany burn injuries even where immediate signs of inhalation injury are not obvious. A 20-year survey at the Massachusetts General Hospital showed that 88 per cent of burn patients developed respiratory complications (Phillips & Cope, 1962).[10]

Pulmonary complications take a number of forms, the most important of which are inhalation injuries due to smoke and toxic fumes, pneumonia and pulmonary oedema.

Inhalation injury resulting from smoke and toxic products of combustion is characterized by severe inflammation of the trachea and bronchi due to the chemical irritation of the mucous membrane lining these respiratory passages. This inflammation may lead to severe breathing difficulties. Clinical indications include the presence of carbon particles in the sputum, wheezing, hoarseness and coughing. Striking changes may be visible on a chest X-ray. The patient with inhalation injury is particularly susceptible to bacterial infection of the tracheobronchial tree (Pruitt *et al.*, 1970).

[10] This institution did not use mafenide acetate cream, which may lead to additional respiratory complications. See page 176.

Such injuries are similar to those caused by the type of chemical warfare agent known as the lung irritant (see chapter 4).

Pulmonary oedema most commonly occurs in patients with large burns, especially children and older patients, patients with associated renal failure, and patients to whom inappropriate amounts of fluid were administered at the time of operations performed in their postburn period (Pruitt *et al.*, 1970). Mortality in these cases is high, although it may be accounted for by the large average size of the burns and other associated factors. A potentially fatal lung oedema may occur with considerable rapidity, even quite late in the recovery period (Walder *et al.*, 1967). This in turn may lead to a weakening of the heart and decreased blood circulation. Continuous monitoring of blood pressure and blood volume is required so that, if necessary, early measures can be taken to prevent decreased blood pressure leading to irreversible tissue damage of the heart and other organs.

Pneumonia is a disease of the lungs resulting from infection by bacteria. The burn wound itself acts as a medium for the culture of bacteria which may subsequently infect the lungs either through the blood or through the air. In one study of 70 burned patients who developed pneumonia it was found that 23 (33 per cent) were infected by airborne bacteria, while 47 (67 per cent) were infected through the blood. In a subsequent analysis of 113 patients who were treated with an antibiotic agent it was found that 74 (65 per cent) developed pneumonia from airborne bacteria and 39 (35 per cent) from bacteria in the blood. Nine (13 per cent) of the patients in the first group, and 25 (22 per cent) in the second group, died (Pruitt, DiVicenti, Mason, Foley & Flemma, 1970).

The problem of infection

In spite of many recent advances in medicine, the prevention and treatment of infection—entering the body through wounds from whatever cause—remains a problem of great magnitude. Where advanced medical facilities are available, enabling successful control of the hypovolemic shock phase, infection is generally the major cause of death following burns.

The deep burn is an ideal site for infection (Artz, 1964). The moisture and warmth of the body provide a near perfect medium for the growth of a range of bacteria, which find abundant nutritive material in the dead tissue and multiply rapidly. Thrombosis and oedema in the tissue decrease the flow of blood and thereby inhibit the patient's natural defence mechanisms against bacterial invasion. For these reasons, all deep burns become infected to a greater or lesser degree. A large burn wound may contain thousands of grams of highly infected tissue, and organisms from this tissue may enter the blood stream or be breathed in by the patient, causing generalized infection, or septicaemia. When infection reaches this stage

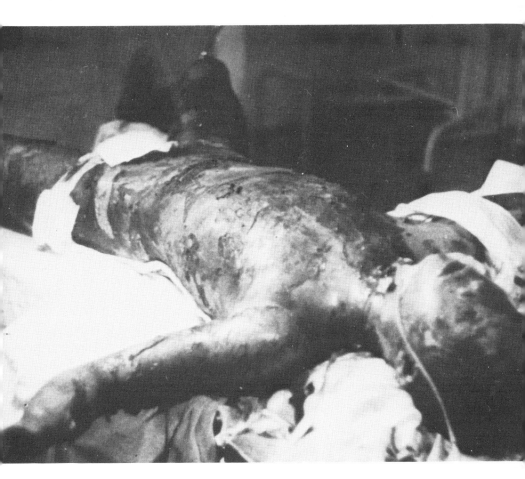

"The severity of a cutaneous burn wound depends not only upon the depth of the burn but also upon the extent of the body surface area affected, which determines the loss of body fluids and heat, and therefore the impact on the major physiological systems of the body." (p. 126)

"There is a direct relationship between the extent of a burn of a given depth and the chance of survival." (p. 128 ff)

"While there is little doubt that war burns have a high immediate mortality, in many cases death may not ensue for days or even weeks." (p. 134)

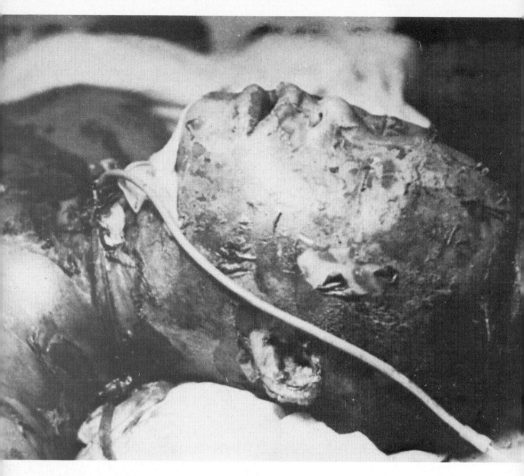

"There is no doubt that pulmonary complications are a significant cause of death. In many cases, pulmonary complications arise as a direct sequel to burns of the face, nose, mouth and throat, or the inhalation of large amounts of smoke or fumes, particularly in a closed space ... However, pulmonary complications frequently accompany burn injuries even where immediate signs of inhalation injury are not obvious." (p. 142 ff)

"Where there are signs of upper respiratory tract obstruction, large amounts of liquid in the respiratory passages or shallow breathing, tracheotomy—the operation of making an opening directly in the trachea ('windpipe') so that oxygen may be administered by tube—may be required. This should only be done where it is clearly warranted by the observed symptoms, since tracheotomy may be itself a factor in pulmonary infection." (p. 171)

"The severly burned person, who frequently develops complications in the digestive tract, has great difficulty assimilating sufficient quantities of nutrients (p. 142) ... Since it is difficult to supply sufficient additional energy from external sources, the body turns to metabolizing its own proteins ... and the patient's weight declines rapidly ...' (p. 138)

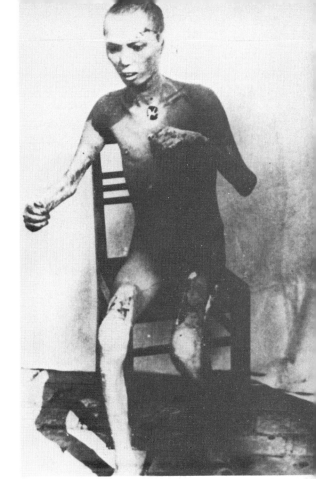

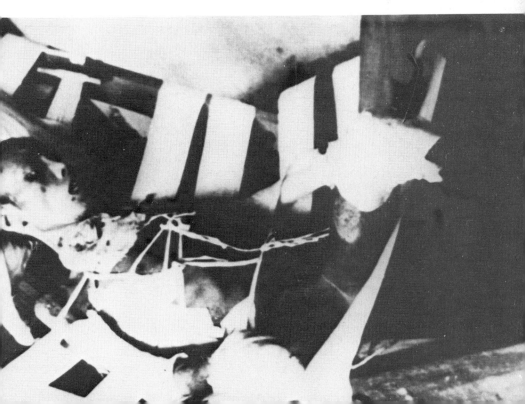

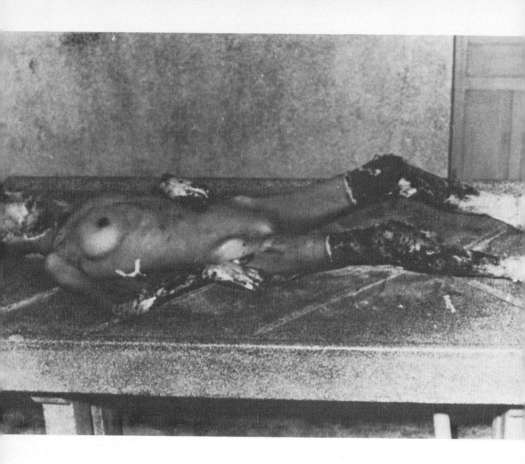

"Burns from napalm most typically occur on the unclothed areas of the body, particularly the hands, head and face, and feet and legs. Because of the thin layer of tissue over these areas napalm burns rapidly affect the underlying muscles, tendons and bones which greatly complicates the surgical problem. Reconstructive surgery to treat such conditions requires a long series of operations over several years and is unlikely to be available to ordinary people in most societies in wartime conditions." (p. 154)

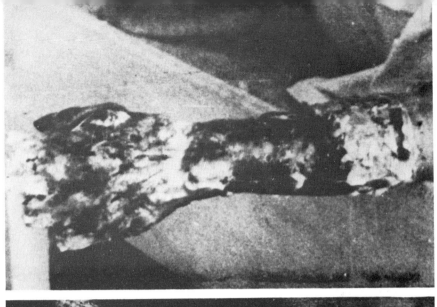
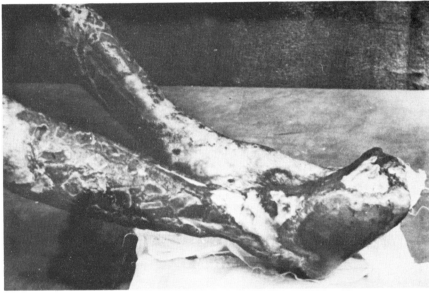
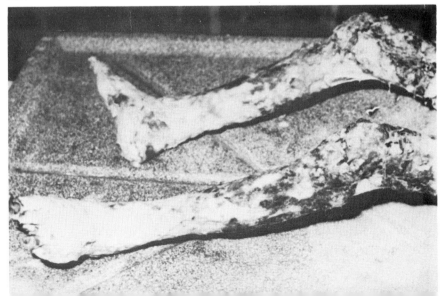

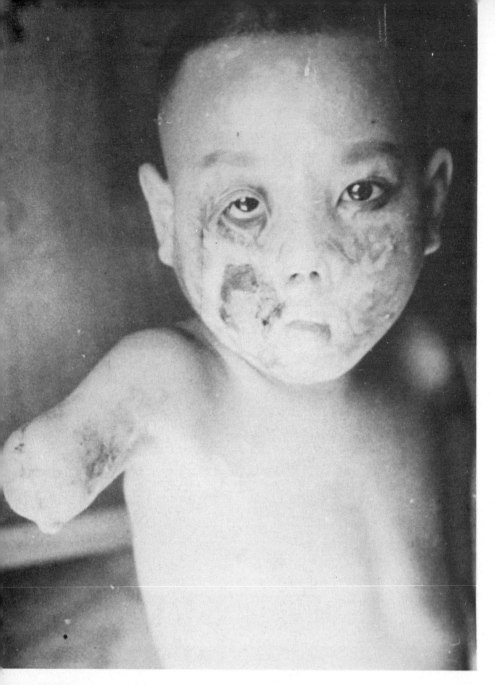

"Hypertrophic scar is ... thickened, raised and grotesque ... Keloids ... may progressively extend beyond the site of the original trauma ... Skin cancer is much more prone to develop in scars caused by burns than in normal skin." (p. 146*ff*)

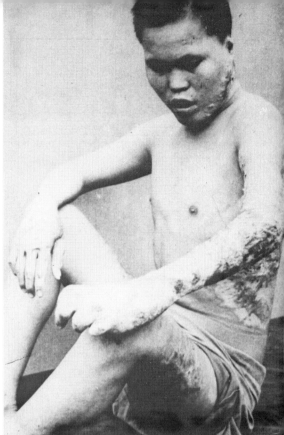

"All full thickness burns heal with some degree of scar . . ." (p. 146)

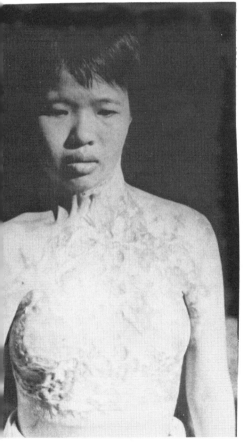

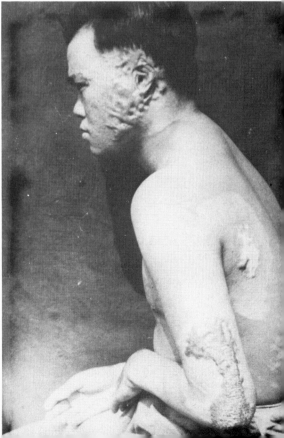

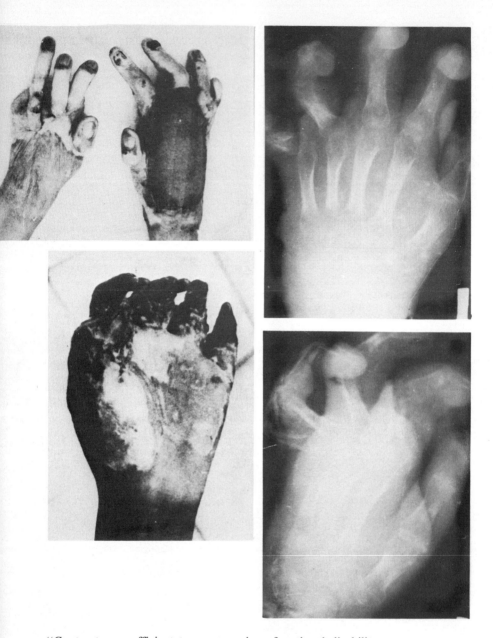

"Contractures sufficient to cause serious functional disability frequently occur in the case of deep burn wounds of the hands and the head and neck ... Burns in these locations are particularly common in the military context." (p. 147)

the chances of survival are not great. According to Moncrief & Teplitz (1964) over 80 per cent of late deaths following burns result from septicaemia.

Large burn wounds are particularly prone to infection because of the extent of necrotic tissue. Infection of clean mechanical wounds, for example those resulting from low velocity bullets, is relatively easy to contain. The bullet itself, or pieces of clothing or dirt carried into the wound, may infect it, but the area affected is generally restricted to the immediate vicinity of the bullet path. Dum-dum bullets and very high velocity bullets, on the other hand, cause an "explosive-type" wound, where tissue is damaged at a considerable distance from the point of contact with the projectile itself; and this type is much more liable to become infected due to the much greater volume of necrotic tissue acting as a culture medium for infective bacteria. Given that in general there is a direct relationship between the size of an open wound and the amounts of infective bacteria which grow, it is obvious that there are very large quantitative increases in the amounts of infection resulting from the entry wound of a bullet, which is less than one square centimetre in area, the exit wound of a high velocity bullet, which may be many square centimetres in area, and a burn wound which may, potentially, cover the total body area of approximately 1.5–2.0 square metres.

The nature of bacterial infection is highly dependent upon the circumstances and geographical location of the patient. In heavily populated and highly cultivated areas the likelihood of infection from grit and dirt in wounds is greater, a major factor to consider in combat conditions. A World War II study of the bacterial infection of comparable wounds showed that only 30 per cent of wounds incurred in the Libyan desert were infected with *Clostridium welchii,* whereas in France 80 per cent were so infected (McLennan, cited in Cope, 1953, p. 15).

The development and utilization of new antimicrobial agents during the past 30 years have resulted in changes in the types of organisms responsible for fatal infection of burn patients. Streptococcal and staphylococcal septicaemia predominated prior to the availability of antibacterial agents effective against these organisms. Since the late 1950s other organisms, predominantly *Pseudomonas aeruginosa,* have emerged as the principal offenders (Pruitt & Curreri, 1971).

Thus, the exact nature of the bacterial infection depends very much upon the circumstances in which a particular patient finds himself, including the type of treatment available. Whatever the cause of infection, however, burn patients tend to be particularly susceptible. This is due to the other effects of the burn on the body, including an initial loss of circulating antibodies and decreased ability of white blood corpuscles to kill bacteria, representing a decline in all of the body's normal defence mechanisms against infection (Liljedahl, 1967).

Disabilities resulting from burns

Severe burn wounds usually result in disability even after the wound has healed.

The disability following the healing of the burn is due to a number of factors. The most common ones are disabilities due to scar formation, to the development of keloids, to contractures in general, to lowered resitance to other diseases, to psychic trauma, to the development of unwanted emotional complexes, to inability to assume former roles in society, and the loss of strength and activity (Aldrich, 1943, p. 581).

Scarring occurs when the burn involves the full thickness of the skin and underlying tissues. All full thickness burns heal with some degree of scar. Skin grafts, if used, never perfectly match the adjacent skin and are surrounded with a rim of scar, especially if grafting is delayed or if infection prevents prompt healing of the burn. In a large burn these areas of scar are very extensive and conspicuous.

This scarred tissue may develop a number of abnormalities. Hypertrophic scar is defined as "a pink, white, or telangiectatic[11] scar which is hard, taut, unyielding, and more or less fixed to deep tissues" (Wells & Tsukifuji, 1952, p. 130). Although they may be thickened, raised and grotesque, they do not normally extend into undamaged skin, and if tension is reduced by releasing contracture, or if adequate skin grafts are applied, over the course of time they generally soften and become much thinner. Keloid is a term introduced by Alibert in 1806 and has been defined as "a movable, superficial lesion, presenting an exuberant, lobulated, overhanging profile, a glistering, inflamed or acrocyanotic[11] surface, a rubbery consistency, and characterized symptomatically by a prickly, burning itch" (*Ibid.*). Keloids are cumulative masses of scar tissue that may progressively extend beyond the site of the original trauma; characteristically, if keloids are excised, a larger keloid results. There is therefore an important surgical distinction between these two types of scar, although "difficulties in clinical interpretation can arise when one approaches the other in appearance or when the two extremes coexist in the same patient" (*Ibid.*). In addition there may be scarring which presents a raised or irregular surface, or a thickness greater than the surrounding normal skin, which is somewhat different again from keloid or hypertrophic scarring as defined above.

It is generally agreed that the incidence of such abnormal scarring depends upon the severity of the initial injury, the inadequacy of early treatment, the incidence of infection, and delays in healing due to mal-

---

[11] *Telangiectasis* (from the Greek *telos,* end; *aggeion,* vessel; *ektasis,* extension) is the dilation of groups of capillaries, forming raised, dark red, wart-like growths; *acrocyanotic* (from the Greek *akron,* extremity; *kyonosis,* dark blue colour) means discoloured blue or dark purple at the finger tips or other extremities, due to the presence of abnormal amounts of reduced haemoglobin in the blood.

nutrition or absence of skin-grafting and other factors (Block & Tsuzuki, 1948; Wells & Tsukifuji, 1952). Such factors may explain the high incidence of keloids following the incendiary and atomic bomb attacks on Japan, although some authors suggest that racial characteristics may also be involved.

A secondary factor is the known disposition for keloid formation to occur among the Japanese and other dark-skinned people as a racial characteristic. Many spectacular keloids, for example, were formed after the healing of burns produced in the incendiary bomb attacks on Tokyo (US Department of Defense, 1962, p. 570).

Keloids, which are extremely rare in the patient populations typical of most of the present-day medical literature, have been noted in Viet-Namese burn victims by Liljedahl (1967) and Constable (1973).

Wells & Tsukifuji (1952) noted a tendency for abnormal scars to disappear over a period of years unless provoked by infection, foreign bodies, such as retained fragments, contractures or abnormal skin tension.

Contractures are due to the restriction of underlying muscles and joints by superimposed scar or inadequate grafts. Contracture bands of fibroblastic cells are formed in the granulation tissue that builds up in the burned areas. These contracture bands may be very dense and can produce many untoward results. Contractures sufficient to cause serious functional disability frequently occur in the case of deep burn wounds of the hands and the head and neck, where they may cause hideous deformity. Burns in these locations are particularly common in the military context (table 3.9).

Disabilities such as contractures and keloids may not develop until weeks or months after the wound has healed.

If such disabilities interfere with the movements of the body, it is impossible for the individual to assume all of his former functions and duties. Frequently, contractures can occur around orifices of the body preventing or interfering with natural functions such as defecation, urination, sexual intercourse and even eating. Late disabilities are prone to produce a lack of social adjustment, thus having a direct bearing on the emotional stability of the patient (Aldrich, 1943, p. 582).

Such complications demand a long series of reconstructive surgical operations coupled with physio- and occupational therapy in order to produce a functional result. This process, spread over many months or even years, is both painful and stressing to the patient. It places great demands on hospital facilities. As a result adequate treatment may only be available to those able to call upon considerable economic resources and is least likely to be available to those most prone to such complications.

Further, it is a well established fact that skin cancer is much more liable to develop in scars caused by burns than in normal skin (Bang, 1925; Johnson, 1926; Treves & Pack, 1930; Lawrence, 1952). There is evidence that this is even more likely to occur where burn wounds have not been

Table 3.10. Location of military burn wounds compared with locations of wounds from penetrat[ing] and blast weapons: US forces in Viet-Nam, February–November 1967[a]

Wounding agent	Wound location (per cent)						Number of wounds per agent	Number patients
	Head and neck	Thorax	Ab-domen	Upper extremi-ties	Lower extremi-ties	Geni-talia		
Burns[b]	23.2	13.3	7.1	36.1	7.6	7.6	224	118
Small arms	10.2	12.8	9.8	25.8	38.6	2.6	1 093	882
Mortar	16.3	15.6	6.9	25.6	32.1	3.3	1 728	1 170
Mine	17.7	10.0	6.8	26.3	35.8	3.2	1 060	660
Punji stake[c]	0.0	0.0	1.0	9.0	85.0	3.0	65	65
Native[d]	11.8	11.8	3.0	34.0	36.0	3.0	68	44
Other[e]	27.5	19.4	5.5	26.4	35.6	5.6	1 339	1 014
All wounds	15.7	12.2	7.1	26.3	34.8	3.9	5 577	3 953
Normal per cent body surface	9.0	18.0	18.0	18.0	36.0	1.0	–	–

[a] The 3 954 patients in this survey were wounded in a total of 5 577 body regions, that is, an average c 1.4 per patient. The data do not include *killed in action,* because this category is not brought to hospitals

[b] Of the 118 burns patients, 68 (57.7 per cent) were victims of accidents rather than of hostile action.

[c] A fire-hardened, sharpened bamboo stake, concealed in foliage, which readily penetrates combat boot and heavy clothing, injuring lower extremities.

[d] "Native" refers to injuries resulting from such weapons as arrows and spikes.

[e] The large "other" category includes 398 non-battle injured patients; the remainder include patient wounded by "unspecified mechanisms such as knifings, phosphorus grenades, home-made bombs, blas injuries, blunt trauma, or otherwise unclassified type incidents"

Source: Kovaric, Aaby, Hamit & Hardaway (1969).

grafted at an early stage, when it may well be that, instead of healing, the wound becomes ulcerous for a period of months or years before becoming cancerous. Lawrence (1952) records 11 such cases, with periods of ulceration ranging from 4 months to 61 years. The latent period before the onset of cancer may be many years and is inversely correlated to the age of the person at the time of burn injury. For example, a person burned in childhood may suffer from a cancerous growth of the scar when he is 40 or 50 years old. This kind of complication is now rare where modern treatment facilities are available, but may be more frequent where such facilities are not available, for example in underdeveloped countries, or in industrialized countries following mass destruction.

Additional long-term pathophysiological problems result from the effects of shock and infection which may affect the kidneys, liver, heart and lungs, resulting in a permanent weakening of the individual's ability to resist disease, and facing the victim of serious burns with a further intermediate and long-term hazard. Renal complications, such as nephritis, may have a permanent influence on the health of the patient and his life expectancy. Prolonged infection which injures the heart may force the patient into a sedentary life.

Psychological effects of burns

The immediate psychic impact of the burn wound may be followed by intermediate and long-term psychological effects on the patient.

A number of factors contribute to a very severe psychological burden on the burned person (Hamburg, Artz, Reiss, Amspacher & Chambers, 1953; Hamburg, Hamburg & de Goza, 1953). The event itself, due to the relatively long time involved in inflicting a burn compared with, say, a bullet wound, is likely to have been particularly traumatic. Extensive second degree burns, where the nerve endings are bared but not destroyed, are excruciatingly painful, and may give rise to profound mental and physical disturbances.

The problems of combating pain and infection may themselves create psychiatric problems for the patient. Easing pain by the administration of analgesics such as morphine may create drug-dependency, and withdrawal from these drugs may cause additional pain and distress. Topical treatment with silver nitrate[12] to prevent infection causes the healthy skin to turn black; though this is temporary it may be an additional source of anxiety for the patient and relatives.

Particularly in the case of a child, the patient who is isolated and receiving only occasional visits by masked and robed hospital staff must also cope with resulting emotional problems.

With some trepidation we have permitted nurses on our Children's Burn Service to work unmasked. The psychological effect of masked attendents is undesirable, and thus far we have observed no evidence of a deleterious effect on the wounds by having the nurses unmasked (Phillips & Constable, undated).

The psychological problem of isolation is exacerbated by the more sophisticated treatment facilities and is most extreme where the patient is completely isolated and observed by television cameras and remote measuring instruments. The emotional strain of having to confront alone the sight of one's own naked and burned body lying on a bare plastic bed, and the stench of one's own rotting flesh, observed only by the cold eye of the television camera, is difficult for the uninitiated to envisage.[13]

In many underdeveloped countries it is common for the patient to be attended by his family, thereby gaining considerably in psychological reassurance and emotional support—factors which may be overlooked in advanced industrial societies. On the other hand, the limited methods of treatment available to the burn patient in most underdeveloped countries greatly diminish the prospects of recovery, thereby multiplying the attendant emotional strain that this implies.

The sum of the psychiatric effects upon the severely burned may be

[12] See page 176.
[13] The emotional strain on the attending personnel is also enormous and even experienced medical personnel have been known to ask for transfers from burn units.

149

overwhelming. At best, the patient with extensive burns will be seriously scarred in spite of all efforts at reconstructive surgery. Many of these disfigured patients, even in cases where function has been restored, will psychologically withdraw and never make an adequate social readjustment.

It is an unfortunate fact that little can be done to ease the psychological problem since it is to a large degree a function of the emotional shock elicited among the social contacts of the patient by his severe disfigurement. Burned persons may find themselves socially stigmatized, as in the case of the survivors of the atomic bomb attacks on Japan, whose keloid deformities resulting from burns rather than radiation mark them as *hibakusha,* a name connoting disease, defect and disgrace (Lifton, 1967).

III. *Casualty effects of incendiary weapons*

In this section a description of the known effects of incendiary weapons is given. In this connection, it should be borne in mind that the specific effects of incendiary weapons depend upon the circumstances of use, the quantity and types of agent used, and factors in the target population such as age, general health and nutritional status, degree of protection, and medical facilities available.

Metal incendiary burns

The metal incendiaries are characterized by high burning temperatures and the tendency to splatter small particles of molten or burning metal on the victim. These small particles may cause small but deep burns. Such burns are rare in civilian life; they normally occur only among workers in munitions factories and among persons subjected to incendiary bombing (Artz & Moncrief, 1969).

Magnesium burns produce ulcers which are small at first but which gradually enlarge to form extensive lesions. According to Wilson & Egeberg (1942) the deeper part of the lesion is usually quite irregular. Tissue destruction may be increased by the formation of small bubbles of hydrogen in the wound (US Army, 1968). The outer layers of the skin must be scraped under local anaesthesia soon after injury in order to remove the magnesium. However, depending on the size of the particles, magnesium may form a rapid or a slow burning ember. If the larger slow-burning particles penetrate deeper than the outer layers of the skin they must be thoroughly excised surgically (Artz & Moncrief, 1969).

Burning thermite produces particles of iron which at the temperature of combustion are molten. Thus, while not actually burning, the drops of molten iron are capable of causing small, deep burns until they cool and solidify. These particles must then be surgically removed. In practice the heat and flame from thermite close enough to shed drops of molten iron on a victim would probably have greater clinical effects, causing severe burns or death from hyperthermia.

Napalm burns

The thickened oil incendiary agents which are collectively grouped under the name "napalm" are intended to cause burns by means of direct adhesion of the burning agent to the body and by instigating combustion of clothes, houses, vegetation and so on. Burning hydrocarbon fuels are characterized by the production of thick, black smoke (carbon particles), considerable heat and a tendency to produce carbon monoxide unless there is very good ventilation. Thus the casualty effects of napalm are due to a variety of causes, the significance of a particular cause depending upon the circumstances of use, such as the quantity of the incendiary agent used, the amount of oxygen available, and so on.

These factors are illustrated in a pilot experiment by Moritz and his colleagues (Moritz, Henriques, Dutra & Weisiger, 1947). They concluded that exposure to burning hydrocarbon fuel in an enclosed space with good ventilation may lead to death within two minutes at 600°C and five to six minutes at 250°C. Death may be due to two mechanisms. First, systemic hyperthermia (heatstroke) results from the overheating of the blood during its circulation through the superficial network of subcutaneous blood vessels. Second, respiration is prevented by severe burning of the mouth and pharynx, followed by an obstructive oedema of the pharynx, trachea and lungs. Where there is bad ventilation, the hydrocarbon fuel will burn more slowly and may even go out. This results in a lower temperature than where there is good ventilation and there is therefore less likelihood of death from heatstroke. On the other hand, the bad ventilation increases the danger from carbon monoxide and other toxic fumes.

According to a US Army Field Manual, the casualty effects of napalm are as follows:

Personnel casualties result from a number of flame effects. First of course is contact with the burning fuel. Thickened fuel sticks to and burns hot on the target. It is difficult to extinguish, thus deterring the individual from accomplishing his combat mission. Casualties are also caused by the extreme heat (1 200°F–1 400°F). Inhalation of flame, hot vapours, carbon monoxide, and unburned hydrocarbons can also produce casualties. Personnel in a pillbox or other closed space will suffer due to the withdrawal of oxygen from the air. The shock effect of flame on the individual is great (US Army, 1960, pp. 3–4).

A Swedish handbook states:

In addition to an increase in the number of burn wounds, war conditions also produce an increase in the proportion of burn wounds with associated injuries (soft tissue wounds, fractures, etc.) and burns with a special aetiology. As an example of the latter can be mentioned the typically very deep wounds caused by phosphorus and napalm. These agents also add the risk of systemic poisoning from white phosphorus and carbon monoxide, respectively (Arturson, 1966, p. 329; trans. from Swedish).

More specifically, the various effects of napalm may be summarized as follows:

1. *Heatstroke* (hyperthermia). Some evidence suggests that immediate death from napalm attack may be less frequent than has otherwise been supposed, since the short duration of the fireball (about 6–10 seconds) is too short to cause heatstroke. However, the air temperature close to the burning napalm rises to some 800–1200°C and persons exposed to this temperature for more than a very few minutes may die rapidly from heatstroke.

2. *Pulmonary burns.* Those close to the fire may suffer severe burning of the nose, mouth and pharynx within a short time as a result of breathing in the hot air and fumes. The physical damage to the tissues, combined with the oedema which this produces, obstructs respiration and may cause rapid death.

The dense black smoke from burning napalm and other incomplete products of combustion may cause *delayed* pulmonary oedema, even in persons not apparently burned by the immediate fireball or by direct contact of napalm on the body. As noted above, such pulmonary complications have come to be recognized as a major cause of death in peacetime experience, and very likely contribute at least as much to deaths from napalm attack.

3. *Carbon monoxide poisoning.* Hydrocarbon fuels, such as napalm, produce carbon monoxide when they burn. Where a victim is confined in a badly ventilated space containing carbon monoxide the proportion of carboxyhaemoglobin in the blood may reach a lethal concentration (66 per cent; see chapter 4). This circumstance is likely to occur relatively infrequently in the case of attack by napalm from the air, but relatively frequently where napalm is projected by flamethrowers into closed spaces such as pillboxes. The effects of carbon monoxide and other toxic substances are discussed further in chapter 4.

4. *Oxygen starvation.* Burning napalm uses up large quantities of oxygen, and in confined areas there is a possibility that the level of oxygen may sink below that necessary to support life (see chapter 4).

5. *Shock.* Shock due to the loss of body fluids is a function of the extent of the body surface area burned. According to Do Xuan Hop (1967), even when napalm burns do not exceed 10 per cent of the body surface area of the persons affected, shock conditions are nevertheless usual and serious. This may be due to the fact that hypovolemic shock is complicated by neurogenic shock as a result of the intense pain or fear, inhalation injuries and the toxic effects of carbon monoxide, benzene and phosphorus.

Gestewitz (1968) reports that 71.4 per cent of early deaths are due to irreversible shock or acute carbon monoxide poisoning.

6. *Burn wounds.* Napalm is spread in clumps of burning jelly, which may burn for up to some 10–15 minutes at temperatures exceeding 800°C, depending on the composition (see chapter 2). Beneath the clump of napalm, the temperature is relatively low, unless slag has been added to increase the downward heat flow. Unless the victim inadvertently spreads the napalm in an attempt to remove or extinguish it, napalm burns are typically round, with an area of inflammation and swelling around the burn and a less damaged area in the middle. According to Hashimoto (1971) it has been demonstrated that the tissues beneath the burned area remain above the normal temperature for five or six minutes after the fire is quenched. This causes further tissue damage and local thrombosis and necrosis spreads rapidly in the first hours and days, the wound becoming easily infected.

Because of the high burning temperature and extended burning time of thickened gasoline fuels, burn wounds resulting from them are typically deep and extensive. According to Do Xuan Hop (1967) and Hashimoto (1971) some 75 per cent of napalm burns extend into the subcutaneous tissue and involve muscles and bones in a further 10–15 per cent. The reports of Gestewitz (1968) and Hashimoto (1971) suggest that some two-thirds of the victims have total areas of burn of up to 25 per cent of the body surface area and one-third have burns of more than 25 per cent.

7. *Physiological complications.* The physiological complications of the burn injury as outlined above (pages 136–142) also occur in the case of napalm burns. The characteristic weight loss in the patient may be as much as 1 kg per day. In the Democratic Republic of Viet-Nam burn injuries have been reported as incurring weight losses averaging 15 per cent of normal weight (Gestewitz, 1968). This is due both to evaporation of water from the burned area and mobilization of the body's fat and proteins to compensate for the heat loss resulting from the evaporation. Such changes are likely to be particularly difficult to compensate for in patients who are initially undernourished and anaemic.

These metabolic changes are frequently complicated by injury to the kidneys and liver, gastric ulcers, decreases in the blood protein levels, disturbances of the hormone balance, psychiatric disturbances, and so on, as described above. Such developments are particularly likely where only limited medical facilities are available, as in many of the combat situations where napalm weapons have been used.

8. *Infection.* The area of dead tissue caused by the burn is easily infected. Sepsis of the wound may extend the depth of the necrotic tissue, converting a less serious burn into a full thickness injury. Due to the general decline in the patient's physiological and nutritional status as a result of the burn, infection is particularly liable to develop rapidly from local sepsis to generalised septicaemia, threatening the life of the patient. As noted

above, exceptional medical resources are required to prevent and treat burn wound sepsis, resources which are unlikely to be immediately available in an embattled area.

It may be concluded that the extensive tactical use of napalm in the Pacific theatre in World War II, in Korea, in Indo-China and elsewhere has resulted in a high mortality amongst the persons affected. Yet there is too little published information to enable an accurate assessment of the mortality to be made. Some authors have gone so far as to describe napalm as an "all-or-nothing" weapon (Dudley, Knight, McNeur & Rosengarten, 1968).

The common offensive agent is napalm (jellied petroleum) dropped from aircraft. However, this is an all-or-nothing weapon and just as it was not usual to be called upon to treat bayonet wounds in World War I or II (Taylor, 1953) it is rare to see napalm burns; in 3 months we did not encounter a single instance. (Dudley, Knight, McNeur & Rosengarten, 1968, p. 334)

Other authors, such as Do Xuan Hop (1967) and Gestewitz (1968), report on the basis of studies carried out in the Democratic Republic of Viet-Nam that 35 per cent of the persons affected died immediately, that is, within 15 to 20 minutes. (Unfortunately, neither author gives details as to the circumstances under which the victims were affected.)

Those who survive the initial infliction of serious burns are faced with a great variety of potentially fatal complications over a period of weeks or months. Do Xuan Hop (1967) reports that in addition to an average of 35 per cent immediate mortality, a further 21.8 per cent of victims die in hospital—a total of 56.8 per cent. After an investigation in the Democratic Republic of Viet-Nam, Gestewitz (1968) reported that 62 per cent of affected persons die before the wounds heal. Dreyfus (1971) says: "I do not have definitive statistics, but it seems that only about 30 per cent of those wounded by napalm and not killed outright can be saved" (p. 198).

The minority of victims whose lives are saved are faced with varying degrees of physical disability, characterized by ugly scars and contractions. Burns from napalm most typically occur on the unclothed areas of the body, particularly the hands, head and face, and feet and legs. Because of the thin layer of tissue over these areas, napalm burns rapidly affect the underlying muscles, tendons and bones which greatly complicates the surgical problem. Reconstructive surgery to treat such conditions requires a long series of operations over several years and is unlikely to be available to ordinary people in most societies in wartime conditions. Thus, in the Democratic Republic of Viet-Nam,

a limited number of gravely burned persons can be treated in a general hospital, especially those in Hanoi, but the majority of victims are treated in the village maternity infirmaries and the district hospitals where skin grafting is not possible. Instead of grafting, wounds are left to heal by slow skin extension from the wound periphery. (Dreyfus, 1971, p. 198)

154

In these conditions, a wound which might heal in two months where grafting is carried out might take a year or more to heal without grafting. A child whose entire scalp was an open wound one year after the burn took place was observed by Constable (personal communication) in a South Viet-Namese hospital. Do Xuan Hop (1967) reported that with the treatment facilities available in North Viet-Nam at that time, 67.1 per cent of wounds in survivors healed within 3 months, 19.8 per cent between 3 and 6 months, and 13.1 per cent took longer than 6 months to heal.[14]

Dreyfus (1971) sums up the situation of the surviving casualty of napalm attack as follows:

Poor grafting also leaves serious after-effects. Retractile skin and contraction of scars form huge welts which will need further treatment. Keloid and hypertrophic scars will form to limit and inhibit the normal elasticity of the skin, which in turn inhibits the normal movements of the member. These scars are prone to pyodermic and microdermic infections. The new skin is extremely fragile, and sclero-atrophied skin will always be susceptible to minor infections that a normal skin would easily combat.

Lastly, concerning the medical effects of napalm recovery, there is the spectre of secondary cancers. Old burn scars show a frequency of skin cancer out of proportion to such appearance in normal skin. This cancer consists of spino-cellular epithelioma with a negative prognosis because of the rapid invasion by the malignant cells of the related ganglion areas.

Though some of the victims may partially recuperate after long and costly treatment, nothing much can be done for the majority of napalm-burned persons. (Dreyfus, 1971, pp. 198–99)

Compared with single penetrating weapons such as low velocity bullets, napalm must be regarded as an exceptionally cruel weapon. There is also fragmentary evidence that a higher proportion of casualties die from napalm burns compared with projectile injuries, that the advent of death is more prolonged, and that rehabilitation of the survivor is more difficult. If this is so, then napalm may also be regarded as more "effective" from a military point of view. Since no comparative study has appeared in the public literature any judgement as to whether the excessive cruelty can be justified by the claim of military necessity is likely to be subjective.

White phosphorus burns

White phosphorus has been used extensively as a smoke, incendiary and anti-personnel weapon in small arms ammunition, grenades, artillery shells, rockets, bombs, and antipersonnel mines.

[14] Of 3 977 admissions due to burns and scalds (all causes) amongst British troops during World War I, 76.87 per cent were hospitalized for less than 3 months, 6.61 per cent for between 3 and 6 months, and 1.97 per cent for more than 6 months (Mitchell & Smith, 1931). It seems likely that the figures reported by Do Xuan Hop reflect both the depth of napalm burns compared with many other burns, and the limited medical facilities available in the Democratic Republic of Viet-Nam, particularly for long-term surgical treatment.

White phosphorus burns have certain characteristics. Because the particles of white phosphorus are usually distributed by an explosive charge, these particles may penetrate deeply into the skin. Secondly, the phosphorus may continue to burn for hours, and in some cases days, until it is neutralized by some means. For these reasons, phosphorus burns tend to be made up of small, deep lesions.

During World War II there were several reports of deaths from the toxic action of white phosphorus contained in tracer bullets (Rabinowitch, 1943; Cope, 1953), which made up 2 per cent of all missile wounds (C. G. Rob, in Porritt, 1953). Porritt (1953) reported:

Wounds due to incendiary or tracer bullets need special management because the phosphorus they contain causes chemical destruction of the tissues, early and progressive shock, and a risk of fatal hepatic and renal damage if not removed early (Porritt, 1953, p. 29).

The 30-lb incendiary bombs dropped by the British on Germany contained white phosphorus, and Bauer (cited in Bond, 1946) reported that "not only laymen but also doctors called every burn a phosphorus burn". However, Bauer states that "no cases have been reported in which organic damage resulting from the absorption of phosphorus through the skin could be proved".

Thirty years ago any toxicity of phosphorus in burns would probably not have been observed since severely burned patients usually died. Since World War II, the treatment of burns has improved considerably, with the result that the death rate in the best modern conditions has decreased. With this decline in mortality the severity of white phosphorus burns compared with wounds from other burning substances has become apparent from a number of recent studies. Because of its importance the question of the toxicity of white phosphorus weapons is discussed in depth in chapter 4, while this section is restricted to a description of the burn wounds resulting from these weapons.

Many authors distinguish between thermal burns, due to heat and flame, and chemical burns, due to the action of a chemical substance on the skin. This terminology is ambiguous, since the production of heat and flame is the result of a chemical reaction. Nevertheless, for clinical purposes it is useful to make the distinction since, in general, flames must be extinguished by the exclusion of oxygen, whereas chemical substances must be neutralized or diluted.

In the case of white phosphorus burns initial injury is largely "thermal" rather than "chemical", but elemental phosphorus, or phosphorus compounds produced in the wound, may be responsible for subsequent complications. For this reason, most authors classify white phosphorus burns as chemical rather than purely thermal (for example, Curreri, Asch & Pruitt, 1970).

156

The principal difference between thermal and chemical burns, including white phosphorus burns, is the length of time during which tissue destruction continues, since the chemical agent continues to cause damage until inactivated by reaction with the tissue, neutralizing agents or dilution with water (Curreri, Asch & Pruitt, 1970). White phosphorus tends to burn its way through the skin and, even days after the original injury, spontaneously igniting particles may be found deep in the wound (Jones, Peters & Gasior, 1968). That is, white phosphorus burns are usually of second or third degree. These burns are most frequently localized on the arm, hand, thigh, lower leg and head. Because phosphorus is lipid soluble it spreads rapidly through the fatty tissue underlying the dermis (Summerlin, Walder & Moncrief, 1967) and the phosphorus-derived acids produced in the wound may cause further tissue damage (Rabinowitch, 1943).

The most frequent complications are contractures of the joints with resultant functional loss. Injuries to the head lead to a significantly high incidence of eye complications. Other complications such as inflammation of the cartilage of the ears, gangrene of the fingers and pneumonia can be observed in 10 per cent or more of the patients (Curreri et al., 1970).

The estimation of burn depth by clinical observation following chemical injury is difficult. The severe full thickness chemical burn may appear deceptively superficial with only a greyish-brown discolouration of intact skin during the first few days (Curreri et al., 1970).

Surveying the surgical literature resulting from World War II, Cope (1953) reported cases of wounds caused by explosive bullets which deposited phosphorus in deeper tissues. Healing of these wounds was slower than normal (Cope, 1953, p. 308).

During World War II phosphorus was used in bombs as well as in bullets and shells. Cope (1953) records the case of two children injured while playing with an unexploded phosphorus bomb:

The two children, aged 7 and 8 were accidentally burned while playing with a phosphorus bomb on July 27, 1943 . . . Child A had extensive second degree burns on the backs of the legs and thighs and a patch of full thickness destruction on the back of the left thigh about 4 in. square. Child B was more severely burned and had lost the skin from the greater part of the back of the right leg from the gluteal region to the ankle and on the left side from the gluteal region of the knee. She also had splash burns on the face and right hand and arm . . . The rate of healing was slow in both cases and multiple grafting operations were done but it was not until December of the same year that epithelialisation was complete. The scars which arose from these burns were in both cases keloidal and unstable. Active contraction took place necessitating re-excision and Thiersch grafting in one case and X-ray therapy in the other (Rooksdown House Centre Hospital account, cited in Cope, 1953, p. 310).

The longer time required to heal phosphorus burns was reported by Obermer (1943) and Sinilo (1961). This has been recently confirmed by Currieri et al. (1970), who analysed 111 cases of white phosphorus and other chemical burn patients admitted to the US Army Institute of Surgical Research during the period from 1950 to 1968.

The mean total body surface area of the burns was 19.5 per cent as compared with 28.5 per cent for all burn patients admitted during the same period, although the mean area of third degree (full thickness) burns was 10.5 per cent for both groups. The lower total burn area in the chemical burns was reflected in a lower mortality: 5.4 per cent compared with 19.3 per cent for the non-chemical burn admissions. However, longer hospitalization was required for complete skin healing of the chemical burns than for the overall group: an average of 104 hospital days compared with 74, or an increase of 40.5 per cent.

An average of 5.8 surgical operations per patient was required, 78 per cent involving homo- or autografting of third degree burn sites. Table 3.10 shows the 227 complications that were recognized in the 111 patients, the most frequent being contractures of joints (52 cases), and complications of the eye and eyelids (36 cases). Table 3.11 shows the distribution of the contractures which resulted.

Systemic complications such as pneumonia (10 cases), upper gastrointestinal bleeding (seven cases), septicaemia (five cases), acute renal failure (four cases), jaundice (three cases) and urinary tract infections (three cases) further complicated treatment. Systemic complications resulting from phosphorus burns may be due to hypovolemic shock, or to the toxic effects of phosphorus absorbed in the body fluids through the burn wound, to toxic effects of substances, such as copper sulphate, used to treat the wound, or to a combination of these factors.

White phosphorus burns from exploding munitions are often associated with other injuries such as lacerations, fragment wounds, traumatic amputation of one or more digits, and fractures of the long bones. Table 3.12 shows the distribution of such associated injuries in the US Army study.

In some cases particles of phosphorus may penetrate deep into soft tissue or into the chest or abdominal cavities. There is usually a need for radical debridement because of the depth of the penetration and it is extremely difficult to remove all the particles. US Army recommendations in Viet-Nam state that re-debridement should be planned after 6–24 hours, by which time the continued burning of previously undetected particles will have created more clearly circumscribed areas of burned tissue, enabling the particles to be located more readily (Whelan, Burkhalter & Gomez, 1968).

There is no doubt that burns due to white phosphorus weapons are extremely serious. Not only do they share the characteristics of thermal burns but the wounds take longer to heal. By continuing to burn in the wound, phosphorus presents serious problems of treatment and results in deep wounds which may require extensive surgical excision. In addition, the known toxicity of white phosphorus is a hazard which may result in complications such as kidney and liver damage, although published

Table 3.10. Classification of 227 complications following white phosphorus and other chemical burns in a total of 111 patients[a]

Complication	Number of complications	Per cent
Contracture of joints[b]	52[b]	22.9[b]
Ectropion	18	7.9
Chondritis of ears	17	7.5
Gangrene, one or more fingers	17	7.5
Cataract	11	4.8
Pneumonia	10	4.4
Ankylosis, one or more inter-phalangeal joints	7	3.0
Upper gastrointestinal bleeding	7	3.0
Corneal ulcer	7	3.0
Cellulitis or lymphangitis	6	2.6
Cutaneous abscess	6	2.6
Septicaemia	5	2.2
Acute renal failure	4	1.8
Infected fragment wounds	4	1.8
Osteomyelitis	3	1.3
Jaundice	3	1.3
Urinary tract infection	3	1.3
Others	47	20.7
Total	**227**	**100.0**

[a] Ninety-six of the 111 patients had wounds caused by white phosphorus, 5 by concentrated sulphuric acid, 3 by lye, 3 by mustard gas and 4 by other causes. Sixty-four of the injuries were sustained in the Republic of Viet-Nam. Fifty-nine of the 111 cases were due to hostile action, and 52 to accidental causes (of which 36 involved exploding phosphorus grenades, shells, bombs or booby traps).

[b] See table 2.11. below.

Source: Curreri, Asch & Pruitt (1970).

Table 3.11. Contractures resulting in functional disability as a result of white phosphorus and other chemical burns[a]

Location	Number of cases
Hand	11
Fingers	10
Neck	9
Elbow	7
Axilla	5
Wrist	3
Mouth	3
Ankle	2
Knee	1
Perineum	1
Total	**52**

[a] See footnote *a*, table 3.10 for explanation.

Source: Curreri, Asch & Pruitt (1970).

Table 3.12. Mechanical injuries associated with white phosphorus and other chemical burns in a total of 111 patients[a]

Type of injury	Number of injuries
Multiple lacerations or superficial fragment wounds	17
Amputation of one or more fingers	11
Fracture, open	7
Fracture, closed	5
Major nerve or artery injury	5
Penetrating wound of the cornea	4
Penetrating wound of the abdomen	3
Perforation of tympanic membrane (unilateral or bilateral)	3
Penetrating wound of the chest	2
Loss of teeth	2
Total	**59**

[a] See footnote a, table 3.10 for explanation.

Source: Curreri, Asch & Pruitt (1970).

research does not indicate clearly the extent to which this hazard is a major factor in battlefield casualties. The question is further examined in chapter 4.

Thermal radiation burns from nuclear weapons

No account of thermal effects of modern weapons would be complete without reference to the thermal effects of nuclear weapons.

Depending upon the nature of the weapon, the fraction of the nuclear explosion yield emitted as thermal energy ranges from 30 to 40 per cent at an altitude below 30 000 metres. The distribution of energy may be roughly estimated as in table 3.13. This thermal radiation is emitted as a pulse of extremely high energy of short duration. For a 1-kiloton[15] air burst, the effective duration of the thermal pulse is 0.3 seconds. For a 10-megaton air burst it may be as long as 30 seconds. Roughly speaking, assuming approximately one-third of the energy is emitted as thermal radiation, it may be estimated that for every kiloton exploded some 3.3×10^{11} calories are released in the form of thermal radiation (US Department of Defense, 1962).

It has been estimated that on the ground immediately below the Hiroshima bomb explosion, which had an effect of some 12.5 kilotons and took place at a height of 560 metres, solid materials were heated to about 3 000–4 000°C, and at 1 200 metres away temperatures exceeded 1 600°C. However, the thermal pulse from a nuclear explosion is so short that while some porous materials such as lightweight fabrics, paper and dry grass may ignite, wood may only char but not ignite. Surface temperatures are

[15] A kiloton is the nuclear equivalent of 1 000 tons of TNT high explosive; a megaton is the equivalent of one million tons of TNT.

Table 3.13. Distribution of total energy released by a typical nuclear explosion in air at an altitude below 30 000 metres

Source	Per cent energy
Shock and blast	50
Thermal radiation	35
Initial ionizing radiation	5
Residual ionizing radiation	10

Source: US Department of Defense (1962).

highly dependent on the reflective properties of the material: light coloured material reflects the heat rather than absorbing it, whereas dark material absorbs the heat.

Nuclear explosions may cause burns both directly and indirectly:

One of the most serious consequences of the thermal radiation from a nuclear explosion is the production of "flash burns" resulting from the absorption of radiant energy by the skin of exposed individuals. In addition, because of the focussing action of the lens of the eye, thermal radiation can cause permanent damage to the eyes of persons who happen to be looking directly at the burst[16] (US Department of Defense, 1962, p. 328).

It is estimated that 20–30 per cent of the fatal casualties in Hiroshima and Nagasaki were caused by flash burns.

In spite of the thousands of cases experienced in the Japanese explosions only the general features of flash burns have been described. These observations have since been supplemented with experimental studies using the skin of pigs which has many similar characteristics to human skin (Pearse, Payne & Hogg, 1949). In addition to being largely limited to exposed areas of the body, flash burns generally show a smaller depth of penetration than do flame burns because of the short exposure time (less than one second in the Japanese explosions). Severity of flash burns in Japan ranged from mild erythema (reddening) to charring of the outermost layers of the skin. Healing of burns in survivors was hampered by inadequate care, poor sanitation and general lack of proper facilities resulting from the general widespread destruction.

In addition to the primary effects of thermal radiation, nuclear weapons may ignite fires in two ways. First, thermal radiation may ignite combustible materials, typically paper, rubbish, curtains and dried grass, which in turn ignite more solid fuels such as wood, plastics and bitumen. Second, the blast wave can upset stoves and furnaces, cause electrical short-circuits and break gas mains. The outbreak of such secondary fires is diffi-

---

[16] A recent report of a group of experts convened by the International Committe of the Red Cross points to the fact that laser weapons, which are at present being developed (Meyer-Arendt, 1968), may have similar effects on the eyes (ICRC, 1973 a). An experimental study of flash-blindness is described by Chisum (1968).

161

Table 3.14. Comparative mortality due to heat, blast and ionizing radiation in first-day survivors in Hiroshima

| | Casualties by major cause of injury | | | |
	Heat	Blast	Radiation	**Total**
Number of survivors on first day	41 992	45 356	37 657	**125 005**
Per cent of total number of first-day survivors	*33.6*	*36.3*	*30.1*	*100.0*
Number of deaths on subsequent days	9 776	3 475	5 649	**18 900**
Per cent of all deaths	*51.7*	*18.4*	*29.9*	*100.0*

Source: Oughterson & Warren (1956).

cult to predict since it is dependent on the density of ignition points, humidity, wind and other prevailing conditions.

The secondary incendiary effects from a nuclear attack do not differ significantly from those due to a massive use of conventional incendiary and high explosive bombs.[17]

The incendiary effects of a nuclear explosion do not present any especially characteristic features. In principle, the same overall result as regards destruction by fire and blast might be achieved by the use of conventional incendiary and high-explosive bombs. It has been estimated, for example, that the fire damage to buildings and other structures suffered at Hiroshima could have been produced by about 1 000 tons of incendiary bombs distributed over the city. It can be seen, however, that since this damage was caused by a single nuclear bomb of only 20 kilotons energy yield, nuclear weapons are capable of causing tremendous destruction by fire, as well as by blast (US Department of Defense, 1962, p. 345).

According to Oughterson and Warren (1956), 45 000 people died on the first day at Hiroshima, while 22 000 died at Nagasaki:

Burns and blast effects were responsible for most of the effects on the first day, but since the effects were interrelated, it is impossible to know what proportion of deaths was due to each of them. However, all observers are agreed that heat was the major cause of death on the first day (Oughterson & Warren, 1956, p. 95).

According to the US Department of Defense (1962) about two-thirds of the casualties at Hiroshima and Nagasaki who died during the first 24 hours suffered from burns the effects of which were often augmented by other injuries, and there were many deaths from burns during the first week. It is estimated that roughly 50 per cent of all deaths were due to burns of one kind or another. Among the survivors after the first day, 65 per cent suffered from burns, 95 per cent of which were flash burns. The reason for the low proportion of flame burns among the survivors is that "most

[17] It is estimated that 83 000 people died in the incendiary raids on Tokyo. However, rather little has been published on the effects of the incendiary raids on Japan, in contrast to the wealth of material on the atomic bomb attacks.

of those who suffered flame burns did not survive, since they were caught in burning buildings and could not escape'' (US Department of Defense, 1962, p. 565).

In Hiroshima alone nearly 42 000 fairly serious burn cases were reported among the survivors of the first day. Of these, 23.3 per cent died subsequently, compared with 7.7 per cent of the 45 000 blast wounded survivors, and 15.0 per cent of the 38 000 ionizing radiation-affected survivors (table 3.14).

Thus there is good reason to regard the Hiroshima and Nagasaki bombs as largely, and perhaps even primarily, incendiary weapons, and only secondarily as blast and radiation weapons. Further, the exceptionally large casualty statistics which resulted indicate that incendiary weapons may be the cause of more serious injuries than either blast or radiation weapons. This conclusion is largely borne out by studies made of the casualty effects of the strategic bombing of German cities, described in the next section.

Mass casualties from incendiary attack

The air attacks on German cities during World War II led to the deaths of between 500 000 and 800 000 people.[18] Several reports were prepared on the causes of death in these raids, during which the British Royal Air Force dropped 196 335 tons of incendiary bombs and 234 312 tons of high explosive bombs (Harris, 1947) and the US Army Air Force a further 80 000 tons of bombs (US Strategic Bombing Survey, 1945) on German population centres—a total of 510 747 tons, or approximately one ton for every fatality.

The Medical Branch of the Morale Division of the US Strategic Bombing Survey published a report in December 1945 on *The Effect of Bombing on Health and Medical Care in Germany* which included a chapter on the nature of air raid casualties by Captain Franz K. Bauer. Bauer concluded in part:

. . . It can be stated that there is a definite relationship between the type of bomb dropped, and the type of death or injury to be expected. An incendiary raid was expected to cause more dead than wounded, through the effects of heat and carbon monoxide; in bombings with high explosives, mechanical injuries outnumbered deaths.
. . . In all the cities visited carbon monoxide poisoning was regarded as the primary cause of death or injury, sometimes reaching to as much as 80 per cent of all incendiary raid casualties. Air blast was found to be a relatively infrequent cause of death and affected only people within a radius of 30 meters from the explosion of a bomb (Bauer, cited in Bond, 1946, p. 113).

Bauer's report contains considerable interesting detail. It became apparent to leading German pathologists that the air war was leading to

---

[18] See chapter 1.

Table 3.15. Most prominent causes of death as a result of the incendiary raids on Hamburg, July and August 1943

Causes of death from external injury
1. Burial under rubble and debris and injury from flying fragments
2. Secondary injuries through explosions (drowning, scalding, chemical burns, poisoning from the by-products of exploded bombs)
3. Burns
4. Tetanus secondary to burns where no serum was given prophylactically

Causes of death from internal injury
1. Carbon monoxide poisoning in air raid shelters and occurring during rescue work
2. Effect of heat through conduction and radiation in the presence of very high temperatures
3. Overheating over a prolonged period of time through temperatures which, normally, can be tolerated for short periods only
4. Dust inhalation; blocking of the upper respiratory passages and inhalation, with damage of the small bronchi and alveoli
5. Carbon monoxide poisoning from bursting gas mains
6. Sudden heart death through fright and exhaustion in cardiac patients
7. Blast injuries in which external injuries may be absent or which may be masked by external injuries

Source: Conclusions of a meeting of experts called by the inspector of sanitary and medical matters of the Luftwaffe held in Jüterborg, December 1943; reported by Captain Franz K. Bauer, US Army Medical Corps, "The nature of air raid casualties", in US Strategic Bombing Survey, Morale Division, Medical Branch, *The Effect of Bombing on Health and Medical Care in Germany* December 1945; cited by Bond (1946).

causes of death which were not at first obvious. In 1943 measures were taken to ensure correct diagnoses. All persons with unclear diagnoses were subjected to autopsy: between 20 000 and 30 000 autopsies were carried out during the war. Physicians from the Luftwaffe were appointed to supervise commissions whose task was to study the causes of death. Prior to the establishment of these commissions a meeting of experts was called in Jüterborg in December 1943 to discuss the effects of the raids on Hamburg in July and August 1943. Their conclusions as to the most prominent causes of death at that time are shown in table 3.16. Several theories regarding deaths from anoxia, "carbon dioxide poisoning", "gas poisoning" (that is, "phosphorus gas") or from high frequency waves subsequent to explosions were disproven.

Additional studies after 1943 led to more understanding of the causes of death. In addition to mechanical injuries, only heat and carbon monoxide proved to be of statistical importance. In large-scale fires, deaths resulting from heat and carbon monoxide poisoning outnumbered those from mechanical causes.

The effects of heat were of two kinds in large-scale incendiary attacks such as those on Hamburg:

(1) The effect of direct heat of short duration through conduction or radiation with production of burns proper.
(2) The effect of high temperatures over long periods of time which did not immediately lead to protein coagulation, but which caused a syndrome identical to that of heatstroke. (Bauer, cited by Bond, 1946, p. 115)

Heatstroke depends on a number of factors such as the humidity of the air, the cessation of sweat production and the amount of heat to which the body has been exposed. In humid air heatstroke may occur at a temperature of 60°C and is not necessarily associated with subjective complaints.

This accounts for the many bodies which were found dead in rooms from which escape would have been possible, and which were in a position not suggestive of agony before death occurred (Bauer, cited by Bond, 1946, p. 115).

According to Bauer, police engineers in Hamburg estimated that temperatures in the burning city blocks rose as high as 800°C.

Literally hundreds of people were seen leaving shelters after the heat became intense. They ran across the street and were seen to collapse very slowly like people who were thoroughly exhausted. They could not get up (Dr. Helmuth Baniecki of Hamburg) . . .

Most of these people were not burnt to ashes when recovered, but dry and shrunken, resembling mummies. In many the intense heat had caused the skin to burst and retract over typical areas such as the elbow, the knee, the scalp and the orbit. Baniecki thought that the cause of death in these cases was shock. In approximately 80 autopsies he found all organs shrunken, showing venous stasis with increased permeability of the small blood vessels. . . .

Professor Rose, chief consultant to the Air Ministry, summarized the effects of heat. Besides immediate contact with flames, he wrote, the effect of heat through hot air as well as radiation of hot gases and from objects is important. This accounts for the severe heat changes in women who do not wear more than stockings on their legs, or not even stockings. In many cases, when stockings were worn, they were not even singed, although the skin and underlying structures were severely damaged. Radiation heat of over 225°C can inflame clothes and [hair]. Besides this local effect of heat, overburdening of the heat-regulating mechanisms of the body is important . . .

During escape from overheated shelters through burning city blocks, the danger was chiefly from radiated heat. The inhalation of hot air can cause severe damage to the respiratory passages such as ulcerous necroses of the mucous membranes. Whether this is a separate entity or the changes a part of the whole picture which leads to death is as yet unsolved. It should be kept in mind that the inhalation of dangerous gases or by-products or fire must be considered . . .

The degree of temperatures produced in incendiary raids gave rise to a question from the office of Professor Karl Brandt, commissar for sanitary and health matters for Germany. Professor Shuetz, a physiologist of Muenster, answered from the Institute of Aviation Medicine: The question concerned is the effect on the human body of overheating to 41°C for eight hours. The answer is: in the tissues increased temperature up to 50°C is followed by death of all cells, with subsequent vacuolization; higher temperatures are followed by shrinking and falling apart of the cells. According to Ludwig Aschoff, human cells die at 50°C, vesicles form in the tissues at 51°C, and haemolysis occurs at 60°C. Ganglionic cells are destroyed at 43°C. Animals die exposed to temperatures of from 60°C to 100°C in overheated rooms, usually in convulsions, after a few minutes to half an hour (Bauer, in Bond, 1946, p. 116).

Bauer gives the following description of the victims of the Hamburg attacks on 27–28 July 1943, taken from an account of Professor Graeff, consulting pathologist to the *Wehrkreis X* (military defence area) in Hamburg:

Many of the bodies were lying in the street half-clothed or nude. The only covering that they always had on was their shoes. The victims' hair was often burned, but preserved. A few hours after the start of the raid the corpses had a peculiar aspect; they seemed blown up, lying on their stomachs. The buttocks were enlarged and the male sex organs were swollen to the size of a child's head. Occasionally the skin was broken and indurated in many places and in the majority of cases was a waxen colour. The face was pale. This picture lasted only a few hours; after this time the bodies shrank to small objects, with a hard brownish black skin and charring of different parts and frequently to ashes and complete disappearance . . .

In the shelters bodies assumed various aspects corresponding to the circumstances under which death had set in. Nowhere were bodies found naked or without clothing as they were in the streets. The clothes, however, often showed burned out holes which exposed the skin. Bodies were frequently found lying in a thick, greasy black mass, which was without a doubt melted fat tissue. The fat coagulated on the floors as the temperature decreased. The head hair as a rule was unchanged or only slightly singed. The bodies were not bloated except for a few which were found floating in water which had seeped into the shelters from broken mains. All were shrunken so that the clothes appeared to be too large. Those bodies were *Bombenbrandschrumpfleichen* ("incendiary-bomb-shrunken bodies"). These were not always in one piece. Sleeves and trouser legs were frequently burned off and with them the limbs were burned to the bones. Frequently such bodies burned to a crisp weeks after death—apparently after oxygen had become available. In the same rooms with such bodies were found other more or less preserved or shrunken corpses and also some which had fallen to ashes and could hardly be recognised. Many basements contained only bits of ashes and in these cases the number of casualties could only be estimated (Bauer, in Bond, 1946, p. 119).

While Bauer makes no reference to death by asphyxiation due to the withdrawal of oxygen from the air, many survivors stated that the air "just didn't come anymore" and breathing became very difficult. In the shelters levels of oxygen fell so low that matches or candles would not burn, and people lay on the floor where, because of a higher concentration of oxygen, breathing was easier. Outside, in the city streets, the firestorm drew in a mass of fresh air with sufficient force to blow people to the ground.

According to Bauer, carbon monoxide as a major cause of death was a possibility which few had expected before the war. However, carbon monoxide deaths assumed such proportions that the high command of the Luftwaffe issued an order to examining commissions to procure statistical evidence of carbon monoxide poisoning. The question of carbon monoxide poisoning is examined in chapter 4.

IV. *The medical treatment of war burns*

In this section an outline of some of the problems of the medical treatment of victims of burns is presented. Such information is necessary for an adequate understanding of the humanitarian issues involved in the use of fire as a weapon of war, since prospects for casualties caused by incendiary weapons are particularly dependent upon the quality of the medical treatment available to survivors.

The treatment procedures outlined below explain what can be done for the victim of burns with the best facilities currently known to medical science. Even with such facilities, the treatment of the severely burned is long, tedious and exceptionally painful—a severe emotional burden on the patient and his family, and indeed, in many cases, on the medical staff as well. The complexity of a severe burn wound is such that exceptional medical resources are required to give the patient a reasonable chance of recovering a sufficient degree of functional ability to be able to perform normally in society. Even where an adequate functional result is obtained, scars and disfigurement often present a psychological and social barrier to normal social life.

The nature of many recent conflicts has meant that the medical equipment and expertise available to the conflicting parties has been highly variable. Many of the facilities required to treat severe burns are not available or are destroyed in combat. Such conditions are tantamount to increasing the "effectiveness" of the weapons employed, since a greater proportion of the victims will die or be permanently disabled. To this end, efforts may be made to reduce the medical support available to an adversary. Suffering will thereby be considerably increased. Due to inadequate treatment by skin grafting and associated surgical measures, a third degree burn wound may never heal and the patient will have to bear a permanently open wound as a continual source of infection, subsequently liable to become cancerous. By contrast, a wound caused by a low-velocity bullet or fragment may in general be treated by relatively simple means and the prognosis for the patient is not so vitally dependent upon the quality of medical treatment available, except when his major organs are damaged.

Because of wide variations in the facilities available no precise course of treatment can be described. The following outline refers to the best treatment possible but it should be borne in mind that such facilities are not available to a high proportion of the victims of incendiary attack.

First aid

It may be assumed that some form of first aid is available to the majority of war wounded, although it may be the only treatment available. The major points to note in first aid are as follows:

1. Where possible, flames should be "suffocated" by excluding air, for example, by covering them with a thick cloth. Where napalm is burning on the skin, great care should be taken to exclude the air by covering it without spreading the sticky jelly. Once the flames are extinguished, simple napalm will not ignite spontaneously. However, it may contain white phosphorus in order to reignite it in air, or sodium to ignite it in water. Phosphorus

fragments should be bathed in water or covered with a wet cloth until they can be removed.

2. To protect the sore from infection and further trauma, it should preferably be covered with large, sterile, absorbent dressings or, failing that, the patient may be wrapped entirely in a sheet, blanket or coat. It is important to keep the patient warm.

3. Particularly if he is unconscious, the patient may have breathing difficulties. The respiratory channels may be blocked by blood, saliva, vomit or the tongue. It is easiest to open the air passages with the patient lying on his side with the neck bent backwards. If the patient does not breathe spontaneously, artificial respiration by the "mouth-to-mouth" method or, if available, the administration of oxygen, may be called for.

4. In the event of great pain, which may contribute to neurogenic shock, analgesics such as morphine may be slowly (over a period of one to two minutes) injected intravenously for adults. Codein may be given to children for the same purpose.

Hospital treatment of burns

The hospital treatment of burn wounds is a specialized field of considerable complexity, enabling a certain variation in treatment methods (e.g. Liljedahl, 1967; Phillips & Constable, undated; Pruitt & Curreri, 1971; NATO, 1958). A brief outline of basic therapeutic measures is given to indicate the extent of the requirements for the adequate treatment of burn wounds.

The initial therapeutic objectives are:

(*a*) the prevention of shock,

(*b*) the maintenance of adequate oxygen supply in the event of respiratory complications, and

(*c*) the prevention of infection.

Subsequently attention may be given to the surgical treatment of the wound, to psychiatric care and finally to rehabilitation.

The prevention and treatment of shock

The first two to three days after the infliction of the burn injury normally bring fluid loss and oedema, leading to hypovolemic shock which is brought on by too little fluid in the body. Replacement or substitution of lost fluids is the obvious treatment.

The administration of fluid volume in shock should have as its goal: (1) an adequate blood volume based on the central venous pressure measurements; and, (2) a normal red cell mass, adequate protein and colloid, the replacement of deficiencies in extracellular fluid, the correction of electrolyte and pH abnormalities in the blood and supply of caloric requirements. No one fluid is adequate, but a combination of different fluids, tailor-made to keep a normal blood composition, is needed. Protein and other colloids are essential to maintain water in the blood and prevent edema. Whole blood colloids and electrolytes are all needed in proper amount and proportion. (Hardaway, 1969, p. 653)

168

Table 3.16. Typical replacement fluids for a severely burned adult during the first 24-hour period

Colloid (blood plasma or substitute)	0.5–1.5 ml × kg body weight × per cent body burned
Electrolyte (e.g. Ringer's lactate) solution	0.5–1.5 ml × kg body weight × per cent body burned
Metabolic requirement (5 per cent sugar solution)	1 000–2 000 ml

Sources: Phillips & Constable (undated); NATO (1958).

It is usual to administer fluids intravenously where burns exceed 10 per cent of a child's body surface area or 15 per cent of an adult's. These fluids have three main components. To compensate for the fluids lost from the wound, replacement fluids must contain electrolytes, especially sodium ions, and plasma or a colloidal solution made up of plasma proteins or a plasma substitute such as dextran.[19] The most preferred electrolyte solution is Ringer's lactate,[20] a solution of electrolytes resembling the electrolyte composition of the blood. Finally, because of the difficulties of administering food by mouth in sufficient quantities (due to the danger of the food getting into the lungs and causing serious complications), solutions of sugar (for example, dextrose) and fat emulsions[21] must be administered intravenously.

Typical replacement fluids for an adult during the first 24-hour period are shown in table 3.16. These proportions are calculated on the basis of body weight in kilogrammes. Because the ratio of body surface area to body weight is different in children, Phillips & Constable (undated) recommend a formula based on the area of the body surface of the child. For each square metre of the body surface area of the child, whether burned or unburned, they suggest 90 ml plasma and 10 ml saline per percentage of the burn.[22] In addition 1 500 ml water (by mouth) or 1 500 ml of a 5 per cent concentration of dextrose (intravenously) should be given for each square metre of the body surface area, whether burned or not.

In general an adult requires about 150 ml of electrolyte and colloid solu-

[19] Dextran is a water-soluble, high molecular weight (average 75 000) glucose polymer produced by the action of *Leuconostoc mesenteroides* on sucrose. It is used as a 6 per cent solution in sodium chloride in the treatment of shock.

[20] Ringer's lactate solution is made up of 5.7–6.3 per cent sodium chloride, 2.9–3.3 per cent sodium lactate, 0.27–0.33 per cent potassium chloride and 0.18–0.22 per cent calcium chloride.

[21] Fat emulsions were introduced by Wretlind (Schubert & Wretlind, 1961; Wretlind, 1962). A recent composition tried successfully by the US Army Brooke Medical Center contains soybean oil, egg yolk, phosphatides and glycerol, and provides one Calorie/ml. Single 500 ml units of the 10 per cent soybean emulsion were administered to patients over a 4-hour period through a forearm vein (Wilmore, Moylan & Pruitt, 1972).

[22] For example, a nine-year-old child, with a body surface area of 1.0 m² and a 30 per cent burn, would receive 1.0×30×90=2 700 ml plasma and 1.0×30×10=300 ml saline in the first 24 hours.

tion per percentage of the burn. Phillips & Constable (undated) recommend a ratio of five parts colloid to one part electrolyte, but the ratio depends upon the individual needs of the patient, the method of treatment and the availability of plasma or plasma substitutes. Due to shortages of plasma in the United States as a result of the war in Viet-Nam, many patients have had to be treated entirely with electrolyte solution (Ringer's lactate). Where electrolyte solution alone is used, no formula can be given and the amount is determined by urinary output and venous pressure as measured with a central venous catheter.

In many cases fluid therapy can be reduced after the first 24 hours, usually reducing the electrolyte and colloid solutions to one-half of the initial amount. After the first few days the infusion of sugar solution or fat emulsion for basal metabolism is required. Careful observation and measurement is necessary to compensate for individual differences. The most valuable indication of an adequate rate of intravenous infusion is the urinary output, which should be maintained at 30–50 ml per hour in adults and 15–25 ml per hour in children. A catheter is inserted into the bladder in order to monitor the flow of urine accurately every hour. Where the flow of urine is inadequate a 12.5 per cent solution of mannitol is sometimes recommended in order to initiate or maintain diuresis and prevent renal damage associated with haemoglobinuria.

After the initial shock phase, lasting two to three days and characterised by loss of fluid and oedema, the burn wounds, if they do not become infected, dry out and the oedema begins to subside. This is known as the resorption phase and lasts from approximately the third to the eighth day.

Moderate burns usually require only three days of intravenous infusion of fluids. For serious burns, infusions may be reduced successively, but the quantity and composition of the fluids may require considerable variation, depending on the tendency to lung oedema, pneumonia and sepsis. A new shock phase may occur due to heart damage or a combination of heart damage and fluid deficiency. Digitalis[23] may be required where there are indications of heart failure. Urine flow and blood potassium and sodium levels require continual monitoring.

Maintenance of respiration

Maintenance of the individual's ability to absorb oxygen is of primary importance. Administration of 95 per cent warmed and humidified oxygen, by mask or nasal tube, may be indicated if:

(*a*) there are breathing difficulties (dyspnoea), a bluish or purple colouration of the skin and mucous membrane, indicating oxygen deficiency (cyanosis), or sounds in the chest detectable with a stethoscope (rales);

[23] Digitalis is a powerful heart stimulant obtained from the dried leaves of *Digitalis purpurea* (foxglove) plants.

(*b*) there are second and/or third degree flame burns about the nose or mouth;

(*c*) there is evidence that the patient was overcome by smoke or is restless, confused or panicky;

(*d*) the patient has a cherry-red colour or was close to a smouldering fire when rescued, indicating the possibility of carbon monoxide intoxification;

(*e*) there is a history of heart disease; or

(*f*) the burn is spread over more than 50 per cent of the body area (Phillips & Constable, undated).

Where the patient is breathing well on reaching the hospital, oxygen may not be necessary even where there are burns around the nose and mouth or some possibility of limited carbon monoxide poisoning. The best current measure of the patient's need of oxygen is the oxygen and carbon dioxide concentration in the blood, which can be monitored by methods which are available in most large hospitals. There is some danger of oxygen toxicity from excessive or prolonged use at high concentrations.

Where there are signs of upper respiratory tract obstruction, large amounts of liquid in the respiratory passages or shallow breathing, tracheotomy—the operation of making an opening directly in the "windpipe" so that oxygen can be administered by tube—may be required. This should only be done when it is clearly warranted by the observed symptoms, since tracheotomy may itself be a factor in pulmonary infection (Foley, Moncrief & Mason, 1968). In circumferential deep burns of the chest it may on rare occasions be necessary to incise burn eschar to permit adequate chest expansion.

Treatment of white phosphorus burns

Irrigation with a plentiful supply of water, immersion in water or placing water-soaked pads on the burn surface stops the combustion of phosphorus instantaneously (Norberg & Rosenqvist, 1944). Often a combination of these methods must be used, since if the surface is allowed to dry the phosphorus reignites. Although warm water is sometimes recommended it may be dangerous since it can liquefy phosphorus particles (Mendelson in Curreri *et al.*, 1970) and speed up absorption making phosphorus penetrate deeper into the tissue. Cold water makes phosphorus solidify, relieves some of the severe pain, and slows the blood circulation beneath and around the wound, thus minimizing oedema and resulting tissue damage. Water also dilutes acids formed by phosphorus combustion. Physiologic saline or weak sodium bicarbonate solution is a better choice but seldom available in large quantities in an emergency.

The standard means of initial treatment has been to irrigate the phosphorus wound with a solution of copper sulphate, usually at 5 per cent

171

strength (cf. NATO, 1958; *Voennyi Vestnik* **48**, May 1968, pp. 95–101), which reacts with the outer layer of the phosphorus particles to form a dark coating of copper phosphide which excludes air, thereby preventing further combustion of the phosphorus and helping to identify the particles.

In practice, this treatment has been disappointing (see below); moreover, copper sulphate is itself toxic and can be absorbed from the wound (Summerlin, Walder, & Moncrief, 1967). Whelan, Burkhalter & Gomez (1968) report that this treatment unequivocally caused the death of at least one soldier with a 10 per cent burn. This man collapsed with renal failure after treatment with copper sulphate for suspected phosphorus burns—a suspicion which turned out to be unfounded. Five of seven patients treated at renal units at the Clark Air Base in the Philippines and the Third Field Hospital in Saigon died; the two survivors had not been treated with copper sulphate at any time.

Since copper sulphate poisoning may be very similar to phosphorus poisoning, the possibility arises that symptoms attributed to phosphorus in fact arise from the copper sulphate used in treatment. Accordingly this question is further examined in chapter 4.

Since other methods are available for detecting and inactivating phosphorus, many recent writers conclude that there now seems to be no reason to place the burden of copper toxicity on patients already threatened with phosphorus toxicity and other stresses of the burn wound (Whelan *et al.*, 1968). Copper sulphate is not very adequate as a means of excluding air and preventing combustion (Norberg & Rosenqvist, 1944; Ben-Hur, Galidi, Appelbaum & Neuman, 1972). Norberg & Rosenqvist (1944) detected the luminosity of phosphorus in the wound four hours after vigorous surgical treatment with scalpels and forceps, combined with the application of pads soaked in 2 per cent copper sulphate, or 22 per cent copper sulphate dissolved in glycerine. Copper sulphate was no more effective than irrigation with water (Norberg & Rosenquist, 1944; Curreri *et al.*, 1970).

To inactivate any residual phosphorus resistant to mechanical treatment, oxidizing agents such as hydrogen peroxide have been suggested (Summerlin *et al.*, 1967). Animal experiments have been conducted which show that a 1 per cent solution of potassium permanganate in a 5 per cent sodium bicarbonate solution neutralizes the phosphorus and removes all nonoxidized elemental phosphorus (Norberg & Rosenqvist, 1944). Residual phosphorus can be detected by means of fluorescence caused by ultraviolet light irradiation (Frye & Cucuel, 1969). Whelan *et al.* (1968) report that lithium iodate-isopropanol is also being investigated as a possible means of treatment.

Other debridement compositions have been proposed for treatment of burns caused by various liquefied white phosphorus mixtures. These mixtures are considered to be more troublesome than solid white phosphorus to remove from the wound surface. The compositions recommended are suspensions of copper sulphate, various oils and organic solvents, or solutions of glycerine, copper sulphate, starch and detergents (Rabinowitch, 1943; Godding & Notton, 1942). The use of copper sulphate and organic solvents must be considered unwise because of the deleterious effects of copper salts and the risk of speeding up absorption of white phosphorus with the use of lipid solvents.

In the face of certain technical possibilities for "improving" white phosphorus incendiary agents, which would make proper debridement more time-consuming, the aim of the treatment must be fast removal of phosphorus from the wound. This must be done with non-toxic solutions which do not interfere with other surgical wounds or cause systemic poisoning or further damage to the tissues.

Animal experiments by Ben-Hur *et al.* (1972) (see also chapter 4) showed that, within the experimental conditions, a solution of 5 per cent sodium bicarbonate and 1 per cent hydroxy-ethyl-cellulose in 5 per cent copper sulphate solution prevents both systemic phosphorus and copper poisoning.

Early mortality in severe chemical burns is usually related to hypotension and acute tubular necrosis as a result of underestimation of the burn area and the depth of tissue necrosis (Curreri *et al.*, 1970). This underestimation, in combination with the possibility of phosphorus absorption, makes fluid resuscitation and careful monitoring of urinary output necessary, with scrupulous attention to serum sodium concentration and serum osmolarity.

The following general treatment schedule is recommended by the authors cited:

1. Remove contaminated clothes and irrigate with large amounts of cold water, or immerse the affected parts of the body in cold water. Care must be taken to maintain normal body temperature.

2. All visible white phosphorus particles should be removed with the aid of scalpel, forceps and pads. Physiologic saline or sodium bicarbonate (5 per cent solution in water) should be used if available. This treatment is extremely painful and is best done under anaesthesia.

3. Intense mechanical treatment under irrigation or immersion with a 1 per cent potassium permanganate in 5 per cent sodium bicarbonate solution should be performed until luminosity or fluorescence ceases, indicating that all the white phosphorus has been neutralized.

4. Pads soaked with the permanganate solution should be left on the wound for some hours.

5. In case of occular injury irrigation should consist of water or physiological saline for at least half an hour. No pads should be placed on the eye since it is important to maintain its mobility.

6. Further treatment continues as for thermal burns.

It must be emphasized that this treatment is to be carried out without delay if the risk of phosphorus poisoning is to be avoided. Thus, correct treatment in battlefield conditions demands substantial medical facilities.

The prevention and treatment of infection includes the following three measures: (*a*) the reduction of sources of infection by asepsis in the patient's environment, (*b*) the treatment of the burn wound itself to prevent infection (sepsis) of the wound, and (*c*) prophylactic and curative measures to prevent generalized infection of the body system (septicaemia) resulting from microorganisms and toxins in the circulating blood.

Asepsis. The need for complex and thorough asepsis is particularly important in the treatment of burn wounds. Measures include not only usual precautions of sterile clothing, scrubbing, masks, gloves, and so on for medical personnel, but preferably treatment of the patient in an isolated sterile chamber, well ventilated by filtered air.

A further means of reducing the threat of bacterial infection is ultraviolet irradiation. Usually this requires the provision of an ante-room, provided with ultraviolet lamps, through which all staff must pass before they reach the patient's isolation room. Considerable success has been reported in reducing infection by such means (Hart, 1936; Hart, Postlethwait, Brown, Smith & Johnson, 1968).

A noteworthy improvement in reducing infection was achieved by Colebrook and his colleagues at the Birmingham Accident Hospital, England, towards the end of World War II. Dressings were changed in special aseptic chambers devised by Bourdillon, ventilated by about 305 cubic metres per minute of warmed, twice-filtered air. This rapid air flow carried with it out of the chamber particles and bacteria liberated from the patient's dressings which might otherwise have contaminated the new dressings (Bourdillon & Colebrook, 1946). This approach has been developed in recent years. Some promising results have been obtained with a plastic ventilated isolator. The isolator is a large, transparent box-like construction in which the patient lies. The patient can thus both be readily observed and have the opportunity to see out, which may be psychologically beneficial in contrast to isolation rooms, where the patient is observed by television cameras but may suffer from lack of social contact. The isolator is equipped with glove ports and transfer pouches on both sides of the patient, making it possible to treat the patient but protect him from contamination by contact or from the air (Haynes & Hench, 1965; Lowbury, 1967; Levitan, Seidler, Strong & Herman, 1968).

Another method has been developed where patients are treated in isolated rooms through which filtered warm dry air is pumped continuously (Liljedahl, 1971). This air is warmed to 32–36°C and its humidity is controlled. Medical personnel must pass through an ultraviolet irradiation chamber before entering the patient's room, and the patient is mainly observed via television cameras and other remote means. In this method, not only is the patient protected from bacteria in the air, but the warm, dry

Table 3.17. Decline in mortality following treatment of burn wounds with mafenide acetate

	Mortality	
Per cent of body burned	Without topical therapy (1962–1963)	With topical therapy (1964–1970)
0–30	4.3	2.0
30–40	44.4	12.6
40–50	61.1	23.1
50–60	78.3	41.0
60–100	89.1	79.5

Source: Pruitt & Curreri (1971).

air rapidly dries out the open wound which forms a protective crust in a few hours. This has enabled an *open* method of treatment to be developed, in contrast to the traditional closed method of covering the patient with dressings. The patient lies on a special bed enabling him to be turned without being moved from the bed. The bed is covered with a sheet of aluminized fibre, which does not adhere to the wound and in addition provides a certain protection against infection. Use of this method avoids the continual changes of dressings which are a major source of excrutiating pain to the patient. Very few of these patients develop *Pseudomonas* infection which has been a major clinical problem (Liljedahl, 1967, 1971; Coriell, Blakemore & McGarrity, 1968).

Medicinal treatment of the wound. There are two reasons why such measures as those above are not sufficient. First, even with the most elaborate facilities, some cases of infection occur. Second, facilities such as those described above are so elaborate and so costly that they are simply not available in most areas of the world, or are not available on a scale applicable to large numbers of battle casualties. The development of surface means of treatment, such as antibiotic creams which can be put on the wound, is therefore of considerable importance.

During World War I a local application of picric acid was used to treat burn wounds. Davidson (1925) introduced the use of tannic acid in Detroit, a method which remained common until World War II. Burn casualties at Pearl Harbour and at the Coconut Grove night club fire in Boston[24] were treated with intravenous injection of sulphonamides (Evans & Hoover 1943; Cope, 1943). Later, sulphonamide-penicillin and penicillin creams were used for local application, before applying a dressing.

More recently a group at the US Army Institute of Surgical Research

[24] On 20 November 1942, 491 people died in a fire at a Boston, Massachusetts nightclub. The Massachusetts General Hospital received 114 dead and injured. A classic series of papers on these cases was published in the *Annals of Surgery* **117** (6) 1943.

175

has developed an antibiotic cream, containing mafenide acetate, known as Sulphamylon, which has resulted in a considerable decrease in mortality (table 3.17) (Lindberg, Moncrief, Switzer, Order & Mills, 1965; Moncrief, Lindberg & Switzer, 1966).[25] This treatment is now widely used. Mafenide is a methylated sulpha compound which, in the form of the acetate salt, is suspended in a soluble base. This suspension is regarded as critically important in order to permit continued absorption into the eschar and maintenance of effective concentrations of the medicament at the level of the interface between the viable and the non-viable tissue—the characteristic site of bacterial proliferation (Pruitt & Curreri, 1971). Mafenide acetate cream is a bacteriostatic rather than a bacteriocide; that is, it does not sterilize the wound by destroying the bacteria but it prevents them spreading and infecting non-burned tissue (Moncrief *et al.,* 1966). Mafenide acetate cream is spread over the entire wound with a sterile tongue blade or a sterile gloved hand, following daily cleansing, wound debridement, physiotherapy and hydrotherapy carried out in a special tank (Hubbard tank) in the ward. Twelve hours later the cream may be reapplied to areas where it has been removed by contact with the bed clothes.

A number of side effects have been noted with the use of mafenide acetate cream. The cream causes some initial pain and discomfort to the patient. Hypersensitivity reactions occur in some 7 per cent of patients (Pruitt & Curreri, 1971). More serious is the development of respiratory complications due to inhibition of the enzyme carbonic anhydrase, which is responsible for the normal process of excretion of carbon dioxide from the blood into the air to be exhaled from the lungs.[26] Mafenide may also delay epithelialization.

A second means of topical treatment which has been widely used in recent years is the application of thick sterile dressings soaked in a solution of 0.5 per cent silver nitrate (Monafo & Moyer, 1965; Polk 1966; Polk, Monafo & Moyer, 1969). Hypersensitivity reactions have not been attributed to the use of this agent and no development of resistant organisms has been noted. It is most effective when applied within 24 hours of the injury, and is active against the entire spectrum of wound bacteria, although some cases of clostridial myositis have been noted (Monafo, Brentano & Gravens, 1966). On the other hand, silver nitrate does not penetrate as deeply as

[25] Arthur D. Mason, Jr., and Robert B. Lindberg won the 1972 US Army Research and Development Achievement Award for their discovery and development of Sulphamylon cream (*US Army Medical Department Newsletter* 4 (1), 1972).
[26] "Alveolar-arterial carbon dioxide gradients of significance have been measured in patients with extensive burns who have elevated serum levels of mafenide acetate and its primary breakdown product *p*-carboxybenzene sulfonamide. In such a situation supervening pulmonary complications, further interfering with carbon dioxide excretion, may cause rapid change from respiratory alkalosis to acidosis. The mafenide acetate cream should then be removed from the burn wound and buffering carried out as necessary" (Pruitt & Curreri, 1971, p. 464).

mafenide and requires the application of thick occlusive dressings, and on contact it discolours not only the patient's unburned skin but bedclothes and attending personnel as well. A number of side effects have been reported, including deficits of electrolytes (sodium, potassium and calcium), methaemoglobinaemia (a form of blood poisoning), and a restriction of the movement of joints, due largely to the dressings (Turnberg & Luce, 1968; Polk, 1966).

The Chinese news agency Hsinhua reported on 8 August 1973 that the teaching hospital of the Nantung Medical College in eastern China's Kiangsu province has treated extensive burns with a herb, *Ilex chinensis sims* (a species of holly), for over three years with good effect. The herb had been used by practitioners of traditional Chinese medicine for many years. Topical treatment of the wound with a solution or cream containing the herb had an antibacterial effect, confirmed by bacterial cultures from 60 patients on 240 occasions, and had the advantage of rapid formation of crusts on the wounds, little exudation, slight infection, rapid healing and few complications. By preventing a large amount of exudation, fluid requirements were also reduced. In addition, the herb has the advantage of being abundant, inexpensive and easy to use.

Other recent topical treatments include gentamicin sulphate (Stone, 1966), sulphadiazine silver cream (Fox, Roppole & Stanford, 1969) and various silver creams (Butcher, Margraf & Gravens, 1969).

Burn wounds may also be infected by fungi, such as *Candida,* and by viruses, such as *Herpesvirus hominus.* Systemic antifungal agents have not been particularly effective in combating fungal infection and the infected area may have to be removed surgically. However, topical application of nystatin (Mycostatin) is being evaluated in the laboratory (Pruitt & Curreri 1971). Several patients have died due to *H. hominus* and post mortem examination has shown systemic lesions in the oesophagus, lung, gastrointestinal tract and liver. Since no adequate means of treatment is presently available it is fortunate that most viral burn wound infections do not spread in this way. Topical application of idoxuridine is being investigated as a therapeutic measure (Pruitt & Curreri, 1971).

General prophylactic measures. In addition to direct treatment of the wound, measures to prevent general bodily infection by bacteria and their toxins may be required. Three general approaches are available. The first is to replace the deficit in the body's natural means of defence by administration of replacements of gammaglobulin. The second approach is the administration of antibiotic drugs such as penicillin. The third approach is the administration of a vaccine.

Liljedahl (1967) recommended that the prophylactic administration of 20–40 ml of a 12 per cent solution of human gammaglobulin be administered between the third and the eighth to tenth day after the burn injury. No definite clinical confirmation of its effectiveness had been recorded, although Birke *et al.* (1964) previously demonstrated the considerable initial loss of gammaglobulin and a rate of breakdown five to six times the normal rate in burn-injured patients. In the four years of consistent treatment with gammaglobulin, mortality due to infection decreased considerably, although other factors were also involved.

As in many aspects of the treatment of burns there is some variation in medical opinion regarding the use of antibiotics. Many authorities agree on the value of prophylactic penicillin doses of from 300 000 to one million units a day for all patients with significant burns (Phillips & Constable, undated). This applies particularly to patients with pulmonary complications. However, antibiotics are no substitute for meticulous wound care. In particular there is a danger that general antibiotic treatment may change the bacterial flora of the wound so that if septicaemia develops later it will be from an organism resistant to normal antibiotics. There is a trend away from prophylactic antibiotic treatment in many burn units (Liljedahl, 1967), and the reservation of antibiotics for the treatment of infections due to specific, identified organisms is recommended (Phillips & Constable, undated).

Alexander & Fisher (1970) report the development of an antigen vaccine against *Pseudomonas* bacteria, a major cause of death from burns.

Skin grafting

The first stage in the surgical treatment of the burn wound is the removal of dead tissue. In some cases dead tissue may be removed by scrubbing (Litvine, 1970) or washing with a jet of water (*US Army Research and Development News,* August 1972). In other cases surgical excision is required. While some authors (Jackson *et al*, 1960) advocate early excisions, this procedure is perhaps to be preferred only in the case of clearly delineated deep burns covering less than 5 per cent of the body (Bäckdahl, Liljedahl & Troell, 1962). Other authors recommend excision after 20–25 days, when it can be carried out with considerably less loss of blood (Liljedahl, 1967).

The ultimate objective of all burn wound care is to replace the lost skin as soon as possible. Although the skin may regenerate itself, in a full thickness burn it does so only at the edges of the wound, where the old skin remains intact. In large third degree burns, the rate of regrowth of the skin may never be sufficient to cover the wound. For this reason it is necessary to resort to surgical measures to replace the skin, following cleansing and preparation of the wound.

In order to cover the large burn wound, pieces of skin are transplanted from other areas of the body, a procedure known as autografting. The most common technique is to remove "split-thickness" skin from a donor site with a special instrument. The split-thickness graft is a thin layer of skin which includes the epidermis and part of the dermis, but leaves a sufficient depth of dermis to enable rapid degeneration. During this period the donor site is an additional source of pain and discomfort, and may itself become infected. For this reason surgeons working in primitive or combat conditions may prefer not to transplant skin, even though they may be technically competent to do so.

Functional and cosmetic considerations dictate priority to areas such as the hands, feet, joints and face, which should be covered before nonfunctional surfaces. In patients with extensive burns and limited donor sites, "meshed" autografts may be used (Tanner, Vandeput & Olley, 1964; Stone & Hobby, 1965). In this technique the skin is perforated by a series of small cuts so that it can be drawn out into a "lace" or "net" up to nine times the original area. The interstices of this mesh regenerate rapidly. However, the resulting skin is not cosmetically satisfactory and is thinner than normal; thus the technique is not recommended for the face or for joints, feet and other areas exposed to constant wear (Pruitt & Curreri, 1971).

It may take several months of skin-grafting operations to cover an extensive burn, since the patient will have little remaining skin to donate to the burned area. In such cases successive "crops" of skin must be transplanted from the same healthy areas. Because of this problem, several other materials have been used for temporarily covering the burn, including skin from other persons or animals, and synthetic materials.

The first clinical use of animal skin grafts was described in the seventeenth century and the transfer of temporary skin grafts from one person to another was first recorded in the nineteenth century (Davis, 1910). Skin grafts from other persons may be taken from cadavers, amputated parts or living volunteers, in that order of preference (Pruitt & Curreri, 1971). Such pieces of skin may be treated and kept for a short time under refrigeration. They will serve as acceptable dressings for up to two weeks.

Less satisfactory but also acceptable are grafts from dogs (Switzer, Moncrief & Mills, 1966) and pigs (Bramberg, Song & Mohn, 1965). Pig skin grafts treated by electron-beam irradiation may be stored under refrigeration until needed. These grafts are more difficult to apply and show less adhesiveness. They may have the advantage of being more readily available, at least in the case of pig skin, which can now be obtained commercially. Vishnevskii (1966) reports that frog skin has been used in the same way in the Democratic Republic of Viet-Nam.

A synthetic polymer burn covering has recently been described by Gregory, Schwope & Wise (1973).

The common uses of such temporary "physiological dressings" are given by Pruitt & Curreri (1971) as follows: (a) debridement of untidy wounds, (b) protection and "stimulation" of granulation tissue following eschar separation, (c) immediate coverage of excised burn wounds, (d) coverage of eschar-free burns between autografting procedures in patients with large burns and limited donor sites, (*e*) as a "test material" to determine readiness of full-thickness burns to accept an autograft of the patient's own skin, and (*f*) provision of temporary coverage for any other surgical wound which cannot or should not be closed immediately.

The application of temporary grafts decreases the loss of water and heat by evaporation, and diminishes the exudation of proteins and blood. Wound pain is strikingly decreased, particularly in children, with the decrease in discomfort enhancing the use of joints, thus helping to ensure maximum functional results (Pruitt & Curreri, 1971; Shuck, Pruitt & Moncrief, 1969).

Reconstructive surgery and rehabilitation

Burned tissue of the hands, face and neck, which is particularly common in war burns casualties, is the most likely to result in disfigurement and functional impairment, the most difficult to reconstruct, and the most essential to normal social life. One of the leading specialists on the reconstruction of the face after burn deformities has summarized the situation as follows:

In the face and neck, contractures and scars, the result of tissue destruction from burns, distort the soft tissue structures and may result in severe facial disfigurement and functional impairment . . . The reconstructive surgical rehabilitation of the patient who bears scars and contractures following burns of the face and neck is a major task for the plastic surgeon. As important as the relief of functional disabilities is the reduction of the severity of facial disfigurement and its attendant sociological, psychological, and vocational implications (Converse, 1967, p. 323).

The initial period of treatment in the hospital has concentrated upon the ensurance of survival; facial disfigurement now becomes a major problem if contractures and hypertrophic scars mar the patient's facial features . . . The return of a patient to his home after a long period of hospitalization may be a traumatic experience. It is essential that the patient be forewarned of the reaction of members of the family, friends, and neighbours. A thorough understanding on the part of the patient's spouse and other members of his family is equally important. One of our patients recalls that when he returned home his two children recoiled, screaming, at the sight of their disfigured father. (*Ibid.,* p. 333)

In these circumstances it is understandable that there is often a clamour for early treatment. But the surgeon must resist the pressure placed upon him both by the patient and the family to undertake early reconstructive procedures, since time must be allowed for the maturation of the scar tissue and metabolic and immunological stabilization, after the severe strains which have been placed upon the normal physiological functions of the body (Converse, 1967). Mathews (1964) reports that the best results were obtained in repatriated prisoners of war who had had a forced delay of perhaps two years before reconstructive surgery could be undertaken.

A few other general points may be made about the problems of reconstructive surgery. Early skin grafting is generally recognized to reduce the problem of hypertrophic scarring and contractions, but not to remove it. The most common type of graft in current practice, the split-thickness skin graft, contracts both during and after the period of healing. The younger the patient the greater the amount of contraction.

Hypertrophic scars are also more common in children:

The propensity of children to hypertrophic scars is well known and similar scars occur in donor areas, following the removal of split-thickness skin grafts of excessive thickness. In the child, the skin is relatively thinner because it is distended over a subcutaneous adipose layer which is thicker than in the adult and penetrates into the base of the dermis through larger and more numerous "columnae adiposae" (Converse, 1967, p. 332).

Hypertrophic scars can occur in various areas of the face. There are indications that certain individuals or racial types may be more predisposed than others to such scars, although the state of nutrition and general health are also determining factors. The most serious deformities occur in those patients in whom initial skin grafting has been delayed or unsuccessful.

After a waiting period to enable such scars to stabilize, the difficult, tedious, drawn-out and costly process of reconstructive surgery can begin.[27]

For the patient, the numerous and repeated operations may represent a test for the most courageous . . . Because of the often protracted period of treatment and numerous operations, the importance of the psychological management of the severely burned patient is obvious; most of this management will rest upon the surgeon in whom the patient has placed his confidence and who must also act as his psychiatrist (Converse, 1967, p. 336).

One illustration of the length and tediousness of the treatment is the problem of preventing contractures of the neck after corrective surgery. A great advance in the treatment of such contracture was made by Cronin (1957), who put his patients into a moulded neck splint after skin grafting. This splint had to be worn continuously for five to six months. Deformities around the eyes are particularly common, due to the thin tissue of the eye lids. Further, the eyes are particularly liable to infection after burns. Residual scars present difficult problems in the final stages of rehabilitation. The removal of these scars, where possible, is psychologically beneficial to the patient.

[27] Dr John Constable, plastic surgeon at the Massachusetts General Hospital, Boston, Mass., estimated that the current cost of such a hospital stay in the United States may be as much as $100 000. The running costs of treatment at the burn clinic at the Karolinska Hospital in Stockholm were Sw. cr. 1 018 000 ($254 000) in 1972. The clinic reported 3 147 patient-days of treatment, that is, an average of 8–9 patients at any time, which gives a daily cost of Sw. cr. 323.5 ($80) per patient. The treatment period ranged from a minimum of 1 month to 8–9 months, giving a treatment cost of Sw. cr. 9 705 ($2 400) to Sw. cr. 87 345 ($21 700). This includes staff salaries and medicines, but not overhead costs such as rent, electricity, heat, food, administration, and so on. Thus the total costs are even higher.

V. Additional military medical considerations

The foregoing section described some of the basic problems in the treatment of burns, based on the best methods available in ideal conditions. In combat conditions, the treatment of burns is complicated by associated mechanical injuries from blast and fragmentation weapons, and by limited or damaged facilities. The state of nutrition and of public health of the population affected by incendiary attack are significant factors in their susceptibility to injury.

It is common military practice to use incendiary weapons in combination with other weapons, such as machine-guns and fragmentation grenades; population centres may be bombed with a combination of high explosive and incendiary bombs. As a result, many victims may suffer from both burn wounds and blast and penetrating wounds. In some cases, such as an exploding white phosphorus munition, the particles of incendiary agent may themselves cause multiple penetrating wounds (Pruitt, 1970). This hazard may be increased as research continues into the development of "reactive fragments" (see chapter 2).

Experimental studies have demonstrated that combined injuries from thermal and mechanical trauma may cause a much greater rate of death than either form of injury alone. The mortality rate in mice following mechanical injury with a normal death rate of 10 per cent was increased eight-to-tenfold if preceded by a sublethal burn injury 0–3 days earlier (Schildt, 1972).

Table 3.18 shows the proportion of burn cases suffering from additional injuries treated at the US Army Institute of Surgical Research between 1965 and 1969, which includes injuries incurred in both combat and noncombat conditions. In the majority of these cases the burns were inflicted through the ignition of fuel in combat vehicles rather than by incendiary weapons. Even so, it is apparent that burns resulting from hostile action are more serious than those from accidental events. A study of 1963 burn patients

Table 3.18. Burn patients with associated injuries admitted to the US Army Institute of Surgical Research, 1965–69

Year	Total burn admissions	Patients with associated injuries	
		Number	per cent of total
1965	174	20	*11.5*
1966	311	67	*21.6*
1967	389	96	*24.7*
1968	389	106	*27.2*
1969	301	80	*26.6*
Total	**1 564**	**369**	**23.6**

Source: Pruitt (1970).

treated at a US Army hospital at Yokohama, Japan, showed that hostile causes accounted for 43.2 per cent of the hospital admissions and 69.3 per cent of the deaths, while accidental causes accounted for 51.2 and 30.7 per cent, respectively (Allen, in DiVicenti *et al.*, 1971). The combat casualties, in most cases the trapped crews of armoured vehicles or helicopters in which the fuel exploded, were usually more severe and associated with mechanical injuries and inhalation injuries due to large amounts of smoke and carbonaceous products. It is likely that the combat use of napalm together with conventional munitions creates a somewhat similar pattern of injury.

The treatment of the burn wound by methods such as those outlined above is in general compatible with the treatment of associated mechanical injuries. Conversely, however, Pruitt (1970) concludes that the presence of burns in the multiple injury patient greatly increases the possibility of septic complications and necessitates modifications in many of the standard surgical techniques and principles of wound care.

A second factor of great importance in combat conditions is the general state of health and nutrition of the population at risk. The prognosis for a burned patient is highly dependent not only upon his age, as noted earlier, but upon his general physical condition. Persons with anaemia or a low state of nutrition have greatly reduced ability to survive a severe burn. In some wars a substantial part of the target population may suffer from food shortages, either as a result of their state of economic development or as a result of the destruction of food supplies or means of distribution.[28] A low state of nutrition not only increases the death rate from burns but also makes wounds more difficult to heal and more liable to hypertrophic scarring and other forms of disfigurement.

In wartime conditions, the possibilities for optimal treatment are often greatly diminished. Widespread use of incendiaries may result in a rate of burn casualties far greater than can be coped with by available medical facilities. Indeed, the experience of civilian air crashes shows that the burn treatment facilities over a wide area may be stretched to their limits by an influx of, say, some 50 seriously burned patients. In military medicine fine judgements may be required concerning how best to utilize limited resources (Wallace, 1969).

The problem of limited resources is highlighted in two types of warfare in which incendiaries have been widely used. The mass destruction of ad-

---

[28] Oughterson & Warren (1956) report that towards the end of the war in Japan "the inhabitants of the cities were seriously undernourished . . . Malnutrition was responsible for many deaths among injured people already weakened by undernourishment . . ." (p. 81). Dudley *et al.* (1968) say "our experience leads us to believe that the Southeast Asian civilian, perhaps because of marginal subnutrition, perhaps because of some undetected specific deficiency has inherently less ability to respond to massive trauma than either his fitter, better-fed military counterpart, or the Westerner" (p. 339).

vanced industrial cities by the combined used of incendiary and high explosive bombs not only creates many casualties, but also destroys a large proportion of the medical facilities which tend to be concentrated in these areas.[29] In the second type of combat situation, incendiaries have been used against guerilla liberation armies in areas which only possess the most rudimentary medical facilities.[30] In neither case is evacuation from the theatre of operations a possible solution to the problem of limited medical resources, and only simple forms of treatment can be attempted. By removing any hope of adequate treatment, the suffering of the burned person is magnified, since the problem of treating severe burn wounds becomes almost insurmountable. Victims will either be left to die, or if they recover from lesser burns, they will be left to cope with their own disabilities and disfigurements, including in some cases open wounds which never heal.

In order to make a complete humanitarian assessment of incendiary weapons it is necessary to consider all these aspects of the circumstances in which they are used.

---

[29] Oughterson & Warren (1956) report that "In Hiroshima most of the medical facilities were in the devastated area, and the larger part of them were extremely vulnerable to blast and fire; consequently casualties were heavy. Ninety percent of the 200 to 300 physicians were killed or injured . . . Almost every hospital in Hiroshima within 1 mile of the hypocenter was so severely damaged that it could not function as a hospital. Only 3 of the 45 civilian hospitals were usable . . ." (p. 71 ff). More recently, extensive damage to hospitals in North Viet-Nam has been well documented (US Senate Committee on the Judiciary, 1972). It is unclear from the published information on target selection whether these attacks are the result of imprecise "precision bombing" or precise attacks intended to undermine morale. The problem has in any case reached such proportions that the International Committee of the Red Cross (1973a) is seeking to strengthen the provisions in the Geneva Conventions designed to protect medical resources from attack.

[30] The medical services of the National Liberation Forces of Yugoslavia, for example, had to face the following problem during World War II: "Doctors had to flee as refugees or face death, imprisonment or deportation . . . The Germans seemed to have made a special point of destroying hospitals, or any other buildings capable of being used as such . . . the enemy on many occasions slaughtered all the patients and staff they captured before destroying the hospital. Under such circumstances the wastage of medical personnel, scanty to begin with, was enormous." (Hirst, 1945, p. 106).

More recently, a staff report prepared for the subcommittee on refugees of the US Senate Committee on the Judiciary (1970), described bombing raids in Laos with as many as 600 planes a day, dropping napalm, phosphorus, antipersonnel bombs and high explosive bombs and concluded that "with a very low standard of medical care generally, and with a near total absence of adequate government hospitals, the burden of war casualty treatment in Laos is specially heavy" (pp. 32–33). A report prepared by the General Accounting Office of the US Senate estimated that there were "about 36 Laotian doctors, of which 17 are in the military and 19 are administrators of the Royal Lao Government" (*Congressional Record*, 3 May 1972). According to Webb (1968), a former surgeon at the US John F. Kennedy Center for Special Warfare, the "denial of medical resources to insurgents" is an important facet of counter-guerilla warfare. It is noteworthy that the Draft Additional Protocols to the Four Geneva Conventions of 1949 contain the paragraph: "In no circumstances shall any person be punished for carrying out medical activities compatible with professional ethics, regardless of the person benefiting therefrom." (ICRC, 1973a).

184

VI. *The question of suffering*

The purpose of this chapter has been to describe the mode of action of incendiary weapons on the human body. This mode of action is complex and dependent upon the circumstances of the burn, the depth and extent, the parts of the body affected, the presence of other injuries, as well as upon the age and condition of the victim, and the quality of the medical resources available.

Military incendiary agents in general cause deep and extensive burns, since they have been developed to the levels necessary to ignite or damage materials, such as metals, much more durable than the human body. Further, their use is typically combined with explosive and fragmentation weapons mutually to enhance the effects.

The medical treatment of severe burns such as those caused by incendiary weapons is more costly, difficult, tedious and demanding both for the patient and the medical staff than is treatment of most other types of injury or sickness. Such treatment is not likely to be available to the majority of incendiary casualties, either in rural areas, or following strategic incendiary or nuclear attacks on cities leading to mass casualties.

The victim of a very serious burn does not necessarily die immediately. He may live for hours, days, or even weeks, depending upon the quality of the accessible medical treatment since even a large area of damage to the skin does not have the immediate impact of, say, a bullet wound in the heart or brain. Death follows in due course from infection, from the complex physiological effects of shock consequent upon loss of fluids, from respiratory complications, or from subsequent strain on other organs leading to heart, kidney or lung failure, or gastric or duodenal ulcers. Except where exceptional medical facilities are available on such a grand scale as are found in only some tens of specialist burn units around the world, the death of the victim of serious burns is rendered probable, if not inevitable, but not necessarily rapid.

The victim of deep, third degree burns may suffer little immediate pain since the pain receptors of the skin are themselves destroyed. The patient may even die without feeling much pain. For those who survive and for those with areas of less severe burn, pain is excruciating, intensifying over a long period during recovery. Deep burns require skin transplantation which itself creates painful donor sites on other areas of the body. In many parts of the world such essential surgery may not be undertaken either because surgical facilities are not available, or because the donor sites may themselves become a source of infection. In these circumstances, the burn wound may never heal, placing the patient under permanent threat of infection as well as under an enormous psychological burden.

The constitution of the World Health Organization (WHO) defines health as "a state of physical, mental and social well-being and not merely the absence of disease or infirmity". Suffering may be defined by the converse as "a state of physical, mental and social distress, and not merely the presence of disease or infirmity". There can be no doubt that incendiary weapons cause excessive suffering in the fullest sense of this definition.

In view of these facts, the verdict of the Special Committee of the League of Nations disarmament conference in 1932 was that "the cruelty inherent in the uses of these appliances [causes] suffering that cannot be regarded as necessary from a military standpoint" (see chapter 1). It is difficult to see any reason to reverse this judgement.

Chapter 4. Toxic effects of incendiary weapons on the human body

I. *Introduction*

When materials are burnt or decomposed by heat, a variety of gaseous, liquid and solid substances are produced. Many of these substances, particularly certain gases and smoke made up of solid particles or droplets of acid, have toxic effects which in certain circumstances have proved to be the predominant cause of death and injury resulting from fire. Examples of toxic agents produced by or in fires include phosphine, hydrogen chloride, hydrogen cyanide, phosphoric acid, metal oxides and carbon monoxide. The toxic hazards of fire can thus no longer be overlooked either in the civilian or in the military context. This chapter reviews a number of the products of combustion or thermal decomposition of incendiary agents, and considers the toxicity of these products.

Toxic effects may also be produced by the direct action of certain incendiary agents on the human body. Recent clinical and experimental studies have shown that white phosphorus may be an agent of this kind. The available literature on the toxicity of white phosphorus burns has been extensively reviewed in appendix 4A.

In appendix 4B the toxicity of various incendiary agents and products of combustion are presented.

II. *Incendiary agents as asphyxiants*

Oxygen is essential both for human life and combustion. With the exception of the pyrotechnic incendiaries (which obtain oxygen from an oxidizing agent in the composition) incendiaries draw oxygen from the air. Where the supply of air is limited, as in a building, insufficient oxygen may be available to ensure complete combustion, while at the same time a variety of potentially lethal and toxic products may be generated.

In exceptional circumstances the amount of oxygen remaining in the confined space may be insufficient to support life, so that persons caught in the space become asphyxiated. Burning hydrocarbon fuels are themselves extinguished when the level of oxygen sinks below some 16 per cent, whereas human beings can continue breathing in an atmosphere with as little as 8–10 per cent oxygen. More frequently the diminished level of oxygen results in the production of carbon monoxide, carbon particles (black smoke) and other products of incomplete combustion. Where the hydrocarbon fuel is extinguished, toxic fumes of, for example, unburned gasoline will also be produced. Carbon monoxide is a well-known poison, which starves the blood of oxygen leading to asphyxiation. Smoke and other products of incomplete combustion are recognized as a major cause of death from fires in enclosed spaces, since they cause potentially fatal lung oedema, which can lead to asphyxiation.

The toxic effects may be increased where, as is usually the case, combustion results in several products:

There is ample evidence to show that the sum of the toxicity potential of two or more gases or vapours may synergistically affect life ... Carbon dioxide, for example, causes stimulation of the respiratory center of the brain ... [and] abnormally high intake of other gases causing toxic or lethal concentrations which might have been avoided if carbon dioxide had been absent. (Einhorn, 1973, p. 43)

In addition to the noxious products of combustion, the victim of burns has a variety of other problems to contend with in maintaining adequate respiration. These factors are described in further detail in chapter 3, but they may be summarized as follows: (*a*) obstruction to oxygen inflow through the airway; (*b*) insufficient functioning lung tissue; (*c*) poor diffusion of oxygen across alveolar capillaries; (*d*) diminution in haemoglobin available for oxygen transport; (*e*) inadequate circulation of blood; (*f*) increased tissue demands; and (*g*) interference with oxygen delivery (Phillips, Tanner & Cope, 1963, p. 807).

When all these factors are combined with the effects of the noxious products of combustion it will be realized that the toxic and asphyxiating effects of incendiary weapons are considerable.

The asphyxiating effects of incendiary attacks were apparently well-known to soldiers. One general,[1] reporting his experience in Luzon during World War II, said: "We'd slap a napalm bomb into the mouth of a cave and the enemy inside would all suffocate" (R. W. Volckmann, in Peterson, Reinhardt & Conger, 1963, p. 18). A US Army manual points out that "personnel in pillboxes or other confined spaces will suffer from the withdrawal of oxygen from the air" (US Army, 1960, pp. 3–4) when attacked with flame-throwers or napalm bombs. Following such an attack, one account records: "Japanese bodies, victims of burns and suffocation, were found along the smouldering corridors in the most remote parts of the tunnels" (Kleber & Birdsell, 1966).

Hypoxaemia (lack of oxygen)

In the normal process of combustion of organic materials, oxygen is consumed and carbon dioxide and water are produced. To achieve complete combustion, hydrocarbon fuels need large quantities of oxygen which is normally drawn from the surrounding air.

[1] Brigadier General Russell W. Volckmann, USA (rtd.), commanded the US Armed Forces in the Philippines, North Luzon, 1942–1945; author of Field Manual 31–20 *Combatting Guerilla Forces* and Field Manual 31–21 *Organization and Conduct of Guerilla Forces*.

There are three ways in which asphyxia or hypoxaemia (insufficient oxygen in the blood) can arise. First, the concentration of oxygen in the air breathed may decrease. Second, oxygen in the air may be replaced by carbon dioxide. Third, asphyxiation may result from carbon monoxide poisoning.

When the proportion of oxygen in the air decreases from the normal level of 20–21 per cent to 16 per cent, many burning fuels are extinguished. When the level falls below 14 per cent human beings begin to show increased heartbeat and breathing rates and muscular effort leads to rapid fatigue. At 6–8 per cent collapse occurs quickly but rapid treatment can prevent a fatal outcome; below 6 per cent death will occur in six to eight minutes.

The level of oxygen may fall below 16 per cent in certain types of fire. First, some fuels such as wood and carbon monoxide continue to burn at much lower levels of oxygen. Second, depending on the nature and extent of the fire inside and outside the building, oxygen may be drawn out of the enclosed space by the continuing fire outside, as in the case of the shelters in German cities during World War II (see above p. 166). In other words, the level of oxygen (and of carbon dioxide and carbon monoxide) depends not so much upon the type of fuel being burned, as upon the circumstances of the fire.

Carbon monoxide (CO) poisoning

The burning of hydrocarbon fuels, including napalm, is normally so rapid that there is insufficient oxygen at the burning surface to ensure complete combustion and large amounts of carbon monoxide, carbon smoke and other products of incomplete combustion are produced.

Carbon monoxide is a very poisonous gas and it has been used both for executions and for suicides. It is similar in action to the class of chemical warfare agents known as blood gases.[2]

Carbon monoxide poisoning frequently accompanies the use of incendiary weapons. A NATO handbook points out that "[w]artime burns are frequently complicated by poisoning. Napalm, for instance, not only causes serious burns but is often lethal from the carbon monoxide produced by imperfect combustion" (NATO, 1958, p. 25).

According to Dreyfus (1971), the Surgeon-General of the French Army has ascribed the high death rate of those in the central strike area of a napalm attack to carbon monoxide poisoning and lack of oxygen rather than to burns, and he offers the following explanation:

An examination of some of the methods of execution practised during the Middle Ages sheds some light on these effects. In executions by burning at the stake, when large fires were used, the victim died rapidly from carbon monoxide poison-

---

[2] Blood gases include hydrogen cyanide (prussic acid), hydrogen sulphide, methyl and ethyl cyanoformate, cyanogen bromide, cyanogen chloride and arsine (cf. SIPRI, 1971, p. 36).

ing before being actually burned by the flames; when small fires were used, a longer and much crueller death by flame resulted. (From this has come the popular French expression for being on tenderhooks: bruler à petit feu, to roast over a slow fire.) (Dreyfus, 1971, p. 193).

Bond (1946) reports that the best estimates of the cause of death during the attacks on German cities were obtained in Kassel.

Deaths due to HE [high explosive] bombs cause the smallest part of the loss of life, only about 15 per cent. Deaths due to burns and inhalation of hot gases were also small, 15 per cent. By far the largest proportion of deaths, 70 per cent, were due to carbon monoxide poisoning. This appeared to be typical of fire deaths in all of the cities which experienced fire storms (Bond, 1946, p. 94).

A US Strategic Bombing Survey report states that in a fire which developed after a raid on Westermünde, 175 out of 210 corpses, that is, 83 per cent, showed acute carbon monoxide poisoning (Bauer, cited in Bond, 1946). Carbon monoxide poisoning came to be recognized as typical of the "shelter or cellar dead".

Medical commissions working under the direction of the German Air Ministry during World War II reported that "[i]n all the cities visited carbon monoxide was regarded as the primary cause of death, sometimes reaching to as much as 80 per cent of all incendiary casualties" (Bauer, cited in Bond, 1946, p. 113).

Perhaps the major difference between the combustion of a high explosive (HE) and an incendiary bomb is the time taken for the chemical reaction to be carried out. Because of the short time of reaction in an HE bomb explosion, the supply of oxygen, in spite of the incorporation of oxidizing agents in the explosive composition, is too limited, and a large amount of carbon monoxide is produced. However, unless in a confined space, this carbon monoxide is normally rapidly dispersed, largely by the blast itself. But Cope (1952) concludes that "carbon monoxide should always be kept in mind in treating casualties from aerial bombing, and ... preference should be given to the treatment of unconscious victims before those with physical injuries ..." He adds that in World War II, "Public prominence was not given to the hazard because of possible adverse effects on morale". Incendiary agents, though they may produce relatively less carbon monoxide than high explosives, do so over an extended period so that victims of incendiary attack are likely to be exposed to carbon monoxide for a much longer time.

During World War I carbon monoxide was considered as a chemical warfare agent. However, it proved impractical because of the difficulty in administering it at concentrations adequate for incapacitating personnel, since it diffuses rapidly, and the toxic reaction is reversible (Prentiss, 1937). During World War II it was suggested that the addition of metallic carbonyls to flame-thrower fuels would produce a high concentration of carbon monoxide and thereby increase the effectiveness of flamethrowers against per-

190

sonnel in fortified positions (Zapp, 1946).[3] Related experiments apparently continued after World War II.[4]

The toxic effects of carbon monoxide have been known since at least the time of Leblanc[5] who attributed accidents resulting from burning coal to carbon monoxide in 1842. Bernard (1870) discovered that carbon monoxide combines with the haemoglobin of the blood to form carboxyhaemoglobin, which he deduced to be the mechanism of poisoning.

Oxygen is normally inhaled into the lungs where it passes through the thin membranes of the alveoli into the blood. The oxygen, which is required to maintain the life of every cell in the body, is then transported throughout the body attached to the haemoglobin of the red blood cells.

Where carbon monoxide is present in the inhaled air it combines with the haemoglobin in preference to oxygen, thereby inhibiting the transport of oxygen to the cells. According to Caughey (1970), at equal concentrations of oxygen and carbon monoxide, there may be as much as 120–550 times as much carbon monoxide as oxygen bound by a given amount of haemoglobin. Because of this, even a low concentration of carbon monoxide in the inhaled air can rapidly displace the oxygen in the blood, leading to asphyxiation.

Further, recent work has shown that carbon monoxide may also attach itself to certain other proteins, such as myoglobins and cytochromes, thus inhibiting cell respiration (Chance, Erecinska & Wagner, 1970).

The lethal dose of carbon monoxide has been accurately determined as that dose which combines with 60 per cent of the blood's haemoglobin. That is, death will occur when 60 per cent of the total haemoglobin has been converted to carboxyhaemoglobin. This ratio is known as the Balthazard-Nicloux poisoning coefficient (Bour, Tutin & Pasquier, 1967).

A number of problems arise in assessing the actual contribution of carbon monoxide poisoning to deaths from incendiary warfare. Firstly, there are

[3] Metallic carbonyls were examined by the chemical warfare laboratories between the two world wars, since they seemed to offer a means of exploiting the toxic effects of carbon monoxide. Most carbonyls decompose in contact with respirator charcoal to yield carbon monoxide which is not thereafter retained by the charcoal. In addition, some of the metallic carbonyls were highly toxic in their own right and showed a marked ability to penetrate the skin (SIPRI, 1971).

[4] For example, Donohue (1947), working for the US Army Chemical Center, reported a study on the lethal effectiveness of 10 special flamethrower fuels containing substances other than petroleum products and napalm, such as iron carbonyl, carbon disulphide, carbothermic magnesium with oxidizing agents, and silica gels. These compositions were fired into fortifications so as to test the "intrinsic lethality" of changes in the levels of carbon monoxide, oxygen and temperature on goats (From the author's abstract, no. 473 138, in *Technical Abstracts Bulletin*).

[5] A review of the literature of carbon monoxide poisoning by Lilienthal (1950) revealed more than 3 000 bibliographic references, and the volume of studies has increased considerably since then. Amongst the major classic accounts of carbon monoxide poisoning are Bernard (1870), Haldane (1922), Flury & Zernick (1931), Henderson & Haggard (1943), von Oettingen (1944). More recent reviews include Finck (1966) and Bour & Ledingham (1967).

other sources of carbon monoxide such as cigarette smoke in the blood of victims. Blackmore (1970), after studies of more than a hundred victims of aircraft accidents, concludes that up to 8 per cent carboxyhaemoglobin may be due to smoking, but concentrations beyond that level are related to carbon monoxide produced by the fire. Secondly, there are difficulties in measuring the concentration of carbon monoxide in the blood accurately, particularly if there are delays, as may well occur in combat conditions: high temperatures may destroy carboxyhaemoglobin, though putrefaction does not. Stored but decomposing blood may produce carbon monoxide sporadically which complicates measurements even further (Blackmore, 1970). Bauer (cited in Bond, 1946) points out that the German findings of the significance of carbon monoxide in World War II bombing deaths are plainly dependent upon the validity of the rather simple laboratory examinations conducted at a considerable time after death. Nowadays, much more complex cytological techniques are recommended (Betke & Kleihauer, 1967; Blackmore, 1970).

In a remarkable series of experiments, Haldane (1922) exposed himself to carbon monoxide and measured the level in his blood. At 20 per cent saturation he noted no symptoms when he was at rest, but dizziness and palpitations occured after he had run upstairs. At 30 per cent, his heart rate increased, accompanied by heavy breathing, and rapid activity produced dizziness and dimness of vision within 30 seconds. At 40 per cent the symptoms were more marked and Haldane feared he would lose consciousness upon exertion. At 56 per cent, he was able to stand but unable to walk.

Henderson & Haggard (1943) published a useful formula relating the concentration of carbon monoxide in air to various symptoms. Headache and nausea occur when c (concentration of carbon monoxide in air in ppm), multiplied by t (time of exposure in hours), reaches 900. A value of 1 500 for ct is lethal.

In 1903 Nicloux established that the association of carbon monoxide with haemoglobin is not permanent. The erythrocytes are not destroyed by carbon monoxide, and the carbon monoxide may be replaced by administration of oxygen. When no treatment is given and the air is not polluted, carbon monoxide is spontaneously and progressively eliminated from the body over a period of up to 18 hours.

Despite improvements in methods of resuscitation, carbon monoxide remains a serious poison, since even a sub-lethal dose may have deleterious effects, depending on the time of exposure. Due to the neutralization of the haemoglobin, a local lack of oxygen may occur in the tissues of the body, leading to the death of the tissues and secondary disorders of vital organs. A number of cases have been reported of "burn-like" erythema and colouring of the skin, which was later revealed to be due to the necrosis of the underlying skeletal muscle following carbon monoxide poisoning (Hedinger, 1948), though these muscular lesions are rare (Finck, 1966).

More usual is damage to the organs most dependent on oxygen supply, such as the liver, kidneys, heart and brain.

According to Bour *et al.* (1967) the heart frequently shows symptoms of being affected during carbon monoxide poisoning. Ayres, Gionelli & Mueller (1970) report that significant myocardial changes were detected in patients when as little as 6 per cent of the haemoglobin had combined with carbon monoxide.

The brain is the organ most sensitive to lack of oxygen since it consumes the largest proportion of oxygen of the whole organism.[6] An oxygen deficiency lasting for more than about six minutes is fatal to brain cells. Diffuse degenerative lesions of the brain which may result from carbon monoxide poisoning can lead to coma and death; in some cases where improved methods of resuscitation have saved the life of the comatose patient, the patient remains in a vegetative state. In less severe cases the person may suffer loss of memory or other specific brain damage.

There seem to be a number of factors operating to cause brain damage. According to Brucher (1967) these are:

1. *Hypoxidosis,* the shortage of oxygen available to the brain cells from the blood.

2. *Oedema,* resulting from lesions of the walls of the blood vessels in the brain. This oedema may cause damage to the nerve and glial cells and even diffuse necrosis of the white matter. Further, because of the increased volume caused by the oedema within the skull, intracranial pressure increases, which in turn compresses blood vessels and decreases blood circulation.

3. Additional *circulatory disorders* which result from paralysis, stasis or spasms of the blood vessels, and the lowering of the blood pressure due to weakening of the heart muscle, all caused by hypoxia. Such circulatory disorders have been shown to play a role in causing lesions of the grey and white matter.

4. A possible direct *toxic action* of carbon monoxide on the brain cells which has been suggested by some authors.

Because of the complexity of these interacting factors, the patterns of brain lesions may vary from one case to another. After an intensive study of 22 autopsies, Lapresle & Fardeau (1967) concluded that the distribution and severity of the necroses strongly suggested that the causal mechanism in each case was circulatory disorder and oedema.

Deficits in mental functioning resulting from discrete lesions in one hemisphere of the cerebral cortex (such as might occur, for example, from a low velocity missile wound) can often be partly compensated for in time by re-

---

[6] According to McIlwain (1955) the brain of the adult human consumes about 25 per cent of the oxygen inhaled; in the nursing infant and child up to about four years of age this proportion is about one-third.

learning with the other hemisphere. Such relearning is not possible where circulatory disorders lead to diffuse lesions in both hemispheres.

In recent years considerable attention has been given to the physiological effects of low concentrations of carbon monoxide, as it was realized that the small quantities of carbon monoxide produced by internal combustion engines, and even cigarettes, may be sufficient to affect the normal functioning of the brain (Beard & Grandstaff, 1970). Experiments by McFarland (1970) showed that small quantities of carbon monoxide affect vision, and that recovery from these detrimental effects lags behind the elimination of carbon monoxide from the blood. Impairment of higher types of mental functioning such as the types of judgement and control required to operate a motor vehicle, have been noted by Schulte (1963) and by Beard & Wertheim (1967). Several other authors (for example, Hanks, 1970, and Mikulka *et al.,* 1970) have not observed such deleterious effects on the cognitive functions in their experiments, but Coburn (1970) concludes that these negative findings may be related to differences in the testing situation. Sjöstrand (1951) showed that minute quantities of carbon monoxide may always be present in the blood as a result of the normal process of haemolysis. This source of carbon monoxide will not normally produce a carboxyhaemoglobin concentration of more than 0.2–1.0 per cent. This is in equilibrium with a concentration in the air of 4 – 7 ppm. Carbon monoxide will be expired if there is none in the air. It is clear that it is well-nigh impossible to establish threshold levels at which carbon monoxide affects performance since there are indications that the brain may be affected at levels as low as 2–4 per cent (Beard & Wertheim, 1967)—levels common amongst smokers and those living in areas of dense motor traffic (DuBois, 1970).

Experimental studies such as those referred to above are typically performed on young healthy adults with normal baseline oxygenation. Though for obvious reasons it is difficult to provide experimental confirmation, it is reasonable to assume that carbon monoxide poisoning will be relatively more serious for persons already suffering from chronic lung disease or anaemia. These persons will already have a reduced capacity to transport oxygen in the tissues, and the lower oxygen tension in the blood will increase their susceptibility to carbon monoxide which in turn decreases their available oxygen. In addition it appears that the decrease is even greater in organs where there are large differences in the arterial and venous oxygen concentration, such as the brain, heart, liver and kidneys (Permutt & Farhi, 1969).

Pregnant women and their foetuses may also be particularly susceptible to carbon monoxide poisoning. Longo (1970) reviewed the literature on the effect of carbon monoxide on the pregnant woman and foetus and concluded that there are a number of possible mechanisms by which carbon monoxide poisoning of the mother can lead to the foetus receiving lower concentrations of oxygen with consequent damage to the developing tissues. Among a reported number of infants born to mothers suffering from carbon monoxide poisoning, all but one showed either neurological or pathological evidence of brain damage.

The main conclusions to be drawn from this brief review of the literature are that:

1. Incendiary weapons tend to produce large quantities of carbon monoxide particularly in confined spaces or when used in very large quantities.

2. Carbon monoxide is a very poisonous gas, acting on the blood to prevent the supply of oxygen to the tissues; concentrations of 0.5–1.0 per cent in air rapidly lead to unconsciousness and death.

3. Even where life is saved, the decrease in the supply of oxygen to the brain for more than some six minutes leads to permanent brain damage. Other tissues may also suffer permanent damage.

4. Certain groups of people, such as those with anaemia, lung disease or reduced blood flow, and pregnant women and their foetuses may be more susceptible to carbon monoxide poisoning.

5. Even low concentrations of carbon monoxide may impair mental performance. In the military situation, this means that even a non-lethal dose may reduce the combat effectiveness of the soldier, making him more susceptible to conventional attack in the same way as non-lethal doses of other chemical agents used in combat.

III. *Incendiary agents as irritants*

A further result of combustion or thermal decomposition is the production of smoke. Smoke consists of small particles of solid material or small droplets of liquid suspended in air and gases. The actual composition varies greatly according to the substances burned and the circumstances of combustion. The inhalation of smoke may be very dangerous and is associated with a high mortality. Smoke may cause prolonged functional deficits and even anatomical sequelae (Pruitt, Flemma, Di Vincente, Foley & Mason, 1970).

Inorganic oxide smokes produced by the combustion of metals, such as magnesium, zinc, cadmium, selenium and uranium, or their compounds, cause lung oedema and other complications, when inhaled.[7]

[7] Military smoke agents are widely used for screening and target-marking purposes, and these are generally claimed to be non-toxic, but in confined spaces they may be fatal. Two military smoke agents, zinc oxide and zinc chloride, have lung-irritant effects which may lead to bronchopneumonia and pulmonary oedema. A number of fatal accidents have been reported in the open literature. (Delamotte (1969), Fischer (1969), Francois (1969), Hedener (1957), Helm (1969), Helm, Renovants, Schmal & von Clarmann (1971), Johnson & Stonehill (1961), Linderholm & Strandberg (1956), Lumsden & Weir (1945), Macaulay & Mant (1964), Pare & Sandler (1954), Williot (1969), Whitaker (1945); this literature has recently been reviewed by Sörbo (1973).

The toxicity of soluble uranium compounds was described by Woroschilsky as long ago as 1899. According to Haven & Hodge (1949) the LD_{50} [8] for intraperitoneal injection of soluble uranium nitrate in the rat is 2.37 mg per kg body weight, and for the rabbit 2 mg per kg. However, Dygert et al. (1951) concluded that the toxicity of the insoluble uranium compounds, such as uranium oxide, was considerably less. Subsequent research has shown that feeding dogs with up to 100 grams of uranium oxide produces little effect, but the finely divided powder introduced into the lungs results in severe poisoning similar to that produced by the soluble uranium salts. Doses range between 300–100 mg per kg body weight.

During the 10–12 days after the administration of the compound a picture of severe kidney damage developed. In the blood there was a sharp rise in non-protein nitrogen (up to 350 mg per cent and in one case one day before death 600 mg per cent) with appearance in the urine of albumin, hyaline cylinders and a large number of leucocytes. The dogs lost appetite and subsequently refused all food, vomited and rapidly lost weight; some died, others gradually recovered (Rubanovskaya, 1970, p. 93).

Kidney damage resulting from inhalation of uranium oxide dust has also been reported by Pozzani (1949), Wilson et al. (1955) and Fish (1961). Several of these authors report that the uranium oxide particles are slowly removed from the lungs, but that this process takes a long time. Fish (1961) reported that the lungs of a person who accidentally inhaled uranium oxide still contained about 3 per cent of the original amount after one and a half years.

A recent chemical handbook recommends that the maximum allowable concentration of soluble uranium compounds in air, based on the chemical toxicity is 0.05 mg per cubic metre for soluble compounds, and 0.25 mg per cubic metre for insoluble compounds (Weast, 1974).

Based on the radio-toxicity, the permissible body level is 0.2 microcurie for soluble uranium compounds and 0.009 microcurie for insoluble compounds; the maximum allowable concentration is 1.7×10^{-11} microcurie per ml for uranium compounds in the air (Weast, 1974).

The addition to incendiary agents of certain compounds which are known to produce toxic smokes has been considered, though apparently they have not so far been used in combat (see chapter 2). Such weapons were thought to be potentially useful because the toxic smoke, usually produced by cadmium or selenium compounds, would impede firefighting activities. Selenium and cadmium smokes when inhaled or swallowed produce lung oedema and other injuries (Prodan, 1932; Christensen & Olsen, 1957; Bonell, 1965).

The combustion of organic substances also produces smoke particles (for the most part carbon) and gases. According to some authors the par-

[8] Lethal dose for 50 per cent of a given statistical sample.

196

ticles are themselves relatively innocuous since they are often large enough to be filtered out in the nose and mouth and trapped in the mucus (Thomas, 1969). This is particularly the case for wood smoke, which has relatively large particles. Particles from petroleum smoke are small, increasing the risk that they will be inhaled into the lungs. The smoke particles are usually coated with other products of combustion, mostly acrylic aldehydes such as acrolein in the case of petroleum products and acetaldehyde in wood smoke.

These aldehydes irritate the mucous membranes of the eyes, nose, mouth, throat and respiratory tract, which become congested and inflamed, producing familiar symptoms such as running nose, sore throat and a burning sensation in the eyes. Acrolein, for example, has an extreme lachrymatory effect. Irritation of the upper respiratory tract may be caused by a concentration of 5.5 ppm. Higher concentrations lead to pulmonary oedema and a concentration of 10 ppm may cause death within a few minutes (Einhorn, 1973). As more particles are trapped in the mucus of the nose and mouth, they are swallowed, irritating the stomach and frequently producing nausea and vomiting. According to Thomas (1969), the particulate fraction in the smoke incapacitates more victims by its action on the gastrointestinal tract than by any action it has on the respiratory tract. Smoke particles which are small enough to enter the lungs may produce coughing and minor chest pain. All these characteristics are typical of the class of military chemical agents sometimes known as *harassing agents,* the most common of which are the so-called "tear gases".

The gaseous fraction of the smoke may contain very many toxic products. Some of these act directly on the lungs, while others enter the body via the lungs to produce toxic effects elsewhere. Some of these gases are produced by the incendiary agent itself, and others result from the combustion of other substances, such as wood, cotton, wool, plastics and other materials in the environment.

Among the most well known lung-irritant gases which may be produced by combustion of common materials are chlorine, phosgene, hydrogen chloride, sulphur dioxide, and ammonia (see appendix 4B). When these gases are inhaled they react with the moisture in the lungs to form acids or alkalis. There is a characteristic delay of one to six hours between exposure to these gases and the onset of symptoms, though once the symptoms appear deterioration may be rapid, and death may follow within an hour or two. A person who survives a moderate to severe exposure to these gases may be left with serious permanent lung damage; exposure to small quantities over a period of years may result in chronic lung disease (Thomas, 1969).

Organic polymers may also produce many toxic products when they undergo thermal decomposition. Polystyrene, which is used as a thickener in napalm-B, may break down into styrene which in concentrations of 100 ppm can cause irritation of the mucous membranes, impairment of neurological functions and other symptoms of toxicity (Einhorn, 1973). Organic fluorine compounds (for example, polytetrafluoroethylene (Teflon) which has been tested as a coating for magnesium incendiary pellets), produce toxic fluorine compounds (for example octafluoroisobutylene).

... Fluorocarbons exposed to pyrolysis of combustion cause severe opacification of the cornea of test animals exposed to their degradation products ... humans exposed in a similar environment might have their sight hampered to an extent that they would not be able to escape a fire area in time to prevent exposure to lethal concentrations of toxic fumes or temperatures sufficient to cause death (Einhorn, 1973, p. 44).

With the increasing use of plastics in modern society, the toxic hazards of incendiary attack are increased. A common plastic such as polyvinyl chloride, for example, produces nearly 60 per cent by weight of hydrogen chloride gas when it decomposes in a fire, as well as carbon monoxide, carbon dioxide, and traces of chlorine and phosgene (Thomas, 1969).[9]

The toxic hazards associated with the pyrolysis of many common synthetic materials have been identified, but the proliferation of these materials is so great that in very many cases the toxic hazard has not been studied. Einhorn, in his recent review of the literature, states:

Not too surprising, however, is the fact that research on the toxicological aspects of pyrolysis and combustion during fire exposure has lagged so far behind other aspects pertaining to the flammability characteristics of polymeric materials that even a fair assessment of the toxic hazards cannot be adequately described at this time except in great generalities. The time has passed for the toxic consequences during combustion to be ignored or minimized (Einhorn, 1973, pp. 8–9).

Zikria *et al.* (1968) showed that smoke poisoning and/or asphyxiation were the cause of a high proportion of early deaths resulting from exposure to fire (see table 4.1). Respiratory tract and pulmonary damage and other aspects of burn wounds were more associated with death occurring after a period of 12 hours or more (see chapter 3).

IV. *Incendiary agents as systemic poisons*

Several classes of incendiary material or their products act as systemic poisons, that is, they are absorbed into the blood stream through the skin, lungs or stomach and intestines and injure vital organs such as the liver, kidneys, heart, brain or bone marrow. Two classes are of particular im-

---

[9] Phosgene dissolves in moisture to form hydrochloric acid, which is highly corrosive. The amount of acid which is formed depends on the amount of water available, but corresponds roughly to 10 kg of 5 per cent hydrochloric acid solution per kg PVC. This is sufficient to cover a surface area of 2 000 square metres with 10 000 1 mm drops per square metre. Hydrogen chloride produced in this way has been shown to cause considerable secondary damage to building materials and equipment following fires (Joint Fire Research Organization, 1968; Atterby, 1972).

Table 4.1. Post-burn survival times with and without smoke poisoning

	Under 12 hours	Over 12 hours
A. Smoke poisoning and/or asphyxia only	99	4
B. Respiratory tract damage and/or pulmonary damage only	11	28
C. Both A and B	20	1
D. Neither A nor B (see chapter 3)	55	39
Total	**185**	**72**

Source: Zikria *et al.* (1968).

portance in this respect: inorganic substances, such as white phosporus and heavy metals and their oxides; and organic compounds, such as benzene. Organometallic compounds, some of which like triethyl aluminium and diethyl zinc have incendiary applications, may also act as systemic poisons.

White phosphorus

As pointed out in chapter 3, there is no doubt that white phosphorus may cause serious burns—burns which frequently require a longer time to heal than purely thermal lesions. However, the evidence from World War II regarding the possibility of systemic poisoning from white phosphorus burns was equivocal. Some authors (for example, Porrit, 1953) reported that there was a risk of fatal hepatic or renal damage from the phosphorus contained in tracer bullets, while others (for example, Bauer, cited in Bond, 1946) reported that systemic damage following attack by phosphorus-containing incendiary bombs could not be proved on the available evidence.

In view of the extensive use of white phosphorus munitions in some recent armed conflicts, this problem has taxed a number of researchers and the resulting body of literature is surveyed in appendix 4A. These studies are complex and any conclusions to be drawn from them are subject to revision.

With this in mind, the results of recent research surveyed in appendix 4A may be summarized as follows:

1. The absorption into the body of about 1 mg white phosphorus per kg body weight (by whatever route) is likely to be lethal, although some individuals may survive slightly higher doses.

2. The location of the various organs relative to the site of absorption accounts for certain differences in the manifest symptoms. Liver damage is most obvious following oral ingestion since the phosphorus absorbed by the stomach and intestines is transported to the liver by direct venous blood flow. White phosphorus absorbed through a surface burn may affect other organs before the liver. For example, the heart may be affected, in some cases fatally, before the cells of other organs are damaged. For this reason some of the symptoms associated with phosphorus poisoning due to oral

ingestion may not be obvious when death is caused by white phosphorus burns.

3. Burns from white phosphorus take longer to heal than thermal burns and are in this respect similar to burns from mustard gas (*bis*-(2-chloroethyl) sulphide) and other vesicant agents.

4. There is at present no standardized treatment that fully removes the possibility of local or systemic poisoning from white phosphorus. Copper sulphate solution which is widely recommended to counteract white phosphorus may itself be toxic. While a number of alternative treatments are being investigated, *cold* water appears at present to be safer than copper sulphate solution and as effective.

While the focus here has been on the absorption of white phosphorus through a skin burn, it is also possible that phosphorus vapour may be breathed in or swallowed. In this case absorption is more rapid and toxic effects become manifest sooner. Furthermore, while the white smoke from burning white phosphorus is not dangerous in low concentrations, at higher concentrations it may cause potentially fatal lung oedema.

Metal incendiary agents, additives and their products

The alkaline metals, sodium, potassium, lithium and barium, which are added to some incendiary compositions (see chapter 2), form strongly alkaline solutions with a caustic effect on contact with the moisture of the skin, capable of causing chemical burns in addition to thermal burns. Absorption of these substances also causes grave disturbance of the electrolytic equilibrium of the body, with repercussions on the nervous system and the heart and skeletal muscles, leading to tetanic symptoms, paralysis, and finally death from circulatory collapse.

Metal incendiary or smoke agents or additives burn to produce metallic oxide dusts and aerosols which when inhaled not only cause manifold lesions of the lungs but also impairment of liver and renal functions, leading to a drop in blood pressure and circulatory difficulties, as well as gastroenteritic symptoms and general nausea, headache, giddiness and even convulsions.

Organic compounds

Fuels such as petrol and benzene are themselves poisonous. In liquid form they may cause chemical burns of the skin, if the skin is soaked in the liquid long enough, as when poured onto clothes or into shoes. These liquids are highly volatile. The fumes are both irritating and anaesthetic. The margin between the anaesthetic and the fatal dose is small, and delay in rescue work or in adopting measures for self-protection may prove fatal (Cope, 1952).

Several deaths from petrol fumes on board ship are reported by Cope and "those who were not fatally poisoned sustained severe skin burns where their clothes were soaked with petrol".

High concentrations of vapour, while they are very dangerous, are so irritant to the upper respiratory passages that men exposed will always try to withdraw from a compartment. A slowly rising concentration from a leak may prove more dangerous in effect, for the sense of smell tires after working in a petrol-ridden atmosphere for some time, so that workers will miss this warning sign, may be unaware of their danger, and pass through a phase of intoxication and impaired judgement to collapse later (Cope, 1952, p. 313).

Normally in combat conditions, these incendiary agents burn, and therefore this particular hazard does not arise. However, in confined spaces the fuel may be extinguished due to an inadequate supply of oxygen. In such circumstances, the liquid will continue to evaporate, producing toxic fumes with effects which may range from mild intoxication to death.

Persons inhaling hydrocarbon vapours suffer from lesions of the nervous system and liver, renal injuries, impairment of gastrointestinal, cardiac and circulatory functions, irritations of the mucous membrane and possibly pulmonary oedema.

Benzene, which is used in some modern napalm compositions, can produce symptoms such as giddiness and excitement. "In the stage of excitement the victim may shriek, sing madly, and fight with the rescuer, who, on account of his greater exertions, runs more risk than the rescued" (Hunter, 1959, p. 149). At higher concentrations these symptoms may be followed by convulsions, coma and death. Chronic benzene poisoning may also arise, particularly amongst industrial workers exposed frequently to the fumes. Some persons are particularly susceptible, including young women.

Acute benzene poisoning may be treated with the usual methods of resuscitation, rest and warmth, together with the injection of nikethamide as a respiratory stimulant. Treatment of chronic benzene poisoning requires repeated blood transfusions, though results are "so poor as to convince all who have studied the subject that the use of benzene in industry must be ruthlessly suppressed, except where the process is entirely enclosed" (Hunter, 1959, p. 151). Recent studies have shown that benzene can cause cancer and chromosomal changes (Deutsche Forschungsgemeinschaft, 1974). Clearly, the use of benzene in munitions introduces an additional hazard for the munition workers, the ordnance personnel, and those who are subject to attack or "accidental drops".

A benzene concentration in air of 7 500 ppm presents an acute danger to life. A concentration of 20 000 ppm produces death within five to ten minutes (Klinkmüller, 1965). A maximum allowable concentration of 100 ppm is recommended as an industrial norm in older books, but this standard is now rejected because of the possibility of carcinogenic and mutagenic effects at even lower concentrations (Deutsche Forschungsgemeinschaft, 1974).

V. Incendiary agents and chemical warfare

There can be no unequivocal answer to the question of whether the use of incendiary weapons should, in some circumstances, be described as chemical warfare.

In the first place there is no universally agreed definition as to what constitutes chemical warfare. The early, pre-World War I legal conventions used terms such as "employment of poison or poisoned weapons" (Brussels Declaration of 1874), and "diffusion of asphyxiating or deleterious gases" (First Hague Declaration of 1899). The Versailles Treaty, the Washington Treaty of 1922 and the Geneva Protocol of 1925 used the terms "asphyxiating, poisonous or other gases and all analogous liquids, materials or devices".

The League of Nations Disarmament Conference in the early 1930s discussed incendiary weapons as a separate category from chemical and bacteriological weapons but nevertheless at one and the same conference. This has been interpreted by some authors as an attempt to extend the prohibition on chemical and biological weapons to incendiaries because of their analogous effects (SIPRI 1971*b*, p. 22), but by others as a recognition that incendiary weapons were indeed a separate category not included by the earlier definitions of chemical warfare. In any event, since existing international rules do not specifically mention incendiary weapons, and the draft proposals of 1933 were never agreed upon, the legal situation with regard to incendiaries remains open (see chapter 1).

The political complexity of disarmament negotiations makes the question of chemical warfare even more convoluted. The inclusion or exclusion of incendiary weapons in the category of chemical weapons is likely to have some bearing on the drawing up of a chemical disarmament treaty. Here it is sufficient to point out a number of similarities between chemical and incendiary weapons. These similarities suggest: (*a*) that insofar as chemical weapons may be regarded as inhumane, such a judgement might also be applied to incendiaries; and (*b*) that any disarmament treaty relating to the production, development, stockpiling and so on of incendiary weapons will face many of the problems of a chemical disarmament treaty.

Definitions of chemical weapons

Definitions of chemical weapons vary from the less to the more inclusive.

A US Army and Air Force technical manual (1957) defines a chemical bomb as "... a missile which contains a chemical filling and is designed to be dropped from an aircraft. The chemical filling may be toxic gas, screening smoke, or incendiary" (p. 3).

A manual supplied to all branches of the US Forces (1961), the *Armed Forces Doctrine for Chemical and Biological Weapons Employment and Defense,* states as policy that:

(a) The decision for US Forces to use chemical and biological weapons rests with the President of the United States. Commanders receive directives relating to the employment of CB munitions through command channels . . .
(b) Commanders are currently authorized to use certain chemical agents such as flame, incendiaries, smoke, riot control agents, and defoliants (pp. 3–4).

These examples of US military terminology seem to reflect a rather general military usage. For example, Hanslian (1937) reports that during World War I, the task of operating flamethrowers was given to the chemical warfare services by a number of states, including both the United States and Russia. But during World War II, though the development of flame weapons was often the responsibility of chemical warfare services, the weapons which resulted were widely used by "regular" troops, rather than specially trained chemical units. Since "poison gases" as such were not used during World War II, incendiaries, which were widely used, came to be regarded by many soldiers as "conventional" rather than as "chemical" weapons. In recent years there has been a trend towards a more restrictive definition of chemical agents, which excludes rather than includes incendiaries.

Thus, in the United Nations Secretary-General's report on chemical and biological weapons (1969) it was decided (though without necessarily prejudicing any definition which might subsequently be generally recognized) to adopt a more exclusive definition:

For the purposes of this report, chemical agents of warfare are taken to be chemical substances, whether gaseous, liquid, or solid, which might be employed because of their direct toxic effects on man, animals and plants . . . We also recognise that there is a dividing line between chemical agents of warfare, in the sense in which we use the terms, and incendiary substances, such as napalm and smoke, which exercise their effects through fire, temporary deprivation of air or reduced visibility. We regard these latter as weapons which are better classified with high explosives than with the substances with which we are concerned. They are therefore not dealt with in this report (pp. 5,6).

A similar approach was taken in the World Health Organization (1970) report, and in the SIPRI (1971) studies: in each case the *direct toxic effect* was emphasized, and both incendiaries and smokes were omitted from the definitions of chemical warfare agents. In the present study the same distinction is made between the thermal effects of incendiaries (chapter 3) and the direct toxic effects of incendiaries.

A broad definition of chemical warfare agents includes incendiaries, perhaps for historical reasons, along with gases and smokes, without reference to the mode of action. A narrow definition excludes incendiaries insofar as their effects are thermal. But the evidence presented above is sufficiently compelling to warrant further examination of the possibility that incendiary agents may, in certain circumstances, be reasonably said to be chemical warfare agents, not simply for historical or terminological reasons but also because they may have a direct toxic effect or other effects (such as the lung irritant effect) which renders them more properly classifiable as chemical warfare agents than as conventional blast and penetrating weapons.

Comparison of chemical and incendiary agents according to their toxic effects

Traditionally, chemical warfare services have divided chemical agents into a number of classes.[10] These include harassing agents on the one hand and casualty agents such as the so-called respiratory and percutaneous agents and nerve gases[11] on the other. The category of respiratory agents may be further subdivided into lung irritants and blood gases.

Comparing this typology with the above review of the effects of incendiaries makes it clear that the toxic effects of incendiaries, or their products of combustion, are such that they should be included in some or all of the categories in the typology except for the category of nerve gases. More specifically:

1. The smoke, heat and fumes produced by fire, particularly from burning hydrocarbon fuels such as napalm, act as *harassing agents,* blinding, choking and terrifying personnel, effects similar to the use of lachrymators (tear gases).

2. These same products also act as *lung irritants,* causing inhalation injury leading to pulmonary oedema, which is a major cause of death. Indeed, one of the classic studies of burns injury specifically noted the similarity between pulmonary complications resulting from exposure to burning materials and the effects of phosgene in World War I (Beecher, in Cope & Rhinelander, 1943).

3. Carbon monoxide, which results, for example, from the use of hydrocarbon incendiaries in closed spaces (such as pilboxes, tunnels or air raid shelters) or in mass incendiary attacks on built-up areas, is a *blood gas,* as is hydrogen cyanide. Both France and the USA specifically included carbon monoxide in their typologies of chemical warfare agents prior to World War II, though it proved impractical as a battlefield agent.

4. White phosphorus acts as a *percutaneous* agent. It not only causes burns but also, by dissolving in the fatty tissues, may be absorbed into the

---

[10] The pre-World War II French classification had eight classes: major poisons, (hydrogen cyanide was the only member of the class); asphyxiants (such as chlorine and phosgene); lachrymators (for example, bromide compounds); vesicants (for example, mustard gas); sternutators (such as aromatic arsenic compounds); labyrinthines (agents which affect the organs of the ear such as dichlormethylether); and carbon monoxide. The Americans had six categories: lung irritants (such as chlorine, phosgene); sternutators (such as diphenylchlorarsine); lachrymators (such as benzylbromide); vesicants (such as mustard gas); direct poisons of the nervous system (such as hydrogen cyanide); and gases interfering with the respiratory properties of the blood (carbon monoxide).

[11] Nerve gases are organic derivatives of phosphorus, with a very high toxicity.

body system where it can have toxic and even lethal effects. It is thus analogous in its mode of action to mustard gas and other vesicants.

It may be noted that phosphorus and carbon monoxide are related to major chemical warfare agents since each can be used in combination with other chemicals to produce a series of potent war gases.

Comparison of chemical and incendiary agents according to their military use

There are a considerable number of parellels between the military uses of incendiary and chemical agents.

1. Both incendiaries and chemical agents may be used as weapons of mass destruction, that is as strategic area weapons.

2. Both may be used on the battlefield as tactical area weapons, either for their direct casualty effects, or in order to enhance the effectiveness of conventional munitions.

3. Both may be used for penetrating confined areas (pillboxes, buildings, tunnels, and so on) not readily accessible to conventional munitions.

4. The military manuals stress the "psychological effect" of both chemicals and incendiaries.

Combined use of chemical and incendiary agents

Mixing various munitions, such as fragmentation, high explosive, napalm and phosphorus bombs, has been widely practiced as a means of mutually enhancing the effectiveness of the weapons (see chapter 1). Similarly, non-lethal gases, such as CS,[12] may in practice be combined with lethal fire from conventional weapons (see SIPRI, 1971a).

A similar rationale might be applied to the combined use of an incendiary weapon such as napalm, and a harassing agent such as CS. In this case, however, the possibility arises of a chemical reaction between the two, producing hydrogen cyanide.[13]

Another possible combined use of chemical and incendiary agents is to dessicate an area of vegetation with herbicides containing sodium chlorate or metaborate. Grass and weeds in particular become highly inflammable after this treatment (Forman & Longacre, 1970). The defoliants used in Viet-Nam were not of the dessicant type and it is reported that

---

[12] CS, orthochlorobenzalmalonitrile, is named after its two inventors, Corson and Stroughton. It should be noted that, while CS is supposedly a non-lethal "riot control agent", in confined spaces it may be lethal and the pyrotechnic agent used to disperse the CS may also generate a lethal concentration of carbon monoxide.

[13] Allegations that BLU-52 chemical bombs containing CS were followed by BLU-27 napalm-B bombs in some attacks in Viet-Nam with the deliberate intention of producing a poisonous gas have been made by some US veterans of the Viet-Nam War. A US Department of Defense spokesman is said to have confirmed that the combination of CS and napalm would produce hydrogen cyanide (*The Guardian* (US), 29 August 1973). Recent studies indicate that CS may be converted to cyanide in the body (Frankenberg & Sörbo, 1973).

they did not contribute significantly to the inflammability of forested areas attacked with incendiaries (Lukasik, 1970). However, there is some evidence that when wood treated with the herbicides 2,4-D and 2,4,5-T is burned, small quantities of dioxin are produced (Buu-Hoi *et al.*, 1971). Dioxin is a powerful poison and teratogenic agent, producing birth defects.

VI. *Conclusions*

Both chemical explosives and incendiaries depend for their effects on a class of chemical reactions known as oxidation. Both classes of military agents may produce toxic by-products, such as carbon monoxide.

Nevertheless, there are considerable differences in the two classes of agent. The major effects of explosives are due to the blast wave which travels a considerable distance from the site of the original chemical reaction. In general, explosives do not depend upon direct contact with the target in order to achieve their antipersonnel effects.[14]

By contrast, incendiaries depend upon direct contact with the target, or inflammable materials surrounding the target. This means, first, that toxic incendiary substances such as white phosphorus may come into direct contact with the human body; and second, any toxic by-products such as carbon monoxide will be produced in the immediate neighbourhood of the victim.

In many cases the thermal effects of incendiary weapons will be the dominant threat to the victims. However, where the fire is extinguished by lack of oxygen (either because of limited ventilation, or by active fire-fighting measures), toxic substances often become the greater hazard.

Thus particles of phosphorus embedded in the body may be prevented from burning, but they will then provide a relatively larger amount of elemental phosphorus for absorption into the organs of the body. Closing off the ventilation into a confined space may help to extinguish or diminish a fire, thereby reducing the threat to the inhabitants from heat, but is likely to increase the concentration of carbon monoxide, smoke and other toxic products.

The major uses of incendiary weapons no doubt depend upon their thermal reactions, but the toxic hazard, though usually secondary, is indisputable. Whether this amounts to chemical warfare then becomes a matter of whether such compound effects are to be included in the definition of chemical weapons or not.

The problem of compound effects arises in relation to many other classes of weapons. For example, blast weapons often produce fragments, and fragmentation weapons usually utilize blast to create and disperse the frag-

---

[14] The use of small exploding projectiles against personnel was prohibited in the St. Petersburg Declaration of 1868. Certain antipersonnel mines explode in direct contact with the body.

ments. Chemical and incendiary agents may also be dispersed by an explosive charge. The problem of compound effects was discussed at the 1899 Hague conference in the context of certain fragmentation weapons which produced a considerable amount of poisonous gas when they exploded. In order to exempt them from the prohibition of weapons which depended for their effect on the emission of asphyxiating or deleterious gases, it was specified that such weapons should be so designed as to ensure that the fragmentation effect was more substantial than the toxic effect.

The limitations of this approach to the problem become readily apparent when the question of poison-tipped penetrating weapons is considered. If only the primary effect of a weapon is considered in its classification, bullets or other penetrating weapons contaminated with irritating, algogenic (pain-producing), or wound-inflaming substances would not be included as chemical means of warfare. In fact, though poison-tipped projectiles have sometimes been investigated by the military research and development establishments of certain "civilized" nations, contaminated projectiles have only been used in recent wars by so-called "uncivilized" tribesmen in non-industrial societies. That is to say, there would appear to be a general understanding that the contamination of projectiles is prohibited, because it is inhumane, causes superfluous injury and is contrary to the "dictates of human conscience"; or in other words that secondary toxic characteristics of weapons are to be taken into account.

If this is so, then similar reasoning should apply to white phosphorus weapons, which, by means of an explosive charge disperse fragments of phosphorus which may penetrate the body, as well as burn their way into it, where they may have systemic as well as local toxic effects.

The same considerations may reasonably be applied to such materials as uranium, though, in the normal state, solid elemental uranium is much more stable than white phosphorus: that is, it would not normally be readily absorbed into the body. In finely divided form it is, however, pyrophoric, and accounts of its use in projectiles emphasize this pyrophoric characteristic. On combustion, it produces uranium oxide smoke which is highly toxic since it is readily absorbed into the body through the lungs and stomach.

It may be said, therefore, that both white phosphorus and depleted uranium projectiles are directly analogous to poison-tipped weapons or contaminated projectiles.

The question of definition is more complex where the toxic effects of the incendiary weapon derive from the products of combustion rather than the initial agent. The problem is even more difficult where the generation of toxic by-products depends upon the circumstances of use, rather than the composition of the incendiary agent as such.

There is some evidence that, while carbon monoxide turned out to be a major lethal agent in incendiary attacks on German cities during World War II, neither the British nor the German authorities expected this result.

That is, to the extent that these attacks amounted to "chemical warfare", it was a question of chemical warfare by default rather than by design. Because of the experience of World War II, however, the excuse of ignorance would not be available to any future perpetrator of mass incendiary attacks.

The question as to whether carbon monoxide is a chemical agent is particularly interesting, since it had been investigated as a potential military chemical agent by a number of powers. The use of incendiary agents in circumstances where there is insufficient air to ensure complete combustion is so likely to produce carbon monoxide that it amounts to the use of a binary chemical weapon where the one component is provided by the munition and the other by the surrounding atmosphere. That is, while carbon monoxide proved impracticable as a military chemical agent because of difficulties due to diffusion, incendiary agents provide a means of generating it *in situ,* thereby solving the problems of dispersal. The addition of metal carbonyls to flamethrower fuels is a means of deliberately increasing the production of carbon monoxide.

Finally there is the question of the casualty effects of smoke, which is now recognized to be a major cause of death as a result of fire. The status of smoke in the military-legal literature is also somewhat equivocal. It has been argued, for instance, that CS, as so-called "tear gas", is not a gas but a smoke, and that while gases may be prohibited, non-lethal smokes are not. CS smoke is indeed made up of small solid particles, just as the thick black smoke from napalm is made up of solid particles of carbon. (By contrast, the white smoke from burning phosphorus is made up of droplets of phosphorus pentoxide dissolved in water.) Like CS, carbon smoke irritates the lining of the nose, throat, eyes and lungs. In low concentrations, both act as "tear gases" or "harassing agents". In higher concentrations, they act as lung irritants, precipitating potentially lethal pulmonary oedemas.

All this suggests, that while it may sometimes be convenient to classify incendiary agents as a separate category of weapons, they are capable of acting in ways similar to chemical weapons, and therefore merit due attention on this score also.

Appendix 4A

Toxic effects of white phosphorus (WP) munitions

I. *Introduction*

White phosphorus (WP) munitions have been widely used not only for smoke screening and target marking but also as incendiary and antipersonnel weapons (Beller, 1969). White phosphorus is well-known as a systemic poison but the possibility that toxic complications may arise as a result of burns from white phosphorus munitions has not always received sufficient emphasis in the military medical literature.

The toxicity of elemental white phosphorus has been known since shortly after Henning Brandt's discovery of *phosphorus mirabilis* in 1669. Acute phosphorus poisoning, usually resulting from the suicidal or accidental ingestion of phosphorus-containing rat poisons or fireworks, is well described in the literature (for example, Diaz-Rivera, Collazo, Pons & Torregrosa, 1950; Marin, Montoya, Sierra & Senior, 1971). Cases of chronic phosphorus poisoning among match workers, resulting in necrosis of the jaw, were described as early as 1839 (Childs, 1970), and the threat to workers in phosphorus plants still exists (see Ozerova, Rusakova & Korenevskaya, 1971).

World War II reports of the effects of phosphorus munitions were contradictory. While some reports (for example, Porritt, 1953) warned of potentially fatal renal and hepatic damage from the phosphorus contained in incendiary bullets, others (for example, Bauer, cited in Bond, 1946) claimed that phosphorus poisoning following incendiary bomb attacks had not been proved, despite many fears at the time. One US military manual (US Departments of the Army and the Air Force, 1963) reports that the vapours of white phosphorus are toxic, producing bone decay, and that phosphorus burn wounds heal very slowly; slow wound healing has been reported by Obermer (1943), Cope (1953), Sinilo (1961) and Curreri, Asch & Pruitt (1970). Another US manual (1968) warns that the phosphorus burn wounds should be debrided immediately to remove bits of phosphorus which "might be absorbed later and possibly produce systemic poisoning" (p. 81). But an experimental study in 1945 (Walker, Wexler & Hill, reprinted 1969)[1] implied that toxic quantities of white phosphorus or its products were unlikely to remain in the wound caused by burning particles of white phosphorus. However, these implications are contentious (see below, pp. 215*ff* and 220*ff*).

---

[1] The study was authorized by the US Chemical Warfare Service, as part of a project on the prevention and treatment of chemical warfare casualties. Originally produced in only 90 copies, it was reprinted in 1969 by the Biomedical Department of the US Army's Edgewood Arsenal Research Laboratories.

More recently, as a result of new experiences in Viet-Nam and in the Middle East, a number of reports have appeared of rapid deaths from phosphorus burns even where only a small area of the body surface was involved (Bowen, Whelan & Nelson, 1971; Ben-Hur, Giladi, Neuman, Shugerman & Appelbaum, 1972). These reports have in turn generated several series of experimental studies aimed at elucidating the physiological mechanisms following phosphorus burns.

There are a number of reasons why possible toxic effects of white phosphorus burns may have been masked in the past. During World War II, particularly in the case of mass bombing attacks which resulted both in large numbers of casualties and in the destruction of medical facilities, it was likely that the victim of moderate to severe burns from phosphorus bombs would die from the thermal injury, regardless of any additional toxic complications. Improvements in the treatment of burns since World War II have revealed the seriousness of even moderate white phosphorus burns (Summerlin, Walder & Moncrief, 1967).

Secondly many of the physiological reactions to phosphorus which are now being described in the literature, such as haemolysis leading to renal failure (Summerlin et al., 1967) and disturbances of the heart leading to death from cardiac failure (Bowen et al., 1971), may also result from purely thermal injury (see chapter 3). The one symptom which might distinguish phosphorus poisoning from a thermal burn is liver damage. This is a characteristic of phosphorus poisoning following oral ingestion, where phosphorus is transported from the intestines to the liver by direct blood flow. But this symptom may not be obvious at the post mortem where rapid death from cardiac or renal failure has occured. It is understandable, therefore, if surgeons working in combat conditions may not have observed toxic reactions in phosphorus burns.

Thirdly, diagnosis of phosphorus poisoning is complicated by the fact that a widely-used treatment for phosphorus burns, irrigating the wound with a dilute solution of copper sulphate (NATO, 1958; Voennyj vestnick, 48, May 1968, pp. 95–101) may itself lead to reactions such as renal failure as a result of copper poisoning (Summerlin et al., 1967). Only recently with a more sophisticated analysis of the phosphorus and copper poisoning syndromes has it proved possible to distinguish between the two (Summerlin et al., 1967).

All these reasons may help to explain why the possible toxic effects of phosphorus munitions have not been greatly emphasized. For the same reasons, the design of definitive experimental research has proved extremely difficult. While it is possible to administer white phosphorus in a variety of ways which do not involve burns, this would not answer the question of whether it was possible to absorb a toxic or lethal dose of phosphorus through a burn wound. Further, all the evidence points to a great variety of physiological reactions to phosphorus affecting the heart, liver, kidneys, brain, bone marrow, and so on. In the absence of an enormous and complicated multivariate experimental design, it is necessary to piece together the results of a variety of experiments in order to approach an overall explanation of the physiological mechanism of poisoning following phosphorus burns.

In this review, general studies of phosphorus poisoning, usually following oral ingestion, are described first. This is followed by descriptions of more recent studies where elemental and radioactively-labelled phosphorus are administered by intraperitoneal or subcutaneous injection. Finally several recent studies of white phosphorus burns are reviewed.

II. *Phosphorus poisoning following gastric/intestinal absorption*

Much of the clinical literature on phosphorus poisoning describes the effects of accidental or suicidal oral ingestion of white phosphorus, such as that contained in certain rat poisons. In one study of 56 cases of attempted suicides, 29 recovered and 27 died after ingesting an estimated average of 1.13 grams, a gross mortality rate of 48 per cent (Diaz-Rivera, Collazo, Pons & Torregrosa, 1950). There was a clear correlation between the amount consumed and the likelihood of death. All the patients vomited sooner or later, but this did not prevent the absorption of sufficient phosphorus to cause death in many cases. A number of symptoms appeared to indicate impending death. Seventeen patients showed haematemesis, of whom 13 (77 per cent) died; of the 39 patients who did not show haematemesis, 14 (36 per cent) died. Many patients showed a severe drop in blood pressure. Mortality of patients who on admission had a systolic blood pressure of less than 100 mm was 70 per cent; between 100–140 mm, 32.5 per cent.

One of the symptoms most frequently reported after oral ingestion of phosphorus is damage to the liver, since it is the liver which receives much of the phosphorus after absorption through the gastrointestinal tract. In small quantities the liver is able to extract phosphorus from the blood and it is subsequently removed from the body in the faeces. Where large quantities are absorbed rapidly, the liver is not able to cope. Forty-one (71 per cent) of the patients in the sample of Diaz-Rivera *et al.* (1950) showed enlargement of the liver, and these authors concluded that if this is noticeable within the first 24 hours the prognosis is negative. Jaundice occurred in 20 (36 per cent) of the cases, again with a high mortality.

Several experimental studies of the effects of phosphorus in the liver have been reported, where oral ingestion is simulated in a more controlled fashion by passing phosphorus in an oil solution through a tube into the stomach of experimental animals. In one such study, Goshal, Porta & Hartroft (1969) showed that the weight of the liver increased significantly from the fourth to the twenty-fourth hour (the longest time period recorded in the experiment). Light microscopy showed a nearly normal picture at four hours. At six hours the liver cells (hepatocytes) contained moderately large droplets of fat. At 12 hours the fatty changes were severe and practically all hepatocytes contained numerous globules of various sizes. Small foci of necrotic hepatocytes were intermingled with more numerous inflamed mesenchymal cells. The frequency of these foci was higher at 24 hours than at 12 hours.

Electron microscopy revealed a diversity of changes in the hepatocytes from four hours and onwards, while liver cells other than hepatocytes appeared normal throughout the experimental period.

Biochemical analysis showed that the level of triglycerides in the liver increased rapidly from the sixth to the twenty-fourth hour, while triglyceride levels in the blood plasma decreased. Similar results are reported by Pani, Gravela, Mazzarino & Burdino (1972), who showed that administration of propyl gallate or glutathione lowered the increased levels of hepatic triglycerides to normal levels.

In order to further explore the distribution of phosphorus in the tissues a number of experimental studies have been carried out using radioactively-labelled white phosphorus. Cameron & Patrick (1966) showed in this way the distribution of labelled phosphorus in the organs of mice, rats and rabbits following administration of phosphorus dissolved in oil through a tube into the stomach. They concluded that in general the fatty degeneration of the liver, kidneys and heart was histologically akin to that noted in clinical reports of human cases. A radiographic analysis showed that the uptake of phosphorus varied in different organs. The authors noted that in the liver the uptake had a zonal distribution and that this was greater in the centrilobular areas. In both the kidneys and the adrenal glands the cortex was more heavily labelled than the medulla. In the spleen the greater intensity of radiation seemed to correspond with the red pulp and in the lungs it was associated with the small vessels and bronchi. Since these differences might have been due to the amount of blood contained in each organ, some animals were perfused with a saline solution before radiographic analysis, but the results were the same, thus indicating that the phosphorus is indeed taken up in the tissues of these organs.

These authors prepared homogenates of the tissue of the liver, kidneys, heart and brain and then examined the phosphorus content of the water-soluble, fat-soluble and dry residue fractions following an extraction procedure. Since phosphorus is fat-soluble it might be expected that the major proportion of the phosphorus was to be found in the fat-soluble fraction. This was the case in the heart and brain, but, surprisingly, was not so in the liver and kidney, where a greater proportion was found in the dry residue, made up mainly of protein. This finding, it was suggested, indicated that in the liver and kidneys the phosphorus reacts directly with the protein of the cells in some way.

Goshal, Porta & Hartroft (1971) in a further study using labelled phosphorus reported that two hours after administration 65 per cent of the radioactivity detected was in the liver, 12 per cent in the blood, 4 per cent in the kidneys, 0.4 per cent in the spleen, 0.4 per cent in the pancreas and 0.39 per cent in the brain. These authors also reported findings which suggested to them that phosphorus was slowly transformed to some as yet unknown toxic metabolite before injuring the liver.

The study of Cameron & Patrick (1966) shows some minor differences to that of Goshal *et al.* (1971), which reflects differences in the time-scales used in the experiments. Since phosphorus is oxidized by the oxygen in the tissues it ends up finally as common phosphate transported in the blood. Thus it is not suprising to see that Cameron & Patrick found a large part of the radioactivity after 48 hours in the blood, while in the Goshal study only a minor part of the isotope was in circulation at the moment of maximal hepatic incorporation (two hours). The incorporation into different hepatic subcellular fractions must therefore be associated with two different mechanisms, one reflecting incorporation of incompletely oxidized phosphorus, which accounts for the toxic effect, and the other being dependent upon the naturally occurring turnover of orthophosphate.

Ganote & Otis (1969) injected solutions of phosphorus in oil into the peritoneum of rats. In addition to the signs of cellular injury noted in the previous studies, an electron microscope examination of the liver revealed changes at the subcellular level. The authors concluded that the accumulation of rough endoplasmic reticulum (RER) which often forms concentric whorls, is a characteristic feature of phosphorus poisoning of the liver, and furthermore, that the time taken for hepatic changes to become manifest may be longer following intraperitoneal injection than following absorption through the gastrointestinal tract.

A previous study by Diaz-Rivera *et al.* (1950) had reported that the increase of urea in the blood (azotaemia) was a valuable prognostic sign, since its early appearance and persistence indicated a fatal outcome. Azotaemia was encountered in 30 (54 per cent) of their patients, and of these 13 (43 per cent) died. Electrocardiograms (ECG) from 16 patients showed that in 12 of these there were significant changes. Whereas minor changes could persist for several weeks, acute changes to the myocardium often resulted in early death. Moreover they noted changes in the blood chemistry which included a number of cases of increased levels of phosphates and decreased blood sugar levels. The red blood cell count was higher than normal, markedly so in patients who had ingested larger doses of phosphorus, whereas white cells were within the normal range in most cases.

Restlessness, toxic delirium, toxic psychosis, hallucinations and maniacal manifestations, all of which are indications of direct or indirect effects (such as anoxia) on the brain, heralded the approach of death in a high proportion of cases.

These authors therefore concluded that intoxication by white phosphorus has a high mortality; that the rate at which symptoms develop depends upon the rate of phosphorus absorption (which in the case of oral ingestion is related to the quantity and form in which the phosphorus is ingested—solid, paste, dissolved in liquid, etc.); and that phosphorus poisoning affects the liver, kidneys, heart, brain and blood.

They further reported that early deaths result from collapse of the peripheral blood circulation (hypovolemic shock); that after 24–48 hours renal or cardiac failure may be the cause of death; and that *therefore the majority of those who die do so before a clear-cut picture of hepatic damage emerges.*

The latter fact is of great importance to the present discussion, since it shows that the mechanism of death in the victim of phosphorus poisoning —in the absence of burns or mechanical injury—may be the same as that in early deaths from burns or mechanical injury. Where these injuries are concurrent, as from a phosphorus munition, it is difficult to attribute the cause of death to any one of the factors in the absence of any additional identifying symptom. Such a symptom—characteristic forms of damage to the liver —may not be present at the time of death in the majority of cases.

III. *Phosphorus poisoning following subcutaneous injection*

A number of experiments have been reported where solutions of phosphorus are injected under the skin. Phosphorus is soluble in the fatty tissue underlying the skin and in this form is readily absorbed into the blood.[2] These experiments are important for the present discussion since the mechanism of absorption is more similar to that in a skin burn than is the case where phosphorus is ingested orally, introduced into the stomach by tube, or injected into the peritoneum.

In one study, Truhaut, Claude & Warnet (1969) reported that following subcutaneous injection of white phosphorus in rats the level of hepatic triglycerides increased and the plasma triglyceride level decreased. This symptom is characteristic of phosphorus poisoning following other forms of administration.

---

[2] In this respect white phosphorus is analogous to mustard gas (or liquid mustard), which is also absorbed into the body through chemical burns of the skin (as well as through the lungs and mucous membranes). Like phosphorus, mustard is lipid soluble and a protoplasmic poison, and the chemical burns caused by it take an exceptionally long time to heal. According to Vedder (1925), the long healing time of mustard burns is explained by "... this action of mustard on the blood vessels which are rendered incapable of carrying out their functions of repair; and by the fact that necrotic tissue acts as a good culture medium. Hence the great liability to infection of mustard burns" (Vedder, 1925, p. 134).

The same authors investigated the triglyceride changes in the liver in a further study using the same method of injecting phosphorus. Palmitinic acid is normally incorporated together with triglycerides into the β-lipoproteins by the hepatocytes in the liver from which they are released into the blood serum. Truhaut *et al.* (1971), following the injection of phosphorus, administered radioactive tritium-labelled palmitinic acid 18 hours before the rats were killed. A significant reduction in the presence of radioactivity in the serum β-lipoproteins was noted, compared to the control group of animals, while the fatty content of the livers of the experimental group was increased. Thus it seems reasonable to believe that phosphorus blocks the release of the triglycerides into the blood in the form of β-lipoproteins. As suggested by other authors such a mechanism would explain the accumulation of triglycerides in the liver and the decrease of triglycerides in the circulating blood.

In a third paper, Truhaut *et al.* (1972) extended their observations to a longer period of time. They reported that few changes were recorded in the livers at 18 hours but that after that time, serum lipids decreased and hepatic liquids increased, with some signs of reversal of this process in those animals which survived 48 hours. These findings are similar to those reported by Diaz-Rivera *et al.* (1950) in the case of humans who had ingested phosphorus orally.

IV. *Phosphorus poisoning following cutaneous burns*

During World War II there were sporadic reports of the possibility of systemic poisoning following burns inflicted by phosphorus munitions (e.g. Cope, 1953). More recently as a result of the use of these munitions in Viet-Nam and the Middle East, further reports have appeared in the medical literature. These in turn have inspired a number of experimental studies.

In an earlier experimental study, Walker, Wexler & Hill (1945, reprinted 1969) allowed 25-mg pellets of white phosphorus to burn on the skin of pigs and on glass and the products of combustion were collected, analyzed and measured. The pellets burned for an average of 22 seconds, and the skin was washed with water immediately afterwards. In these conditions the authors concluded that 66 per cent of the phosphorus was converted to phosphorus pentoxide smoke (79 per cent when burned on glass) and 24 per cent was left in the skin as acid (mostly orthophosphoric acid). The residue in the skin consisted of a small amount (0.5 mg) of unoxidized phosphorus, some of it as elemental white phosphorus, and some as the isomorphic but less toxic red phosphorus. The authors calculated that on average 2.7 mg of the phosphorus entered the skin as orthophosphoric acid. This was only sufficient to alter the pH to a depth of 1.5 mm whereas thermal coagulation extended to a depth of 3 mm. They therefore concluded that the heat of reaction, rather than any chemical action, was "probably primarily responsible for the tissue damage in the WP burn".

These results must be interpreted with some care. The pellets burned for a very short time (22 seconds) in optimal conditions (on the surface of the skin, rather than deeply embedded in it). Even so about 0.5 mg of elemental phosphorus remained on the skin after burning—but this was immediately washed off by water. All these factors mean that the white phosphorus was in contact with the tissues for a very short period of time. It is questionable whether these conditions can be compared with combat conditions. In this study no attempt was made to follow possible systemic effects, which may not arise for many hours.

Nevertheless, these results are interesting from another point of view. Although the authors do not give the area of full thickness burn caused by the 25-mg pellets of white phosphorus, it may be estimated from the indications provided that such a pellet would cause a third degree burn wound of between roughly 0.3–1.2 cm² in area. That is, approximately 20–80 mg of white phosphorus is required to burn 1 cm² of body surface. By extrapolation it may be calculated that 5–20 gm would be required to cause a 15 per cent burn in an adult man weighing 70 kg and with a body surface area of 1.73 m² (Guyton, 1966). In their study Walker *et al.* calculated that 1.7 per cent of the phosphorus remained in the wounds as elemental white phosphorus after spontaneous extinction. Thus, in the case of a 15 per cent burn wound in a 70-kg man, between 1.25–5 mg of white phosphorus per kg body weight would remain in the wound. This figure assumes small particles of white phosphorus (25 mg) burning in optimal conditions on the surface of the skin. Where particles were larger, embedded in the tissues, or artificially extinguished, the amount of white phosphorus remaining in the wound would be higher.

This figure may be compared with the estimates of the lethal dose of white phosphorus as 1–1.4 mg per kg body weight (Diaz-Rivera, 1950; US Department of Health, Education & Welfare, 1972). Walker *et al.* drew the conclusion that the amount of white phosphorus left in the wound was insignificant; presumably it was for this reason that the US Army's Edgewood Arsenal Laboratory chose to reprint the paper in 1969. But far from demonstrating that the residual phosphorus can be dismissed, the study would seem to indicate that potentially lethal doses of white phosphorus may remain in a burn wound of average severity.

In a more recent clinical report, Summerlin *et al.* (1967) studied 11 military patients with phosphorus burns, eight of whom had been treated with copper sulphate solution. Three of these patients suffered from massive haemolysis and other signs of phosphorus and/or copper poisoning. The authors concluded that even relatively minor phosphorus burns were more serious than had been thought, but that it was not possible in this material to separate fully the effects of phosphorus from those of the copper sulphate solution used in treatment. However, the authors did present a useful list of symptoms caused by phosphorus and copper poisoning respectively.

Bonelli & Varotti (1971) reported a clinical study of six boys burned by phosphorus when they accidentally set off a dud white phosphorus munition. Though in this case the patients recovered, there were clear indications that phosphorus may be absorbed into the body through the burn wound and produce symptoms, such as enlargement of the liver and increased blood and urine levels of phosphorus, which are similar to symptoms produced by phosphorus poisoning following oral ingestion and other means of absorption.

As a result of all these indications of possible toxic effects of white phosphorus burns, several series of experiments have been reported in recent years.

In one experiment, Bowen et al. (1971) created "standard white phosphorus burns" (SWPB) in anaesthetized rabbits weighing about 3.5 kg.[3] The effects of these burns were compared with thermal burns of similar depth and extent caused by placing a branding iron on the back and flanks of the anaesthetized animals. In each group some animals were given no further treatment, while in others the wound was excised and closed one hour after burning. In a further control group only the surgical operations (anaesthesis, excision and closure) were carried out, without burning.

The main focus of this study was on decreases in the levels of calcium in the blood serum and increases in the levels of phosphate, a phenomenon described as the calcium-phosphorus shift. Of the 130 animals in one SWPB group, 90 received no treatment, while 40 received excision and closure. Sixty-five per cent of the animals died within three days regardless of treatment, half of them within 18 hours. All 45 animals in the control groups survived. In the SWPB group, serum calcium levels were depressed in 80 per cent of cases, more so in the cases of those which died. All animals which died showed elevated levels of serum phosphate.

In a second series 24 rabbits were subjected to standard white phosphorus burns and this time hourly electrocardiograms were recorded in 85 per cent of these animals, in 90 per cent of cases within 24 hours. All animals that died showed profound calcium-phosphate shifts, which became

---

[3] The animals were shaved and treated with a depilatory agent on the back and flanks. The burns were produced by placing a metal well three inches in diameter on one flank of the anaesthetized animal. In the metal well a wafer of white phosphorus weighing 10 grams, 2 cm in diameter, was placed. The phosphorus was ignited by heating with a hairdryer and allowed to burn for one minute. Thereafter the phosphorus was extinguished with iced water and the residue removed immediately. The procedure was repeated again on the other flank. The paired burns produced were well demarcated, of full-thickness, representing an estimated involvement of 10 to 20 per cent of total body area. This experimental method was named standard white phosphorus burn (SWPB).

noticeable as early as one hour after the burn. Seventy per cent of the animals showed electrocardiographic abnormalities (prolongation of the Q-T interval, ST segment depression, T-wave changes, bradycardia and low QRS complex voltage). Control animals receiving branding iron burns instead of white phosphorus burns survived, and did not show calcium-phosphate shifts or abnormal ECG recordings. All animals underwent histological examination of the heart, liver, kidney and lungs at death or at sacrifice after five days. No morphological changes were observed.

It must be noted here that, as the authors point out, the measure of serum phosphate used does not include unoxidized elemental white phosphorus or other oxidation products. Indeed, an attempt was made to remove any such residues from the wound after one minute when the burning phosphorus was extinguished with iced water. Therefore it is not surprising that post mortem investigation failed to reveal any morphological changes to the heart, lungs, liver and kidneys. The importance of this study is that it revealed an *additional* physiological mechanism following phosphorus burns.

Because of the importance of this finding, the authors attempted to check on a number of clinical cases in Viet-Nam. The calcium-phosphorus shift was revealed in one patient who died 10 hours after receiving moderate white phosphorus burns, but electrocardiographic abnormalities did not develop. In two other patients fatal cardiac arrhythmias were recorded eight hours after the burn, but serum calcium and phosphorus determinations had not been carried out. Cases were also reported where, despite extensive white phosphorus burns, the calcium-phosphorus shift and electrocardiographic changes did not occur, as was also the case in a minority of the experimental animals. The authors therefore concluded that on this admittedly limited basis it seems likely that some, but not all, patients burned with white phosphorus may rapidly develop hypocalcaemia and hyperphosphataemia and occasionally cardiac arrhythmias serious enough to cause death. Cardiac abnormalities following oral ingestion of white phosphorus were also reported by Diaz-Rivera *et al.* (1950, 1961) and other authors.

From this experiment it can be seen that the phosphate level increases even after burn excision, which implies two possibilities. First, phosphorus may enter the circulation after absorption from the wound without being detected before it is oxidized to phosphate. Second, it is possible that minimal amounts of white phosphorus or partly oxidized phosphorus compounds interact with the phosphate-calcium regulatory mechanism of the body.

In another experiment, Ben-Hur *et al.* (1971) compared phosphorus burns in rats with third degree thermal burns caused by a hot brass plate. The phosphorus-burned rats showed a rise in the serum phosphate level as early as two hours after burning, with no decrease in calcium ion concentration. In addition the level of glutamic pyruvic transaminase in the serum (SGPT) showed a marked increase (from 10 to 100 units per ml); this was probably related to extensive liver cell damage found on histological examination:

The liver was swollen, yellow-brown in colour with patchy areas of haemorrhage scattered over its surface. Histologically, the liver showed diffuse areas of necrosis ... periportal infiltration with inflamatory cells ... [and] areas of ballooning degeneration of hepatic cells and microthrombi of partal veins ... In the kidneys there was swelling of cells, desquamation and perinuclear vacuolisation and necrosis ... and vacuolar degeneration of proximal convoluted tubules, with debris in their lumen (Ben-Hur *et al.*, 1971, pp. 241–42).

The phosphorus burns covering 12–15 per cent of the body surface caused death in approximately 50 per cent of the cases within 24–48 hours. In this short period it is unlikely that liver damage was responsible and these authors suggest that death was more likely to have been the result of renal changes, leading to renal failure. These authors point out that high levels of serum phosphate cause highly acidic urine, which may cause necrosis of the tubules of the kidneys (cf. Artz, 1960; Phillips & Cope, 1962; Schreiner & Maher, 1965). Renal failure in turn might lead to cardiac failure as a result of increased levels of potassium in the blood. A number of additional causes of renal failure following phosphorus burns are suggested: (*a*) elemental phosphorus that has not undergone oxidation; (*b*) phosphoric acids; and (*c*) other products or toxins from the burn wound, phosphated or otherwise. The second possibility seemed the least likely since Mason, Teschan & Muirhead (1963) have shown that loading with phosphoric acids does not produce lesions of the liver or kidneys. Ben-Hur *et al.* therefore concluded that unoxidized phosphorus was the most likely explanation, though in this study other burn toxins were not specifically investigated.

Knowing the small lethal dose of elemental unoxidised phosphorus, its absorption even in small quantities is capable of causing these lesions. They are similar to those described in the literature on acute phosphorus poisoning ... (Ben-Hur *et al.*, 1972, p. 242).

In a second paper, Ben-Hur, Giladi, Appelbaum & Neuman (1972) confirmed the findings of Summerlin *et al.* (1967) that copper sulphate solution may cause toxic effects similar to those of phosphorus itself. However, in this experiment, Ben-Hur *et al.* showed that the treatment of the white phosphorus particles with a *suspension* of copper sulphate resulted in the successful neutralization of the phosphorus without causing the toxic changes shown in the rats treated with copper sulphate *solution* alone. The addition of lauryl sulphate detergent, by reducing the surface tension of the phosphorus particles, greatly improved the process of coating the particles with a neutralizing layer of copper phosphide. By contrast, lithium iodate, as proposed by Summerlin *et al.*, proved either too toxic, or if used in lower concentrations, had no effect at all.

In a third paper Ben-Hur & Appelbaum (1973) confirmed that both renal and hepatic changes may follow phosphorus burns. They reported that renal damage occurs first and is likely to be the major cause of death. Hepatic damage follows later, and appears less likely to be fatal than in the case of phosphorus poisoning following oral ingestion. Biochemical changes were recorded which paralleled the histological changes. The alterations in serum phosphate, sodium and potassium levels correspond to the chemical alterations usually seen after acute renal failure. Further evidence of kidney involvement was given by the high volume of urine output three days after the burn with low osmolarity as opposed to the elevation of serum osmolarity and high water intake. This conclusion was further reinforced by the sharp decrease in creatinine clearance. In this experiment, where 25-mg pellets of phosphorus were introduced into an incision in the inguinal region and allowed to burn for four minutes by opening and closing the wound, 50 per cent of the rats died.

These authors also described what appears to be the most promising means of treatment reported so far. The basic reaction of copper sulphate with phosphorus, producing a coating of copper phosphide on the particles which prevents further combustion, is modified by suspending the 3 per cent copper sulphate and 5 per cent sodium bicarbonate solution in 1 per cent hydroxyethyl cellulose. This solution prevents the sedimentation of copper salts in the wound, while the sodium bicarbonate neutralizes any acids of phosphorus formed. In addition 1 per cent lauryl sulphate solution is added to the suspension to reduce the surface tension of the phosphorus granules, ensuring total coverage. In the animals treated with this method no deaths occurred and wound healing was noticeable within four to five days; in the untreated phosphorus burns, the wounds showed no tendency to heal until six days after the burn.

V. *Discussion*

The above material is presented in order to enable an assessment to be made of the current state of knowledge with regard to the toxic effects of phosphorus, whether the absorption into the body is by means of cutaneous burns, subcutaneous or peritoneal injection, or oral ingestion.

The figures given by Walker *et al.* (1945) enable the calculation to be made that at least 1–5 mg of white phosphorus and 4–23 mg of red phosphorus per kg body weight are likely to remain in the wound in an average adult male suffering a 15 per cent white phosphorus burn, if combustion is allowed to proceed to completion. This must be compared with the commonly accepted estimate that the lethal dose for man is 1.4 mg per kg body weight (US Department of Health, Education and Welfare, 1972). If combustion is stopped early, or if phosphorus is driven into the skin by means of explosives, more elemental white phosphorus and phosphorus compounds will remain in the tissues because embedded phosphorus particles will not oxidize completely in the absence of free access to oxygen. Therefore it must be concluded that there may well be enough phosphorus present in the wound to cause systemic poisoning or even death.

It is evident that white phosphorus, red phosphorus and orthophosphoric acid will all be present in the wound (Walker *et al.*, 1945). This means that other intermediate phosphorus compounds, inorganic or organic, may also be present. Some of these substances may be present in sufficient concentration to impede wound healing; even correct treatment with oxidizing and neutralizing agents may impair the regeneration of wound tissue (Brånemark *et al.*, 1968).

The absorption of white phosphorus is governed by its lipid solubility. In a third degree burn the injury may extend into the subcutaneous tissue, which contains numerous fat cells. Some of these will be ruptured by the heat of combustion, releasing the fat content in which white phosphorus is soluble. Fat-soluble substances penetrate cell membranes and other membranous structures more readily than water-soluble substances. Thus there will be little difference between a subcutaneous injection of white phosphorus dissolved in oil and white phosphorus dissolved in subcutaneous fat tissue except the time taken to dissolve the phosphorus particles and the fact that solubility of phosphorus in fat is not unlimited.

The rate of solvation depends upon the size of the particle and the amount of fat present. Small particles dissolve more rapidly than large particles. This may explain why patients sometimes not only survive with large pieces of white phosphorus embedded deep in the muscular tissue, but show no signs of systemic phosphorus poisoning (cf. Erskin, in Curerri *et al.*, 1970, p. 641), but such reports cannot be used to prove the innocuousness of WP munitions.

The animal experiments described indicate that the major difference between oral, gastric, intubation, intraperitoneal and subcutaneous administration of phosphorus is the time which elapses before clinical symptoms and histological and biochemical alterations become manifest. The rate of uptake in different organs and the toxic effects are related to the path of the blood flow through the body.

Phosphorus is transported in the blood as a colloidal suspension in combination with micelles, fat droplets or lipoproteins and is not removable by haemodialysis, as is free orthophosphate (Goodman & Gilman, 1955). The phosphorus transported in the blood is absorbed by the tissues, particularly the liver, within two or three hours. The serum phosphorus level, measured as orthophosphate, reaches a maximum level after one to three days, demonstrating that phosphorus is carried by the bloodstream throughout the body before being taken up in the most well-perfused tissues and then being slowly transformed by oxidation or orthophosphate, causing increased serum levels of phosphate after a few days.

Several explanations of the elevation of serum phosphate levels are possible. For example, acidosis and renal function disturbances may mobilize skeletal phosphate and calcium. Phosphorus or phosphorus compounds may interfere with the phosphate-calcium regulatory mechanisms, or phosphate imbalance may arise as a consequence of renal failure. Nevertheless, the animal experiments show that the elevation of serum phosphate level is a unique feature of the white phosphorus-burned animals, since control animals subjected to branding-iron burns or skin removal do not show any change in phosphate levels. Thus at the present level of research the most satisfactory explanation must be that the increase in serum phosphate originates from phosphorus absorbed through the burn wound.

During the time phosphorus is located in the tissues, cell damage and metabolic disorders occur. The mechanism of hepatocytic damage has been extensively studied, yielding results which suggest that phosphorus impairs the synthesis of lipoproteins and thereby blocks the release of hepatic triglycerides into the blood. Some authors report that they have detected diene conjugation in the lipid fraction of liver cells. The histological pattern of liver damage is a proven characteristic of phosphorus poisoning and different from changes induced by other hepatic poisons (Ganote et al., 1969). The liver appears to be the most vulnerable organ if the phosphorus is ingested, perhaps because the venous blood flow from the gastrointestinal tract passes the liver before entering the main circulation.

However, if phosphorus is absorbed through a burn wound, other organs, such as the heart and kidneys, may suffer metabolic disorders before the liver. Heart disturbances may lead to death before any histological changes occur. The increase in phosphate in the serum produces a highly acidic urine which in burned animals may produce tubular necrosis, particularly where hypovolaemia results in reduced perfusion of blood through the kidneys. Renal and cardiac failure appear to be the primary causes of early deaths following phosphorus burns.

It is evident that current knowledge of the physiological and biochemical effects of phosphorus burns is not complete and that further studies are required. Two types of experiment would seem to be of particular importance in addition to full analyses of any clinical material which may become available as a result of continued use of white phosphorus munitions. First, valuable information could be obtained by combining the use of labelled phosphorus and thermal burn techniques used by Bowen et al. (1971) and Ben-Hur et al. (1972).[4] This would enable the absorption and distribu-

---

[4] Druckrey (1973) reports an experiment where radioactive phosphorus (^{32}P), in the form of sodium phosphate, was injected intravenously into pregnant rats as early as the second day of gestation. Malignant tumours developed in 17 of the 130 offspring, 11 in the nervous system,

tion of phosphorus in the tissues following the burn to be plotted. Since this technique alone would not reveal the chemical form of the phosphorus, a laboratory method is required to measure the various forms of phosphorus in the blood and tissues in both experimental and clinical studies. Second, possible toxic oxidation products might be detected by agitating tissue homogenates or blood together with white phosphorus at physiological oxygen pressure and temperature; after centrifugation or filtration the clear solution could be tested on laboratory animals. If toxic reactions were recorded, biochemical separation methods could be applied in an effort to identify the toxic agent or agents.

VI. *Conclusion*

In spite of incomplete knowledge of the toxicological mechanisms involved in the white phosphorus burn syndrome, it must be concluded that the toxic manifestations of white phosphorus burns are of greater importance than has sometimes been judged in the past. There is compelling experimental evidence that sufficient quantities of white phosphorus may be absorbed through a surface burn wound to cause lethal or toxic effects, such as renal or cardiac failure or liver damage. There are a number of clinical reports of early deaths from white phosphorus burns in combat conditions. Further, white phosphorus burns take longer to heal than purely thermal burns.

White phosphorus munitions must therefore be considered to have both an incendiary and a chemical mode of action on the human body. Certain technological developments, such as high-velocity shells and more powerful explosives, giving white phosphorus particles a higher velocity, plasticized white phosphorus which better maintains the integrity of the particles, and liquefied white phosphorus which dissolves more rapidly in the body fats, tend to facilitate the penetration of white phosphorus into the body, thereby increasing the risk of poisoning.

two in the liver, two in the lungs and two in the skin. These results are probably due to the radioactivity rather than to the phosphorus as such. Nevertheless, they point to a further complication which would have to be controlled in any further experimentation on the effects of phosphorus using labelled atoms.

Appendix 4B

Toxicity of incendiary agents, additives and products of combustion

I. *Measurement of toxicity*

Reliable measures of toxicity are difficult to obtain, since for obvious reasons it is not possible to carry out experiments with poisonous substances on human beings. Instead, a variety of laboratory animals are used (usually rats, mice and rabbits). Often the toxicity figures are derived from only one species, such as the rat; only rarely is accurate data available for man. Such estimates for man as do exist are usually derived from a relatively small number of clinical cases resulting from accidents, suicide attempts or (rarely) combat; in each of these situations it is difficult to determine precisely how much of a substance has actually been absorbed into the body. The species used in the determination is thus one source of variation in the results, since some species are more sensitive than others to a particular toxic substance.

Another source of variation is the route of administration used in experiments. Again data is not available for all possible routes of administration in all species. The most common routes are oral (including eating or drinking, or in some experiments passing the substance into the stomach through a tube), intraperitoneal (usually by injection from a hyperdermic syringe directly into the abdominal cavity), subcutaneous (by injection under the skin) and inhalation (either by filling a chamber with the toxic gas or vapour, or through a face mask or tubes into the trachea). Other means of administration include intravenous, occular and intramuscular methods.

Because of differences in the physical state of the toxic substance and the route of administration, it is not possible to give the toxic dose in the same units of measurement. Where the dose is administered orally, subcutaneously or intraperitoneally, it is usual to give the dose as the number of milligrams (mg) for each kilogram (kg) of the body weight of the animal required to produce a toxic or lethal effect.

Where the toxic substance is inhaled, it is more difficult to determine the amount of the substance actually absorbed. It is of interest to know what the concentration of the substance in the atmosphere must be before symptoms appear within a given time. Therefore concentration figures are given as parts per million parts of air by volume (ppm) where the substance is a vapour or gas. Where the substance is a smoke made up of solid particles or liquid droplets, the unit is the number of milligrams (mg) of the substance in a cubic metre (m^3) of air.

The problem of estimating the toxic dose is especially difficult in the case of the thermal decomposition products of organic substances, such as plastics. The pyrolysis of plastics is often a complex process resulting in a great variety of possible products, depending upon the circumstances. It is very difficult to measure the toxicity of the resulting mixture of products, since the composition of the mixture may vary. (This problem is admirably described by MacFarland, 1968.)

There are four main measures of toxicity, though not all of them are appropriate to a given substance. They are (*a*) the *toxic concentration* (TC), that is, the concentration of the substance in the air which has been reported to produce any indication of a physiological reaction in a given time, or to produce any carcinogenic (cancerous), teratogenic (affecting the development of the foetus), mutagenic (affecting the genes) or neoplastic (affecting the development of the young) effects; (*b*) *the lethal concentration* (LC), that is, the concentration which has been reported to cause death in man after exposure of a given time, or which has caused death in animals after an exposure eight hours or less; (*c*) the *toxic dose* (TD), that is, the dose of a substance introduced by any route other than inhalation which has been reported to produce any toxic effects in man or animals; and (*d*) the *lethal dose* (LD), that is, the dose of a substance introduced by any route other than inhalation over any given period of time which has been reported to have caused death in man or a single dose introduced in one or more portions which has been reported to have caused death in animals. LD_{50} is a common measure which refers to the dose which has caused death in 50 per cent of a sample of experimental animals. Table 4B.1 gives the available measures of toxicity for a variety of incendiary agents, additives and products of combustion.

Table 4B.1. Toxicity of some incendiary agents, additives and products of combustion

Substance	Produced by combustion of	Dose/concentration[a]	Quantity[b]	Route of administration[c]	Species[d]
Acetaldehyde	wood, cotton, paper	TD	60 kg	scu	rat
		LD	500 mg/kg	ipr	rat
		LD	1 900 mg/kg	orl	rat
Acrolein	napalm, petroleum products	LD	46 mg/kg	orl	rat
		TC	504 mg/kg	skn	mus
		LC	24 mg/m³	ihl	mus
Aluminium oxide	aluminium, elektron	LC	500 mg/m³	ihl	mus
Ammonia	wool, silk, melamine & other resins	LC	2 000 ppm	ihl	rat
Benzene	(incendiary agent additive)	TD	48 mg/kg	skn	mus
Carbon black	napalm, petroleum products	LD	4 080 mg/kg	orl	rat
		LD	120 mg/kg	scu	rat
Carbon monoxide	napalm, petroleum products, wood, plastics	LC	2 000 ppm	ihl	mus
Chlorine	polyvinyl chloride (PVC)	TC	5 ppm	ihl	man
Hydrogen chloride	polyvinyl chloride	LC	1 000 mg/m³	ihl	rbt
Hydrogen cyanide	wool, silk, acryl, polyurethane foam, phenolic & melamine resins, 2-chloro-benzalmalononitrile (CS)	LD	4 mg/kg	orl	mus
		LD	0.57 mg/kg	orl	man
		LC	5 000 ppm	ihl	man
Hydrogen sulphide	wool, silk	LC	1 500 mg/m³	ihl	rat
Magnesium oxide	elektron, magnesium	TC	400 mg/m³	ihl	man
Nitrogen oxides	nitrocellulose	LC	250 mg/kg	ihl	mus
Octafluoroiso-butylene	polyfluorocarbons	LD	180 mg/kg	ipr	rat
Phosgene	polyvinyl chloride	LC	50 ppm	ihl	rat
Phosphine	phosphorus (in absence of air)	LC	8 ppm	ihl	man
Phosphoric acid	phosphorus (in air)	TC	100 mg/m³	ihl	man
Phosphorus	(incendiary agent, igniter)	LD	1.4 mg/kg	orl	man
Sodium hydroxide	sodium (igniter)	LD	500 mg/kg	orl	rbt
Tetraethyl lead	(additive)	LC	6 ppm	ihl	rat
Uranium oxide 3-37	depleted uranium	LD	6 mg/kg	ipr	mus

[a] LC=lethal concentration; LD=lethal dose; TC=toxic concentration; TD=toxic dose; see text for explanation.
[b] Dose measurements are given in milligrams (mg) per kilogram (kg) body weight of the test animal. Concentration measurements are given in parts of vapour or gas per million parts of air by volume (ppm), or if solid (particles) or liquid (droplets) in milligrams (mg) per cubic metre (m³).
[c] Ihl=inhalation; ipr=intraperitoneal; orl=oral; scu=subcutaneous; skn=application on intact skin.
[d] Man=man; mus=mouse; rat; rbt=rabbit.

Source: US Department of Health, Education and Welfare (1972).

Bibliography and references

Adler, F., 1971, *Behandling av Bomullsuniformer med Flamskyddsmedel i Kem-tvättvätska* [Treatment of cotton uniforms with a flame retardant substance in a dry-cleaning solvent]. FOA 1 rapport C 1419-H2. Försvarets Forskningsanstalt, (FOA) Stockholm.

Aldrich, R. H., 1943, Forensic aspects of burns: Special reference to appraisal of terminal disability. *Annals of Surgery* **117** (4), 576–584.

Alexander, J. W. & Fisher, M. W., 1970, Immunological determinants of pseudo-monas infections of man accompanying severe burn injury. *Journal of Trauma* **10** (7), pp. 565–574.

Allen, H. R., 1972, *The Legacy of Lord Trenchard*. Cassell, London.

Andersson, R. (United Aircraft Corporation), 1969, *Process for forming a gel within a container*. Patent No. 3 427 368. US Patent Office.

Arturson, G., 1961, Pathophysiological aspects of the burn syndrome with special reference to liver injury and alterations of capillary permeability. *Acta Chirurgica Scandinavica,* Supplement 274.

Arturson, G., 1966, Brännskador [Burn wounds]. In *Försvars- och Katastrofmedicin,* pp. 329–339. Medicinalstyrelsens sjukvårdsberedskapsnämnd, Stockholm.

Artz, C. P., 1960, Complications in surgery and their management. In *The Treatment of Burns,* 1st edition (ed. C. P. Artz & J. D. Harley). Saunders, Philadelphia.

Artz, C. P., 1964, Recent developments in burns. *American Journal of Surgery* **108,** p. 649.

Artz, C. P. & Moncrief, J. A., 1969, *The Treatment of Burns,* 2nd edition. Saunders, Philadelphia.

Atterby, P., 1972, Plastics on fire—corrosion. *FOA Reports* **6** (5), pp. 1–7. Försvarets Forskningsanstalt (FOA), Stockholm.

Aviation Studies Atlantic, *Armament Data Sheets* (passim). London.

Ayres, S. M., Gianelli, S., Jr & Mueller, H., 1970, Part IV. Effects of low concentrations of carbon monoxide. Myocardial and systemic responses to carboxyhemoglobin. Annals of the New York Academy of Sciences **174** (1), pp. 268–293.

Bachelder, R. B. & Hirt, H. F., 1966, *Fire in Tropical Forests and Grasslands.* ES-23, Earth Sciences Division, Natick Army Laboratories, Massachusetts.

Bäckdahl, M., Liljedahl, S.-O. & Troell, L., 1962, Excision of deep burns. *Acta Chirurgica Scandinavica* **123** (January), pp. 351–359.

Baer, Lt.-col., 1957, Pourquoi l'Armée égyptienne a été battue. *Revue Militaire Générale* **5** (May), p. 642.

Balke, C. C. & Graff, W. S. (US Army), 1957, *Pyrophoric element.* Patent No. 2 801 590. US Patent Office.

Bang, F., 1925, Le cancer des circatrices; étude clinique et expérimental. *Bulletin d'Association francaise de Cancer* **14,** pp. 203–218.

Banks, D., 1946, *Flame Over Britain.* Sampson Low, Marston, London.

Barr, P.-O., Birke, G., Liljedahl, S.-O. & Plantin, L.-O., 1967, Treatment of burns with warm dry air. *Lancet,* 10 June, p. 1276.

Barr, P.-O., Birke, G., Liljedahl, S.-O. & Plantin, L.-O., 1968, Oxygen consumption and water loss during treatment of burns with warm dry air. *Lancet,* 27 January, p. 164.

Batdorf, J. W., Cammack, K. V. & Colquitt, R. D., 1969, The silicone dressing management of the burned hand. *Archives of Surgery* **98** (April), pp. 469–471.

Baum, B. M., 1973*a*, Flame retardant fabrics, part I. *Chemical Technology* **3** (3), pp. 167–170.

Baum, B. M., 1973*b*, Flame retardant fabrics, part II. *Chemical Technology* **3** (5), pp. 311–16.

Baum, B. M., 1973*c*, Flame retardant fabrics, part III. *Chemical Technology* **3** (7), pp. 416–21.

Baxter, C. R. & Shires, T., 1968, Physiological response to crystalloid resuscitation of severe burns. *Annals of the New York Academy of Sciences* **150**, p. 874.

Beard, R. R. & Grandstaff, N., 1970, Carbon monoxide exposure and cerebral function. *Annals of the New York Academy of Sciences* **174** (1), pp. 385–395.

Beard, R. R. & Werteim, G. A., 1967, Behavioral impairment associated with small doses of carbon monoxide. *American Journal of Public Health* **57**, p. 11.

Beerbower, A. & Philippoff, W., 1967, History of gelled fuels: Their chemistry and rheology. *Esso Air World* **19** (4), pp. 93–97.

Beller, W. S., 1969, *Arsenal for the Brave: A History of the US Army Munitions Command, 1962–1968*. Washington, DC.

Ben-Hur, N. & Appelbaum, J., 1973, Biochemistry, histopathology and treatment of phosphorus burns. *Israel Journal of Medical Sciences* **9** (1), pp. 40–48.

Ben-Hur, N., Giladi, A., Appelbaum, J. & Neuman, Z., 1972, Phosphorus burns. The antidote: A new approach. *British Journal of Plastic Surgery* **25**, pp. 245–249.

Ben-Hur, N., Giladi, A., Neuman, Z., Shugerman, B. & Appelbaum, J., 1972, Phosphorus burns—a pathophysiological study. *British Journal of Plastic Surgery* **25**, pp. 238–244.

Berkow, S. G., 1924, Method of estimating extensiveness of lesions (burns and scalds) based on body surface proportions. *Archives of Surgery* **138** (8).

Bernard, C., 1870, *Leçons sur les Anesthésiques et sur l'Asphyxie*. Paris.

Bertholet, M., 1893, *Histoire des Sciences, La Chimie au Moyen Age*. Paris.

Betke, K. & Kleihauer, E., 1967, Cytological demonstration of carboxyhaemoglobin in human erythrocytes. *Nature* **214**, p. 188.

Birke, G. & Liljedahl, S.-O., 1966, Nierenschädigungen bei ausgedehnten Verbrennungen mit Berücksichtigung der Behandlung mit Rheomacrodex. *Schweizerische Medizinische Wochenschrift* **96**, p. 925.

Birke, G. & Liljedahl, S.-O., 1968, The influence of different types of early treatment on the prognosis of severe burns—early treatment of severe burns. *Annals of the New York Academy of Sciences* **150**, p. 711.

Birke, G. & Liljedahl, S.-O., 1971, Studies on burns: XV. Treatment with warm dry air, clinical results compared with those of earlier treatment series. *Acta Chirurgica Scandinavica*, Supplement 422.

Birke, Ḡ., Liljedahl, S.-O., Bäckdahl, M. & Nylén, B., 1964, Studies on burns: VIII. Analysis of mortality and length of hospital care for 603 burned patients referred for primary treatment. *Acta Chirurgica Scandinavica*, Supplement 337.

Birke, G., Liljedahl, S.-O. & Linderholm, H., 1958/1959, Studies on burns: V. Clinical and patho-physiological aspects on circulation and respiration. *Acta Chirurgica Scandinavica* **116**, pp. 370–381.

Birke, G., Liljedahl, S.-O. & Nylén, B., 1970, Behandling av mycket utbredda brännskador [Treatment of very extensive burn wounds]. *Läkartidningen* **67** (34), pp. 3760–3770.

Birke, G., Liljedahl, S.-O. & Wickman, K., 1960, Studies in burns: VI. Bacteriology. *Acta Chirurgica Scandinavica*, Supplement 309.

Birnstigl, M., 1968, North Vietnam, 1967. In *Medicine in Vietnam at War,* pp. 5–8. Medical Aid Committee for Vietnam, London.

Bismuth, C., Pebay-Peyroula, F., Fréjaville, J. P., Crabie, P. & Sicot, C., 1971, Syndromes ictéro-rénaux toxiques. *European Journal of Toxicology* **3** (5–6), pp. 223–231.

Blackett, P. M. S., 1948, *Military and Political Consequences of Atomic Energy.* Turnstile Press, London.

Blackmore, J. J., 1970, Interpretation of carboxyhaemoglobin found at post mortem in victims of aircraft accidents. *Aerospace Medicine* (July), pp. 757–59.

Block, M. A. & Tsuzuku, M., 1948, Observations on burn scars sustained by atomic bomb survivors. *American Journal of Surgery* **75,** pp. 417–434.

Bond, H. (ed.), 1966, *Fire and the Air War.* National Fire Protection Association, Boston, Massachusetts.

Bonnell, J. A., 1965, Cadmium poisoning. *Annals of Occupational Hygiene* **8,** p. 45.

Bonnelli, U. & Varotti, C., 1971, Aspetti clinici e terapeutici delle ustiono da residuati bellici al fosforo. *Archivo italiano di dermatologia, venerelogia e sessuologia* **36,** pp. 287–296.

Botteri, B. P. & Manheim, J., Fire and explosion suppression techniques. *Aerospace Medicine* **40** (11), pp. 1186–93.

Bour, H. & Ledingham, I. McA. (eds.), 1967, *Carbon Monoxide Poisoning.* Progress in Brain Research, volume 24. Elsevier, Amsterdam.

Bour, H., Tutin, N. & Pasquier, P., 1967, The central nervous system and carbon monoxide poisoning. I. Clinical data with reference to 20 fatal cases. In *Carbon Monoxide Poisoning* (ed. H. Bour & I. McA. Ledingham). Progress in Brain Research, volume 24. Elsevier, Amsterdam.

Bourdillon, R. B. & Colebrook, L., 1946, Air hygiene in dressing rooms for burns or major wounds. *Lancet* **1** (April), pp. 561–565.

Bowen, T. E., Whelan, T. J. & Nelson, T. G., 1971, Sudden death after phosphorus burns: Experimental observations of hypocalcemia, hyperphosphatemia and electrocardiographic abnormalities following production of a standard white phosphorus burn. *Annals of Surgery* **174** (5), pp. 779–784.

Bradford, E., 1964, *The Great Siege: Malta 1565.* Penguin Books, Harmondsworth (UK).

Bramberg, B. E., Song, I. C. & Mohn, M. P., 1965, The use of pig skin as a temporary biological dressing. *Plastic & Reconstructive Surgery* **36,** p. 50.

Brånemark, P.-I., Breine, U., Joshi, M. & Urbaschek, B., 1962, Microvascular pathophysiology of burned tissue. *Annals of the New York Academy of Sciences* **150,** pp. 474–494.

Brophy, L. P., Miles, W. D. & Cochrane, R. C., 1959, *United States Army in World War II, The Technical Services: The Chemical Warfare Service, Vol. 2: From Laboratory to Field.* Office of the Chief of Military History, United States Army, Washington, DC.

Broughton, S. & Byfield, A., 1943, *The manufacture, properties and testing, of napalm soaps.* Report OSRD No. 2036 (17 November) and Supplement Report.

Brucher, J. M., 1967, Neuropathological problems posed by carbon monoxide poisoning and anoxia. In *Carbon Monoxide Poisoning* (ed. H. Bour & I. McA. Ledingham). Progress in Brain Research, volume 24. Elsevier, Amsterdam.

Buck, G., 1967, *Incendiary compositions containing highly inflammable liquid carbon compounds and a thickener and a process for the production of such compositions.* Patent Specification 1 061 631. Patent Office, London.

Buettner, K., 1950, Effects of extreme heat on man. *Journal of the American Medical Association* **144,** pp. 732–738.

Bull, J.P., 1971, Revised analysis of mortality due to burns. *Lancet,* 20 November, pp. 1133–1134.

Bull, J. P. & Fisher, A. J., 1954, A study of mortality in a burns unit: A revised estimate. *Annals of Surgery* **139** p. 269.

Bull, J. P. & Squire, J. R., 1949, A study of mortality in a burns unit: Standards for the evaluation of alternative methods of treatment. *Annals of Surgery* **130** (2), pp. 160–173.

Burke, J. F. & Bondoc, C. C., 1968, Combined burn therapy utilizing immediate skin allografts and 0,5 % $AgNo_3$. *Archives of Surgery* **97** (November), pp. 716–721.

Butcher, H. R., Margraf, H. W. & Gravens, O. L., 1969, The treatment of large cutaneous burns with silver creams. *Journal of Trauma* **9**, pp. 359–376.

Butterfield, F., 1972, South Vietnamese drop napalm on own troops. *New York Times,* 9 June.

Buu-Hoi, N. P., Saint-Ruf, G., Bigot, P. & Mangane, M., 1971, Préparation, propriétés et identification de la "dioxine" (tétrachloro-2,3,7,8 dibenzo-p-dioxine) dans les pyrolysats de défoliants à base d'acide trichloro-2,4,5 phénoxyacétique et de ses esters et des végétaux contaminés. *Comptes rendus de l'Academie des Sciences de Paris* **273**, pp. 708–711.

Cagle, M. W. & Manson, F. A., 1957, *The Sea War in Korea.* United States Naval Institute, Annapolis, Maryland.

Cameron, J. M. & Patrick, R. S., 1966, Acute phosphorus poisoning—the distribution of toxic doses of yellow phosphorus in the tissue of experimental animals. *Medicine, Science & Law* **6** (4), pp. 209–214.

Cameron, J. S., 1969, Disturbances of renal function in burnt patients. *Proceedings of the Royal Society of Medicine* **62** (January), pp. 49–50.

Cannon, B. & Cope, O., 1943, Rate of epithelial regeneration: A clinical method of measurement, and the effect of various agents recommended in the treatment of burns. *Annals of Surgery* **117** (1), pp. 85–92.

Caroff, J., Breton, J., Hadengue, A. & Dérobert, L., 1968, Aspects histologiques du foie dans l'intoxication par le phosphore. *Médicine légale et dommage corporel* **1**, pp. 178–179.

Caughey, W. S., 1970, Carbon monoxide bonding in hemeproteins. *Annals of the New York Academy of Sciences* **174** (1), pp. 148–153.

Chance, B., Erecinska, M. & Wagner, M., 1970, Mitochondrial responses to carbon monoxide toxicity. *Annals of the New York Academy of Sciences* **174** (1), pp. 193–204.

Chassin, L. M., 1954, *Aviation Indochine.* Paris.

Cheronis, N. D., 1937, Chemical warfare in the Middle Ages. *Journal of Chemical Education* **14**, pp. 360–365.

Childs, A. F., 1970, A matter of life and death. *Chemistry and Industry* (March), pp. 383–384.

Chisum, G. T., 1968, Intraocular effects on flashblindness. *Aerospace Medicine* (August), pp. 860–868.

Christensen, F. C. & Olsen, E 1957, Cadmium poisoning. *Archives of Industrial Health* **16**, p. 8.

Chuttani, H. K., Gupta, P. S., Gulati, S. & Gupta, D. N., 1965, Acute copper sulphate poisoning. *American Journal of Medicine* **39** (November), pp. 849–854.

Clarke, A. M. & Keogh, E. J., 1970, Progress in the treatment of burned children. *Medical Journal of Australia* (1), pp. 240–243.

230

Coburn, R. F. (ed.), 1970, Biological effects of carbon monoxide. *Annals of the New York Academy of Sciences* **174** (1), pp. 1–430.

Constable, J. D., (Massachusetts General Hospital, Boston, Massachusetts), 1973. Personal communication.

Converse, J. M., 1967, Plastic Surgery: The twentieth century: The period of growth (1914–1939). *The Surgical Clinics of North America* **47** (2), pp. 261–278.

Converse, J. M., 1967, Burn deformities of the face and neck: Reconstructive surgery and rehabilitation. *The Surgical Clinics of North America* **47** (2), pp. 323–354.

Cope, O., 1943, The treatment of the surface burns. *Annals of Surgery* **117**, p. 185.

Cope, O., Nathanson, I. T., Rourke, G. M. & Wilson, H., 1943, Metabolic observations. *Annals of Surgery* **117** (6), pp. 937–958.

Cope, O. & Rhinelander, F. W., 1943, The problem of burn shock complicated by pulmonary damage. *Annals of Surgery* **117** (6), pp. 915–928.

Cope, V. Z. (ed.), 1952, *Medicine and Pathology*. History of the Second World War, United Kingdom Medical Series. HMSO, London.

Cope, V. Z. (ed.), 1953, *Surgery*, History of the Second World War, United Kingdom Medical Series. HMSO, London.

Coriell, L. L., Blakemore, W. S. & McGarrity, G. J., 1968, Medical applications of dust-free rooms: II. Elimination of airborne bacteria from an operating theater. *Journal of the American Medical Association* **203** (12), pp. 134–142.

Craven, W. F. & Cate, J. L., 1950, *The Army Air Forces in World War II*, vols. 4–5. University of Chicago Press, Chicago.

Cronin, T. D., 1957, Successful correction of extensive scar contractures of the neck using split thickness grafts. *Transactions of the International Society of Plastic Surgery 1st Congress*, p. 123. William & Wilkins, Baltimore.

Crook, J. C., 1966, Some hazards of accidental gassing. *Medicine, Science & Law* **6** (1), pp. 29–36.

Curreri, P. W., Ash, M. J. & Pruitt, B. A., Jr., 1970, The treatment of chemical burns: Specialized diagnostic, therapeutic and prognostic considerations. *Journal of Trauma* **10** (8), pp. 634–642.

Cushmac, G. E., 1968, Enemy napalm in Vietnam. *Army* (August), pp. 58–59.

Cutforth, R., 1952. *Manchester Guardian*, 1 March.

Davidson, B., 1969, *The Liberation of Guiné*. Penguin, Harmondsworth (UK).

Davidson, B., 1972, *In the Eye of the Storm: Angola's People*. Doubleday, New York.

Davidson, E. C., 1925, The tannic acid treatment of burns. *Surgery, Gynecology & Obstetrics* **41**, p. 202.

Davis, J. S., 1910, Skin transplantation. *Johns Hopkins Hospital Reports* **15**, 307.

Davis, K. P., 1959, *Forest Fire: Control and Use*. McGraw-Hill, New York.

Delamotte, F. T., 1969, Voorstelling van klinische gevallen. *Revue du Service de Santé Militaire belge* **15**, pp. 197–209.

Deutsche Forschungsgemeinschaft, 1974, *Benzol am Arbeitsplatz: Zur Frage Unbedenklicher Konzentrationen von Benzol am Arbeitsplatz (MAK-Wert)*. Mitteilung der Arbeitsgruppe "Aufstellung von MAK-Werten" der Senatskommission zur Prüfung gesundheitsschädlicher Arbeitsstoffe, unter Mitwirkung von Dr. Gertrud Büttner. Harald Boldt, Boppard (FRG).

Deutsche Forschungsgemeinschaft, 1974, *Maximale Arbeitsplatzkonzentrationen*. Kommission zur Prüfung gesundheitsschädlicher Arbeitsstoffe, Mitteilung X. Bonn-Bad Godesberg.

Diaz-Rivera, R. S., Collazo, P. J., Pons, E. R., & Torregrosa, M. V., 1950, Acute phosphorus poisoning in man: A study of 56 cases. *Medicine* **29**, pp. 269–298.

Diaz-Rivera, R. S., Ramos-Morales, F., Garcia-Palmieri, M. R. & Ramirez, E. A., 1961, The electrocardiographic changes in acute phosphorus poisoning in man. *American Journal of Medical Science*, (June), pp. 758–765.

Divincenti, F. C., Moncrief, J. A. & Pruitt, B. A., Jr., 1969, Electrical injuries: A review of 65 cases. *Journal of Trauma* **9** (6), pp. 497–507.

Divincenti, F. C., Pruitt, B. A., Jr. & Reckler, J. M., 1971, Inhalation injuries. *Journal of Trauma* **11** (2), pp. 109–117.

Divine, D., 1966, *The Broken Wing: A Study in the British Exercise of Air Power.* Hutchinson, London.

DMS, 1974, *Designation Handbook: Aerospace, Defense, Technology,* Greenwich, Connecticut.

DMS, *Market Intelligence Report: Ships/Vehicles/Ordnance* (passim). Greenwich, Connecticut.

Donohue, E. B., 1947, *Flame Attack Study, III. The Lethal Effectiveness of Special Flamethrower Fuels (iron carbonyl, carbon disulphide, carbothermic magnesium with oxidizing agents and silica gels).* US Army Chemical Corps, Army Chemical Center, Maryland.

Dowling, J. A., Omer, G. E. & Moncrief, J. A., 1968, Treatment of fracture in burn patients. *Journal of Trauma* **8**, pp. 465–474.

Do Xuan Hop, 1967, Napalm- och fosforbomber. In *Napalm* (ed. J. Takman), pp. 16–25. Rabén & Sjögren, Stockholm.

Dreyfus, J.-C., 1971, Napalm and its effects on human beings. In *Prevent the Crime of Silence* (ed. K. Coates, P. Limqueco, & P. Weiss), pp. 191–198. Allen Lane, The Penguin Press, London.

Druckrey, H., 1973, Chemical structure and action in transplacental carcinogenesis and teratogenesis. *Transplacental Carcinogenesis,* pp. 45–53. International Agency for Research of Cancer.

Dryer, J. E., 1965, *Annex B (flamethrowers) to addendum, mechanized rifle troop carrier (M-113).* Final report, 1 November 1964 – 31 May 1965, Project JRATA-1B-150.1. Army Concept Team in Viet-Nam, San Francisco. (Classified. Author's unclassified abstract in *Technical Abstracts Bulletin*, 1965, No. 367371.)

DuBois, A. B., 1970, Establishment of "threshold" exposure levels. *Annals of the New York Academy of Sciences* **174** (1), pp. 425–428.

Dudley, H. A., Knight, R. J., McNeur, J. C. & Rosengarten, D. S., 1968, Civilian battle casualties in South Vietnam. *British Journal of Surgery* **55** (5), pp. 332–334.

Dufour, R. E., 1963, *Survey of Available Information on the Toxicity of the Combustion and Thermal Decomposition Products of Certain Building Materials under Fire Conditions.* Bulletin of Research No. 54. Underwriters' Laboratories, New York.

Dunant, H., 1859, *Un Souvenir de Solferino.*

Dygert, H. P., Labelle, C. W., Laskin, S., Pozzani, U. C., Roberts, E., Rothermel, J. J., Rothstein, A., Spiegl, C. J., Sprague, G. F. & Stockinger, H. E., 1951, Toxicity following inhalation. In *The Pharmacology and Toxicology of Uranium Compounds,* vol. 1, p. 423. Foreign Literature Publishing House, Moscow.

Einhorn, I. N., 1973, *Physio-chemical study of Smoke Emission by Aircraft Interior Materials, Part I. Physiological and Toxicological Aspects of Smoke during Fire Exposure.* US Department of Transportation, Federal Aviation Administration, Washington, DC. (AD-763 602).

Enthoven, A. C. & Smith, K. W., 1971, *How Much is Enough? Shaping the Defense Program, 1961–1969.* Harper & Row, New York.

Epstein, B. S., Hardy, D. L., Harrison, H. N., Teplitz, C., Villarreal, Y. & Mason, A. D., Jr., 1963, Hypoxemia in the burned patient: A clinical-pathologic study. *Annals of Surgery* **158** (6), pp. 924–932.

Erskine, L. A., 1970, Discussion of "Treatment of chemical burns" by Curreri, Asch & Pruitt. *Journal of Trauma* **10** (8), pp. 641–642.

Evans, E. I. & Hoover, M. J., 1943, The sulfanilamide ointment treatment of severe burns. *Surgery, Gynecology & Obstetrics* **77**, 367–375.

Fall, B., 1961, *Street without Joy*. Stackpole, Harrisburg.

Favrod, C.-H., 1962, *Le FLN et l'Algérie*. Paris.

Feller, I., 1962, A second look at adrenal cortical function in burn stress. In *Research in Burns* (ed. C. P. Artz), pp. 163–170. American Institute of Biological Sciences, Washington, DC.

Feller, I. & Pierson, C., 1968, Pseudomonas vaccine and hyperimmune plasma for burned patients. *Archives of Surgery* **97** (August), pp. 225–229.

Fieser, L. F., 1952, *Incendiary gels*. Patent No. 2 606 107. US Patent Office.

Fieser, L. F., 1964, *The Scientific Method: A Personal Account of Unusual Projects in War and Peace*. Reinhold, New York.

Fieser, L. F., Harris, G. C., Hershberg, E. B., Morgana, M., Novello, F. C. & Putnam, S. T., 1946, Napalm. *Industrial and Engineering Chemistry* **38** (8), pp. 768–773.

Finck, P., 1966. Exposure to carbon monoxide: Review of the literature and 567 autopsies. *Military Medicine* (December), pp. 1513–1539.

Finney, D. J., 1947, Probit Analysis. University Press, Cambridge (UK).

Fisch, B. R., 1961, Inhalation of uranium aerosols by mouse, rat, dog and man. In *Inhaled Particles and Vapours*. Proceedings of an International Symposium (ed. C. N. Davies). Pergamon, Oxford (UK).

Fischbeck, R., Frenzel, K. & Gehrlicher, W., 1974, Lokalbehandlung oberflächlicher thermischer Hautverbrennungen unter Gefechtsbedingungen. *Zeitschrift für Militärmedizin* **15** (1), pp. 52–56.

Fischer, H., 1969, Unfälle durch Kampf- und Nebelstoffe und ihre Folgen. Pathologisch-anatomischer Beitrag. *Wehrmedizinische Monatschrift* **12**, pp. 355–359.

Fischer, H., 1971, Verbrennungen. *Zeitschrift für Allgemeinmedizin/Der Landarzt* **8**, pp. 415–420.

Fischer, J. B., 1946, *Incendiary Warfare*. McGraw-Hill, New York.

Flüry, F. & Zernick, F., 1931, *Schädliche Gase*. Springer, Berlin.

Foley, F. D., 1969, The burn autopsy: Fatal complications of burns. *American Journal of Clinical Pathology* **52** (1), pp. 1–13.

Foley, F. D., Moncrief, J. A. & Mason, A. D., Jr., 1968, Pathology of the lung in fatally burned patients. *Annals of Surgery* **167** (2), pp. 251–264.

Foley, F. D., Pruitt, B. A.. Jr., Myers, L. T. & Moncrief, J. A., 1967, Adrenal hemorrhage and necrosis in seriously burned patients. *Journal of Trauma* **7** (6), pp. 863–870.

Formal, O. L. & Longacre, D. W., 1970, Fire potential increased by weed killers. *Fire Control Notes* **31** (3), pp. 11–12.

Fox, C. L., Jr. (ed.), 1968, Early treatment of severe burns. *Annals of the New York Academy of Sciences* **150** (August), pp. 469–1012.

Fox, C. L., Ropple, B. W. & Stanford, W., 1969, Control of *Pseudomonas* infection in burns by silver sulfadiazine. *Surgery, Gynecology & Obstetrics* **128**, pp. 1021–1026.

Francois R. J. I., 1969, Présentation d'un cas clinique. *Revue du Service de Santé militaire belge* **15**, pp. 213–215.

Frankenberg, L. & Sörbö, B., 1973, Formation of cyanide from o-chlorobenzylidene malonitrile and its toxicological significance. *Archiv für Toxikologie* **31**, pp. 99–108.

Frankford Arsenal (US Army), 1954, *Historical Summary,* vol. 2, chapter III, pp. 141–142.

Friesen, F. R., 1950, The genesis of gastroduodenal ulcer following burns: An experimental study. *Surgery* **28**.

Frye, F. L. & Cucuel, J.-P. E., 1969, Acute yellow phosphorus poisoning in a cat. *Veterinary Medicine/Small Animal Clinician,* (November), pp. 995–996.

Futrell, R. F., 1961, *The United States Air Force in Korea, 1950–1953.* Duell, Sloan & Pearce, New York.

Gaddum, J. H., 1933, *Special Report Series No. 183.* Medical Research Council, London.

Ganote, Ch. E. & Otis, J. B., 1969, Characteristic lesions of yellow phosphorus-induced liver damage. *Laboratory Investigation* **21** (3), pp. 207–213.

Gestewitz, H.-R., 1968, Uber die Geschädigtenstrukturen, die Organisation der medizinischen Hilfe und den Transport Geschädigter infolge des See-Luftkrieges der Vereinigten Staaten von Nordamerika gegen die Demokratische Republik Vietnam von 1965 bis 1967. *Zeitschrift für Militärmedizin* **9** (5), pp. 259–262.

Gestewitz, H.-R., 1968, Der Einsatz von Brandbomben (-granaten) der US-Flieger-kräfte gegen die Demokratische Republik Vietnam und ihre Wirkung unter besonderer Berücksichtigung von Napalm. *Zeitschrift für Militärmedizin* **9** (5), pp. 275–280.

Ghohal, A. K., Porta, E. A. & Hartroft, W. S., 1969, The role of lipoperoxidation in the pathogenesis of fatty livers induced by phosphorus poisoning in rats. *American Journal of Pathology* **54** (2), pp. 275–290.

Godding, E. W. & Notton, H. E. F., 1942, The treatment of phosphorus burns. *British Medical Journal* **4**, pp. 433–435.

Gomez, A. C., 1967, Phosphorus burns. *USARV Medical Bulletin* (2), pp. 48–49. (USARV Pam 40–2).

Goodman, L. & Gilman, A., 1955, *The Pharmacological Basis of Therapeutics,* 2nd edition. MacMillan, New York.

Goodwin, R. N., 1966, *Triumph or Tragedy: Reflections on Vietnam.* Random House, Vintage Books, New York.

Green, F. H. K. & Covell, G. (eds.), 1953, *Medical Research.* History of the Second World War, United Kingdom Medical Series. HMSO, London.

Greene, F., 1967, *Vietnam! Vietnam!* Penguin Books, Harmondsworth (UK).

Greene, L. W., 1947, Prewar incendiary bomb development. *Chemical Corps Journal* (October), pp. 25–30.

Greene, L. W., 1966, Incendiaries. *Kirk-Othmer Encyclopedia of Chemical Technology,* 2nd edition, vol. 4, pp. 895–900. Interscience, New York.

Gregory, J. B., Settwope, A. D. & Wise, D. L., 1973, *Development of a synthetic polymer burn covering.* Dynatech Corp., Cambridge, Massachusetts (AD-759 381).

Guillain, R., 1947, *Le Peuple japonais et la Guerre.* Juillard, Paris.

Guyton, C., 1966, *Textbook of medical physiology.* Philadelphia.

Haessler, W. M., 1973, Fire extinguishing chemicals. *Chemical Engineering* **80** (5), pp. 95–100.

Hajek, A. V., 1954, Napalm. *Allgemeine Schweizerische Militär Zeitschrift,* pp. 65–66.

Hajek, H. V., 1957, Napalm und seine neuen Anwendungsmöglichkeiten [Napalm and its new possibilities of application] *Explosivstoffe* **6**, pp. 121–126.

Haldane, J. S., 1922, The causes of anoxaemia. In *Respiration,* chapter 7, pp. 158–170. Yale University Press, New Haven, Connecticut.

Hamburg, D. A., Artz, C. P., Reiss, F., Amspacher, W. H. & Chambers, R. E., 1953, Clinical importance of emotional problems in the care of patients with burns. *New England Journal of Medicine* **248**, p. 355.

Hamburg, D. A., Hamburg, B. & de Goza, S., 1953, Adaptive problems and mechanisms in severely burned patients. *Psychiatry* **16**, p. 1.

Hampe, E., 1963, *Der Zivile Luftschutz im zweiten Weltkrieg.* Bernard & Graefe Verlag für Wehrwesen, Frankfurt-am-Main (FRG).

Hanks, T. G., 1970, Human performance of a psychomotor test as a function of exposure to carbon monoxide. *Annals of the New York Academy of Sciences* **174** (1) pp. 421–424.

Hanslian, R., 1937, *Der chemische Krieg.* Mittler, Berlin.

Hardaway, R. M., 1969, Clinical management of shock. *Military Medicine* **134** (9), pp. 643–654.

Harris, A., 1947, *Bomber Offensive.* Collins, London.

Hart, D., 1936, Sterilization of the air in the operating room by special bactericidal radiant energy. *Journal of Thoracic Surgery* **6**, p. 45.

Hart, D., Postlethwait, R. W., Brown, I. W., Jr., Smith, W. W. & Johnson, P. A., 1968, Postoperative wound infections: a further report on ultraviolet irradiation with comments on the recent (1964) National Research Council cooperative study report. *Annals of Surgery* **167** (5), pp. 728–743.

Haven, F. & Hodge, H. C., 1949, Toxicity following parenteral administration of certain soluble uranium salts. In *Pharmacology and Toxicology of Uranium Compounds,* vol. 1, p. 281. McGraw-Hill, New York.

Harvey, P., 1968, Eye witness: North Vietnam. In *Medicine in Vietnam at War,* pp. 9–10. Medical Aid Committee for Vietnam, London.

Hashimoto, M., 1971, The napalm bomb. In *Prevent the Crime of Silence* (ed. K. Coates, P. Limqueco & P. Weiss), pp. 199–202. Allen Lane, The Penguin Press, London.

Haynes, B. W. & Hench, M. E., 1965, Hospital isolation system for preventing cross contamination by staphylococcal and pseudomonas organisms in burn wounds. *Annals of Surgery* **162** (October), pp. 641–649.

Hedener, B., 1957, Förgiftningsskador genom rökgas. *Tidskrift för Militär Hälsovård* **82**, p. 87.

Hedinger, C., 1948, Zur Pathologie der Skelettmuskulatur. *Schweizerische Medizinische Wochenschrift* **78**, p. 145.

Helm, K. U., 1969, *Revue du Service de Santé militaire belge* **15**, p. 170.

Helm, K. U., Renovanz, H. D., Schmahl, K. & von Clarmann, M., 1971, Zinc chloride poisoning and its treatment, II. Symptomatology and progress of the poisoning. *Wehrmedizinische Monatschrift* **15**, pp. 203–217.

Henderson, Y. & Haggard, H. W., 1943, Chemical asphyxiants. In *Noxious Gases and the Principles of Respiration Influencing their Action.* 2nd (rev.) edition, chapter 11, pp. 159–176. Reinhold, New York.

Henriques, F. C., Jr., 1947, Studies of thermal injury: V. The predictability and the significance of thermally induced rate processes leading to irreversible epidermal injury. *Archives of Pathology* **43** (5), pp. 489–502.

Henriques, F. C., Jr. & Moritz, A. R., 1947, Studies of thermal injury: I. The conduction of heat to and through skin and the temperatures attained therein. A theoretical and an experimental investigation. *American Journal of Pathology* **23** (4), pp. 531–549.

235

Heon, N. P., 1964, Flame in war. *Infantry* **54** (5), pp. 28–32.

Herrera, M., 1972, *Giron/Giron* (film). ICAIC, Cuba.

Hime, H. W. L., 1915, *The Origin of Artillery.*

Hirst, J. W., 1945, An account of the medical services of the national liberation army of Jugoslavia and of the R.A.M.C. assistance given to it. *Journal of the Royal Army Medical Corps* **84** (3), pp. 105–114.

Holland, R. A. B., 1970, Reaction rates of carbon monoxide and hemoglobin. *Annals of the New York Academy of Sciences* **174** (1), pp. 154–171.

Hollingsworth, E. W., 1951, The use of thickened gasoline in warfare. *Armed Forces Chemical Journal* **4** (3), pp. 26–32.

Holzmann, R. T., 1969, *Chemical Rockets and Flame and Explosives Technology.* Dekker, New York and London.

Horn, J. S., 1969, *'Away with All Pests': An English Surgeon in People's China.* Paul Hamlyn, London.

Hufferd, R. W., 1946, Spectacular developments in incendiaries. *Chemical Engineering* **53**, pp. 110–113.

Hunter, D., 1959, *Health in Industry.* Penguin, Harmondsworth (UK).

Iklé, F. C., 1958, *The Social Impact of Bomb Destruction.* University of Oklahoma Press, Norman, Oklahoma.

International Committee of the Red Cross, 1955, *Draft Rules for the Protection of the Civilian Population from the Dangers of Indiscriminate Warfare.* Geneva.

International Committee of the Red Cross, 1958*a.* *Draft Rules for the Limitation of the Dangers Incurred by the Civilian Population in Time of War,* 2nd edition, Geneva.

International Committee of the Red Cross, 1958*b,* *Final Record Concerning the Draft Rules for the Limitation of the Dangers Incurred by the Civilian Population in Time of War.* XIXth International Conference of the Red Cross, New Delhi, October–November 1957. Geneva.

International Committee of the Red Cross, 1969, *Reaffirmation and Development of the Laws and Customs Applicable in Armed Conflicts.* Report submitted to the XII International Conference of the Red Cross. Geneva.

International Committee of the Red Cross, 1972*a, Conference of Government Experts on the Reaffirmation and Development of International Humanitarian Law Applicable in Armed Conflicts (second session 3 May – 3 June 1972).* Vol. I. *Basic Texts.* Vol. II. *Commentary.* Geneva.

International Committee of the Red Cross, 1972*b, Conference of Government Experts on the Reaffirmation and Development of International Humanitarian Law Applicable in Armed Conflicts (second session, 3 May – 3 June 1972). Report of the work of the Conference,* Vols. I–II. Geneva.

International Committee of the Red Cross, 1973*a, Draft Additional Protocols to the Geneva Conventions of August 12, 1949.* Geneva.

International Committee of the Red Cross, 1973*b, Draft Additional Protocols to the Geneva Conventions of August 12, 1949: Commentary.* Geneva.

International Committee of the Red Cross, 1973*c, Weapons that may cause Unnecessary Suffering or have Indiscriminate Effects.* Report on the Work of Experts. Geneva.

International Committee of the Red Cross, 1975, *Report on the Work of the Conference of Government Experts on the Use of Certain Conventional Weapons (Lucerne, 24.9 – 18.10.1974).* Geneva.

Irving, 1963, *The Destruction of Dresden.* Kimber, London.

Jackson, D., Topley, E., Cason, J. S. & Lowbury, E. J. L., 1960, Primary excision and grafting of large burns. *Annals of Surgery* **152,** p. 167.

Jackson, R., 1970, *The Red Falcons: The Soviet Air Force, 1919–1969*. Clifton, London.

Jackson, R., 1973, *Air War Over Korea*. Allan, London.

James, W. R. L., 1966, Suicide by burning. *Medicine, Science and Law* **6** (1), p. 43.

Jelenko, C., Smulyan, W. I. & Wheeler, M. L., 1968, VI: Studies in burns: the role of lipids in the transmissivity of membranes. *Annals of Surgery* **167** (4).

Jelenko, C. & Wheeler, M. L., 1969, Production of the experimental burn—a critical technical evaluation. *Journal of Surgical Research* **9** (3), pp. 159–165.

Johnson, F. A. & Stonehill, R. B., 1961, Chemical pneumonitis from inhalation of zinc chloride. *Diseases of the Chest* **40** (6), pp. 619–624.

Johnson, F. M., 1926, The development of carcinoma in scar tissue following burns. *Annals of Surgery* **83,** 165–169.

Joint Fire Research Organization, 1968, *Fire behaviour of PVC and the corrosivity of its combustion products*. Joint Fire Research Organization Library Bibliography No. 85. London.

Joinville, J. S., de (trans. J. Evans), 1938, *The History of St. Louis*. Oxford University Press, London.

Jones, E. L., Peters, A. F. & Gasior, R. M., 1968, Early management of battle casualties in Vietnam. *Achives of Surgery* **97** (1), pp. 1–26.

Kalshoven, F., 1971, *Belligerent Reprisals*. Sijthoff, Leiden.

Karig, W., Cagle, M. W. & Manson, F. A., 1952, *Battle Report: The War in Korea*. Rinehart, New York.

Kefalides, N. A., Arana, J. A., Bazan, A., Velarde, N. & Rosenthal, S. M., 1964, Evaluation of antibiotic prophylaxis and gamma-globulin, plasma, albumin and saline-solution therapy in severe burns. *Annals of Surgery* **159** (4), pp. 496–506.

Kleber, B. E. & Birdsell, D., 1966, *The Chemical Warfare Service: Chemicals in Combat*. Volume 3 in the Technical Services subseries of the United States Army in World War II series. Office of the Chief of Military History, United States Army, Washington, D C.

Klinkmüller, A., 1965, Brandschutz: Rauchvergiftungen bei der Brandbekämpfung. *Zivilschutz* **29,** (2), pp. 56–59.

Koehn, C. J., 1963, Riboflavin content of livers in experimental burns. *Annals of Surgery* **158** (6), pp. 933–935.

Konůpka, F., 1960, *Válka Ohněm*. Naše Vojsko, Prague.

Kovaric, J. J., Aaby, G., Hamit, H. F. & Hardaway, R. M., 1969, Vietnam casualty statistics: February–November 1967. *Archives of Surgery* **98** (February), pp. 150–152.

Kunzman, J., 1970, Management of bleeding stress ulcers. *American Journal of Surgery* **119** (June), pp. 637–639.

Kusterer, D. F., 1966, *The application of air-delivered incendiary weapons to limited war in Southeast Asia*. NOTS Technical Publication 4229. US Naval Ordnance Test Station, China Lake, California.

Lamb, L. E., Kelly, R. J., Smith, W. L., Leblang, A. D. & Johnson, P. C., 1969, Physiological response to steady state hypoxia. *Aerospace Medicine* **40** (i), pp. 943–951.

Lamb, L. E., Leblang, A. D., Kelly, R. J., Smith, W. L. & Johnson, P. C., 1969, Cardiac output and coronary blood flow during steady state hypoxia. *Aerospace Medicine* **40** (10), pp. 1060–1064.

Lamke, L.-O. & Wennberg, L., 1971, Prediction of evaporative water and heat loss from the severely burnt patient. *Försvarsmedicin* (2), pp. 71–77.

Lang, K., 1966, Probleme des Blutersatzes in Vergangenheit und Gegenwart. *Wehrmedizin* **4** (11/12), pp. 203–211.

Lapresle, J. & Fardeau, M., 1967, The central nervous system and carbon monoxide poisoning, II. Anatomical study of brain lesions following intoxication with carbon monoxide (22 cases). In *Carbon Monoxide Poisoning* (ed. H. Bour & I. McA. Ledingham). Studies in Brain Research, volume 24. Elsevier, Amsterdam.

Lawrence, E. A., 1952, Carcinoma arising in the scars of thermal burns. *Surgery, Gynecology and Obstetrics* **95**, pp. 579–588.

de Lesquen, 1954, Le Napalm. *Revue militaire d'Information,* No. 225 (10 Janvier), pp. 16–22.

Letavet, A. A. & Kurlyandskaya, E. B. (eds.), 1970, *The Toxicology of Radioactive Substances. Volume 4: Thorium-232 and Uranium-238* (trans. G. W. Dolphin). Pergamon, Oxford (UK).

Levitan, A. A., Seidler, F. M., Strong, C. D. & Herman, L. G., 1968, The role of supportive services in the operation of an isolator system. *Journal of the American Medical Association* **203** (12), pp. 105–110.

Lieber, F., 1881, *Contributions to political science including lectures on the Constitution of the United States, and other papers.* Miscellanea II, p. 215.

Lifton, R. J., 1967, *Death in Life: The Survivors of Hiroshima.* Random House, New York.

Lilienthal, J. L., 1950, Carbon monoxide. *Pharmacological Review* **2**, p. 324.

Liljedahl, S.-O., 1967, Brännskadebehandling. *Medicinsk Årbog* **X,** pp. 176–203. Munksgaard, Copenhagen.

Liljedahl, S.-O., 1970, Brännskadebehandling. *Opuscula Medica* **15** (6), pp. 179–194.

Liljedahl, S.-O., 1971, Brännskador – nya synpunkter. *Medicinsk Årbog* **XIV,** pp. 159–171. Munksgaard, Copenhagen.

Lindberg, R. B., Moncrief, J. A., Switzer, W. E., Order, S. E. & Mills, W., 1965, The successful control of burn wound sepsis. *Journal of Trauma* **5**, p. 601.

Linderholm, H. & Strandberg, O., 1956, Lungskador i samband med rökgasexplosion, *Tidskrift för Militär Hälsovård* **81,** p. 230.

Lindkvist, K. I., (Fortifikations förvaltning, Stockholm), 1974. Personal communication.

Lindstrand, K., Norden, Å. & Schildt, B. E., 1970, Cobalamin and folate in burned mice. *Scandinavian Journal of Haematology* (7), pp. 435–439.

Littauer, R. & Uphoff, N. (eds), 1972, *The Air War in Indochina,* revised edition. Beacon Press, Boston.

Litvine, J., 1970, Traitement en urgence des brulés en cas de catastrophe. *Revue Internationale des Services de Santé* **43** pp. 121–129.

Livingston, J., Moore, J. & Oldfather, F. (eds.), 1973, *The Japan Reader, I. Imperial Japan, 1800–1945.* Pantheon Books, New York.

Longo, L. D., 1970, Carbon monoxide in the pregnant mother and fetus and its exchange across the placenta. *Annals of the New York Academy of Sciences* **174** (1), pp. 313–341.

Lowbury, E. J. L., 1967, Advances in the control of infection in burns. *British Journal of Plastic Surgery* **20,** pp. 211–217.

Ludewig, R. & Lohs, K.-H., 1970, *Akute Vergiftungen*. VEB Gustav Fischer Verlag, Jena.

Lukasik, S. J. (Director of the US Department of Defense Advanced Research Projects Agency (ARPA)), 1973, letter to Congressman Les Aspin, House of Representatives, 17 September.

Lumsden, R. B. & Weir, C. D., 1945, Subglottic stenosis after exposure to a high concentration of screening smoke (zinc chloride). *British Medical Journal* **1**, 21 April, pp. 554–555.

Lyons, J. W., 1970, *The Chemistry and Uses of Fire Retardants*. Wiley, New York.

Macaulay, M. B. & Mant, A. K., 1964, Smoke-bomb poisoning. A fatal case following the inhalation of zinc chloride smoke. *Journal of the Royal Army Medical Corps* **110** (1), pp. 27–32.

MacFarland, H. N., 1968, The pyrolysis products of plastics—Problems in defining their toxicity. *American Industrial Hygiene Association Journal* **29** (1), pp. 7–9.

Macleod, A., 1970, Adult burns in Melbourne: a five-year survey. *Medical Journal of Australia* (October), pp. 772–777.

Mainichi Newspapers Ltd., 1971, [The Air Raids in Japan] (in Japanese). Tokyo.

Mäkelä, J. K., 1967, *Helsinki liekeissä* [Helsinki on fire]. WSOY, Porvoo (Finland).

Mallory, T. B. & Brickley, W. J., 1963, Pathology: with special reference to the pulmonary lesions. *Annals of Surgery* **117** (6), pp. 865–884.

Marin, G. A., Montoya, C. A., Sierra, J. L. & Senior, J. R., 1971, Evaluation of corticosteroid and exchange-transfusion treatment of acute yellow-phosphorus intoxication. *New England Journal of Medicine* **284** (3), pp. 125–128.

Markley, K. & Smallman, E., 1970, Protection against burn, tourniquet, and endotoxin shock by purine compounds. *Journal of Trauma* **10** (7), pp. 598–607.

Mason, A. D., Jr., Teschan, P. E. & Muirhead, E. E., 1963, Studies in acute renal failure: III. Renal histologic alterations in acute renal failure in the rat. *Journal of Surgical Research* **3** (9), pp. 450–456.

Mathews, D., 1964, The late repair of burns. *Fortschritte der Kiefer- und Gesichts-Chirurgie* (ed., K. Schurchardt). Georg Thieme, Stuttgart.

McClure, R. D. & Lam, C. R., 1943, *Burns, Shock Wound Healing and Vascular Injuries*. Military Surgical Manuals No. 5. Saunders, Philadelphia.

McConnell, A. F., 1970, Mission: Ranch Hand. *Air University Review* **21** (January–February), pp. 89–94.

McFarland, R. A., 1970, The effects of exposure to small quantities of carbon monoxide on vision. *Annals of the New York Academy of Sciences* **174** (1), pp. 301–312.

McIntyre, G. H. & Ellivott, S. B., 1944, *Aluminium soaps for thickening gasoline*. Report OSRD No. 3772 (June 13).

McLean, D. B., 1971, *Guide to Viet Cong Ammunition*. Normount Technical Publications, Forest Grove, Oregon.

Mendelson, J. A., 1971, Some principles of protection against burns from flame and incendiary munitions. *Journal of Trauma* **11** (4), pp. 286–294.

Meyer-Arendt, J. R., 1968, Efficiency and limitations of lasers as weapons. *American Journal of Optometry & Archives of American Academy of Optometry* **45**, pp. 188–191.

Michael, N. W., 1945, *The laboratory evaluation of new formula napalm thickener*. TDM Report No. 1209 (18 December).

Middlebrook, M., 1973, *The Nuremberg Raid*. Allen Lane, London.

Mukulka, P., O'Donnell, R., Heinig, P. & Theodore, J., 1970, The effect of carbon monoxide on human performance. *Annals of the New York Academy of Sciences* **174** (1), pp. 409–420.

Miles, T. D. & Deleanto, A. C., 1968, Durable non-reactive flame retardant finishes for cotton. *Textile Research Journal* **38** (March), p. 273.

Miller, C. F., 1972, *Fire-fighting Operations in Hamburg, Germany, during World War II*. URS Research Co., San Mateo, California. (US Department of Commerce, National Technical Information Service Acquisition No. AD-753 346; see also: AD-632 366; AD-664 523; AD-672 497; AD-680 459; AD-681 075; AD-683 345; AD-726 461 for translations of original German documents and related material.)

Miller, W. L., 1954, The uses of flame in Korea. *Combat Forces Journal* (March), pp. 37–39.

Miller, W. L., 1958, Flame for the infantry. *Infantry* (July–September).

Milsom, J., 1970, *Russian Tanks, 1900–1970*. Arms and Armour Press, London.

Minkowitz, F., 1967, Regression of massive keloid following partial excision and post-operative intralesional administration of triamcinolone. *British Journal of Plastic Surgery* **20**, pp. 432–435.

Mitchell, T. J. & Smith, G. M., 1931, *Medical Services: Casualties and Medical Statistics of the Great War*. HMSO, London.

Monafo, W. W., Brentano, L. & Gravens, D. L., 1966, Gas gangrene and mixed clostridial infections of muscle complicating deep thermal burns. *Archives of Surgery* **92**, pp. 212.

Monafo, W. W. & Moyer, C. A., 1965, Effectiveness of dilute aqueous silver nitrate in the solution of major burns. *Archives of Surgery* **91**, pp. 200–210.

Moncrief, J. A., 1966, Effect of various fluid regimens and pharmacologic agents on the circulatory hemodynamics of the immediate postburn period. *Annals of Surgery* **164** (4), pp. 723–752.

Moncrief, J. A., Lindberg, R. B. & Switzer, W. E., 1966. The use of a topical sulfonamide in the control of burn wound sepsis. *Journal of Trauma* **6,** pp. 407–419.

Moncrief, J. A. & Mason, A. D., 1964, Evaporative water loss in the burned patient. *Journal of Trauma* **4,** pp. 180–185.

Moncrief, J. A. & Pruitt, B. A., Jr., 1970, Electric injury. *Postgraduate Medicine* **48** (3), pp. 189–194.

Moncrief, J. A., Switzer, W. E. & Teplitz, C., 1964, Curling's ulcer. *Journal of Trauma* **4,** p. 481.

Moncrief, J. A. & Teplitz, C., 1964, Changing concepts in burn sepsis. *Journal of Trauma* **4,** p. 233.

Moritz, A. R., 1947, Studies of thermal injury: III. The pathology and pathogenesis of cutaneous burns. An experimental study. *American Journal of Pathology* **23** (6), pp. 915–934.

Moritz, A. R. & Henriques, F. C., J., 1947, Studies of thermal injury: II. The relative importance of time and surface temperature in the causation of cutaneous burns. *American Journal of Pathology* **23** (5), pp. 695–720.

Moritz, A. R., Henriques, F. C., Jr., Dutra, F. R. & Weisiger, J. R., 1947, Studies of thermal injury: IV. An exploration of the casualty-producing attributes of conflagrations; local and systemic effects of general cutaneous exposure to excessive circumambient (air) and circumradiant heat of varying duration and intensity. *Archives of Pathology* **43** (5), pp. 466–488.

Moritz, A. R., Henriques, F. C., Jr. & McLean, R., 1945, The effects of inhaled heat on the air passages and lungs: An experimental investigation. *American Journal of Pathology* **21**, pp. 311–331.

Mourreau, P., Heusgheim, C., Desmarez, J. J., Mannes, P. & Dubois, E., 1968, Les dangers des écrans de fumée, *Bulletin de l'Academie Royale de Medicine de Belgique* (VIIe Série) **8** (9), pp. 671–690.

Moyer, C. A., 1954, Aging and mortality from thermal injury. *Journal of Gerontology* **9**, p. 456.

Moyer, C. A. & Butcher, H. R., Jr., 1967, *Burns, Shock and Plasma Volume Regulation*. Mosby, St. Louis, Missouri.

Naerland, A., 1967, Napalm. *Norsk Militaer Tidskrift* **7**, pp. 359–366.

Nakano, J., 1973, *Prostaglandins: Their Pathophysiological Roles and Therapeutive Applications*. University of Oklahoma, Oklahoma City. (AD-759 410)

Netherlands Ministry for Foreign Affairs, 1899, *Conference internationale de la paix, La Haye 18 mai – 29 juillet, 1899*.

Noel-Baker, P. J., 1958, *The Arms Race*. Calder, London.

Norberg, B. & Rosenqvist, H., 1944, Om fosforbrännskador. *Svenska Läkartidningen* **16**, pp. 1125–1134.

Nordén, G. & Stenberg, T 1962, Studies of the liver function in experimental burns II. Morphological studies of the liver in rabbits after standardized burns. *Acta Chirurgica Scandinavica* **123**, pp. 171–178.

North Atlantic Treaty Organisation, 1958, *Emergency War Surgery*. US Department of Defense, Washington, DC.

NWM De Kruithoorn B. V., undated, *Cartridge, 20 mm, API, MN20A1*. s'Hertogenbosch, Holland.

O'Ballance, E., 1956, *The Arab-Israeli War*. Faber, London.

O'Ballance, E., 1966 *a*, *The Greek Civil War, 1944–49*. Faber, London.

O'Ballance, E., 1966 *b*, *Malaya. The Communist insurgent War, 1948–60*. Faber, London.

O'Ballance, E., 1971, *The War in the Yemen*. Faber, London.

Obermer, E., 1943, Phosphorus burns. *Lancet*, 13 February, p. 202.

Ochsner, H., 1949, *History of German Chemical Warfare in World War II. Part I. The Military Aspect*. Chemical Corps Historical Studies, No. 2. Historical Office of the Chief of the US Chemical Corps.

O'Neill, J. A., Jr., Pruitt, B. A., Jr. & Moncrief, J. A., 1968, Surgical treatment of Curling's ulcer. *Surgery, Gynecology & Obstetrics* **126**, p. 40.

Order, S. E. & Moncrief, J. A., 1965, *The Burn Wound*. Thomas, Springfield, Illinois.

Oughterson, A. W. & Warren, S., 1956, *Medical Effects of the Atomic Bomb in Japan*. McGraw-Hill, New York.

Ozerova, V. V., Rusakova, G. S. & Korenevskaya, S. P., 1970, On the action of yellow phosphorus on the human organism under conditions currently prevailing in its production. Institute of Industrial Hygiene and Occupational Diseases, Moscow.

Pajari, R., 1971, *Talvisota ilmassa* [The Winter War in the Air]. WSOY, Porvoo (Finland).

Pani, P., Gravela, E., Mazzarino, C. & Burdino, E., 1972, On the mechanism of fatty liver in white phosphorus poisoned rats. *Experimental and Molecular Pathology* **16**, pp. 201–209.

Pare, C. M. B. & Sandler, M., 1954, Smoke-bomb pneumonitis: Description of a case. *Journal of the Royal Army Medical Corps* **100**, pp. 320–22.

Partington, J. R., 1960, *A History of Greek Fire and Gunpowder*. Heffer, Cambridge (UK).

Payne, R., 1966, *Lawrence of Arabia*. Robert Hale, London.

Pearse, H. E., Payne, J. T. & Hogg, L., 1949, The experimental study of flashburns. *Annals of Surgery* **130** (4), pp. 776–789.

Permutt, S. & Farhi, L., 1969, Tissue hypoxia and carbon monoxide. In *Effects of Chronic Exposure to Low Levels of Carbon Monoxide on Human Health, Behavior and Performance.* National Academy of Science & National Academy of Engineering, Washington, D.C.

Peterson, A. H., Reinhardt, G. C. & Conger, E. E. (eds.), 1963, *Symposium on the Role of Airpower in Counterinsurgency and Unconventional Warfare:* RM-3651-PR, The Malayan emergency; RM-3652-PR, The Philippine Huk Campaign; RM-3653-PR, The Algerian War; RM-3654-PR, Chindit Operations in Burma; RM-3655-PR, Allied Resistance to the Japanese on Luzon, World War II; RM-3656-PR, Unconventional Warfare in the Mediterranean Theater. The Rand Corporation, Santa Monica, for United States Air Force.

Phillips, A. W. & Constable, J. D., (undated.), Burns: Method of the Massachusetts General Hospital. *Physical and Chemical Injuries* (section 15), pp. 807–818.

Phillips, A. W. & Cope, O., 1962, Burn therapy: II. The revelation of respiratory tract damage as a principal killer of the burned patient. *Annals of Surgery* **155**, p. 1.

Phillips, A. W., Tanner, J. W. & Cope, O., 1963, Burn therapy: IV. Respiratory tract damage (an account of the clinical, x-ray and postmortem findings) and the meaning of restlessness. *Annals of Surgery* **158** (5), pp. 799–811.

Pietras, R., Stavrakos, C., Gunnar, R. M. & Tobin, J. R., 1968, Phosphorus poisoning simulating acute myocardial infarction. *Archives of International Medicine* **122** (11), pp. 430–434.

Polk, H. C., 1966, Treatment of severe burns with aqueous silver nitrate (0.5%). *Annals of Surgery* **164** (6), pp. 753–770.

Polk, H. C., Monafo, W. W., Jr. & Moyer, C. A., 1969, Human burn survival: study of efficacy of 0.5% aqueous silver nitrate. *Archives of Surgery* **98** (March), pp. 262–265.

Polk, H. C., Ward, C. G., Clarkson, J. G. & Taplin, D., 1969, Early detection of pseudomonas burn infection: Clinical experience with Wood's light fluorescende. *Archives of Surgery* **98** (March), pp. 292–295.

Porritt, A., 1953, The treatment of war wounds. In *Surgery* (ed. Z. Cope). History of the Second World War, United Kingdom Medical Series. HMSO, London.

Posey, K. & Schleicher, R., 1966, *Feasibility Study of Turbine Fuel Gels for Reduction of Crash Fire Hazards.* Final Report, Contract FA-64-WA-5053. Western Co. of North America, Research Division, Dallas, Texas. (From authors' abstract in *Scientific and Technical Aerospace Reports,* 8 December 1966, p. 3609.)

Pouggouras, P., Karoutsos, K., Dariotis, A. & Pombodakis, N. 1971, Hépatite aigue par intoxication phosphorée. *La Presse Médicale* **79** (14), pp. 634.

Pozzani, U. C., 1949, High-grade ores. In *Pharmacology and Toxicology of Uranium Compounds,* vol. 1 (ed. C. Voegtlin & H. C. Hodge), pp. 423–524. McGraw-Hill, New York.

Prentiss, A. M., 1937, *Chemicals in War.* McGraw-Hill, New York.

Prodan, L., 1932, Cadmium poisoning, *Journal of Industrial Hygeine* **14**, p. 174.

Prokosch, E., 1973, *Inventory of US Incendiary and Antipersonnel Munitions.* NARMIC, Philadelphia.

Pruitt, B. A., Jr., 1970, Management of burns in the multiple injury patient. *Surgical Clinics of North America* **50** (6), pp. 1283–1300.

Pruitt, B. A., Jr. (Commander and Director, US Army Institute of Surgical Research, Brooke Army Medical Center, Houston, Texas), 1972. Personal communication.

Pruitt, B. A., Jr. & Curreri, P. W., 1971, The burn wound and its care. *Archives of Surgery* **103** (October), pp. 461–468.

Pruitt, B. A., Jr., DiVincenti, F. C., Mason, A. D., Foley, F. D. & Flemma, R. J.,

242

1970, The occurrence and significance of pneumonia and other pulmonary complications in burned patients: comparison of conventional and topical treatments. *Journal of Trauma* **10** (7), pp. 510–531.

Pruitt, B. A., Jr., Flemma, R. J., DiVincenti, F. C., Foley, F. D. & Mason, A. D., 1970, Pulmonary complications in burn patients—A comparative study of 697 patients. *Journal of Thoracic and Cardiovascular Surgery* **59** (1), pp. 7–20.

Pruitt, B. A., Jr., O'Neill, J. A., Jr., Moncrief, J. A. & Lindberg, R. B., 1968, Successful control of burn-wound sepsis. *Journal of the American Medical Association* **203** (12), pp. 150–152.

Pruitt, B. A., Jr., Tumbusch, W. T., Mason, A. D. & Pearson, E., 1964, Mortality in 1100 consecutive burns treated at a burns unit. *Annals of Surgery* **159,** pp. 396–401.

Rabinowitch, I. M., 1943, Treatment of phosphorus burns. *Canadian Medical Association Journal* **48** (4), pp. 291–296.

Rapaport, F. T., Converse, J. M., Horn, L., Ballantyne, D. L. & Mulholland, J. H., 1966, Altered reactivity to skin homografts in severe thermal injury. *Annals of Surgery* **159** (3), pp. 390–395.

Read, R. C. & White, H. J., 1969, Corrosive stricture of the stomach in a phosphorus worker. *Journal of the Arkansas Medical Society* **66** (3), pp. 96–99.

Reinhold, R., 1972, US attempted to ignite Vietnam forests in '66–67. *New York Times,* 21 July.

Republic of Cyprus Public Information Office, 1969, *The Cyprus Question: A Brief Analysis.* Nicosia.

Rittenbury, M. S., Maddox, R. W., Schmidt, F. H., Ham, W. T., Jr. & Haynes, B. W., Jr., 1966, Probit analysis of burn mortality in 1,831 patients: Comparison with other large series. *Annals of Surgery* **164** (1), pp. 123–138.

Roberts, J. D. & Caserio, M. C., 1964, *Basic Principles of Organic Chemistry.* Benjamin, New York.

Robinson, J. P. P., 1973, *Data on United States Aircraft Weapons.* Science Policy Research Unit, University of Sussex, Brighton (UK) (Mimeo).

Rodrigues-Iturbe, B., 1971, Acute yellow-phosphorus poisoning. *New England Journal of Medicine* **284** (3), p. 157.

Roe, C. F., Kinney, J. M. & Blair, C. S., 1964, Water and heat exchange in third-degree burns. *Surgery* **56,** p. 212.

Röse, W., 1969, Die Bedeutung der Infusionstherapie bei der Erstbehandlung von Verbrennungsgeschädigten. *Zeitschrift für Militärmedizin* **10** (7), pp. 401–405.

Rubanovskaya, A. A., 1970, The effect of uranous-uranic oxide (U_3O_8) in experimental work. In *The Toxicology of Radioactive Substances: Volume 4. Thorium-232 and Uranium-238* (ed. A. A. Letavet & E. B. Kurlyandskaya), pp. 87–100. Pergamon, Oxford (UK).

Rueggeberg, W., 1948, Use of aluminium soaps and other fuel thickeners in gelling gasoline. *Physical and Colloidal Chemistry* **52,** p. 1944.

Rumpf, H., 1952, *Der hochrote Hahn.* Mittler, Darmstadt (FRG).

Rumpf, H., 1961, *Das war der Bombenkrieg.* Gerhard Stalling Verlag, Oldenburg (FRG).

Rusk, H. A., 1967, Vietnam medicine I. Visiting American team, on its return, reports to Johnson on napalm burns. *New York Times,* 1 October 1967.

Saliba, M. J., Jr., 1970, Heparin efficacy in burns: II. Human thermal burn treatment with large doses of topical and parenteral heparin. *Aerospace Medicine* (November), pp. 1302–1306.

Saliba, M. Jr. & Griner, L. A., 1970, Heparin efficacy in burns: I. Significant early modification of experimental third degree guinea pig thermal burn and ancillary findings. A double blind study. *Aerospace Medicine* (February), pp. 179–187.

Schappel, J. W., 1968, *Modern Textiles* **49** (7), p. 54.

Schildt, B. E., 1970, Function of the RES after thermal and mechanical trauma in mice. *Acta Chirurgica Scandinavica* **136**, pp. 359–364.

Schildt, B. E., 1971, The role of the RES in shock states. *Annales Chirurgiae et Gynaecologiae Fenniae* **60**, pp. 165–174.

Schildt, B. E., 1972, Mortality rate in quantified combined injuries. *Strahlentherapie* **144** (1), pp. 40–49.

Schildt, B. E., 1972, Liver blood flow in traumatized mice. *Acta Chirurgica Scandinavica* **138**, pp. 59–68.

Schildt, B., Bouveng, R. & Sörbo, B., 1971, Inverkan av brännskador på några folsyra- och B_{12}-beroende processer [Effects of burns on some folic acid- and B_{12}-dependent processes]. FOA 1 Rapport C (December). Försvarets Forskningsanstalt (FOA), Stockholm.

Schmidt, D. A. 1968, *Yemen. The Unknown War*. London.

Schönrock, D., 1969, Ein Trainingsplatz für die Ausbildung im Schutz vor Brandmitteln. *Militärtechnik* **9** (11), pp. 498–501.

Schreiner, G. E. & Maher, J. F., 1965, Toxic nephropathy. *American Journal of Medicine* **38**, pp. 409–449.

Schuberth, O. & Wretlind, A., 1961, Intravenous infusion of fat emulsions, phosphatides and emulsifying agents. Clinical and experimental studies. *Acta Chirurgica Scandinavica*, Supplement 278, pp. 2–21.

Schulte, J. H., 1963, Effects of mild carbon monoxide intoxication. *Archives of Environmental Health* **7**, pp. 524–30.

Schunk, J., 1973, Brandmittel: Anwendung, Wirkung, Schutzmöglichkeiten. *Zivilverteidigung* **37** (III), pp. 7–9, 64–66; (IV), pp. 10–12, 15–18.

Sedlácek, J., 1969, Eye burns with phosphorus. *Ceskoslovenska Oftamologie* **25** (1), pp. 36–38.

Sevitt, S., 1966, Death after burning. *Medicine, Science & Law* **6** (1), pp. 36–44.

Shapley, D., 1972, Technology in Vietnam: Fire storm project fizzled out. *Science* **177**, 21 July, pp. 239–241.

Shirer, W. L., 1962, *The Rise and Fall of the Third Reich*. Secker & Warburg, London.

Shook, C. D., MacMillan, B. G. & Altemeier, W. A., 1968, Pulmonary complications of the burn patient. *Archives of Surgery* **97** (August), pp. 215–224.

Shuck, J. M., Pruitt, B. A., Jr. & Moncrief, J. A., 1969, Homograft skin for wound coverage: A study in versatility. *Archives of Surgery* **98** (April), pp. 472–479.

Silversides, R. G., 1964, New approaches to fire protection. *Discovery* (March) pp. 23–27.

Simeone, F. A., 1963, Shock, trauma and the surgeon. *Annals of Surgery* **158** (5), pp. 759–774.

Sinilo, M. I., 1961, Chemical burns and their treatment. *Acta Chirurgica Plastica* **3**, pp. 311–317.

Siscot, C., Bismuth, C., Frejaville, Z. P., *et al.*, 1969, Les héptatites toxiques. *Revue francaise d'Études cliniques et biologiques* **14** (2), pp. 200–212.

Sjöstrand, T., 1951, Endogenous formation of carbon monoxide. The CO concentration in the inspired and expired air of hospital patients. *Acta Physiologica Scandinavica* **22**, p. 137.

Slessor, J., 1956, *The Central Blue*. Cassell, London.

Smith, A. D., 1953, Air evacuation—medical obligation and military necessity. US Air Force. *Air University Quarterly Review* VI (2), pp. 98–111.

Smith, E. I. & DeWeese, M. S., 1969, The topical therapy of burns in children. *Archives of Surgery* 98 (April), pp. 462–469.

Snow, C. P., 1962, *Science and Government*. Mentor Books, New York.

Sörbo, B., 1973, Skador från rökammunition. *Försvarsmedicin* 9 (1), pp. 167–171.

Sorenson, H., 1949, Flame warfare. *Canadian Army Journal* 2 (7–8).

Stenberg, T., 1962, Studies of the liver function in experimental burns: I. A standardized back burn procedure for the rabbit and observations on blood volume and some blood components after a 10 per cent burn. *Acta Chirurgica Scandinavica* 123, pp. 159–170.

Stepniczka, H. E., 1973, Flame-retarded nylon textiles. *Industrial & Engineering Chemistry, Product Research & Development* 12 (1).

Stettbacher, A., 1944, Über die durch Brandbomben entstehende Wärme und die Erstickungsgefahr infolge Sauerstoffentzuges der Luft. *Protar*, pp. 158–64.

Stettbacher, A., 1948, *Sprent- und Schiesstoffe. Atomzerfallselemente und ihre Entladungserscheinungen*. Rascher, Zürich.

Stockholm International Peace Research Institute, 1971 a, *The Problem of Chemical and Biological Warfare*, vol. I. Almqvist & Wiksell, Stockholm.

Stockholm International Peace Research Institute, 1971 b, *The Problem of Chemical and Biological Warfare*, vol. IV. Almqvist & Wiksell, Stockholm.

Stockholm International Peace Research Institute, 1971 c, *The Arms Trade with the Third World*. Almqvist & Wiksell, Stockholm.

Stoll, A. M. & Greene, L. C., 1959, Relationship between pain and tissue damage due to thermal radiation. *Journal of Applied Physiology* 14 (3), pp. 373–382.

Stone, H. H., 1966, Review of Pseudomonas sepsis in thermal burns: Verdoglobin determination and gentamicin therapy. *Annals of Surgery* 163, 297–305.

Stone, H. H. & Hobby, L. W., 1965, Use of the mesh dermatome with split-thickness grafts for major burns. *American Surgeon* 31, pp. 583–586.

Sullivan, C. D., Eliot, G. F., Gayle, G. D. & Corson, W. R., 1968, *The Vietnam War: Its Conduct and Higher Direction*. The Center for Strategic Studies, Georgetown University, Washington, DC.

Summerlin, W. T., Walder, A. I. & Moncrief, J. A., 1967, White phosphorus burns and massive hemolysis. *Journal of Trauma* 7 (3), pp. 476–484.

Switzer, W. E., Moncrief, J. A. & Mills, W., 1966, The use of canine heterografts in the therapy of thermal injury. *Journal of Trauma* 6, 391–398.

Tanner, J. C., Vandeput, J. & Olley, J. F., 1964, The mesh skin graft. *Plastic and Reconstructive Surgery* 34, pp. 287–292.

Taylor, G., 1953. In *Surgery* (ed. Z. Cope). History of the Second World War, United Kingdom Medical Services. HMSO, London.

Tchad, 1971. Oeuvre collectif. Editions Git-le-Coeur, Paris.

Teschan, P. E. & Mason, A. D., 1963, Studies in acute renal failure: II. Incidence, mortality, urinary and plasma chemical alterations and clinical characteristics of reversible acute renal failure in the rat. *Journal of Surgical Research* 3 (9), pp. 442–449.

Thomas, D. M., 1969, What smoke can do to your body. *Fire Engineering* 122 (8), pp. 46–7; (9), pp. 52–53.

Thomas, H., 1961, *The Spanish Civil War*. Eyre, London.

Thomas, H., 1971, *Cuba; or Pursuit of Freedom*. Eyre, London.

Treves, N. & Pack, G. T., 1930, The development of cancer in burns scars. *Surgery, Gynecology & Obstetrics* 51, pp. 749–782.

Truhaut, R., Claude, J.-R. & Warnet, J.-M., 1971, Etude de l'incorporation de

245

l'acide palmitique ^{3}H-9-10 dans les triglycérides et les lipoprotéines du rat intoxique par le phosphore blanc. *Comptes Rendus Hebdomaires des Sciences* **272** (5), pp. 2400–2403.

Truhaut, R., Claude, J.-R. & Warnet, J.-M., 1969, Etude des modifications biochimiques provoquées par des intoxications aigues et subaigues au phosphore blanc chez le Rat: I. Action de doses répetées administrées par voie parentérale. *Annales Pharmaceutiques françaises* **27** (1), pp. 17–23.

Truhaut, R., Claude, J.-R. & Warnet, J.-M., 1972, Etude des modifications biochimiques provoquées par des intoxications aigues et subaigues au phosphore blanc chez le Rat: II. Action d'une dose unique administrée par voie parentérale. *Annales Pharmaceutiques francaises* **30** (1), pp. 35–44.

Tubiana, R., Bauz, S. & Kenesi, C., 1967, A propos de 300 brûlures thermiques récentes des mains. *Annales de Chirurgie* **21** (2), pp. 1387–1395.

Tunney, J. V., 1968, *Measuring Hamlet Security.* Report of a Special Study Mission, Committee of Foreign Affairs, US House of Representatives. US Government Printing Office, Washington, DC.

Turnburg, J. L. & Luce, E., 1968, Methemoglobinemia: A complication of silver nitrate treatment of burns. *Surgery* **63,** p. 328.

United Nations, 1969, *Chemical and Bacteriological (Biological) Weapons and the Effects of their Possible Use.* Report of the Secretary-General. A/7575. New York.

United Nations, 1973 a, *Napalm and other Incendiary Weapons and all Aspects of their Possible Use.* Report of the Secretary-General. A/8803/Rev.1. New York.

United Nations, 1973 b, *Napalm and other Incendiary Weapons and all Aspects of their Possible Use.* Report of the Secretary-General. A/9207. New York.

United Nations, 1973 c, *Existing Rules of International Law Concerning the Prohibition or Restriction of Use of Specific Weapons.* Survey prepared by the Secretariat. A/9215 (Vols. I–II). New York.

Urlanis, B., 1971, *Wars and Population.* Progress Publishers, Moscow.

US Air Force Armament Laboratory, 1970, *Guide to non-nuclear munitions and associated munitions under cognizance of AFATL,* Part I.

US Army Institute of Surgical Research, 1972, *Annual Research Progress Report, 1971–72.* Brooke Army Medical Center, Fort Sam Houston, Texas.

US Army Munitions Command, 1972, *Laboratory Posture Report.* Research, Development and Engineering Directorate. Dover, New Jersey.

US Army Munitions Command, 1973, *Laboratory Posture Report.* Research, Development and Engineering Directorate. Dover, New Jersey.

US Bureau of Naval Personnel, 1970, *Aviation Ordnanceman 3 & 2.* Rate Training Manual Navpers 10345-C.

US Commander in Chief Pacific, 1968, *Report on the War in Vietnam.* US Government Printing Office, Washington, DC.

US Department of Agriculture, Forest Service, 1966, *Forest Fire Research, Final Report-Phase I,* vol. 1. ARPA Order No. 818. Washington DC.

US Department of the Army, 1956, *The Law of Land Warfare.* Field Manual FM 27-10. Washington, DC.

US Department of the Army, 1960, *Ground Flame Warfare.* Field Manual FM 20–33. Washington, DC.

US Department of the Army, 1966, *Bombs and Bomb Components.* Technical Manual TM 9-1325-200.

US Department of the Army, 1967, *Artillery Ammunition: Guns, Howitzers, Mortars and Recoilless Rifles.* Technical Manual TM 9-1300-203.

US Department of the Army, 1969, *Jungle Operations.* Field Manual FM 31–35.

US Department of the Army, 1969, *Employment of Riot Control Agents, Flame, Smoke, Antiplant Agents and Personnel Detectors in Counterguerilla Operations.* Training Circular TC-3-16. Washington, DC.

US Department of the Army, 1970, *Combat Flame Operations.* Field Manual FM 20–33.

US Department of the Army, 1971, *Identification List.* Supply Catalog SC 1305/30-IL.

US Departments of the Army & the Air Force, 1957, *Chemical Bombs and Clusters.* Technical Manual No. 3–400/Technical Order No. 11C2-1-1.

US Departments of the Army & the Air Force, 1963, *Military Chemistry and Chemical Agents.* Technical Manual No. 3-215/Air Force Manual No. 355–7. Washington, DC.

US Departments of the Army & the Navy, 1971, *Grenades, Hand and Rifle.* TM 9-1330-200/OP 3833 1st Rev Vol 1/TM-1330-15/1.

US Departments of the Army, the Navy & the Air Force, 1961, *Armed Forces Doctrine for Chemical and Biological Weapons Employment and Defense.* FM 101-40/NWP 36 (C)/AFM 355-2/LFM 03. Washington, DC.

US Departments of the Army, the Navy & the Air Force, 1967, *Handling, Maintenance, Storage and Inspection, (Including Repair Parts and Special Tool Lists). Dispenser and Bomb, Aircraft: CUB-1A/A, CBU-2/A, CBU-2A/A, CBU-2B/A, CBU-2C/A, CBU-3/A, CBU-3A/A, CBU-8A/A, CBU-9/A, CBU-9A/A, CBU-9B/A, CBU-12/A, CBU-12A/A, and CBU-26/A.* TM 9-1325-202-50/1/Navair 11-5A-2, Vol. 1/TO 11A1-5-1-7.

US Departments of the Army, the Navy & the Air Force, 1968, *Treatment of Chemical Agent Casualties.* TM S-285/NAVMED P-5041/AFM 160-12. Washington, DC.

US Department of Defense, 1962, *The Effects of Nuclear Weapons.* US Government Printing Office, Washington, DC.

US Department of Health, Education & Welfare, 1972, *Toxic Substances List.* Washington, DC.

US National Academy of Sciences & National Academy of Engineering, 1969, *Effects of Chronic Exposure to Low Levels of Carbon Monoxide on Human Health, Behavior and Performance.* A report prepared by the Committee on Effects of Atmospheric Contaminants on Human Health and Welfare of the Division of Medical Sciences, National Research Council for the Environmental Studies Board of the National Academy of Sciences and National Academy of Engineering. Washington, DC.

US Senate Committee on Armed Services & Committee on Foreign Relations, 1951, *Military Situation in the Far East.* Hearings to Conduct an Inquiry into the Military Situation in the Far East and the Facts Surrounding the Relief of General of the Army Douglas MacArthur from his Assignments in that Area. Eighty-second Congress, First Session. US Government Printing Office, Washington, DC.

US Senate Committee on Armed Services, 1971, *Investigation into Electronic Battlefield Program.* Hearings before the Electronic Battlefield Subcommittee of the Preparedness Investigating Subcommittee. Ninety-first Congress, Second Session. US Government Printing Office, Washington, DC.

US Senate Committee on Armed Services, 1974, *Fiscal Year 1975 Authorization for Military Procurement, Research and Development, and Active Duty, Selected Reserve and Civilian Personnel Strengths.* Hearings. Ninety-third Congress, Second Session. US Government Printing Office, Washington, DC.

US Senate Committee on Foreign Relations, 1971, *Impact of the Vietnam War.*

Report prepared by the Foreign Affairs Division, Congressional Research Service, Library of Congress. US Government Printing Office, Washington, DC.

US Senate Committee on Foreign Relations, 1971, *Laos: April 1971*. Staff report for the Subcommittee on US Security Agreements and Commitments Abroad. US Government Printing Office, Washington, DC.

US Senate Committee on Foreign Relations, 1972, *Vietnam Commitments, 1961*. A Staff Study based on the Pentagon Papers, No. 1. US Government Printing Office, Washington, DC.

US Senate Committee on the Judiciary, 1968, *Civilian Casualty, Social Welfare and Refugee Problems in South Vietnam*. Hearings before the Subcommittee to Investigate Problems Connected with Refugees and Escapees. Ninetieth Congress, First Session. US Government Printing Office, Washington, DC.

US Senate Committee on the Judiciary, 1970, *Refugee and Civilian War Casualty Problems in Indochina*. A Staff Report prepared for the use of the Subcommittee to Investigate Problems Connected with Refugees and Escapes. US Government Printing Office, Washington, DC.

US Senate Committee on the Judiciary, 1972, *Problems of War Victims in Indochina Part IV: North Vietnam*. Hearings before the Subcommittee to Investigate Problems Connected with Refugees and Escapees. US Government Printing Office, Washington, DC.

US Senate Committee on the Judiciary, 1974, *Relief and Rehabilitation of War Victims in Indochina: One Year after the Ceasefire*. A Study Mission report prepared for the use of the Subcommittee to Investigate Problems Connected with Refugees and Escapees. Ninety-third Congress, Second Session. US Government Printing Office, Washington, DC.

US Strategic Bombing Survey, 1945, *Overall Report: European War*. Washington, DC.

US Strategic Bombing Survey, Morale Division, Medical Branch, 1945, *The Effect of Bombing on Health & Medical Care in Germany,* Washington, DC.

US Strategic Bombing Survey, 1946. The effects of atomic bombs on Hiroshima and Nagasaki. In *Fire and the Air War* (ed. H. Bond). National Fire Protection Association, Boston, Massachusetts.

US Tactical Air Command, 1966, *Operational Test and Evaluation BONE STEW (Napalm B)*. TAC-TR-64-65. Headquarters Tactical Air Command, US Air Force, Langley Air Force Base, Virginia. (AD-372483)

US War Department, 1943, *Unexploded Bombs. Organization and Operation for Disposal*. Field Manual 9-40. US Government Printing Office, Washington, DC.

Vedder, E. B., 1925, *The Medical Aspects of Chemical Warfare*. William & Wilkins, Baltimore.

Verrier, A., 1968, *The Bomber Offensive*. Batsford, London.

Vishnevskii, A. A., 1966, Ten days in the Democratic Republic of Vietnam (in Russian). *Eksperimental Khirurgiai Anesteziologiia* **2** (Sept–Oct), pp. 85–90.

Vertel, R. M., Summerlin, W. T., Pruitt, B. A., Jr. & O'Neill, J. A., 1967, Coombs tests after thermal burns. *Journal of Trauma* **7** (6), pp. 871–876.

von Clausewitz, C., 1832, *On War,* (trans. J. Graham, 1908). Penguin Books, Harmondsworth (UK), 1968.

von Oettingen W. F., 1944, *Carbon Monoxide: Its Hazards and the Mechanisms of its Action*. Bulletin 290, US Public Health Service. US Government Printing Office, Washington, DC.

Walder, A. I., Summerlin, W. T., Mason. A. D., Jr., Foley, F. D. & Moncrief, J. A., 1967, Respiratory complications in the acutely burned patient: A clinical study. *Military Medicine* (May), pp. 379–387.

Walker, J., Jr., Wexler, J. & Hill, M. L., 1945 (reprinted 1969), *Quantitative analysis of phosphorus-containing compounds formed in WP burns*. Edgewood Arsenal Special Publication EASP 100-49. US Department of the Army, Edgewood Arsenal Research Laboratories, Maryland. (AD-687270).

Wallace, A. F., 1969, Mass burns casualties. *Journal of the Royal Army Medical Corps* **115** (6), pp. 191–194.

Weast, R. C. (ed.), 1974, *Handbook of Chemistry and Physics*. Chemical Rubber Co., Cleveland, Ohio.

Weaver, J. A. & Stoll, A. M., 1969, Mathematical model of skin exposed to thermal radiation. *Aerospace Medicine* (January), pp. 24–30.

Webb, C. R., 1968, Medical considerations in internal defense and development. *Military Medicine* (May), pp. 391–396.

Webster, C. & Frankland, N., 1961, *The Strategic Air Offensive against Germany, 1939–1945*, vols. I–IV. HMSO, London.

Wells, W. & Tsukifuju, N., 1952, Scars remaining in atom bomb survivors: A four year follow-up study. *Surgery, Gynecology and Obstetrics* **95** (2), 129–141.

Whelan, T. J., Burkhalter, W. E. & Gomes, A., 1968, Management of war wounds. In *Advances in Surgery* **3** (ed. E. E. Welch), pp. 227–350. Yearbook Medical Publishers, Chicago.

Whitaker, P. H., 1945, Radiological appearances of the chest following partial asphyxiation by a smoke screen. *British Journal of Radiology* **18**, pp. 396–397.

Williot, J., 1969, Intoxication par un pot fumigène. *Revue du Service de Santé militaire belge* 15, pp. 217–259.

Wilmore, D. A., Moylan, J. A. & Pruitt, B. A., Jr., 1972, Safety of parenteral fat emulsion as a calorific source in thermally injured soldiers. In US Army Institute of Surgical Research, *Annual Research Progress Report*, 30 June 1972. Brooke Army Medical Center, Fort Sam Houston, Texas.

Wilson, A., 1956, *Flame Thrower*. Kimber, London.

Wilson, J. A. & Egeberg, B., 1942, Treatment of burns of the skin due to molten magnesium. *Industrial Medicine* **11**, p. 443.

Wilson, H. B., Sylvester, G. E., Laskin, S., La Belle, C. W., Scott, J. K. & Stokinger, H. E., 1955, Relation of particle size of U_3O_8 to toxicity following inhalation by animals. *Archives of Industry & Health* **11**, p. 11.

Winterscheid, L. C. & Merendino, V. A., 1960, Etiology and mortality of burns at a general hospital. *American Journal of Surgery* **100**, p. 375.

World Health Organization, 1970, *Health Aspects of Chemical and Biological Weapons*. Report of a WHO Group of Consultants, Geneva.

Woroschilsky, L., 1899, *Wirkung des Urans*. Dissertation. Dorpat.

Wretlind, A., 1962, The pharmacological basis for the use of fat emulsions in intravenous nutrition. *Acta Chirurgica Scandinavica,* Supplement 325, pp. 21–42.

Zanetti, J. E., 1936, The forgotten enemy. *The Independent Journal of Columbia University* **3** (b).

Zapp, J. A., 1946, Cadmium, selenium, and the carbonyls of iron and nickel. In *Summary Technical Report of Division 9* (ed. B. Renshaw) vol. 1, chapter 11. National Defense Research Committee, Washington, DC. (PB 158507–8)

Zavyalov, P. V., 1969, Postburn contractures and deformations in children (in Russian). *Khirurgija* **45** (7), pp. 112–115.

Zawacki, B. E. & Pruitt, B. A., Jr., 1970, Emergency treatment of burns. *American Family Physician/GP* **2** (1), pp. 60–68.

Zikria, B. A., Sturner, W. A., Astarjeon, N. K., Fox, C. L. & Ferrer, J. M., 1968, Respiratory tract damage in burns. *Pathophysiology & Therapy Annals* **150**, New York Academy of Sciences, p. 618.

INDEX

A

Africa 26–28, 48–49, 66–68, 72
African Party for the Independence of Guinea and Cape Verde. *See* PAIGC
Air raids: on Shrewsbury 21; on London 21; total in WWI 22; on German cities in WWII (*see also* Hamburg) 120 ff; on Japanese cities (*see also* Tokyo, Hiroshima) 35–36, 121
"Alecto" (napalm-B) 50
Algeria 48–49, 72
Aluminum, as incendiary agent 89, 109; soaps (constituents of napalm gels) 93
Alunat (thickener). *See* Sweden
American Electric Co., *See* United States
Angola 66, 68
Antimony 89
Arab-Israeli conflict 63–64
Area bombing: in WWII 30–37; rationale of 33, effectiveness of 35, 37; in Korean War 45–47; in Viet-Nam War 57–59, 82. *See also* Morale; Fire-storms; Atomic bomb; Civilian casualties
"Area denial" 57, 57 (fn)
Arrows, incendiary 15–17, 29
Asia 25, 28–29, 36, 42–47, 49–66, 72
Atomic bomb 42; effects of on Hiroshima and Nagasaki 35 (fn), 37, 134–35, 134 (table), 147, 150, 160–63, 184
Australia 70, 100, 135–36
Austria 66, 109

B

Belgium 30, 31, 38, 40, 70
Benzene 76–78 (table), 95, 152, 200–201; benzene sulphohydrazide 97
Binary chemical weapons 208
Blitzkrieg 29
Blood gases 204
Bombs, antipersonnel 42, 62, 184 (fn); delayed action 33–34; fragmentation 33–34, 54, 56; 60, 113, 114 (tables), 182, 206–207; high explosive 60, 121, 190. *See also* Incendiary bombs; Napalm bombs; White phosphorus
Booby traps 54, 105, 159 (table)
Boron compounds 103
Brazil 100
Burma 36, 38

Burns, flash and flame 161–62; primary and secondary 124; first, second and third degree 126–27; temperature limits for 126; extent of 128–29, 130 (table); severity of 122, 185; mortality from 129–32; day of death from 134–36; causes of death from 122, 123 (table); complications from 123 (table), 136–42, 158, 159 (tables); disabilities from 146–48, 154–55; psychological effects of 149–50, 180–81; due to metal incendiaries 150–51; due to napalm 151–55; due to white phosphorous 155–60, 215–20; due to thermal radiation 102, 161, 165; treatment of 166–81. *See also* "Pulmonary" burns

C

Cadmium, added to incendiaries to produce toxic smoke 195–96
Cambodia (Khmer Republic), napalm bombs in 62 ff
Canada 38, 70
Carbon monoxide poisoning 121, 122, 155–52, 163–64, 166, 171, 187–95; as chemical warfare 190–91, 204, 206–208; addition of metallic carbonyls to incendiaries 190–91 (fn), 208
Catapult, mechanical 22, 111
Cerium 100
Chad 67
"Chemical fireball" 102
Chemical warfare 24, 41, 57 (fn); chemical weapons, definitions of 202–204; and incendiary agents 190–91, 202–208. *See also* Herbicides; Mustard gas; CS; Blood gases; Nerve gas; Harassing agents; Irritant agents
China 28–29, 36, 44–47, 60, 142, 177
Cherwell, Lord 32
Churchill, Sir W.S. 25, 31
CIA (Central Intelligence Agency) 54 (fn)
Civil defence, against incendiary warfare 120–21
Civilian casualties 17, 21, 28, 30, 31, 34–37, 41, 45, 54, 54 (fn), 55–56, 59, 61, 62, 63, 64, 65, 66, 71, 162, 163
Close air support 29, 39–40, 42, 43, 44, 54
Cluster bombs 52, 52 (table), 55, 62, 77 (table), 79 (table), 112–13, 114 (table), 116–17
"Coercive warfare" 31 (fn), 60